T0339673

A Ruinous and Unhappy War

A Ruinous and Unhappy War

New England and the War of 1812

James H. Ellis

Algora Publishing
New York

Library of Congress Cataloging-in-Publication Data —

Ellis, James H., 1932-
    A ruinous and unhappy war: New England and the War of 1812 / James H. Ellis.
        p. cm.
    Includes bibliographical references and index.
    ISBN 978-0-87586-690-1 (soft cover: alk. paper) — ISBN 978-0-87586-691-8 (hard
cover: alk. paper) — ISBN 978-0-87586-692-5 (ebook) 1. United States—History—War
of 1812. 2. New England—History—1775-1865. 3. New England—History, Military—19th
century. I. Title. II. Title: New England and the War of 1812.

    E354.E465 2009
    973.5'2—dc22
                        2008048535

Front Cover: Boarding and Taking of the American Ship Chesapeake (English lithograph)

Printed in the United States

For Ruthie, again

TABLE OF CONTENTS

The War of 1812 against Great Britain was the first war declared by the United States, and the first, but by no means the last, prosecuted over the objections of a sizeable portion of the citizenry. The most persistent, organized, and vociferous opposition arose from that oldest region of the country — New England. Commercial, political, and religious interests in the region contested the war on multiple grounds, but rested their case on a foundation of States' rights. The Federalists, the minority political party in the country, controlled much of New England and led the contrariness and contention.

The war originated as a side show of the Napoleonic Wars sweeping Europe. The long-running conflict between Britain and France dominated world affairs at a time when American businessmen and farmers relied on European exports and imports, much of it carried by New England shipping. But Napoleon and France objected to outside trade with the English. And, just as naturally, Great Britain disapproved of third-party trade with France. Both countries adopted restrictions and interdicted American and other neutral ships headed to or near their enemy. In the United States, sides were taken. New England tended to consider France the principal antagonist. President James Madison saw it differently. He believed Great Britain to be the real threat and deserving of armed retaliation. Madison outlined his case to a Congress dominated by his Democratic Republican party. And Congress took his side and voted for war in June 1812.

Federalist majorities in Massachusetts, Connecticut, and Rhode Island opposed and resisted the conflict at every stage. Vermont, New Hampshire, and the District of Maine harbored numerous although fewer war critics. Thus, the perception prevailed in other parts of the country and for a time in Great Britain that the region as a whole rejected the war policies of the national government. Truth be told, while war opponents gained a great deal of attention, other elements in the region made considerable contributions to the national war effort. Much of the financing and a substantial portion of the army and navy came from New England. Vice President Elbridge Gerry and Secretary of War William Eustis hailed from Massachusetts. U.S. Army General Henry Dearborn came from New Hampshire and illustrious naval officers such as Isaac Hull, Charles Morris, and Oliver Hazard Perry were native New Englanders. As important, New England vessels formed the backbone of the nation's important and successful private navy — the privateersmen.

Before it ended, the war injured New England more than almost anyone expected. Unemployment deepened, business failures became common, and privation spread. Nantucket entered into a neutrality agreement with the enemy, eastern Maine fell into the hands of Great Britain, and the Royal Navy raided with impunity all along the coast. As significant, the embargoes and blockades associated with the conflict decimated and forever altered the region's economy. During the fighting, shameful smuggling flourished on the borders of eastern Maine and northern Vermont (not to mention northern New York). Further staining the region's name, regional political leaders late in 1814 convened the infamous and divisive Hartford Convention to consider ways to gain relief. And the governor of Massachusetts secretly explored a separate peace settlement with the British.

Historians and writers have experienced more than a little difficulty in treating the War of 1812. Debate lingers over the cause or causes. To cover himself, one writer listed 12 different causes! Many observers feel nationalism was the cause when in fact it was no more than a motivating element. Others point to Canada as the cause. Yet this supposedly vulnerable and nearby part of the British Empire was simply an objective. The primary cause is clear. Hostile British interference in one form or another with the neutral maritime commerce of the United States caused the war. Much against its wishes, this placed seafaring New England in the middle of the disagreeableness that ushered in the war as well as the war itself.

The reach of the conflict thrust common citizens to the forefront of the action. The story is their story. In presenting it, to a great extent, reliance is placed on their obscure diaries, letters, logs, journals, and public records as well as period newspapers. Readers will note that many of these people shared Andrew Jackson's style. This great hero of the war reputedly felt it was a poor mind that was unable to come up with more than one way to spell a word. To avoid clutter, the text that follows for the most part avoids using the Latin word *sic*, meaning "so" or "thus," after the numerous misspelled or misused words found in quoted material. In almost every case the intended meaning is obvious. And in just a few instances does it seem necessary to add bracketed words to complete or clarify a quotation.

With all of the contemporary contributions, New England's contradictory and controversial roles in this peculiar war form a fascinating account worth reviewing for the first time as we approach the bicentennial of the 1812–15 conflict sometimes called the Second War of Independence. The tale begins off the New England shore east of Cape Cod with the first shots of the war.

Chapter 1. The Die is Cast

John Rodgers moved with striking alacrity on the morning of June 21, 1812. Official word arrived in New York from Washington indicating the United States, not altogether unexpectedly, declared war on Great Britain on the 18th. Commodore Rodgers took only an hour to get under way in his 1,576-ton flagship, the 44-gun frigate *President*. Tradition has it that he called all hands to quarters and announced: "Now lads, we have got something to do that will shake the rust from our jackets. War is declared! We shall have another dash at our old enemies. It is the very thing you have wanted." He went on to say: "The rascals have been bullying over us these ten years, and I am glad the time has come when we can have satisfaction."[1]

At the same time, he started the rest of his ships. The frigate *United States*, 44 (i.e., rated for 44 guns), Captain Stephen Decatur; the frigate *Congress*, 36, Captain John Smith; the sloop *Hornet* 18, Master Commandant James Lawrence; and the brig *Argus*, 16, Master Commandant Arthur Sinclair moved rapidly into the stream. By evening the squadron cleared Sandy Hook and stood to the east.

Two reasons dictated haste. The element of surprise was one factor. For a period of days, British ships off America might be attacked unawares. As it turned out, official notice of the war did not reach the main North American Royal Navy base in Halifax, Nova Scotia until July 4, although solid intelligence was in hand late on June 28. The government in Quebec got word by express around June 25.

The second reason involved anticipated strategic policy, a policy alien to Rodgers' makeup. Although otherwise bellicose, as war approached, Secretary of the Navy Paul Hamilton developed plans to employ the navy as

---

1 Lovette, *Naval Customs, Traditions and Usage*, 195-196.

a static coastal defense force. Senior officers wanted to carry the fight to the enemy wherever he could be found. In Washington seeking commands, Captain William Bainbridge and Captain Charles Stewart lobbied for the officers' aggressive plan. Hamilton, supported by his fellow cabinet members, would not budge. So, the two senior officers turned to President James Madison and presented their case in a strongly written letter. Madison was impressed with the officers' reasoning and yielded to their plea for an offensive approach.

Nonetheless, Hamilton remained cautious. On the 18th he wrote to Captain Isaac Hull, fitting out the *Constitution*, 44 at Annapolis, telling him about the state of war. He ordered Hull to sail to New York with "utmost dispatch." The secretary cautioned: "[T]he Belvidera is on our coast, but you are not to understand me as impelling you to battle, previously to your having confidence in your crew unless attacked, or with a reasonable prospect of success, of which you are to be at your discretion the judge." He added: "You are to reply to this and inform me of your progress."[1]

Hamilton did not get around to writing detailed orders for Rodgers until the 22nd. The secretary wanted the commodore to cruise defensively with the *President, Essex*, 32, *John Adams*, 28, *Hornet*, and *Nautilus*, 14 and in concert with Commodore Decatur and his *United States, Congress*, and *Argus*. The two were to operate between New England and the Chesapeake so "as to afford to our returning commerce, all possible protection. . . . The safe return of our commercial vessels, is obviously of the highest importance."[2] By the time the secretary's directive arrived in New York, Rodgers, as noted, was long gone. He did not see the orders until he returned to the country in September. But before long, he did see the British frigate *Belvidera*, 36, Captain Richard Byron.

Once at sea, Rodgers, the second most senior officer in the U.S. Navy and about to turn 40, positioned himself to intercept British merchantmen sailing out of the West Indies. Prior to departing New York, he received a report of a British merchant convoy moving to the east. And in the wee hours of the 23rd, the master of an American brig bound for New York said he had passed such a fleet three days earlier. Rodgers shaped a course in its direction.

Well east of Abercon Inlet and south of Tiverton, Rhode Island, at 6:00 a.m., the Americans spotted a frigate standing to the southwest. The commodore signaled a general chase, and the quarry turned tail and raced to the northeast. The ship proved to be the *Belvidera*. By noon the ships were 48 miles east of Nantucket Shoals, the *President* the closest American to the Briton, and gaining. At 4:20 p.m., Rodgers ordered his bow chase guns fired — the first shots of the War of 1812. Within moments, Byron in the *Belvidera* returned fire with his stern guns.

1 Maloney, *Captain from Connecticut*, 167.
2 Dudley, *Naval War of 1812*, 1:148.

How could this be? The first engagement of the war was playing out in the waters off New England — the one place in the country that did not want the war or anything to do with it.

For certain, Byron did not want anything to do with the area. The initial American shots had some effect, smashing into his cabin and a gun room. As he struggled to get away from his five pursuers, Byron caught a break. Ten minutes into the firing, "one of the Presidents chase guns burst and killed and wounded sixteen persons, among the latter myself" recorded Rodgers.[1] The explosion incapacitated another chase gun for a time. "I now gave orders to put our helm to Starboard and fire the starboard broadside," Rodgers reported. By yawing, or deviating to port, the *President* lost ground, but she recovered before long and opened again with bow-chasers. "At one time, the President was within pistol shot of the Belvidera."[2]

The *Belvidera*'s stern guns firing grape (packaged small round shot) did a fair amount of damage to the American's sails and rigging. Rodgers returned to the tactic of yawing across the Briton's stern and firing broadsides. Byron turned and tried a broadside of his own, without much effect, and then "commenced lightening his Ship by throwing overboard all his boats, waiste, anchors &c &c."[3] Casks and spars littered the water. Niles "supposed most" of the Briton's guns were ditched over the side.[4] At 7:15 p.m., Byron got beyond the reach of the *President*'s guns. By midnight, the *Belvidera* sailed three miles ahead, and Rodgers discontinued the chase. When their ship fell in with a Philadelphia merchantman on the 24th, the "crew of the *Belvidera* expressed some surprise the yankee fleet did not take them." And, they admitted, Byron "used much acrimonious language" during the confrontation.[5]

Although it would be two weeks before the American public learned details of the first clash of the war, news of President Madison's declaration of war reached Boston and Portland on June 23, the day of the sea fight off Cape Cod. An outcry erupted. Church bells tolled throughout New England, and gloom fell over the region's whaling ports since their fleets remained exposed on distant whaling grounds. Before long, the British began stopping and burning returning whalers as they approached the American coast. Nantucket would lose half of its whaling fleet during the war — 23 out of 46 ships.

Editors railed. A New Bedford newspaper lamented the "awful calamity."[6] A Portsmouth, New Hampshire *Oracle* headline declared "THE DIE IS CAST." The paper reported the "Horrid WAR" prompted every citizen thereabouts to hurry "from his house, as if it was on fire," and mingle "with his neighbor at the corners of some street, trying to derive comfort from his friends — the

---

1 Ibid., 155.

2 *Portsmouth* (NH) *Oracle*, July 11, 1812.

3 Dudley, 156.

4 *Niles' Weekly Register* (MD), September 12, 1812.

5 *Columbian Centinel* (MA), July 8, 1812.

6 *New Bedford* (MA) *Mercury*, June 26, 1812.

trembling lips, the *broken* voice and the *faltering* tongue, give answer to eager enquirers, 'THERE IS WAR'."[1] In Boston, a Federalist leaning paper reported: "The overwhelming calamity — so much dreaded by many — so little expected by the community at large — but so long considered inevitable by a few — has befallen OUR COUNTRY."[2]

Many businesses shut down for the day. In protest, flags were lowered to half-mast, and, in a few cases, displayed upside down. After setting the town flag at half-mast, a gang in Augusta, Maine manifested its feelings of disapproval by hanging Madison in effigy. United States soldiers in town cut the flag pole down. "As soon as this was known, the citizens assembled, erected it, and set the flag again at half mast." The soldiers formed once more to get at the flag, but confronted by "the invincible spirit of the citizens dared not cut it away." A local newspaper said cooler heads prevented bloodshed, but the flag remained in its position "*as a proper expression of feeling* for the space of two days."[3]

Not everyone took to the streets. Many throughout the region "turned to 'the strongest of all citadels of civil liberty, the purest of democracies,' the town meeting."[4]

In Buckstown, Maine (now Bucksport), the town voted to send delegates to a special county peace convention in Castine on August 21, and instructed them to "express disapprobation of the measures of the General Government in respect to Commerce, and the interests of the Northern States generally, and particularly the Declaration of War against Great Britain. . . ."[5] At a Deer Isle meeting called for the same purpose, "party feelings ran high and led to acts of indiscretion and violence of language."[6] Nonetheless, the gathering acted to send a two-man delegation to the Castine convention instructed to support measures which would result in "the colunation [culmination] of the War . . . and produce a Speedy, Just & honourable Peace." The heated meeting also resolved declaring war when unprepared stemmed from "gross" ignorance or from "a criminal and base subserviency to the ambitious views and wishes of the French Emperor."[7] Castine itself met before the county conclave in order to contemplate "with pleasure, the patriotic spirit, which animates the Friends of Peace," hailing "it as kindred to the spirit of '75."[8]

At Wells, Maine, only four men voted support for the war while 246 favored peace at a July 7 town meeting which went on to prepare a memorial to the president declaring the war "unjust, unnecessary and inexpedient."[9] Nearby Biddeford also sent a written protest to the president, while the Bath

---

1 *Portsmouth* (NH) *Oracle,* June 27, 1812.

2 *Columbian Centinel* (MA), June 24, 1812.

3 North, *History of Augusta,* 407-408.

4 Fannie S. Chase, *Wiscasset in Pownalborough,* 329-330.

5 *Records of the Town of Buckstown* (ME) No. 1, 183.

6 Hosmer, *Historical Sketch of the Town of Deer Isle,* 223.

7 *Town Clerk's Record of Town Meetings,* Vol. II, Deer Isle, ME, 102-103.

8 *Records, No. 1, 1796-1830,* Castine, ME, 197.

9 *Town Records, Vol. C, 1811-1834,* Wells, ME, 12.

selectmen called a Lincoln County convention in Wiscasset to condemn the war. And a Brunswick, Maine town meeting censured Congressman William Widgery for voting for war.

Widgery was a combative fellow. He had served as a lieutenant on a privateer during the Revolutionary War. In the recent congressional debates leading to the war vote, he uttered one of the memorable lines of the time. Commenting on the growing distress and agony of the Federalist members, and in a reply to remarks of Representative Timothy Pitkin of Connecticut, Widgery began: "Mr. Speaker, It is an old saying among gunners that the wounded pidgeons can be discovered by their fluttering."[1] The other side of the aisle did not appreciate the comparison, and, as noted, Widgery's constituents did not appreciate his support for the war. The Brunswick censure was a barometer of things to come. The voters turned him out of office in the next election.

Farther south, in Massachusetts, a special meeting in Gloucester adopted a statement on "the portentous crisis," and chose delegates for a county convention in Ipswich called to consider the "awful and alarming situation."[2] The town also expressed support for the state government, looking to it "for firm, dignified and prompt measures, such as will do honor to the sons of freemen."[3]

On Cape Cod, a July town meeting in Yarmouth appointed a committee to write a protesting memorial to the president. In nearby Chatham, the townsmen gathered in meeting to express "an unwillingness and disapprobation to enter into the present war." The men also instructed a committee to send a protesting petition to President Madison to include an expression of their "abhorance of an Alliance with France."[4] A Sandwich man observed the declaration of war "appears to create a great anxiety in many peoples minds."[5] And most Cape towns participated in the Barnstable County peace convention held early in August at Barnstable.

At Boston, "long . . . the seat of discontent," once war was declared, civic leaders magnified difficulties "to the highest degree for the purpose of influencing the public passions. . . . [T]hey clamored for peace, and reprobated the war as wicked, unjust, and unnecessary."[6] Three to four thousand met at Faneuil Hall and passed antiwar resolutions, contending the war "is sincerely to be deprecated, as it tends to impair the attachment of the people to the union of these States."[7]

At a July Plymouth meeting, in a show of hands, some 300 men indicated they were for peace, while not a single voter backed war. The assemblage

---

1 Egan, *Historical New Hampshire*, 160.
2 Babson, *Town of Gloucester*, 510.
3 *Columbian Centinel* (MA), July 8, 1812.
4 *Town Records 1789-1823 of Chatham* (MA), Vol. 3, July 16, 1812.
5 *Benjamin Percival Diary*.
6 Barry, *History of Massachusetts: The Commonwealth Period*, 377-378.
7 *Columbian Centinel* (MA), July 18, 1812.

adopted a memorial to the president asking him "to rescue them from scenes of horror from the near prospect of which hope, the solace of the wretched, flees away, and which, in their serious apprehension, will endanger the existence of the social compact when the rulers of a free people persevere in a system of measures directly tending . . . to distress a large and respectable section of the country. . . ."[1] Similarly, Newbury " 'passed at a very full meeting without a dissenting vote,' a series of resolutions in decided opposition to the war."[2] Neighboring Boxford passed comparable antiwar resolves.

Feeling the same distress, a Worcester County peace convention considered the national government beyond reform, and concluded it was useless to send resolutions to Washington. But it did agree to exhort its constituents to withhold discretionary aid to the government and not to assist beyond constitutional mandates. Meanwhile, the little town of Douglas in the county resolved "with but four dissenting voices that we view the Act of War as a wanton sacrifice of our dearest Rights and Interest."[3]

Unlike some communities well inland, Worthington, in the Berkshires, voiced its disapproval of events. At a July 3 meeting, "not one vote was given in favor" of the war, "but all agreed in the necessity of organizing an efficient 'Peace Party' and to abolish all other party distinctions."[4] Reading, Massachusetts likewise advanced nonpartisanship. At its special town meeting, "Party distinctions were happily swallowed" and the men "united in expressing their sentiments against the war."[5] The town of Newburyport prepared an "address" to the governor and legislature expressing their feelings about the "ruinous, . . . unexpected, . . . mad war."[6]

Federalist state officials did not need much prodding. The Massachusetts House of Representatives by a 406 to 240 vote adopted its own address to the people criticizing the war, "an event awful, unexpected, hostile to your interests, menacing to your liberties, and revolting to your feelings."[7] Not to be outdone, the Democratic Republican or minority members issued a report asserting it did not believe "the people of Massachusetts are unmindful of the example of their ancestors, who in the most perilous times 'took' no 'counsel from fear'" and urged support of the national government "with that energy and firmness which becomes a free people."[8] Further demonstrating the divisions of the day, the Massachusetts Senate, controlled by Madison's party, passed a resolution approving the war. The senators asserted: "The rightful authority has decreed. Opposition must cease. He that is not for his country is against it."[9]

---

1 William T. Davis, *History of the Town of Plymouth*, 99.
2 Coffin, *Sketch of the History of Newbury, Newburyport, and West Newbury*, 278.
3 *Boston Gazette*, July 20, 1812.
4 *Columbian Centinel* (MA), July 15, 1812.
5 Ibid.
6 *Connecticut Mirror*, July 27, 1812.
7 Barry, 382.
8 *Niles'*, June 27, 1812.
9 Barry, 381.

Massachusetts Governor Caleb Strong, a prominent Federalist, thought otherwise. He proclaimed July 23rd a fast day to mourn a war "against the nation from which we are descended, and which for many generations has been the bulwark of the religion we profess."[1] Governors Roger Griswold of Connecticut and William Jones of Rhode Island issued similar proclamations.

Public fasts proliferated. The events amounted to public prayer, and ministers throughout New England answered the gubernatorial calls. Their presentations for the most part could not be distinguished from Federalist Party dogma. In New Hampshire, Reverend David Osgood reacted quickly. Believing it his duty to testify "against wickedness," he delivered a discourse on the "dreadful calamity" on the first Sunday after receiving the unhappy news of war.[2] Many clergymen followed suit in the days ahead. Some of the preachers published their antiwar sermons. Reverend Samuel Austin of Worcester did so because of "the desire of some who heard" his discourse "and liked it," and "by the desire of some who heard it, and did not like it."[3] This was just part of the beginning of a long campaign. Throughout the duration, the Congregational clergy of New England deprecated the war and positioned itself at the heart of the peace movement. Many ministers, in fact, served as chaplains for their local chapters of the Washington Benevolent Society, a Federalist fraternal order. As one scholar noted, "Madison and his cohorts gave a war, and the godly refused to come."[4]

Strong, however, did more than agitate against the war. He refused to participate. The governor knew his way around. Sixty-seven years old, a Harvard graduate, and member of the bar since 1772, he served seven years in the United States Senate. More to the issue at hand, he represented Massachusetts at the convention that framed the United States Constitution. He based his opposition to national war efforts on constitutional grounds, especially States' rights aspects.

Partly to offset the complaint that the war amounted to a war of the West and South, President Madison tapped Major General Henry Dearborn, a 61-year-old warhorse from New Hampshire to head the northern army. Promptly, Dearborn requisitioned militiamen from the several states. He asked Strong to provide a detachment of the Massachusetts militia consisting of 41 companies. The general designated eight of the companies for service in Rhode Island, while marking the rest for duty under federal command within the Bay State. Strong did not reply to the request.

As for Connecticut, Governor Griswold on August 6 issued a proclamation explaining his rejection of Dearborn's requisition of state militiamen. Backed by his council, Griswold said the militia could not be withdrawn from his authority except under specific conditions expressed in the United States Constitution. And the conditions did not exist. Rhode Island likewise

1 Mahon, *War of 1812*, 32.

2 Osgood, *Solemn Protest Against the Late Declaration of War*, 1.

3 Austin, *Sermon, Preached in Worcester*.

4 Gribbin, *Church History*, 297.

declined to dispatch militiamen to federal service. Governor Jones asserted the same constitutional position held by his neighboring counterparts. New Hampshire relented somewhat and sent to federal service on its own seacoast and northern border a token 246 men during the year. Congress had earlier set the Granite State quota at 3,500. "These military requisitions profoundly agitated the minds of the quiet citizens of the state."[1]

On the other hand, Vermont Governor Jonas Galusha, a Democratic Republican, supported the war and supplied the national government with 2,434 men. Largely as a result, he lost his job. In the 1813 state election, Galusha failed to gain a popular majority, and the legislature decided the contest in favor of Federalist Martin Chittenden. In a celebrated controversy, Chittenden tried to recall the Vermont troops from the field. But before matters deteriorated to such a degree, the martial spirit crossed party lines in the Green Mountains. The Light Infantry Company of Montpelier demonstrated the point early in July. Captain Jeduthan Loomis, a forceful opponent of the war, paraded his company and addressed the troops, declaring every man had a duty to respond to the national appeal for detached militia to serve under federal control. He ordered those ready to volunteer to step two paces to the front. All but five men stepped forward.

Randolph, to the south, had more difficulty reaching its quota, necessitating a ruse on the part of two elders. Asked to come up with 20 volunteers, the local Madison adherents wanted a strong showing. The town's four militia companies were called out and formed in a line. "Then the music started from the right of the line and passed down in front of the column, around the left wing, and so back to the right again." Patriotic tunes such as "Yankee Doodle" filled the air. The 300 militiamen were asked to fall in behind the musicians, which they did. But when the call went out for volunteers to step forward "to serve their country," nobody moved. The performance was repeated three times without any takers. This prompted old Deacon Flint to declare, "[I]f the boys are all afraid to go, I will go," and he stepped off with the musicians. Old man Tracy followed suit, saying, "If you go, I will go as your waiter." This act so excited some of the younger men that more than 20 jumped in behind the two gents, and soon they all retired to a nearby tavern. Now at ease, the commanding officer asked the deacon if he really wanted to go. "O! no," said he, for he was too old and decrepit for a soldier, "but, if the boys don't want to go that have volunteered, I will."[2] Having served their purpose, Flint and Tracy were discharged by the commander from further service.

Vermont's initial backing of the war seemed to follow a pattern. Opposition Federalists and peace proponents long complained support for the war increased as one moved inland away from the coast and the major impact of embargoes and the enemy warships. Indeed, Massachusetts had its own example of this tendency. To counteract the influence of a July 14 Northampton

---

1 Sanborn, *History of New Hampshire*, 254.
2 Hemenway, *Vermont Historical Gazetteer*, 1024.

antiwar convention attended by 57 towns, 142 Republican delegates from the interior counties of Franklin, Hampden, and Hampshire gathered in the same town a week later. Beforehand, a West Springfield committee studied the causes of the war and prepared a report for the gathering. In short, the committee found: "There is no doubt . . . the United States have just cause of war against England and France; but sound policy required that we should not be burthened by a war with two powerful nations at once, Congress therefore wisely selected England as our enemy, she being the greatest aggressor." The convention passed 11 resolutions supporting the positions of President Madison and the Massachusetts Senate and it condemned "all meetings and conventions for the purpose of opposing the general government and the laws of the union, as dangerous during the existence of the present war and highly criminal. . . ."[1]

In this atmosphere, several days after his initial request, Dearborn renewed his call to Strong. The governor declined again, but did issue a general order directing his militia to prepare to respond hastily to any military threat within Massachusetts. At the end of July, the secretary of war got involved and urged the governor to fulfill Dearborn's request. Once again, Strong refused.

After receiving a supporting decision from a panel of Massachusetts Supreme Judicial Court justices, the governor defended his position most notably in an August 14 message to the legislature. He suggested Massachusetts did not face imminent danger, because Dearborn marched off to Canada on July 22. More to the point, he said he was fully disposed to adhere to the Constitution of the United States and the laws made there under. He regretted an officer of the federal government made an unconstitutional request he was bound to reject. He stressed he found himself under a fundamental obligation to maintain the rights of the Commonwealth.

Beyond the demonstrable chagrin and misgivings, the developing crisis also prompted realistic action in a number of towns, especially along the exposed and somewhat remote coast. The most vulnerable town from a geographic standpoint acted quickly to protect its interests. As soon as the fact of war became known in Eastport, Maine, the residents met and "unanimously agreed to preserve a good understanding with the Inhabitants of New-Brunswick, and to discountenance all depredations on the property of each other."[2] The British authorities responded accordingly. Sir John C. Sherbrooke, the lieutenant governor of Nova Scotia, and his naval chief, Vice Admiral Herbert Sawyer, informed Eastporters that British forces were under orders to respect their persons and property "so long as they shall carry on their usual and accustomed trade and intercourse" with the maritime provinces "and abstain from acts of hostility and molestation towards

---

1 Library of Congress, *Prompt Patriotism.*
2 Joshua M. Smith, *Rogues of Quoddy,* 296.

the inhabitants thereof and their property."[1] A state of neutrality benefited both sides.

At the same time, Machias asked the Commonwealth of Massachusetts for "a supply of Arms & Ammunition for the defence of the Town."[2] Governor Strong also received a plea from the scattered inhabitants of the unincorporated settlements on the Penobscot River north of Orono that constitute present-day Milford, Argyle, Greenbush, and Passadumkeag. Sixty petitioners expressed anxiety over the fact developing plans anticipated dispatching inland militia units to the coast to repel British waterborne forces. This movement would leave the remote territory open to Indian attacks launched from Canada. In just several days, the men explained, the tribes could attack and fade back across the line ahead of any pursuit mounted from away. The petitioners declared they had "no apprehension of a large force but in our present defenceless state three hundred might be as fatal as three thousand." And they noted: "We are very sensible that our property to defend is small when compared to that on the sea coast, but, that our wives and children are as dear to us as to any, your Excellency will readily conceive."[3] The petition requested construction of a stockade fort on Passadumkeag Stream and a supply of arms and ammunition. Selectmen from Bangor and Orono endorsed the request.

After raising and appropriating $150 "for a Stock of powder" in anticipation of the war, once war was declared, Sullivan, like many towns in Maine, appointed "a Committee of Safety and Correspondents."[4] At Deer Isle, a July 12 meeting voted to "lay aside and not read" the widely distributed defensive recommendations of the selectmen of Boston; decided to petition the national government "for one or more companies of United States Soldiers" to be stationed on the island; and agreed to ask Massachusetts "for the Loan of Sixty muskets and four, four pound guns."[5] Buckstown at the same time authorized its selectmen to purchase a "hundred pounds of powder and a quantity of balls proportioned to the same, in addition to the stock required by law."[6] Sensing things to come, Hampden, Maine met on July 11 to consider the adequacy of "the measures adopted by the general government in defence of our Commertial rights." The meeting chose a committee to review the Boston recommendations; voted to pay activated militiamen $12 per month over the federal allowance; voted to "double the quantity of powder and balls that the Law requires"; and moved to procure "Ten stands of arms".[7] Eden (now Bar Harbor) appropriated $50 for powder.

1 *New England Palladium* (MA), July 24, 1812.
2 *Machias* (ME) *Town Records 1795-1823*, 1:221.
3 *Bangor Historical Magazine*, 5:163.
4 *1789-1831 Book of Sullivan* (ME) *Town Records*.
5 *Town Clerk's Record of Town Meetings, Vol. II*, Deer Isle, ME, 101.
6 *Records of the Town of Buckstown* (ME) *No. 1*, 182.
7 *Records, Vol. 1, 1751-1835, Town of Hampden*, ME, 157.

Thomaston "freeholders & other Inhabitants" met and agreed to pay the town's militiamen "when called into actual Service fifteen Dollars per month in addition to their other pay." Also, the town petitioned federal authorities for "one or more gun boats or Batteries as they shall think proper for the protection of Owls head Harbour." Before adjourning, the town meeting set up a process to confer about the situation "with the neighboring Towns on Penobscot Bay."[1]

Nobleboro, Maine, in addition to establishing a committee of safety and correspondence, voted "to pay all those who have been drafted and ordered into the service of the commonwealth by authority $4.00 per month in addition to the Commonwealth pay."[2] Nearby Boothbay on July 7 voted to petition the president "to grant them speedily the aid of a naval or land force as he may in his judgment think most proper and suitable to the situation."[3] A North Yarmouth, Maine town meeting instructed its selectmen to "purchase an additional stock of Ammunition for the use of the town equal to the stock required by law" and to "look up the swivels and small arms belonging to the town."[4] And Industry, Maine added 23 cents to the regular pay of each militiaman who furnished his own arms and equipment. In Washington, Congressman Richard Cutts of the District of Maine moved quickly and received a promise from the navy secretary to assign a government boat to Winter Harbor (now Biddeford Pool).

At the end of July, Dresden, Maine men gathered and by a 68 to 24 vote rejected several antiwar proposals. One failed motion sought a disapproving memorial to the president. A second rejected article expressed a wish for peace and an abhorrence of an alliance with France. Another unsuccessful article sought support for a county peace convention, while still another proposed the adoption of vague and expedient measures to deal with the crisis short of using force. But a few days later, in adjoining Wiscasset, "with deep regret & utter astonishment" a town meeting passed a resolution expressing "the deepest horror" over a perceived alliance with the "despotic tyrant" in France. The gathering also chose four delegates to the county peace convention planned for their town. And in a practical move, reluctant to abuse Madison, the townsmen directed their selectmen to ask the president for "means of defence and . . . further aid and protection."[5]

Meanwhile, Rumford, safely away from the Maine coast, rigorously opposed Governor Strong's anti-administration position. Also away from the shore, Monmouth adopted an equally bellicose stance. But its inland status does not explain. The town laid claim to two of the nation's prominent warriors. Major General Henry Dearborn moved to the rural community west of Augusta in 1784 and appears to have remained until accepting appointment

---

1 *Town Records Vol. 1 1777-1825* Thomaston, ME, 157.

2 Dunbar and Dow, *Nobleboro, Maine – A History*, 110.

3 Greene, *History of Boothbay*, 249-250.

4 *North Yarmouth (ME) Town Records Volume Second*, 400.

5 *Town Records, Vol. 3, 1790-1813*, Wiscasset, ME, 537-538.

as secretary of war in 1801. And Joel Chandler, another New Hampshire native, moved to Monmouth about 1780. At the outbreak of war he served as the major general of the 17th division of the Massachusetts militia. And within a month of the declaration of war, Chandler became a brigadier general in the U.S. Army. Little wonder, on July 6, the town voted, "we do highly approve of the act of Congress declaring war" and "we will consider all persons . . . who shall either by words, deeds or addresses take and pursue measures calculated and intended to create disunion . . . to counteract or oppose . . . the general government . . . as enemies to the best interest and well-being of our common country."[1]

A Carver, Massachusetts meeting in early August refused to appoint a committee of safety or take other defensive steps "in this time of Commotion and Political Division."[2] Instead, the town placed its trust in the national government and voted to pay its militiaman an added $14 a month. Watertown also took steps to improve the lot of its militiamen. The town voted to assure every man received $15 per month by adding to the government allowance. The town additionally agreed "to advance each Man ten dollars, when called to march into actual service."[3] Abington simply adopted a series of resolves favoring the national administration and its war while Hubbardston tried another approach. The inland town called all its men liable to military service together in the meetinghouse. "Plenty of grog was distributed among them, and when they had 'well drunk,' earnest appeals were made to them to volunteer. The fife and drum struck up stirring strains . . . and any who were willing to volunteer, were requested to fall into a certain pew. Only one or two could be found to go."[4]

Unlike some towns, Rye, New Hampshire did not resort to a plea for aid from Washington. While the town exhibited Yankee independence, it did not cast aside Yankee frugality. At a July 7 town meeting, the voters directed the selectmen to deliver to each militiaman "a good fire arm one half pound Powder and balls in proportion." But the meeting added the thrifty proviso, "that each and every man that doth not return the same Powder and balls when demanded by the Selectmen of the Town shall pay the Town a fine of five dollars if they have not fired it away in action with the enemy."[5] Likewise, Providence, Rhode Island acted to care for itself. An August 7 town meeting recommended "to all persons capable of bearing arms forthwith to furnish themselves with arms and ammunition, and be ready at a moment's warning to aid in defence of themselves, their families and their country."[6]

Despite the growing danger, some places remained intractable and bitter. Castine recorded itself against the war and voluntary enlistments. Simi-

1 Cochrane, *History of Monmouth and Wales*, vol. 2, 573.
2 Griffith, *History of the Town of Carver*, 241.
3 Works Progress Administration, *Watertown Records*, 83.
4 Stowe, *History of the Town of Hubbardston*, 74.
5 Parsons, *History of the Town of Rye*, 275.
6 Carroll, *Rhode Island: Three Centuries of Democracy*, 448.

larly, by a 40 to 15 vote, Salisbury, Massachusetts rejected an effort to pay its drafted men a $15 per month supplement. An attempt to give these men an additional $10 a month also failed. Exeter, New Hampshire spent more time on the pay issue, only to reach the same outcome as Salisbury. A group of citizens, "being sensible that duties of a Soldier, when called into actual service, are arduous, fatigueing & respo[n]sible, & that a compensation ought to be provided adequate to the services," petitioned for town meeting action to this end.[1] Somewhat ahead of their time, the town took the now standard course of appointing a study committee. Within the month, the committee returned a sure if not cocksure report.

The group noted Congress provided for militia compensation and no federal or state law "made it the duty of [a] Town to add to such compensation," and "we consider any measures for this purpose, as unnecessary and improper, *if not ellegal*...." More expressive of their core beliefs, the committee added "we deem it improper to take on ourselves burdens, in addition to those laid on the community at large for the support of an offensive war, in which, as a Town, we have no particular interest — and which in our opinion, neither the honour nor the interest of the Nation demanded, and that ... we greatly fear its tendency will be to injure, if not destroy, our system of government." As a final point, the members pledged themselves to the country and the constitution, but felt "bound as friends to the protestant religion, to independence, to national union and happiness ... to forbear any act, which may be considered an approbation of a war, that may produce such calamities."[2] An August town meeting handily voted to accept the report.

In Belfast, Maine, a July special town meeting took like action. The warrant contained articles to see if the town would vote "any Money for the purchase of firearms"; "any thing to be paid" to activated militiamen; and to "authorize those who Volunteer themselves in defence of the Town to draw their supply of ammunition from the Town Stock."[3] The meeting voted to postpone without action each of these war measures. At a Rindge, New Hampshire town meeting only three men stood for war. In Jaffrey, out of 220 voters, only "about ten or twelve" supported the conflict.[4] At Pembroke, New Hampshire, a meeting refused to act on militia pay articles. And the townsmen of Newbury and Newfane, Vermont voted the same way.

Geography allowed some places to sit out or altogether ignore the conflict. Bingham, Maine is one example. Well up the Kennebec River, throughout the duration, the town did not take any official action for or against the war. Despite the impact on their farming and lumbering economy, the absence of a military threat enabled the town fathers to remain detached from national affairs. The stance of nearby Madison is unknown, because, as in several other towns, the period town records were lost in a fire. But it is

1 *Town Records 1796-1815 Pages 100-221*, Exeter, NH, 151.
2 Ibid., 153-154.
3 *The Second Book of Records in the Town of Belfast*, ME, 115.
4 Cutter, *History of the Town of Jaffrey*, 139.

safe to assume there were more than a few townspeople who supported the president. When incorporated in March 1804, the citizens named their town after the founding father from Virginia and then secretary of state.

Beyond all the official and organized hand wringing, opposition, and resistance, right away the war altered and impacted the lives of a great many individuals. Appreciating the hardships to follow, Reverend Alfred Johnson of the First Congregational Parish of Belfast gave "a bond relinquishing his salary during the present war with Great Britain."[1] Other New Englanders saw only opportunity. Wiscasset shipwrights quickly laid down the keel of a 309-ton armed brig. Pierced for 16 guns, she moved off the stocks in 50 days. Sold in Boston and fitted out in Salem, the owners named her the *Grand Turk*. She went on to a celebrated and profitable career as a privateer during the war.

Asa Parker of Jaffrey, New Hampshire felt driven by fraternal concern. He mailed his brother Isaac in Keene a book on cavalry tactics. "[B]ut my Book on Sword Exercise I cannot on the most diligent enquiry find. . . . I likewise send you here a little Book For you to look upon That you may know a Sergeants place When you do one become." Asa went on to lament the country "is in a critical and alarming state for I am well convinced (as you state you are) that there is a *Gallic* influence in our councils." He opined it would be important to elect better men as rulers. And although the country had just cause to engage Britain, "our government acted very imprudently in bringing it upon us in our unprepared state." Asa concluded: "I fear our divisions and animosities will have a tendency to lengthen out this war because if the British find a strong party here that is opposed to it they may probably calculate on an insurrection. . . . For myself I shall neither plan a Rebellion nor join one. I like our Government tho not the administrators of it. . . ."[2]

Other New Englanders moved into the spotlight. Born in Salisbury, New Hampshire in 1782, Daniel Webster became an outstanding lawyer and Federalist Party leader in the years leading up to the war. In the days following the start of hostilities, he took advantage of developments. On July 4, 1812, Webster spoke to the Portsmouth chapter of the Washington Benevolent Society. At every chance, this fraternal order agitated against the administration in office. Webster, however, set a diplomatic tone in his speech. He declared, "If we are taxed, to carry on this war, we shall pay. If our personal services are required, we shall yield them to the precise extent of our constitutional liability." He stressed: "By the exercise of our constitutional right of suffrage, by the peaceable remedy of election, we shall seek to restore wisdom to our councils, and peace to our country."[3]

A month later, a large assembly of Rockingham County citizens gathered at Brentwood, New Hampshire to prepare a protesting memorial to the president. They delegated the task to Webster. Years later, he recalled: "It

---

1 Abbott, *History of Belfast*, 11.
2 Parker, *Letter*.
3 Current, *Daniel Webster and the Rise of National Conservatism*, 13.

was an anti-war paper of some note in its time." Webster thought it proved "of a tone and strain less vulgar than such things are prone to be."[1]

In his learned and detailed protest, Webster advanced all the expected arguments. And he made it clear, New England did not oppose the war purely because of timidity or peaceable tendencies. "We are not, sir, among those who feel an unmanly reluctance to the privations, or a nervous sensibility to the dangers of war. Many of us had the honor of aiding, by our humble efforts, in the establishment of our independence, and of exposing our lives, in more than one field of danger and blood, in our country's service."[2] Before the year passed, Webster moved up. The decennial reapportionment added a sixth seat to New Hampshire's congressional delegation. In the November election, the voters sent Webster to Congress as a Federalist in opposition to the war.

As must be expected, others did not fare well. John French of Newton, New Hampshire found himself in the west marching to Detroit in a 1,300-man regiment of the regular Army "made up with all kinds of People and men of no Learning." He lamented his misfortune and the error of his ways in an August letter to his wife. "I wright to you in my Letter how that I came to be a Soldier it was By drink I have not drink any since I have been Listed nor shant as long as I remain in the Army." As something of an excuse, he noted "there is six Soldiers from Newhampshire with us thay Ware taken in the same that I was. . . ." He did not expect to see his wife "No more till the war is over if ever. O if you New the state of my mind you would freely Forgive me but O my Dear wife if tears would Have brout me back I should have ben to home Long a go. . . ." In the meantime, he prayed the Almighty would take her "under his protection."[3]

Private French, however, did not agonize alone. In the months ahead, citizens of all stations would endure hurt and hardship in an unpopular conflict of unexpected duration.

1 *Writings and Speeches of Daniel Webster*, 599.
2 Ibid., 601.
3 John French, *Letter*.

CHAPTER 2. THE MOST PREJUDICIAL PLANTATION

All of the New England protesting antiwar town meetings, public fasts, county peace conventions, and editorial outrage that erupted in the wake of the declaration of war did not surprise many at the time. The caustic war opposition of large segments of reputable society was understood if not appreciated. Much of the disagreeableness traced to long-standing political, religious, and economical differences between sections of the country. These differences are better appreciated with some understanding of New England's culture — its origins, development, and modes of thought.

At the beginning of the 19th century, New England consisted of its current land area covered by the present five states of Connecticut, Massachusetts, New Hampshire, Rhode Island, and Vermont as well as the eastern part of Massachusetts known as the District of Maine. As an aftereffect of the war, in 1820, Maine separated and became a state, the final step in forming the region as it is known today.

But the most enduring and naturally formed region of the country — the only one with its own semi-official flag — began to take shape much earlier. By the beginning of the 16th century, European explorers were probing the North Atlantic coast of North America, seeking, among other things, the Northwest Passage, the fabled short cut to the Orient. In 1524, the celebrated navigator Giovanni Da Verrazzano, sailing in behalf of France, cruised the coastline from the Carolinas past Maine to Newfoundland. He made a memorable stop at Casco Bay, and, at arms length, traded with the local Abnakis despite their openly hostile behavior. Their unfriendly manner contrasted with the generally well-disposed demeanor of other Indians encountered along the way. This is a fair sign the Maine Abnakis had prior exposure to incompatible Europeans. When Verrazzano left, the Abanakis jeered and several men of the band turned and saluted by bending and exposing bared buttocks, a derisive gesture known today as mooning. Verrazzano retaliated by naming the area " 'Terra Onde di Mala Gente' (land of Bad People)."[1]

In the mid-16th century attention shifted away from the elusive Northwest Passage and in the direction of the mythical and vast but opulent region known as Norumbega. Ill-defined, the name more or less became associated with what is now New England, and, perhaps, parts of Atlantic Canada. The capital, a grand city of houses believed to be constructed on crystal and silver pillars, was thought to be located on the banks of the Penobscot River. The vain search for the fair city continued well into the 17th century. In reality, the fanciful city served as a symbol of a new goal — unlimited natural resources. The region possessed unglittering but boundless wealth — from fish and furs to forest products. As much as anything else, this richness formed and defined the New England region that confronted Jefferson and Madison in the 19th century.

The Frenchman André Thevet visited the Maine coast in 1556 and penned an early promotional piece including a description of the Penobscot. "Here we entered a river which is the finest in the whole world. . . . Several beautiful rivers flow into it."[2] The Englishman David Ingram followed in 1568. Abandoned on the Gulf of Mexico, he and two shipmates walked all the way to the Saint John River to find passage home. He wrote a fanciful narrative about passing through present-day Massachusetts and Maine and described the city of Norumbega, a community full of peltry if not silver and gold. John Walker of England followed up on the reports and sailed to the Penobscot in 1580. He returned by way of France, where he garnered notice by selling a quantity of furs for 40 shillings each.

With his laudatory writings, the chaplain to the British minister in Paris also played an important role in the future of the region. In 1582, Richard Hakluyt published a book recounting many of the remarkable North American voyages. He encouraged English colonization of the region. Two years later, he prepared a pamphlet designed to convince Queen Elizabeth to support the effort.

Bartholomew Gosnold led a 1602 expedition to the Maine coast and the Cape Cod area. In fact, Gosnold applied the name Cape Cod to the tip of the famous peninsula after seeing the astounding amount of cod in nearby waters. As something of an indicator of the growing interaction between the Old and the New Worlds, when Gosnold stopped at Casco Bay, an Abnaki decked out in European garments greeted him as he came ashore. Verrazzano had earlier made the pointed observation that only fur-clad Indians lived thereabouts. At any rate, Gosnold's navigator, John Brereton, wrote a vivid and positive account of the voyage, describing the plentitude of the region. Gosnold's plan to establish a minor post on Cuttyhunk failed when members of his crew would not agree to remain behind.

---

1 Beck, *Sailor Historian*, 64.
2 Calvert, *Dawn Over the Kennebec*, 41.

Energized by Gosnold's experience, Martin Pring left England in 1603 to pursue the commercial possibilities described by his predecessors. He spent a fair amount of time poking into the rivers of southern Maine and New Hampshire, especially the Piscataqua. Venturing south to the Elizabeth Islands, he found stands of the sassafras tree. Pring loaded his boat with sassafras, prized for medicinal purposes in England, and returned home.

Following the reports of Gosnold and Pring, in 1605, Captain George Weymouth explored the Maine coast for a short time. Though his visit turned out to be brief, Weymouth's companion, James Rosier, gathered enough material to write still another glowing account promoting the wonderful abundance of this part of the world.

The French showed continued interest in the region, and, in 1604, initiated the European settlement phase. Pierre Dugua, Sieur de Mons, and his map maker and chronicler Samuel de Champlain, sailed into Passamaquoddy Bay and settled on Saint Croix Island near what is now the town of Calais, Maine. After one harsh winter, the French left Saint Croix in search of a more temperate site. They explored as far south as Cape Cod, and eventually returned north to encamp at Port Royal, Nova Scotia.

After fitful starts, in 1607, the Popham expedition settled at the mouth of Maine's Kennebec River. Promoted by Sir John Popham, Lord Chief Justice of England and Wales, and headed by his nephew George, the company included some 120 colonists. The members came to America to seek their fortune "in the broad and savage wilderness. They knew not what mines of silver and gold, and diamonds, might be found in the depths of the green woods."[1] The venture became the first systematic effort to set up a permanent colony in New England. The group erected several buildings and an elemental fort named St. George. As a prelude to a major New England industry, ample resources at hand, the Popham men built a 30-ton pinnace and called her the *Virginia*, supposedly the first ship built in North America. But, like the French at Saint Croix, the English at Popham experienced overwhelming setbacks. Severe winter weather exacerbated the fact their storehouse burned. And backers in England died, as did their leader, George Popham. Discouraged, the little band gave up and returned to their homeland, some sailing in the *Virginia*.

With the failure of the Popham expedition, colonizing the region lost its appeal for a period. Traders and fishermen, of course, continued to frequent the coast. Then, in 1614, Captain John Smith, the formidable explorer and earlier governor of Jamestown, Virginia took a step with a lasting impact. By the late 16th century, British mariners were calling the place New England. Smith formalized the designation. He came to the region seeking gold and whales, but devoted his best efforts to mapping the coastline from Penobscot Bay to Cape Cod. He labeled the subject of his map "New England." The map appeared in his 1616 published account entitled "A Description of New

---

1 Lilly, *History of New England*, 27.

England." Prince Charles, later Charles I, endorsed the New England name, although he did edit the map to change some 30 "barbarous" Indian names.

The next important event in the settlement of New England may be its most memorable. Late in 1620, the Mayflower Pilgrims landed at Cape Cod, now well-known as Provincetown. After several weeks, the group sailed west across what is now called Cape Cod Bay to permanently settle at Plymouth. Despite travails, the Pilgrims held on and succeeded and revived interest in colonization of the harsh but potentially rich region called New England.

Colonists from Old England, many of them dissenters, prodded by the religious and civil discord of the period, moved in carrying a deep-seated affinity for the mother country. Their primary goals were to worship God and make money. To accomplish the second objective, they tied themselves to the sea. Mountain barriers and the absence of lengthy navigable rivers tended to confine settlers to the coastline and adjacent foothills. While poor and rocky soils ruled out much more than subsistence farming, vast timberlands provided the materials for ship-building and numerous first-rate harbors encouraged and supported maritime pursuits. The draw of the sea proved overwhelming. And by the Federalist period (1765–1815), the region had a single-minded attachment to waterborne "trade and more trade."[1]

Colonization spread from Plymouth and Massachusetts Bay west to the Connecticut River and the Berkshires and east up the Merrimack Valley and down the Maine coast. Puritan idealism and a preeminent regard for religion and order prevailed as settlements took hold. An equal attachment to industry existed and attention to learning developed. As the decades passed, the region produced an inordinate number of national leaders in politics, business, religion, law, literature, philosophy, art, medicine, and science. As a consequence, "New Englanders have long asserted their claim to centrality, a claim that is at the core of a regional identity developed over four centuries."[2]

Early struggles for subsistence bred frugality in the stock. An early historian observed: "Money is hardly got and carefully spent" by New Englanders; "and no man lavishes it or lends it, except on the best security."[3] Generations passed before the trait began to wane. Hezekiah Niles, editor of an influential national newsweekly, irritated at the New England stance during the War of 1812, poked fun at this proclivity. When militiamen arrived in Boston from the interior during the summer of 1814, "it was remarked in the papers of that town, that, 'with characteristic economy' they 'marched barefoot,' carrying their boots and shoes in their hands, or attached to their knapsacks. It is by such 'economies' and the invincible fortitude, and patient industry of the people," that "the thin soil of *New England* . . . sustains its thick population."[4]

---

1 Wilkie and Tague, *Historical Atlas of Massachusetts*, 25.
2 Feintuch and Watters, *Encyclopedia of New England*, xv.
3 Elliott, *New England History*, vol. 2, 14.
4 *Niles' Weekly Register* (MD), November 16, 1814.

Nonetheless, as much as anything, early New Englanders abhorred the idea of accepting charity. For a good many New England generations, to be unable to meet one's basic needs was sinful. "God helps those who help themselves" was practiced doctrine.[1] The national government's embargoes and restrictions on trade associated with the War of 1812 forced even some of the most industrious into idleness. "Many a noble man became a mere wreck of humanity, and many a delicately bred lady descended into an unthrifty, slatternly household drudge, while their offspring, half clad and half fed, mixed unrestrained amongst the very dregs of the population."[2]

This was not what New England was supposed to be about. The firstcomers came as free people intent on self-sufficiency. And above all, they wanted to be left alone to make their own way. Upon moving to Maine, E.B. White observed his neighbors still clinging to this philosophy. "New Englanders are jealous of their right to govern themselves as they like . . .," he wrote in 1940.[3] Modernity has chipped away at this principle, but the spirit remains alive and well in places. New Hampshire still proudly displays its motto "Live Free or Die" on its auto license plates.

Yet the firstcomers were not against organizing themselves for the common good. The Mayflower Compact signed by the Pilgrims at Cape Cod harbor in November 1620 established a social contract under which the people were the state. Two decades later, in 1643, after the Pequot War, the struggling colonies in Connecticut, Massachusetts Bay (including New Hampshire), New Haven, and Plymouth confronted another specific need. They banded together for mutual defense and formed The United Colonies of New England, a prototype of the national union which followed many years later. The Maine and Rhode Island settlements were denied admission on religious grounds. Ironically, the confederation concept originated in Hartford, the seat of the infamous 1814 gathering known as the Hartford Convention.

A council of eight men, two from each colony, managed and ruled the affairs of the confederation. The member entities divided expenses and spoils in proportion to their adult male populations. With only one fourth of the voting power, the arrangement proved unfair to Massachusetts with a population greater than the others combined. As a precursor to its behavior in the War of 1812, when its partners ignored its objections and sought war with the Dutch, Massachusetts simply declined to participate. Although revived as a productive force during King Philip's War in the mid-seventies, the union finally dissolved in 1684.

Recalling Verrazzano's opinion, the region continued to hold the reputation of being different and difficult. Once colonization commenced, the inhabitants behaved in a manner to cement the early judgment. The firstcomers did little to raise or produce commodities but stressed fishing in direct competition with Old England. For this, Sir Josiah Child and his collabora-

1 Elliott, 12.

2 Emery, *Reminiscences of a Nonagenarian*, 275.

3 E.B. White, *One Man's Meat*, 122.

tors in their 1669 essay, *The Nature of Plantations and Their Consequences to Great Britain, Seriously Considered*, thought: "New England is the most prejudicial Plantation in the Kingdom of England."[1]

Charles II certainly shared the assessment. The Massachusetts Declaration of Rights of 1661 drew his ire. This important colonial document enacted by the General Court asserted any attempt to impose laws on Massachusetts contrary to Massachusetts laws not at odds to the laws of England amounted to a violation of the colony's collective rights. The resentment of Charles festered. Massachusetts disregarded his Navigation Acts, denied the English church entrance into the colony, and, in general, acted too independently. After years of political infighting and a lengthy legal fight, the crown withdrew the colony's charter, and, therefore, retracted the independence of Massachusetts.

James II assumed the throne upon the death of Charles. Overtly Catholic and even more of a despot than his predecessor, in 1686, he sent Sir Edmund Andros to govern the dominion of New England and stem its growing autonomy. Andros, assisted by a submissive council, ruled with an iron hand. He curbed popular assemblies, assumed the power of taxation, and limited town meetings as well as the press. He meddled in land titles, touching a particularly raw nerve. Without success, Andros demanded the charters of Rhode Island and Connecticut. Then, in December 1688, across the sea, the Prince of Orange issued his declaration on Protestant religion and liberty, spawning the Glorious Revolution. The fall of James followed within days, and the prince assumed the throne of England as William III. Massachusetts leaders learned of this turn of events, and seized Andros as he tried to flee disguised in women's clothing. He was returned as a prisoner to London, and the earliest substantial effort to curtail the liberties of the colonists came to a failed end. Out of the experience, New Englanders learned lessons and tasted the success of resisting arbitrary authority and asserting independence when their inherent rights and way of life were threatened.

Over the generations to follow, men such as James Otis, John Hancock, Samuel Adams, John Adams, and others would build upon this foundation. Boston and its Faneuil Hall, always the center of New England, became known as the "Cradle of Liberty." And this overriding drive to remain free and unfettered and retain the right to prosper seemed to make New Englanders a little different than many of their countrymen.

Years later, an observer tried in another way to explain this apparent diversity when he wrote: "Nature has made New England different from the other sections of the country, and the circumstances of their ancestry and environment have made New England people somewhat different from the people of other sections."[2] Their tight knitted communities, ruled by open town meetings and the Congregational and Presbyterian churches, engendered a parochialism that approached contempt for the country to the south

---

1 Robert G. Albion, et al., *New England and the Sea*, 28.
2 George French, *New England*, 5.

and west. "Between New England and the Middle States was a gap like that between Scotland and England."[1] The eminent jurist Joseph Story of Massachusetts, a moderate member of Madison's party, spoke to the point when he said: "New England was expected, so far as the Republicans were concerned, to do everything and have nothing. They were to obey, but not to be trusted."[2] New Englanders had little tolerance for subordination of any kind, especially when their interests clashed with the interests of other regions.

Some from outside the region saw other differences. In 1775, the patrician Virginian at the head of the American army criticized what he considered undisciplined New England militia units. George Washington thought New Englanders in general were "an exceedingly dirty & nasty people."[3] During the War of 1812, another military leader, England's Sir John C. Sherbrooke, saw another side of the people of the region. His assessment was not as unkind, but it was not intended as a compliment. At the height of the Hartford Convention when Massachusetts explored a separate armistice with Great Britain, Sherbrooke cautioned Lord Bathurst, "The subtlety of the New Englanders will require a most able Negotiator to treat with them."[4]

Another Englishman in the same year characterized New Englanders or Yankees in much the same terms. While cruising off New Hampshire, Lieutenant Henry Napier made an entry in his journal alluding to the craftiness he observed among the natives. "Self, the great ruling principle, more powerful with Yankees than any people I ever saw. Begin with a dollar and proceed to any amount, you may always buy a Yankee in almost any rank and station!"[5] The renowned Hezekiah Niles put it more bluntly when he opined that New Englanders were of "a class of persons, who, as the *Dutch* merchant said, 'would scorch their sails by trading with h—l, to make a penny.'"[6] Timothy Dwight, himself of the region, put it a little differently. "A New Englander," he thought, "often discerns means of business and profit which elsewhere are chiefly concealed from men of the same class. Hence," he added, "when prevented from pursuing one kind of business, or unfortunate in it, he easily, and in very many instances successfully, commences another."[7]

On the strength of such judgments, over the years, Yankees "became known as a people proud, willful, tenacious, stubborn, often taciturn, always self-reliant, men and women who demanded terribly of themselves. . . . The tradition of nonconformity that had given the culture its birth lived on, too — a perverse independence of mind that would cultivate the flames of

1 Henry Adams, *History of the United States of America During the Administrations of Thomas Jefferson*, 76.
2 Higginson, *Harper's New Monthly Magazine*, 753.
3 Joseph J. Ellis, *His Excellency George Washington*, 78.
4 Martell, *American Historical Review*, 558.
5 Whitehill, *New England Blockaded in 1814*, 18.
6 *Niles'*, November 26, 1814.
7 Dwight, *Travels in New England and New York*, 4:225.

the American Revolution,"[1] and, later, steer the region on a different course during the second war with Great Britain.

Having said this, party politics of the early 19th century played a large role in shaping the antiwar stance of New England. The minority Federalist Party led the opposition to the war. Headed originally by Alexander Hamilton and after by John Adams, the party flourished for a time in New England and showed some strength in the Middle Atlantic States. Conservative in outlook, it believed protection of property was a primary purpose of government. The party advocated a strong central government and a well-ordered society. It drew support from the educated, mercantile, and propertied classes. Openly pro-British, the party considered France the great threat to this country and Napoleon the anti-Christ "at whose perfidy and corruption Lucifer blushes and Hell itself stands astonished."[2] President John Adams, son of Massachusetts, even entered into an undeclared and limited naval war against France in 1798.

The dominant party of the time, first called Anti-Federalist, formed under Thomas Jefferson as Republicans, later called Democratic Republicans. The Federalists derisively called them Jacobins, because of their pro-French policies and views. The party drew initial support from landed interests, especially from the slaveholding regions. However, Jefferson's democratic agenda appealed to the large working classes as well as the less privileged, and his party gained strength and majority status.

Hamilton broke with the more moderate Adams over doctrine, and a weakened Adams lost to Jefferson in the 1800 presidential election. Jefferson's broader appeal and party-building skills led to the so-called Virginia dynasty. Protégés James Madison and James Monroe followed him in the White House. Once Adams lost the presidency, his party went into decline — a fading New England party with its greatest strength in Massachusetts and Connecticut.

As much as anything, the party's minority status in the pre-war and war years can be traced to the fact its leaders were men from the second tier with little national stature or following. Harrison Gray Otis, nephew of James Otis the Patriot, best articulated the Federalist view. His biographer called him the "Urbane Federalist." Previously a congressman, and later a United States senator, he served in the Massachusetts Senate during the important years of 1805 to 1811. Timothy Pickering represented Massachusetts in the U.S. Senate from 1803 to 1811. He used this forum in a relentless attack on the national government's pre-war policies. Massachusetts Governor Strong, who held his key post from 1800 to 1807 and from 1812 to 1816, vexed Madison and Dearborn, and made a greater impact in opposition than his cohorts. A fourth leader from the Bay State — Josiah Quincy — is known as the "Last Federalist." But while in Congress from 1805 to 1813, his opponents considered him no more than a rabble-rouser.

---

1 Pierce, *New England States*, 16.
2 Caffrey, *Twilight's Last Gleaming*, 78.

Although Federalist Roger Griswold occupied the key Connecticut governor's post at the outset of the war, his absolute opposition to Madison did not have sustained effect since he died in office on October 25, 1812. John Cotton Smith succeeded Griswold and served in the position until 1817. While he remained faithful to Federalist antiwar policies, he exerted little influence beyond the Nutmeg State. James Hillhouse played a more active although not great role. He represented Connecticut as a Federalist in the U.S. House from 1791 to 1796 and in the U.S. Senate for the next 13 years.

As well as Chittenden of Vermont, the foregoing men formed the core of the Federalist opposition to Jefferson and Madison. By any standard, they were outmatched.

Never far from the region's party politics of the period, religion played a vociferous and persistent role in the antiwar movement in New England. Public fasts, a pious practice that originated with the early Puritan settlers, became a favorite tool of politicians and clergy alike. Elected leaders called for the fasts, and the ministers performed. A prominent historian of the following generation recalled the clergy of the 1812 period "had . . . inherited all the fervid, stubborn, uncompromising Puritan spirit, and with it the idea of obligations and duties higher than created by human laws."[1] When the ministers applied themselves in this manner and enwrapped religion around divisive political issues, it drew bitter complaints from Madison's party.

At the call of his governor, Timothy Dwight, sarcastically known by his enemies as "The Protestant Pope of Connecticut," gave a two-part peace discourse at Yale on July 23, 1812. He deprecated Napoleon and France along with the war itself. On the same day, in Massachusetts, William Ellery Channing likewise preached about French wickedness and the country's misguided movement in their direction. Down the coast in little Newcastle, Maine, Reverend Kiah Bayley found enough parishioners on the 23rd to require two discourses of his own to make his point that the war was "a calamity greatly to be dreaded."[2]

And so it went, in the meetinghouses of the larger towns such as Worcester and Fitchburg to the smaller towns such as New Braintree and North Yarmouth. A common theme presented by numerous town meeting resolutions found its way into many of the sermons of the clergy. Anyone who aided in the prosecution of the war effort — by service, by funding support, by speech or writing — it was said, "loads his conscience with the blackest crimes."[3] Even though the power of the clergy — especially the Congregational clergy — began to lose its civil authority after the Revolution, it exerted considerable influence in the developing antiwar movement.

Dwight and Channing returned to the pulpit with their now familiar message on August 20, 1812, "the day of humiliation and prayer, appointed by the President of the United States, in consequence of the declaration of

---

1 Hildreth, *History of the United States of America*, 3:324-325.

2 Bayley, *War: A Calamity Greatly to be Dreaded*, 24.

3 Hickey, *War of 1812*, 257.

war against Great Britain."[1] Since Madison called for the fast, the day was not one-sided. As might be expected, a few preachers came to his support. Reverend Reed Paige of Hancock, New Hampshire made the case that obedience to the laws of civil rulers is a duty enjoined by the Scriptures. There was some agreement with this view throughout the region, but most ministers castigated Madison since his national fast appeared to be aimed at gaining a blessing for American forces. In Massachusetts, one detractor said Madison "is not content with forcing upon the nation a war that must destroy it, but he asks you to supplicate your God for its success . . . for success in a battle against your liberties and your God." Despite such criticism, when Republican Governor William Plumer of New Hampshire got around to calling a fast in 1813, he asked "the ruler of all armies to 'teach our hands to war and our fingers to fight.'"[2]

While most ministers stayed on the message of calamity, danger, and hope, several approached treasonable conduct. Elijah Parish placed himself at the head of the few extremists. At Byfield, Massachusetts on the state fast day in July he implored, "[L]et the southern *Heroes* fight their own battles. . . . Break those chains, under which you have sullenly murmured . . . and once more breathe that free, commercial air of New England which your fathers always enjoyed. . . ." Wrapping up, he thundered: "Protest did I say, protest? *Forbid this war to proceed in New England!*"[3]

Though the major sects led the religious response to the war, the Quakers or Society of Friends cannot be overlooked. They played a meaningful part in the opposition to war in New England. A pacifist religion, they interpreted the Scriptures literally, and did not fight evil. Although, on the whole, few in number, Quakers occupied positions of respect and inordinate influence in places such as New Bedford and Nantucket. And they helped direct these communities away from hostile actions against the British.

As the months passed, religious considerations remained in the forefront. In reporting on early army setbacks at the frontier, a Worcester newspaper opined it "must convince all but atheists, that *the finger of God is pointed against the unrighteous war of invasion*, in which the mad administration, and their tools and contractors, have plunged the United States, under the false pretence of vindicating our rights on the oceans."[4]

Throughout the war, New Hampshire clergymen generally displayed moderation. Most opposed the war on moral grounds, but at the same time they cautioned against rash behavior that could be viewed as traitorous or seditious. As a result, they were sensitive to criticism. George Hough eventually found it necessary to pen a defense of the New England clergy. He asserted it was not the case that Congregational and Presbyterian ministers were seeking a religious establishment. "The Clergy are loudly complained

1 Channing, *A Sermon, Preached in Boston*, 15.
2 Gribbin, *Churches Militant*, 21-23.
3 Banner, *To the Hartford Convention*, 307.
4 *Worcester* (MA) *Gazette*, December 23, 1812.

of, because their conduct in this war is different from their conduct during the revolution. At that time they encouraged the men to fight; and prayed for success of our arms; and now they do neither," he said. In that war, Hough argued, the British "sent their armies here to invade us; in the present war, we have sent our armies to invade neighboring provinces which have lived peaceably by us. That was on our part a war of self defence; this is obviously a war for conquest."[1]

The fast sermons continued throughout the duration. To the end, New England ministers challenged the justification for and conduct of the war against Great Britain. As the war entered its third year, Reverend Francis Brown of North Yarmouth thought "that the amount of property wasted in carrying it on is immense and altogether incalculable." He, nonetheless, estimated Europe yearly spent on war "the immense sum" of $786,250,000 and the United States ran up an annual military tab of some $31,450,000. Brown wondered: "And how desirable it seems, that some portion of this expense, which is devoted to the work of destroying men's lives, should be used for the purpose of saving their souls." He thought "that it should be turned into the channel of Christian charity," and "should become the means of putting the Gospel into the hands of the poor, and of carrying its light and grace to those, who are sitting in the region and shadow of death. How acceptable such an offering would be to Him, who is named, 'The Prince of Peace'. . . . "[2]

Brown touched the core of New England war opposition, but did not develop the case. Economic issues — dollars and cents; profits and losses — explain a great deal. Absent the central and underlying economic factors, it is doubtful war opposition would have amounted to much. Jefferson's attempt to combat British and French hostile actions and policies by economic measures, including embargoes, gained little but the lasting enmity of the elements of society that depended on exporting and importing. Madison's general acceptance of his predecessor's policies assured the continuance of the deeply felt antagonism of manufacturers, merchants, mariners, and the like, many of them in New England.

---

1 Hough, *Defence of the Clergy of New-England*, 13.
2 Francis Brown, *Evils of War*, 20-21.

Chapter 3. A Dastardly, Inglorious Policy

New England's economic differences with President Jefferson were rooted in the Old World turmoil of the period. For years, the European powers and their allies were at war with one another. The principal combatants were England and France. In 1802, France came to terms with Britain at the Peace of Amiens. Harmony did not last. Within the year, Napoleon openly prepared to invade the British Isles. In 1803, Britain formalized the renewed hostilities by declaring war on France. In the years leading up to 1812, Europe remained in a state of war. Napoleon swept back and forth over the Continent. He defeated the Austrians, Russians, Prussians, Saxons, and Spaniards; invaded Portugal; and annexed the Papal States, Holland, Westphalia, north-west Germany, and Oldenburg. Little wonder New Englanders of Puritan descent watched in horror. Only the Royal Navy and the English Channel held him at bay.

Both England and France relied heavily on American commercial shipping, much of it with some New England connection. The United States attempted to follow the free ships, free goods theory of international law formulated in 1625 by Hugo Grotius, a Dutch legal scholar. His liberty of the sea or neutrality concept considered the oceans international territory open to neutral shipping as long as it did not carry munitions of war to belligerents. Grotius' unsophisticated principle would be addressed and altered by numerous agreements and treaties, especially with respect to secondary issues such as searches.

Yet, as war intensified between the two principal antagonists, they both harassed and interdicted neutral shipping serving their opponent. Great Britain carried on the economic warfare through adjudications of their admiralty courts and sovereign promulgations known as orders in council, effectively blocking open trade with France. Napoleon countered with the issuance of a set of edicts that became known as the Continental System. Beginning with the Berlin Decree of November 1806, and extended by the Warsaw, Milan, and Fontainebleau decrees, he prohibited trade with Great Britain by France, her allies, and neutrals such as the United States. The British and French restrictions substantially impacted the American merchant marine.

In February 1806, the U.S. Senate, acting on a message from the administration, passed a resolution condemning British actions against American vessels as "unprovoked aggression."[1] In April, Congress responded to the problem by enacting what is referred to as the First Nonimportation Act. Effective November 15, 1806, it became unlawful "to import into the United States, or the territories thereof, from any port or place situated in Great Britain or Ireland, or in any of the colonies or dependencies of Great Britain, any goods, wares or merchandise," of leather, silk, hemp, flax, tin, certain woolen goods, glass, silver and plated wares, "paper of every description," nails, spikes, hats, "clothing ready made," millinery, playing cards, beer, ale and porter, and pictures and prints.[2]

British aggression continued, and, in fact, became more blatant. Nonimportation failed. Jefferson concluded he had three choices. He could submit to the demeaning and costly enforcement actions of the two contending powers. War was an obvious if not sensible second choice. Indeed, in June 1807, an egregious British insult to the American flag prompted a public outcry for war. But the nonviolent Jefferson adopted the third alternative — a self-imposed embargo. "I think one war enough for the life of one man," he said.[3]

In December, the president sent a message to Congress asking for a maritime embargo due to "the great and increasing dangers with which our vessels, our seamen, and merchandise, are threatened, on the high seas, and elsewhere, from the belligerent Powers of Europe."[4] In short order, on December 22, Congress passed an act laying an embargo on all American "ships and vessels in the ports and places within the limits or jurisdiction of the United States, cleared or not cleared." Foreign ships in ballast or loaded "when notified of this act" were free to leave the United States.[5] The administration and Congress strengthened and tweaked the law in January, March, and April 1808 and January 1809.

Jefferson hoped Europe would settle on peace within months and his embargo would become unnecessary within a year or so, long before it would seriously impact his country's economy. He noted, while the United States remained aloof of the conflict between its friends, the nation's maritime commerce fell prey to their edicts and fleets. To submit to prohibition and tribute, he argued, amounted to surrender of American independence. Jeffer-

1 U.S. *Senate Journal.* 9th Cong., 1st sess., February 12, 1806, 37-38.

2 Act of April 18, 1806, ch. 29, 1 *Stat.* 379.

3 Brodie, *Thomas Jefferson*, 417.

4 U.S. *House Journal.* 1807. 10th Cong., 1st sess., December 18, 1216.

5 Act of December 22, 1807, ch. 5, 1 *Stat.* 451.

son thought a suspension of our trade would not only protect and preserve our resources and seamen, but it would give the belligerents time to come to their senses.

The original measure passed the Senate by a 22 to 7 vote and prevailed in the House by a count of 82 to 44. In the Senate debate, Hillhouse of Connecticut opposed the bill, arguing: "I DO not believe ... that the citizens of the United States are yet prepared to surrender their Liberties at the shrine of either *foreign* or *domestic* tyranny." He predicted the people "WILL NOT SUBMIT" to its unconstitutional provisions.[1]

Pickering of Massachusetts, another Senate opponent, detailed his opposition to the embargo in a lengthy February 16, 1808 letter to Governor James Sullivan of Massachusetts, a member of Jefferson's party. Sullivan returned the letter unopened. So, a friend of Pickering's employed a Providence printer to reproduce the letter in the form of a broadside suitable for public distribution. A printer in Utica, New York published the letter in booklet form. Pickering estimated more than 100,000 people got the chance to read his message. "The public mind was in a state singularly fitted to hail the publication," he thought.[2]

Senator Pickering questioned the mystery of Jefferson's reasoning. He thought merchants and seamen, "the preservation of whose persons and property were the *professed* object" of the embargo, were quite aware of and resigned to existing risks. "[T]hey had excited little concern." He saw a certain outcome. "The course we have seen pursued leads on to war — to a war with Great Britain — a war absolutely without necessity — a war which, whether disastrous or successful, must bring misery and ruin to the United States: *Misery*, by the destruction of our navigation and commerce.... And *ruin*, by the loss of our liberty...." He questioned Jefferson's secretiveness about dispatches on the general issue with France, fearing the French emperor was somehow behind the embargo. He felt the proceedings appeared "calculated to mislead the public mind to public ruin." In the end, Pickering asserted, "*those States whose farms are on the ocean, and whose harvests are gathered in every sea, should immediately and seriously consider how to preserve them.*"[3]

Right away, commerce dropped sharply. The smaller providers and merchants suffered early. Henry Willson of Topsham, Maine typified a widespread result. He wrote to John Kittell in Boston and asked about the status of a load of shingles he shipped for sale. "I am sorry to inform you Sir," Kittell replied, "that they yet remain on hand & I fear will while the Embargo continues but you may depend upon my using every exertion to effect a sale of them for your interest. I hope to obtain Two dollars & half for them but I cannot get even that for them until the Embargo is removed."[4] During the

---

1 Library of Congress, *Dignified Patriotism.*
2 Sears, *Jefferson and the Embargo*, 158.
3 Library of Congress, *Important and Alarming Information.*
4 Kittell, *Letter.*

weeks and months to follow, this kind of cheerless exchange was repeated countless times up and down the coast.

Newport, Rhode Island felt uneasy and sensed danger. On March 23, the freemen of the town petitioned Congress to appropriate funds for the defense of the exposed seaport. They decried the "actual neglect and apparent abandonment of this Town and Harbour." They made an early appeal to Washington "that they may not hereafter be obliged to petition in vain for mercy as a favour, to an insolent and inexorable invading foe."[1]

Then, after a Federalist meeting in Salem, Massachusetts on March 25, 1808 passed a resolution condemning the embargo, towns throughout the region got into the act. Surprisingly, inland Northampton found itself at the head of the pack when it sought repeal in a March 29 memorial to Congress. A few days later, 285 Essex County, Massachusetts fishermen along with 324 of their neighbors petitioned the president. In quick succession, places such as Easthampton, Goshen, Greenfield, Hatfield, and Southampton followed suit.

An unsuccessful May 2 petition to the president from Buckstown simply sought special consideration instead of a general repeal. The town asked Jefferson "for permission to export the dry and pickled fish now in this town, if it shall appear that he has the authority to grant the same."[2] Throughout the embargo, the perishable nature of fish was a favorite but unavailing argument for an exception to the restrictions. Boston, for instance, made a similar vain appeal to Congress.

The first prominent political victim of the gathering storm met his fate in June. U.S. Senator John Quincy Adams, a Massachusetts Federalist, not only served on the committee that recommended the embargo, but he voted for the measure when it reached the floor. The resulting vilification of Adams became unrestrained. At the end of 1807, he recorded in his diary, "I am constantly approaching to the certainty of being restored to the situation of a private citizen."[3] The restoration came sooner than expected. Well ahead of the regular date, early in June, the Massachusetts Senate named James Lloyd, a loyal Federalist, to succeed Adams when his term expired in March 1809. The rebuff was intended as an insult, and Adams considered it such. He resigned his seat several days later, and continued to support the administration. In a year, Madison appointed him minister to Russia. Despite predictable Federalist opposition, the Senate confirmed the nomination. In the end, truth be told, his party was happy to see Adams leave the country.

Ironically, John Adams, the father, thought the embargo "a cowardly measure." Long at odds with "that sect," his own Federalist Party, the second president would "raise no clamor." Although his longstanding advocacy of a

---

1 *Newport* (RI) *Mercury*, April 9, 1808.
2 *Records of the Town of Buckstown* (ME) No. 1, 119.
3 James T. Adams, *Adams Family*, 137.

strong naval capability failed to catch hold, he "determined to support the government in whatever hands as far as I can in conscience and honor."[1]

Governor Sullivan, trying to check the mounting opposition, provided a reasoned defense of the embargo in a speech to the legislature. On June 9, the Massachusetts House of Representatives countered with a diplomatic response, agreeing on the merits of national union and the governor's "sentiments of warm attachment to the independence of our country." However, the House stressed, "that if ever it shall be considered criminal to investigate the conduct of our rulers, or to express our opinions of the measures of government with freedom; if ever the mandate of authority shall suppress inquiry, or stifle the voice of publick complaint, the Constitution becomes a dead letter, and the liberties of the people but a name."[2]

At all events, the Washington petitioning subsided for a few weeks after Congress adjourned its 1st Session on April 25, although Barre, Massachusetts celebrated July Fourth by adopting resolutions condemning Jefferson's "decided hostility to commerce."[3] Then, on August 9, a Newburyport town meeting voted to ask the president "to remove the Embargo" and restore "our Country to her former prosperity and happiness."[4] On the same day, a Boston town meeting prepared a similar memorial and directed its selectmen to send a copy to all the towns in the state "to request them, if they see fit" to act in concert.[5] By the next day, the selectmen had the petition in print and in the mails. The *Newport Mercury* editorialized on the Boston meeting. "We are happy in learning . . . that THE PEOPLE are arousing from their lethargy, and turning their undivided attention to *Constitutional Remedies* for the flagrant and almost intolerable Evils which have been inflicted on them by the folly, madness, partiality and wickedness of the . . . National Administration."[6]

As much as anything, Boston shippers wanted at least a partial lifting of the embargo so they could take advantage of a lucrative opening. The war in Europe had shifted to the Iberian Peninsula, and the allied armies were a potential major customer for American provisions. Portugal and Spain were almost on New England's doorstep. Within the next few weeks, some 70 regional towns appealed to either the president or Congress asking for an end to the destructive embargo.

In Maine, Belfast, Boothbay, Bowdoinham, Camden, Gorham, Waldoboro, Warren, and Winthrop were among the towns petitioning during this period, generally patterning their plea after the Boston document. But Lincolnville pleaded its case in its own way. The midcoast town asked the president to rescind the embargo "either wholly or partially" because the "hardness of the soil, severity of the climate and newness of the Country

---

1 McCullough, *John Adams*, 598-599.
2 Library of Congress, *Answer to the Governor's Speech*.
3 *Newport* (RI) *Mercury*, July 16, 1808.
4 *Newburyport* (MA) *Freeholders 1797-1811*.
5 Boston Selectmen, *Petition*, to the Selectmen of the Town of Halifax, MA.
6 *Newport* (RI) *Mercury*, July 16, 1808.

obliges us to depend chiefly on our lumber Fisheries and navigation for support" and the embargo "acted with a paralising influence upon us."[1] Machias made somewhat the same point when it told the president its citizens "ever impressed with a proper sense of their duty to observe and obey the Laws they have submitted with patience to the many embarrassments arising to their wasting trade. . . ."[2] And the men in a Castine meeting simply and boldly told Jefferson his "distressing measure" was an unconstitutional failure to which "their idle ships and perishing commodities unfortunately bear positive testimony."[3]

Wiscasset, the chief lumber shipping port in Maine, in an August 17 petition told Jefferson his embargo had the effect of "checking Industry & enterprise" and, in an astute twist, added, "the evils of the Embargo are daily encreasing that the Dissatisfaction & Complaints of the people are becoming greater under the Distressing effects of this Measure that they shall be wholly Incapable in this state of things either to Discharge personal Demands or to contribute to the Revenue of the Government."[4]

The inhabitants of Topsham got together on August 20 and appealed to the president to suspend the embargo "in whole or in part," stressing the opportunities of the "safe and lucrative" market open on the Iberian Peninsula. The Topsham memorialists added they held to "an anxious hope that when experience should ascertain the extent and degree of their sufferings in common with their fellow citizens," the national government would do the right thing.[5]

Two days later, the town of Wells met and petitioned Jefferson. Wells recognized the president's motives "were pure and patriotic," but they said the embargo "strikes at the roots of our prosperity & happiness." The petitioners explained their soil was "penurious." Thus, they argued: "We have hitherto resorted to the ocean for a supply of what the hand of Nature has denied us from the field."[6]

In Massachusetts, Salisbury likewise focused on its particular situation when it told the president the town was "a Marritime place, tho not of primary importance, And deriving the means of their subsistence, In a great measure from the various occupations of fishing, freighting, & Ship-building, They have felt very sensibly the losses & Inconveniences resulting from the Embargo. . . . From a Just sense of their obligation to obey the laws of their Country, they . . . patiently sustained these Evils & privations. . . ."[7]

The citizens of Dennis, Provincetown, and Yarmouth on Cape Cod sent the president similar appeals. The Provincetown memorial emphasized "the

1 *Town Records Book 1, 1802-1823, Town of Lincolnville,* ME, 64-66.
2 *Machias* (ME) *Town Records 1795-1823,* 1:174.
3 *Records, No. 1, 1796-1830,* Castine, ME, 163.
4 *Town Records, Vol. 3, 1790-1813,* Wiscasset, ME, 341-343.
5 *Town of Topsham* (ME) *Memorial to Thomas Jefferson.*
6 *Town Records, Vol. B. 1775-1810,* Wells, ME.
7 *Records 1797-1815,* Salisbury, MA, 136.

various evils that must result from a total suspention of their business having long habituated to a maritime employment, . . . whose shipping & fish thus left to wast & perish on their hands not only to the loss of their property, but in some instance of health & life."[1]

A Plymouth August 25 town meeting prepared a more learned request to the president. They asserted the embargo was "so novel an experiment in the history of commerce, and is fraught with so numerous a train of political and moral evils, that they would betray not merely a destitution of patriotism, but a want of proper regard for the constituted authorities of their country, did they not remonstrate against the further continuance of the anti-commercial system, and express their ideas of its various tendencies in manly and decent language."[2] Plymouth went on to spell out in such language the harm experienced and asked the president to rescind the embargo, or if necessary, call Congress back for a special session to enact repeal.

As he did from time to time with other communities, North Yarmouth, Maine, Cambridge, Haverhill, Kingston, New Bedford, Stockbridge, and Winchendon, Massachusetts included, Jefferson replied to Plymouth in September. He explained the now familiar reasoning behind the embargo, and added, logistical considerations precluded a special session of Congress. The scattered members would return for the scheduled regular session just as quickly. In closing, the president said: "I should with great willingness have executed the wishes of the inhabitants of Plymouth had peace or a repeal of the obnoxious edicts" of Britain and France been in place.[3] Jefferson's responses to North Yarmouth, Cambridge, and Plymouth, written within the same week, are identical — word for word. As the weeks passed, he refined his answer to petitioners. But the virtual flood of incoming petitions seems to be the reason he turned to a standard printed, signed reply. "There is a pretty well founded conviction" Jefferson made reply to a petition from Gardner, Massachusetts, "but, such was its nature and import, that those who received it, never cared to make it public."[4]

Woodbridge, Connecticut protested the embargo in a memorial to Congress, while New Haven petitioned the president at an "uncommonly full" August 29 meeting.[5] Westport, Massachusetts on the same day went on record seeking at least a partial suspension of the embargo.

Some towns remained detached and did not take the time to express their views one way or the other. And there were those who supported Jefferson. In August, several voters in Barnstable submitted a town meeting article seeking a repeal petition to be sent to the president. The meeting rejected the article, effectively endorsing the embargo for the time. Dresden and Pittston, Maine voters turned down similar town meeting articles.

---

1 *Town Records 1785-1811, Provincetown* (MA), Vol. 5, 90.

2 William T. Davis, *History of the Town of Plymouth*, 96.

3 Ibid., 97.

4 Herrick, *History of the Town of Gardner*, 107.

5 *Newport* (RI) *Mercury*, September 10, 1808.

Pittston took the added step of passing resolves supporting the president's policies. Lynn, Massachusetts likewise rejected a repeal attempt and embraced a pro-administration stance by adopting a resolve supportive of the national government. Dighton, Dorchester, Fairhaven, Sudbury, and Weymouth, Massachusetts were among other communities that sided with the national administration.

Perhaps not surprisingly, two towns that later suffered the wrath of the Royal Navy steadily supported the president's efforts. In March 1809, town meetings in Falmouth, Massachusetts and Stonington, Connecticut denounced opposition to the embargo acts. Falmouth went further, declaring its attachment to the Constitution and its intent to support the national administration "against the unjust of every foreign power."[1]

Marblehead earlier gained national notoriety for similar sentiments. At a December 1808 town meeting, the inhabitants resolved, "That this town continues steadfast in the faith that the Embargo law was a law of wisdom. . . ." The townsmen further asserted they would "use all the energy they possess to carry into full effect" the laws of the land. When Congressman Joseph Story, their townsman, read the Marblehead petition in the House, the "effect was electrical." Story added: "It gave a degree of delight, it awakened a sensation of admiration." A fellow Republican congressman from South Carolina felt so moved that he offered the depressed fishing community a gift of 1,000 bushels of corn from his plantation.[2]

Despite the widespread bitterness and inflamed rhetoric, Portland found time to lighten the swirling controversy with some street theater. A group of alongshore men loaded a long boat stern foremost on a car. Modeled as a ship in distress and disarray with loose rigging flapping in the breeze, its stern and quarter boards carried the name *O-grab-me*, the derisive transposed name for the embargo. A number of wagoners hitched their horses to the car, mounted the animals, and fell in behind a marching band playing doleful music. A crowd of unemployed — from masters to mechanics — followed along to the battery where a popular ship captain held forth. In burlesque fashion, he told the assemblage how easy it was to starve old England by shutting down the American merchant marine. The crowd responded with a spirited rendition of an improvised psalm. As the ceremonies proceeded, a gang of riggers went to the long boat and turned her bow to the forward position. They trimmed her sails, repainted the hull, and raised the American flag at the mastheads. A smartly dressed crew took over the boat as the procession continued through town to Union Wharf. A large segment of the community cheered the launching of the improved vessel. A few months later, Newburyport mariners put on a similar farce accompanied by tolling church bells and banging minute-guns.

A few people who could afford the expense published their criticisms of the embargo in political tracts. A writer who called himself "A Cheshire

1 *Town Records & Vitals, Vol. 2, 1750-1838 Town of Falmouth, MA,* 427.
2 Roads, *History and Traditions of Marblehead,* 234-236.

Farmer" printed an attack on the law curiously entitled *An Enquiry into the State of the Farm.* He made his point in two sentences. "Ten months of Embargo have driven from our country more of our Mariners," he wrote, "than we should have lost by three years of war. Seamen *cannot live* where they *cannot be employed.*"[1]

There is considerable evidence numerous communities in the United States, particularly along shore, suffered greatly from the economic stagnation brought on by the embargo. Yarmouth, Massachusetts offered public assistance to any resident in want of the necessities of life due to the embargo's impact. Newburyport set up soup houses for those in need. Sections of the Maine coastline found more than one out of two men unemployed. The Portland poorhouse could not handle the increased demand. Several merchants in town lost their fortunes, and a Portland bank failed. Portland's import duties dropped from $342,909 to $4,369 in the first year of the embargo. Although it experienced a marked drop in its tax collections, the town managed to set up a soup kitchen at Market Square.

A January 1808 survey found 16 ships and 27 brigs laid up at Bath. A prominent Bath businessman estimated his nine vessels idled by the embargo caused him to lose $5,558 per month. Fishermen, farmers, and lumbermen also felt the squeeze. The Wiscasset collector issued two sea letters to lumber ships in 1808. In the year before the embargo, he issued 67. Cordwood went unshipped and unsold because customers could not afford to pay for the necessity. This was one factor that at the time prompted some residents of practically treeless Nantucket to move away from the island.

Marblehead counted 87 fishing vessels idled, so many, the town felt the need to raise and appropriate $2,000 for the relief of its unemployed fishermen. In Newburyport, the prosperous business of distilling whiskey took a hit when the means of exporting disappeared. And distillers stopped buying rye from area farmers. The thriving occupation of exporting salt pork likewise suffered, and the stock of swine became valueless, "unless to eat the rye which the distillers did not want!"[2]

Rhode Island experienced an 85 percent drop in exports in 1808. In the same year, in New London, customs duties dropped below $100,000 after reaching $214,940 in 1806. And so it went, wherever the sea played some role in the economy. Jefferson felt taken aback by the resulting bitterness and rancor.

Although regular trade and employment dropped sharply due to the embargo, some shrewd Yankees took advantage of loopholes in the law or ineffective enforcement and made out quite well. A few even prospered. Vessels abroad at the time of enactment held an obvious option — stay in business overseas. Many did so, remaining beyond the reach of the law.

Within less than a month after passage of the original act, the government moved to close a major loophole by extending coverage to coasting

---

1 Cheshire Farmer, *An Enquiry into the State of the Farm*, 8.
2 E. Vale Smith, *History of Newburyport*, 183.

and fishing vessels. Owners or masters of these vessels were required to give bond that they would not sail to and unload at a foreign port. Two months later, another amendment required returning fishing captains and mates to declare under oath whether they had sold any part of their catch while away, or forfeit $100. And a month later, Congress authorized public armed vessels to enforce the embargo.

The revisions did not have the intended effect. In the months that followed, many New England coasters and fishermen found themselves "blown off course" and "in distress" in the Canadian Maritimes or even as far away as the Caribbean or Europe. Senator Samuel Mitchill of New York complained, "the southern atmosphere has become so subject to gales and tempests from the north, that our poor coasters, who love to hug their native shores, are by distress of weather often driven to Cuba and Jamaica, and there forced (dire necessity!) to sell their cargoes to repair the damage they have sustained, and refit for return to that land which they are longing and sickening to see."[1] The Bangor sloop *Ploughboy*, for one, left Rhode Island in October 1808 bound for the Penobscot River. She did not arrive in Castine until February 1809. Strong winds, the skipper claimed, struck her as she tried to beat around Cape Cod and drove her all the way to Antigua! A Newburyport observer explained, West Indies "carpenters were so expert and generous" that they could make repairs "in an extraordinary short space of time, and at scarcely no expense!!"[2]

Others sailed without pretext and took their chances. A Bath owner loaded his ship *Sally* with lumber and, without governmental clearance, sent her down the Kennebec on the way to England. The federal battery on Hunnewell's Point, built to keep the enemy out, commenced an ineffective fire as the 342-ton ship slipped out past Popham. This led the crew to understand the *Sally* was an outlaw and the men became mutinous. The captain put down the uprising with a grant of a $50 note to each man. When the ship neared the English coast, the skipper put on shore a junior officer who happened to be the brother of the owner. The man rushed ahead to London and reported a mutiny. When the *Sally* docked at the city, authorities arrested the rebellious crew. The British released the men as soon as they gave up their $50 notes. The owner's brother sold the cargo at a substantial profit and went on to become one of the wealthiest shippers in Bath.

Smuggling proved a greater concern. The borders around Passamaquoddy Bay and the upper reaches of Lake Champlain were porous. Little Eastport became one of the busiest towns in America. As many as 14 vessels appeared off its docks at one time. In a single week, 30,000 barrels of American flour arrived for illicit export. As much as 160,000 barrels passed through town in a year. Other spots along the coast from Machias to Robbinston moved lesser amounts of flour. Worth five dollars a barrel in Eastport, the flour brought twelve dollars a barrel less than two miles across the water in New

1 *Annals of Congress*, 10th Cong., 2nd sess., 86.
2 E. Vale Smith, 180.

Brunswick territory. Smugglers initially charged twelve and a half cents to transport a barrel. As government enforcement increased, the fee jumped to three dollars a barrel. Boats of every description, including skiffs and canoes, carried the contraband. Working alone, a man could earn around fifty dollars in a day.

The government attempted to stop the contraband running, but met with limited success. A company of troops, several gunboats, and even the frigate *Chesapeake*, 38 and the sloop of war *Wasp*, 18 supplemented the uphill efforts of the Eastport collector of customs. Locals referred to the period as the Flour War. A writer described the futile enforcement in an 1872 paper after interviewing men who were around Eastport at the time of the smuggling. He allowed for exaggeration, noting "tales of smugglers and fishermen are always long and frequently adorned." However, he reported: "Persons who intend to measure their words have assured me that every man in the pay of the government, three excepted, would take hush-money, and that even these three would retire or go to sleep while on duty to oblige a friend."[1]

This is not to say the business proceeded quietly. Although nobody was killed around Eastport, there was a fair amount of gunplay. Many smugglers armed themselves. And the Royal Navy stationed ships on the line to offer protection to craft fleeing into British waters. One smuggler claimed enforcers fired 21 shots at him during a chase. Another remembered American gunboats fired 18 cannon balls at him before he reached safety on the other side. Along the coast at Buckstown, customs officers seized a load of contraband rum in a warehouse raid and sailed away taunting the inhabitants by firing salutes and cheering "Jefferson, rum, and embargo!"[2]

Unfortunately, a caper offshore proved deadly. Authorities blocked a vessel full of flour and rice from discharging in Eastport. She was seized and moved to Isle au Haut at the mouth of the Penobscot where her cargo was unloaded and put under guard of the Castine collector's agents. At the behest of some area merchants, a band of more than a dozen armed men sailed from Eastport in the *Peggy* to recover the contraband. A government sentinel challenged the group as they tried to land at Kimball's Harbor on the remote island. A gunfight broke out leading to the death of a guard, one Lazaro Bogdomovitch. Two guards, however, escaped the skirmish and alerted the collector in Castine on the mainland. He hastened out in an armed cutter and pursued and apprehended the culprits. Eight wound up in jail. But, before long, a mob of up to 30 men disguised as women stormed the lockup and managed to release four of the conspirators. The quartet disappeared into the countryside.

Authorities had somewhat more success prosecuting the organizers of the *Peggy* affair. A federal court found Dr. Andrew Webster of Castine, a deputy sheriff no less, guilty of involvement in the plot and fined him $2,500. When he could not pay, he was jailed as a debtor. Before a week passed, Webster

1 Kilby, *Eastport and Passamaquoddy*, 146-149.
2 Joshua M. Smith, *Maine History*, 26.

escaped and fled to Nova Scotia where he lived out his life. John McMasters, a local merchant, also deeply involved in the criminal enterprise, faced similar charges. The court found him guilty, and when he could not cover a $10,000 fine, the government sent him to the Wiscasset jail. There he died in 1815, murdered by a drunken inmate.

A less violent incident took place nearby on relatively peaceful Swan's Island. A pair of brothers named Purdy brought a load of flour in their Chebacco and stored it in an island house in anticipation of moving it to Canada. But some patriot notified customs officials on Deer Isle. The government, aided by David Smith, acted quickly and confiscated the contraband. Needless to say, the Purdys were not happy. Soon, they encountered Smith alone and attacked the gentleman. But, "Much to their surprise, this old Revolutionary hero administered to them a sound thrashing."[1] The Purdys had Smith arrested for assault. Fortunately for him, the head of customs on Deer Isle presided at the trial. And he dismissed the charge, ruling justifiable self-defense.

On the mainland, Frankfort likewise experienced its share of unruliness. Local store owners were reluctant to keep corn and flour on hand, because area settlers did not have money to pay for such goods. And the traders, not wishing to overextend credit, turned to civil suits to collect on overdue accounts. A gang assaulted a deputy sheriff attempting to serve related writs, demanded his papers, "with a cocked gun presented to his breast, threatening him with instant death if he refused; he complied — they searched his pocket book, took what they chose, and released him; threatening him with death if he ever came that way with precepts again." Around this time, about "4 miles from Frankfort, there were seen 400 collected in one body, all in Indian dress, ready for any enterprise that might appear to their advantage."[2] A Boston newspaper lamented the trend. "Open force against the laws of the land, is certainly rebellion, however plausible or urgent the reasons for such conduct."[3]

Vermont smuggling turned out to be as much, if not more, of a problem. Senator Mitchill complained: "While our gunboats and cutters are watching the harbors and sounds of the Atlantic, a strange inversion of business ensues, and by a retrograde motion of all the interior machinery of the country," lumber and potash illicitly move over Lake Champlain and into Canada.[4] Vermont smugglers employed one raft described as more than a half-mile in length. Manned by a few hundred armed men, it included a bullet resistant fort at its center. The militia suffered casualties in a pitched battle when it attempted but failed to stop the raft.

In April 1808, President Jefferson took notice "that sundry persons are combined, or combining and confederating together on Lake Champlain . . . for the purpose of forming insurrection against the authority of the laws of

1 H.W. Small, *History of Swan's Island*, 31.

2 *Newport* (RI) *Mercury*, May 14, 1808.

3 *Boston Gazette*, May 19, 1808.

4 *Annals of Congress*, 10th Cong., 2nd sess., 86.

the United States. . . ." Since judicial proceedings and marshals were not up to the task, he issued a proclamation "commanding such insurgents . . . in-stantly and without delay to disperse and retire peaceably to their respective abodes."[1] Vermonters took great exception. A St. Albans town meeting ratio-nalized the embargo should not apply to their remote hills. After all, the law was expressly designed to protect "vessels, our seamen, and our merchan-dize on the high seas." Moreover, "to a people who stand FRONT GUARD between their country and a foreign kingdom . . . the unmerited imputation of insurrection and rebellion, is, of all things, the most degraded, the most insupportable."[2] They wondered if the president had forgotten the traditions and reputation of the Green Mountain Boys of yore. Others thought his 1791 visit to the state — in which he found too much wind, a sultry clime, and a muddy Lake Champlain — turned him against the place.

A man returning to Vermont from Montreal counted along the way 700 sleighs engaged in the smuggling trade. A news report "calculated that not less than *One Hundred Tons*" of pearl ash "passed within ten days" through Burlington bound for Canada.[3] Pearl ash, like potash, is a form of potassium carbonate. Both were used to make dyes, glass, soap, and, more significant, saltpeter for gunpowder. The first patent issued by the federal government went in 1790 to a Pittsford, Vermont man who invented an improved appara-tus and process for making potash and pearl ash. The abundant hardwoods on northern New England farms were the principal basis of the ash. Many Vermont and New Hampshire farmers turned this offshoot of their regular work into a welcome source of added income, and they did not appreciate Jefferson's interference. One of Vermont's senators predicted the patriotism of the state would end the illicit traffic. Connecticut's Senator Hillhouse ex-claimed: "Why, patriotism, cannon, militia, and all had not stopped it; . . . they were absolutely cutting new roads to carry it on. . . ."[4]

A principal smugglers' road ran between Saint-Armand in Quebec, through Franklin, Vermont to the Missisquoi River in Sheldon. English goods crossed southerly over the line and many droves of cattle moved to the north along this wilderness road. On one occasion, the United States military captured a band of cattle smugglers on the trail after they mistook their captors for British soldiers eager to purchase livestock. The downcast owners, forced to aid in the return drive, retraced their steps back to Shel-don. Once in town, the American commander released the smugglers to their homes. But after the war, the court in Rutland summoned the men to answer to their offense. They retained a wily attorney who argued, 'driving cattle on foot was not *transporting beef*' — and the point being carried, — they were released."[5]

---

1 *American State Papers: Miscellaneous* 1:940.

2 *Newport* (RI) *Mercury*, June 11, 1808.

3 Ibid., June 18, 1808.

4 *Annals of Congress*, 10th Cong., 2nd sess., 24.

5 *Vermont Historical Magazine* 2:222.

Near Craftsbury, a posse confiscated 110 head of cattle headed north, and in the face of threatened armed retaliation drove them to the American forces stationed in Burlington. Following a similar confiscation, a recovery party came out of Canada and reclaimed the herd. A more serious encroachment took place in Derby. Canadians upset with military anti-smuggling efforts were able to set fire to the town's barracks, guardhouse, and officers' quarters and escape back to Stanstead. "But from that time until the close of the war it was not prudent for a Canadian to be seen on the streets of Derby after nightfall unless he was ready for a coat of tar and feathers."[1]

Perhaps apocryphal, a report indicates some smugglers took advantage of novel and unsuspecting means — including gravity. This method required a steep hill just on the American line. Contrabandists would build a crude storage hut on the peak, the shelter so designed that removal of one foundation stone would collapse its northern wall. Then the smugglers secreted barrels of contraband — pork, beef, or potash — inside. At an opportune time, the keystone was pulled and the barrels quickly sent rolling over the wall's remains and down the hill into Quebec, where they became Canadian property.

An incident at Alburgh typified the times. Revenue authorities had stored some 70 barrels of confiscated potash in a barn near Wind-Mill Point. Local men acted quickly when they saw the officer overseeing the contraband depart for Burlington. That night two of the band went to the officer's house and engaged in distracting conversation with the man left in charge and the woman housekeeper. Other plotters found the barn locked, so they ripped away sideboards, and "the ponderous barrels, as if by magic, rolled up the skid-ways, on to the well appointed sleds." One after another, teams raced northward over the ice. One teamster worked fast enough to make three roundtrips before dawn. Years later, a chronicler asked a participant: "Was there ever any stir made about it?"

"Not a word, Sir. Not a word!"

"We see by this," concluded the scribe, "something of the state of things at that period."[2]

Lawlessness became so pronounced by May 1808, Governor Israel Smith mobilized a detachment from the Franklin County militia brigade. They proved ineffective enforcers. Before long, some were sent home protesting and 150 militiamen from Rutland County called to the task. In October, a customs collector found it necessary to appeal to the secretary of war for assistance. "The smugglers are growing daily so bold," he said, "it will be impossible to execute the laws without the aid of the military." But the federal military proved just about helpless. Colonel Zebulon M. Pike found the "thirst for gain" so acute, whenever he apprehended a smuggler, he could "find no court who will take cognizance of the transaction or person concerned."[3]

---

1 Collins, *History of Vermont*, 188.
2 Hemenway, *Vermont Historical Gazetteer*, 495.
3 Everest, *War of 1812 in the Champlain Valley*, 95.

The continuing British demand for beef and other contraband "created an itching palm in many a thrifty farmer's hand."[1] The business developed to the level that in Irasburg smugglers formed an association to handle their affairs.

Gunplay became inevitable. Bill Blake, a prominent entrepreneur of Bellows Falls, used the newspapers to detail his unhappy experience traveling to the border from Lyndon Corner. He complained that soldiers wielding bayonets stopped him six times within the space of one mile and a half. Twenty-five miles from the line, another soldier shot at Blake, chased him for a mile, and stopped him. "He seized my bridle and said, 'Why did you not stop when we fired at you?' I replied, 'Did you fire at me?' 'Yes, and meant to stop you.' 'Why did you not shoot straight? I expected I was in a country where I was not obliged to stop at everyone's call.'"[2]

But the men around Canaan could shoot straight. Samuel Beach, a prominent local farmer, also owned land just over the line in Canada. He would drive a pair of oxen across the border under the guise of working them on his Quebec holdings. He always wound up selling the animals on the other side and returning to Vermont for another pair. Lieutenant Dennett, a special customs officer, confronted Beach. When the farmer persisted in his ploy, the officer shot and killed him. "Great excitement ran all through the county." Local authorities arrested Dennett and charged him with murder. When he escaped, a band of a dozen or so Beach sympathizers followed him to his hiding place in the woods and shot him through the hips. His captors placed him in a wagon "on the bare boards, and hurried back to Guildhall, a distance of nearly 40 miles over very rough roads, where he died in great agony that night in jail."[3] Authorities did not pursue the matter.

A Lake Champlain incident in the first week of August 1808 gained more notoriety. Lieutenant Daniel Farrington and Sergeant David Johnson with a crew of ten privates in the 12-oared revenue cutter *Fly* engaged ten smugglers in a large bateau named the *Black Snake*. Originally the ferry between Charlotte, Vermont and Essex, New York, the *Snake*, at 40 feet, carried one sail and featured as many as 14 oars. She was capable of carrying 100 barrels of potash, at $5 to $6 a barrel. Truman Mudgett commanded the renegade craft, assisted by Samuel Mott, Cyrus Dean, David Sheffield, Francis Ledgard, and five others. In addition to their personal guns, the men possessed a large blunderbuss, a number of clubs and pikes, and a basket of sizeable rocks.

Returning from Canada, Mudgett tried to hide in a stream just above Burlington, but Farrington found his unmanned boat and pulled alongside. "Don't lay hands on that boat," shouted Mudgett from the woods. "I swear by G—d I will blow the first man's brains out who lays hands on her." Undeterred, the lieutenant and several men jumped on the *Snake*, prompting the

---

1 Collins, 187.

2 Hayes, *History of the Town of Rockingham*, 461.

3 Benton, *History of Guildhall*, 186-187.

chief smuggler to call to his men: "Come on, boys! parade yourselves! you are all cowards! they are going to carry the boat off!"

Ledgard appeared at the edge of the bushes "and called, in what was denominated . . . a Methodist tone of voice: 'Lieutenant prepare to meet your God! Your blood shall be spilt before you get out of the river!'"

As the authorities moved the two boats down the river, the smugglers followed along the bank, shouting threats and epithets. And when the procession reached Joy's Landing, the rogues fired into the boats. Private Ellis Drake fell dead. Farrington regrouped and was joined by Captain Jonathan Ormsby of the neighborhood. The government party moved toward their opponents and met a blast from the blunderbuss. "Capt. Ormsby fell, pierced by 5 balls, exclaiming: 'Lord, have mercy on me! I am a dead man!' and instantly expired." Private Asa Marsh suffered the same fate, and Farrington dropped wounded. Sergeant Johnson rallied his men, charged the smugglers, and took eight in custody. Authorities promptly captured the other two.

"The greatest excitement now prevailed throughout the entire region. The people were horror-stricken at crimes like these, in the hitherto quiet and peaceable State of Vermont." Well-attended funerals followed amidst bitter wrangling between the two principal political parties, each blaming the other's policies for the sad turn of events. Before the month passed, the Supreme Court convened a special session leading to indictments against eight of the smugglers. In quick succession, Mott, Dean, and Sheffield were found guilty of murder. Sentenced to the gallows, Dean received a two-week reprieve from the governor. But on November 11 "he was conveyed to the place of execution . . . and at 3 o'clock, p.m., was swung off."[1] Ten thousand spectators reportedly watched as he met his fate. Tradition indicates: "He appeared perfectly composed and hardened; denied his crime, kicked his hat into his grave, spit upon his coffin."[2] Benefiting from legal maneuvering, Mudgett got off altogether while Mott, Sheffield, and Ledgard received sentences of ten years. The governor pardoned the trio before they completed their sentences.

The gravity of the entire episode embarrassed the community. The Chittenden County grand jury promptly issued a statement declaring "beyond the Black Snake affair, in which strangers were principally the actors, we view with satisfaction and admiration, the loyalty and patience of our fellow citizens, and that the charge of Insurrection and Rebellion, lately exhibited against them, are vile aspersions against the honor and the dignity of this county."[3] But those close to the scene knew it was misleading to focus blame on outsiders. Though most of the outlaws came from Franklin County, two of the convicted four — Ledgard and Sheffield — lived in Chittenden County.

1 Dutcher, *History of St. Albans*, 345-347.
2 Sears, 170.
3 Wilbur, *Early History of Vermont*, 3:151.

After weeks of inquiry and resolutions, in November 1808, in time for the opening of the 2nd Session of Congress, the Massachusetts Senate and House forwarded instructions to the state's delegation in Congress, asking them "to use their most strenuous exertions to procure an immediate repeal" of the embargo. The "evils which are menaced by the continuance," according to the legislature, "are enormous and deplorable."[1] The Connecticut governor and legislature decried the embargo in equally vehement language. In Rhode Island, the legislature made its position known in a fairly close 42 to 32 vote against the embargo. Along party lines, both the New Hampshire Senate and House voted to support Jefferson's embargo. Vermont more or less remained outside the embargo dispute, for the time, busying itself with the resulting increased trade across its border with Canada.

Early in January 1809, Congress, to the further dismay of maritime interests, added teeth to the embargo laws by passing the so-called Draconian Enforcement Act. Towns once again called meetings to respond. A Gloucester resolution typified the heightened discontent. The assembled citizens declared "we will mutually watch and protect what little property we have still left . . ." and "we will use all lawful means 'to arrest disturbers and breakers of the peace; or such others as may (under pretence of authority from government) go armed by night,' or utter any menaces or threatening speeches, to the fear and terror of the good people of this town; — and . . . we will ever hold in abhorrence pimping spies and night-walkers, who strive to fatten on the spoils of their suffering fellow-citizens."[2]

Meanwhile, Buckstown passed a set of 14 anti-embargo resolutions, calling the embargo acts unconstitutional, having "originated either from a *dastardly, inglorious* policy towards *foreign powers*, or from a *contemptible* and *wicked* one with regard to the northern section of our own Country." The meeting resolved: "That like the immortal Leonidas and his brave troops who fell at the defile of Thermopylae, we will expose ourselves to certain death, rather than submit tamely to the fetters of slavery, whether forged by foreign or domestic manufactures."[3] Beyond the rhetoric, following after the town of Bath, the meeting established an 11-man committee of public safety and correspondence to work toward the town's goals.

Buckstown's strong language may be traced to a somewhat vindictive action taken by the president just a few weeks earlier. The owner of the schooner *Caroline* out of Buckstown applied to the federal government for a permit to sail despite the embargo, a procedure allowed by the law. Jefferson denied the application because of the widespread embargo opposition in the Maine town. He thought the town "tainted with a general spirit of disobedience."[4] The president would not approve such a waiver short of absolute proof the applicant never agitated against or disobeyed the embargo. Nantucket did

---

1 *American State Papers: Commerce and Navigation* 1:728-729.
2 Library of Congress, *Sedition! Treason!*
3 *Records of the Town of Buckstown* (ME) No. 1, 128-129.
4 McMaster, *History of the People of the United States*, 3:304.

not fare better. The island, firmly opposed to the embargo, applied to import food. Jefferson explained his denial to Levi Lincoln, the acting governor of Massachusetts. "Our opinion here is," he said, "that if it wants it is because it has illegally sent away what it ought to have retained for its own consumption."[1]

Newburyport on January 12 took common action, appointing a committee "to prepare and report resolutions expressive of the sense of the Town on the Calamitous situation of our Country...."[2] A special Plymouth committee at the same time detailed similar unhappiness with the embargo and its impact. "[T]he annihilation of our commerce," they said, "and the consequent failure of our revenue, the unnecessary employment, at exorbitant wages, of a horde of spies, patrols, and informers to watch our empty dismantled ships, is a waste of public money...."[3]

The committee had a couple of troubling incidents in mind. When the embargo came down, government officers pounced on a Plymouth vessel loaded with fish for a foreign market. The agents confiscated her sails and felt she was disabled and not a threat to breach the embargo. Captain Samuel Doten thought otherwise. In the middle of a stormy night, along with a gang of men, he stripped a companion vessel and fitted her rigging and sails to the loaded schooner. Before daylight he was well out in the bay and on his way overseas.

On another night, Doten surreptitiously took a crew across the bay to Provincetown and boarded the Plymouth vessel *Hope* at anchor without officers and crew, but loaded with fish. Captain Thomas Nicholson, commanding a nearby government gunboat, thought the unmanned vessel secure for the time. Quietly, Doten put out to sea and was not noticed until he cleared Wood End on the way to St. Lucia. Nicholson fired a hopeless token shot from his long 18-pounder.

The Plymouth committee drafted a petition to the General Court which asserted "with great confidence that the supplementary law made to enforce" the embargo "contains many provisions that are in direct violation" of the U.S. Constitution. "It is only necessary to read the group of embargo laws to discover, on the face of them, the most flagrant infractions of all those sacred rights." Plymouth somehow concluded the state legislature was "their last hope ... to rescue this unhappy country from the destruction that threatens it."[4]

Provincetown felt it had suffered in "great disproportion" to the rest of the country due to "the baraness" of its "Soil, & almost insulated situation" and its total reliance on marine pursuits. The town fathers appealed to the legislature to consider their "peculiarly suffering situation" and "grant us

---

1 Henry Adams, *History of the United States of America During the Administrations of Thomas Jefferson*, 1105.
2 *Newburyport (MA) Freeholders 1797-1811*.
3 William T. Davis, 98.
4 Ibid.

some relief in any way that your Honorable body may think most expedient."[1] A Beverly meeting seeking help "look[ed] up to their political fathers in the legislature of this state."[2] And in Brewster, the townsmen told the state legislature: "Whilst the mouth of labor is forbidden to eat, the language of complaint is natural." The Cape Cod town went on to "beseech, conjure and implore" the General Court "to obtain redress of the oppressive grievances under which we suffer. . . ."[3]

Augusta, Portland, and other Maine towns expressed the same general position. In a January petition to the General Court, Camden lamented earlier appeals to the national government for relief only led to "new and greater restrictions . . . which in our opinion strikes home at the civil rights of the People, and threatens a total subversion of our Liberties." The town went on to ask the legislature to "interpose in our behalf, and to take such steps as you in your wisdom may judge expedient in order to relieve us from our present distress."[4] A Deer Isle meeting chose a committee to draft a similar plea. A completed "draft of a Petition was twice read, and after some deliberation was almost Unanimously accepted."[5] In Castine, a meeting passed a set of resolves for the legislature making the point "that this part of the State have not attended to Agriculture, and the stubborn soil if cleared up and improved would illy yield sufficient support." As a consequence, the town said "we consider the sea our Farm, and our ships our Store houses — and that our rights therein ought not to be destroyed nor diminished" by an "oppressive and unconstitutional" embargo.[6]

Wells also turned to the state legislature. A January 23 town meeting prepared a petition, "read and accepted by a very large majority," that asked the General Court "to take the awful situation of our Country immediately into consideration." Recognizing this could prove a tall order, the petitioners prayed "may the God of justice and mercy give you wisdom." The Wells petition asserted "the right of navigating the ocean as legitimate as the air we breath — each derived from the same source and equally removed from the rightful control of every power but that from which we inherit them." The Wells meeting went on to vote "no confidence in our national government," and took sharp aim at the congressman for the district — Richard Cutts, a Republican. The meeting described his conduct "as basely servile to Executive will, highly treacherous to his constituents and justly deserving the excoriation of every friend of his Country."[7] In the end, the voters did more than upbraid Cutts. His general support of the administration resulted in his defeat in the 1812 election.

---

1 *Town Meetings 1784-1826, Town of Provincetown*, MA, 98-99.
2 Library of Congress, *Sedition! Treason!*
3 Mary R. Bangs, *Old Cape Cod*, 147.
4 Locke, *Sketches of the History of the Town of Camden*, 90-91.
5 *Town Clerk's Record of Town Meetings, Vol. II.*, Deer Isle, ME, 61.
6 *Records, No. 1, 1796-1830*, Castine, ME, 165-168.
7 *Town Records, Vol. B, 1775-1810*, Wells, ME, 188-189.

Inland Farmington, Maine appointed a three-man committee in January to draft a set of resolutions in opposition to the embargo. Among the best crafted town appeals, in a single paragraph, the Farmington document ably summarized the intense regional discontent. One need not search further to gain an understanding of the intense opposition to the embargo. The committee found it to be the sense of the town "that the feelings, the habits, the necessities and the hopes of the great mass of the people of New England are indispensably founded on the navigation of the ocean; that they ought to retain that right and privilege as sacred and inalienable; that the very finger of nature has pointed them to the prospects, the employments and the benefits derivable from it, and that they ever ought to be in the exercise of this important privilege unembarrassed by too much regulation, and, last of all, to submit to its annihilation."[1]

A few towns, such as Barrington, Rhode Island, felt it enough to simply instruct their state representative to support any legislative measure aimed at relief or repeal. But men in Providence took things in their own hands. After customs authorities seized a local vessel, a band of defiant sailors declared their intention to set her free. The governor called out four state companies to prevent the recovery. The militiamen met in formation and promptly proclaimed they would not aid in the enforcement of the hated embargo law. "Emboldened by this, some three hundred men gathered at the wharf, took the sloop, bent her sails, cut a way through the ice, and sent her to sea."[2]

Along the coast, a late January gathering at the Brick Meetinghouse in New Haven proved frustrating and alarming for at least one advocate of the embargo. William Bristol attempted to rebut the meeting's call to convene the Connecticut legislature. "Before the speaker had uttered two sentences," however, "coughing, and other unusual noises, rendered it impossible to be heard, if not dangerous to proceed." A motion to divide the house resulted in "a scene of tumult . . ., rather uncommon in a meeting-house." The measure passed, and a dismayed Bristol decided to publish his "reply to the reasons urged for requesting His Excellency the governor to convene the General Assembly to take into consideration the alarming situation of public affairs, but prevented from being delivered" at the meeting. "The Embargo is not the principal and efficient cause of your distress — apply to any merchant of candor and honor, and the fact will be acknowledged." The problem, he argued, was the existence of "the hostile decrees of belligerents" and their "implacable war against the rights of neutral commerce."[3] Despite Bristol's printed plea, a solid majority in Connecticut felt the embargo unconstitutional, and Governor Jonathan Trumbull called the legislature into session to deal with the growing crisis. The upshot, Connecticut acted as one with Massachusetts. Both states pledged defiance of the national government and its embargo and hinted at allying with Great Britain.

---

1 Butler, *History of Farmington*, 115.
2 McMaster, 332.
3 Bristol, *An Address*, n.p.

Meanwhile, Lincolnville, like Buckstown, took a somewhat daring step. At a February 1 town meeting it first resolved "that the alarming and deplorable situation of our Country which calls us together at this time is the offspring of unnecessary impolitick, unconstitutional, oppressive and arbitrary acts of the general government laying an embargo on all ships and vessels in the ports and harbors of the united States and the produce of our farms." Then the voters declared: "[W]e will not voluntarily aid or assist in carrying them into effect and will consider all those who do as enemies to the prosperity of this Country."[1] Boston, Topsfield, Newburyport, and Gorham passed similar sets of resolutions, while a Hadley, Massachusetts town meeting advanced the idea that dissolution of the Union was at hand. The Gorham meeting thought it paradoxical and "unconstitutional for Congress, to whom is delegated only a power to regulate commerce, to destroy it."[2] Such defiance and expression amounted to heady behavior at the time, though it would become more common during the war to come. "Altogether, the people of the New England States were growing into a dangerous state of discontent with the government."[3] An early Jefferson biographer thought: "A full collection of the newspapers of the period would probably enable us to multiply to thousands these examples of expressions directly in favor of, or leading to, resistance and disunion."[4]

Thus prodded, in February, the Massachusetts legislature resumed its efforts to gain repeal of the "destructive" embargo. In a "solemn remonstrance" to Congress, the General Court pleaded: "Our husbandmen and mariners cannot, by act of Government, be converted into manufacturers; nor will our merchants and mechanics ever consent to abandon their cities and retire from the seashore, to clear up and cultivate the wilderness." Jefferson, of course, wanted the nation to become, if not agrarian, more self-sufficient and move away from substantial reliance on maritime pursuits and their international hazards. The Massachusetts memorial continued: "The interdiction of foreign commerce, for an indefinite period, by perpetual laws, is justly considered as a total annihilation of it."[5]

A number of editors returned to the fray aiming fresh criticism at the January act designed to "enforce and make more effectual" the embargo. Particularly galling, as the Gloucester resolutions noted, the new law provided informers "shall be entitled to one half the fine" imposed on violators.[6] Boston's *Columbian Centinel* said the revisions "subject us to domiciliary and nocturnal visits, by spies, informers, and military hirelings." The *Centinel* hoped: "If New-England declares firmly, but *temperately*, as one man, that she will not submit to hold out her hands to be *manacled*, and if she shall firmly and

1 *Town Records Book 1, 1802-1833, Town of Lincolnville*, ME, 69-70.

2 McLellan, *History of Gorham*, 155.

3 Edmund Quincy, *Josiah Quincy of Massachusetts*, 138.

4 Randall, *Life of Thomas Jefferson*, 3:283.

5 *American State Papers: Commerce and Navigation* 1:776.

6 Act of January 9, 1809, ch. 5, 2 *Stat.* 506.

steadily act in pursuance of that declaration, she may be yet safe — she may escape the horrors of Civil War, and the *still worse horrors* of Slavery."[1]

Not to be outdone, the *Boston Gazette* editorialized against the "Hateful Measures for Enforcing the Embargo." Boston's acting port collector, it was reported, found it necessary to withhold clearances to all vessels. "This aggravated repression was not generally known until yesterday, when the vessels in the harbor bound their colors in black, and hoisted them half mast. The circumstance has created some considerable agitation in the public mind, but to the honor of the town has been yet unattended with any serious consequences." The *Gazette* warned: "The spirit of New England is slow in rising; but when once inflamed by oppression, it will never be repressed by anything short of complete justice."[2]

By this time it was all too apparent the embargo laws failed to achieve their purpose. France could see and enjoy the fact the American embargo halted more trade to England than France was capable of stopping. Great Britain, on the other hand, managed to get along without open trade with the United States. A Federalist newspaper in Boston likened the situation to the farmer's story about the minister who "sent his boy to the pasture after a horse. He was gone so long that the parson was afraid the horse had kicked his brains out; he went therefore with anxiety to look after him," the editor recalled. "In the field he found the boy standing still with his eyes steadily fixed upon the ground. His master inquired with severity what he was doing there. Why, sir, said he, I saw a woodchuck run into this hole and so I thought I would stand and watch for him until he was starved out, but I declare I am almost starved to death myself."[3]

The severe enforcement provisions enacted in January 1809 turned out to be a last gasp for the embargo. Even Jefferson's party now saw the need to end the experiment. Republican Congressman Roger Nelson of Maryland came to conclude: "The excitement in the East renders it necessary that we should enforce it by bayonet, or repeal."[4] Kentucky Representative Matthew Lyon, once a member of the Green Mountain Boys and a congressman from Vermont, adopted a more measured view when he announced: "The embargo has, like other things, had its day."[5]

Most congressmen agreed with Lyon, but a general fear of war pervaded the capital. Available options promoted deep anxiety. The failed embargo, it seemed, accomplished little beyond setting the stage for war of some kind and riling, perhaps beyond repair, a large section of the country. If the Congress did not repeal the hated law, the growing unrest and defiance in the Northeast threatened civil war. Yet many members felt a repeal to quiet this part of the country must be followed by a war with one or both of the bel-

---

1 Library of Congress, *The Constitution gone!!*
2 *Boston Gazette*, February 2, 1809.
3 *Columbian Centinel* (MA), May 25, 1808.
4 *Annals of Congress*, 10th Cong., 2nd sess., 1258.
5 Ibid., 1411.

ligerent European powers. Repeal without a foreign war to gain the elusive rights of neutral commerce would amount to dishonorable capitulation, or so many believed.

In the end, a March 1 measure raised the embargo, effective on the 15th, except as it applied to Great Britain and France and their colonies and dependencies, and immediately denied public ships of the two countries entrance to the United States. After May 20, the law denied all British and French vessels entrance, and banned importation of goods from the two nations. Thus, as Jefferson left office, the government followed a mixed policy of limited embargo, nonintercourse, and nonimportation. In looking back, Jefferson lamented: "I felt the foundation of the government shaken under my feet by the New England townships."[1]

The inhabitants of Wiscasset certainly felt the ground rumble. Across the Sheepscot River, the new fort at Edgecomb fired its cannons to celebrate the end of the general embargo. Captain John Binney commanding the fort told his wife Wiscasset folks took up the challenge. In a letter to Mrs. Binney, he said the militiamen reported for duty in 15 minutes. Small arms firing kept up until 10:00 p.m. "At 7 a procession was formed . . . and all the citizens of the town followed 4 deep about 250 men, 500 boys, 700 dogs observed by 800 women, 900 children and 1,000 cats besides other animals in great numbers." The parade passed through the principal streets, "Bells a-ringing, marshals hallooing, boys squalling, guns firing, altogether made the most noisome *hurlebello* you ever heard." Then the militia company "went to Fort Hill where grog in pails was given to the common people and they were bid to get roaring drunk as soon as possible."[2]

Similar revelry took place throughout the region. The jubilation, however, ran its course in short order. Ports up and down the coast came to life. Enterprising ship owners anticipated the end of Jefferson's embargo and had their vessels loaded and standing by. They quickly provided the required bonds, and sailed without delay to handsome profits.

A Baltimore newspaper offered a summary of the long and divisive controversy. "After . . . reducing the whole country to a state of wretchedness and poverty," the editor wrote, "our infatuated rulers, blinded by a corrupt predilection for France, have been forced to acknowledge their fatal error, and so far to retrace their steps. To the patriotism of the New England States is due the praise of our salvation. By their courage and virtue have we been saved from entanglements in a fatal alliance with France."[3]

This kind of commentary, of course, amounted to partisan simplification. But the vacillating and imperfect economic warfare of the United States had not resolved its persistent maritime problems or gained the respect and rights of a sovereign neutral. All the while, the matter of impressment smoldered. Within three years, impressment would become a *casus belli*.

---

1 Bailey, *Diplomatic History of the American People*, 129.
2 Fannie S. Chase, *Wiscasset in Pownalborough*, 329.
3 *Federal Republican and Commercial Gazette* (MD), March 1, 1809.

Chapter 4. A Most Unexampled Outrage

When President James Madison sent his war message to Congress in June 1812, he listed impressment of American seamen as the country's foremost grievance with Great Britain. In doing so, he not only tugged at the high sense of patriotism prevalent in a newly fledged sovereign state, but he focused on a human predicament that most of the people could understand and appreciate. "American citizens," he argued, "have been torn from their country, and from every thing dear to them; have been dragged on board ships of war of a foreign nation; and exposed . . . to be exiled to the most distant and deadly climes. . . ." Such conduct by the British, he said, amounted to a "crying enormity."[1] Forever after, the British manning practice of impressment became identified with the War of 1812. In the minds of some, it was the cause of the war.

Seafaring New Englanders possessed mixed feelings about the issue, partly because the practice of impressing — or forcing — a man into the service of the Royal Navy was of ancient date. To some mariners it was an acceptable though unhappy risk. Massachusetts Senator Pickering made the point when he noted, "we seldom hear complaints in the great *navigating* States." He wondered why Washington and the interior states expressed "such extreme sympathy" for seamen impressed by the British.[2]

As late as 1813, The Massachusetts House of Representatives downplayed the issue. A committee took depositions from 51 sea captains, merchants, and others and found, on average, 21,060 seamen were employed each of the previous 15 years. Yet, out of "this vast number,"[3] the committee concluded

---

1 *American State Papers: Foreign Relations* 3:405.

2 Library of Congress, *Important and Alarming Information.*

3 Massachusetts House of Representatives, *Report of the committee of the House of Representatives of Massachusetts on the Subject of Impressed Seamen*, 9.

the total of impressed American seamen amounted to only 107. By sharp contrast, in 1812, a presidential report to Congress indicated over the years 6,057 men filed applications for relief with the United States government claiming to be impressed Americans.

At any rate, the increasing British arrogance associated with impressment during the Napoleonic Wars finally riled most of the United States. A prominent editor summarized American feelings when he observed: "King *George* wants men to support him in his 'abominations,' and he will get them if he can — on the same principle that the robber obtains the purse of the traveller."[1]

Supposition traces the business to feudal England and the French term *prest* meaning *ready* or the Latin *praestitum* signifying *engaged*. The money tendered to recruits for the king's service was called *prest* or *imprest* money. Upon receipt of the money, a man was ready or engaged for duty. In a word, he became impressed. The Royal Navy apparently began impressing seamen as early as 1355.

Over time, compulsive force replaced the seemingly consensual approach to impressment. In 1776, Lord Mansfield, chief justice of the King's Bench, ruled the legal authority for pressing was based on immemorial usage and its justification was the safety of the state. He recognized, nonetheless, the power as it had developed was subject to abuse. The latter point was an understatement.

British navy captains were responsible for their own recruiting, but they often turned to the navy's organized Impress Service and its press-gangs. By the mid-18th century, violence became associated with the gangs. In a landmark 1743 case, one Alexander Broadfoot disputed his seizure, killed a member of a press-gang, and was found guilty of manslaughter. In 1783, a band of sailors, earlier impressed in Sunderland, returned to the site of their misfortune to seek out those who had helped the press-gang. The informers were nabbed, mounted on poles, and carried through the streets, exposed to the taunts and missiles of the citizenry. One informer died of the mistreatment.

A decade later, seamen in North Shields and other eastern coast towns resolved to resist any press-gang. They captured one gang, and after demonstrating their contempt for the gang members, tossed them out of town. A few weeks later some 500 seamen conspired to attack the Newcastle office of the Impress Service. The assault fizzled when it became known the Dragoons and North York Militia were prepared to challenge the foray. The press-gangs enacted their revenge at the end of April. The Tynemouth regiment cordoned off North Shields to prevent escape, and the gangs gathered up some 250 protesting recruits.

"It would be tedious to describe or even enumerate, the various press-gang riots . . . which took place on the Tyne and Wear almost every season down to the peace of Amiens. After the resumption of hostilities in 1803, the

---

1 *Niles' Weekly Register* (MD), November 14, 1812.

like scenes began again to be acted."[1] But the navy did not limit its pressing to the British ports and countryside. When and wherever the need arose, the navy went after able-bodied British subjects. A difference of opinion existed over the meaning of the phrase *British subject*. The definition was at the center of the growing tension with the United States.

The problem began to develop after American independence when sailors deserted at an alarming rate from the repressive Royal Navy. The rapidly expanding and more lucrative United States merchant service attracted more than a few of the British deserters. And Britain understandably felt justified in forcible recovery of these men when found. Recovering deserters detected on American commercial vessels in British waters, by itself, did not create serious discord. Antagonism grew when, as a belligerent, Great Britain exercised its internationally recognized right to board neutral vessels on the high seas and search for goods destined for their enemies, or contraband or servicemen of the enemy. If Royal Navy deserters were found during the boardings, they were fair game. But the navy often expanded its grasp and took British subjects properly employed by an American captain. Too often, when this enlarged field was targeted, American seamen in the mix were grabbed. Officers supervising such highhandedness were known to rationalize their conduct by explaining the protesting seamen spoke English very well; therefore, they must be British. A few officers defended broad sweeps with the argument Britain was trying to save the world, and America ought to help.

At least one Briton spoke out against the impressment of Americans. While actually serving a two-year sentence in Newgate Prison for treasonous libel, William Cobbett, a radical journalist, found time to complain about the practice to the prince regent. Cobbett held a deep-seated distrust of authority. Government officials "were constantly under Cobbett's flail."[2] Cobbett observed: "Our ships of war when they meet an American vessel at sea, board her, and take out of her, by force, any seamen whom our officers assert to be *British subjects*." He summed up the issue, arguing: "There is no *rule* by which they are bound. They act at discretion and the consequence is that great numbers of native Americans have been thus impressed, and great numbers of them are now in our navy."[3]

In his autobiography, Joseph Bates of New Bedford, later a leader in the Adventist Church, provided a vivid firsthand account of the Royal Navy's routine and flagrant disregard of the rights of American seamen who fell within its grasp. Bates' remembrance of the unhappy experience mirrored the personal account published in 1811 by Joshua Davis of Boston. The British impressed Davis while he sailed on the privateer *Dean* off Newfoundland in September 1779. Placed on a frigate at St. John's, the 19-year-old was "put down in the ship's books as a gunner's boy, at 16 shillings 6 pence per month."

1 "The Press-Gang in the Northern Counties," 2.
2 Spater, *William Cobbett*, 1:241-242.
3 *Niles'*, May 30, 1812.

When an officer gave him his assignment, Davis recalled: "I told him that I was a prisoner of war, and would not go. He called me a d—d Yankee rascal, and if I said a word more, he would tie me up to the gangway and give me a dozen lashes." Davis went.[1]

While Bates was held for five years, Davis spent eight years against his wishes in the Royal Navy, serving on six ships. Conditions were poor at best. At one point, while on the H.M.S. *Arrogant*, 74, sickness raged throughout the ship. "[I]n the course of ten days we had seventy two men carried on shore, not being permitted to carry them through the town to the burying ground."[2]

Finally, late in September 1787, he saw his chance to escape while on a shore party in England. Breaking away, he said he ran "as fast as I could run, through Chatham, Rochester, and Strude. When I reached the top of Strude hill, I sat down to rest myself, having came four miles on tiptoe."[3] Before long, he obtained a berth on the *Nonpareil*, Captain Cushing bound for Boston. Cushing was short-handed, having lost some of his crew to a British press-gang.

The United States began to get serious about the matter with passage of "An Act for the relief and protection of American Seamen" in May 1796.[4] Among other things, the law provided for the appointment of agents to live in Great Britain and elsewhere to inquire into cases of alleged impressment of American citizens, work for their release, and report the results. Port collectors in the United States were required to file quarterly accounts of impressments and detentions reported to them. In turn, the secretary of state filed a comprehensive annual report with Congress.

The process turned out to be tedious. As of January 1799, the two agents in Britain filed 651 release applications with the Admiralty. As a consequence, 173 men were discharged, while 172 seamen could not document their citizenship and continued to be detained. Out of the overall total, only 29 men turned out to be British subjects, while another 17 managed to escape. And 93 men foolishly accepted a tendered bounty, and, therefore, the Admiralty would not release them from their obligation.

The issue intensified as a result of a confrontation at Havana in November 1798. A British squadron stopped the United States sloop-of-war *Baltimore*, 20 and impressed 55 of her crew. The House Committee of Defence felt "instances of abuse of this kind excite a lively sensibility. . . ."[5] Unfortunately, the incident did not create enough excitement to leave a lasting impression with the parties. Confronted by an overwhelming British force made up of a 98-gun ship, two 74s, and two frigates of 32 guns, Captain Isaac Phillips of the *Baltimore* did not have many options. When Captain J. Loring of the

1 Joshua Davis, *A Narrative*, 11.
2 Ibid., 18.
3 Ibid., 56.
4 Act of May 28, 1796, ch. 36, 1 *Stat.* 477.
5 *Annals of Congress*, 5th Cong., 3rd sess., 2546.

H.M.S. *Carnatic*, 74 took the 55 American crewmen, Phillips protested he could not defend and handle his ship with such a loss of manpower. Loring reconsidered, and returned 50 of the men. A polite exchange followed, in which Phillips offered to give up all Englishmen on his ship, if Loring would turn over all Americans on the *Carnatic*. Loring rejected the offer, leaving Phillips remonstrating against "such indignity to our flag."[1]

The incident created predictable anti-British sentiment in the United States. President John Adams downplayed the seriousness of the encounter. "I have no doubt that this first instance of misconduct [against a U.S. Navy vessel] will be readily corrected." He directed Secretary of the Navy Benjamin Stoddert to follow up. The secretary issued a circular to his officers declaring, "that on no pretence whatever, you permit the public vessel of war under your command to be detained, or searched, nor any of the officers or men belonging to her to be taken from her, by the ships or vessels of any foreign nation, so long as you are in a capacity to repel such outrage on the honor of the American flag."[2] To make his point, Stoddert dismissed Phillips from the service.

The issue more or less festered well into the next decade. Then, on June 22, 1807, the U.S. frigate *Chesapeake*, Captain James Barron left Norfolk, Virginia. Her aborted trip almost led to immediate war with Britain. Upon reflection, it can be argued, the War of 1812 would not have been fought if the *Chesapeake* had remained quietly in port in June 1807. Her unhappy cruise was not the cause of the war, but it promoted a bellicose climate. For the first time, the war cry sounded loud, and it did not subside until the country got its fill of war.

British treatment of the *Chesapeake* put war in the minds of many Americans.

Early in the morning of the 22nd, the *Chesapeake* cleared Norfolk bound for the Mediterranean. Off Cape Henry, the H.M.S. *Leopard*, 50, Captain Salusbury P. Humphreys, began to follow. Around 4:00 p.m., the *Leopard*, one of numerous British warships in the area, hailed the *Chesapeake*, a ship called by a British historian "a kind of fly-paper for picking up deserters and other wandering British seamen."[3] Barron ordered his ship to hove to for the Briton. Lieutenant John Meade "came on board to demand some men who had deserted from the English navy."[4] He handed Barron a copy of a directive from the commander of the North American Station, Vice Admiral Sir George C. Berkeley. The admiral's standing order called for a search for deserters on the *Chesapeake* if the American ship was encountered outside United States' limits. Meade also provided a letter from Humphreys, stating he wanted specific deserters while expressing "a hope that every circumstance respecting

---

1 Ibid., 2576.
2 Ibid., 2575.
3 Bradford Perkins, *Prologue to War*, 142.
4 *American State Papers: Foreign Relations* 3:20.

them may be adjusted in a manner that the harmony subsisting between the two countries may remain undisturbed."[1]

Barron answered in writing, "I know of no such men as you describe." He added, "I am also instructed never to permit the crew of any ship that I command to be mustered by any other but their own officers."[2] Meade returned with the reply to his ship.

Barron sensed danger, and quietly gave the order to send the men to quarters with as little animation as possible. "[B]ut before a match could be lighted, or the quarter-bill of any division examined, or . . . the gun-deck . . . could be cleared, the commander of the Leopard hailed. . . ."[3] Barron could not make out his words. Humphreys purportedly twice shouted: "Commodore Barron, you must be aware of the necessity I am under of complying with the orders of my commander-in-chief." Barron replied: "I do not understand what you say."[4]

Observing the hurried activity on the *Chesapeake*, Humphreys did not want to lose his advantage. He directed a shot across the American's fore-foot. In a minute, he fired another warning shot. After two minutes of un-responsiveness and apparent evasion, the *Leopard* poured a broadside into the *Chesapeake*. Two more broadsides followed. The Americans managed to fire one gun as their colors came down. Racing from the galley, carrying a hot coal for the purpose, young Lieutenant William Allen, a native of Providence, touched off a token shot. The encounter took some 18 minutes. Barron reported, "[O]ur resistance was but feeble."[5] The frigate suffered substantial hull, rigging, and spar damage. Her log reported three men killed and sixteen wounded.

Barron sent Lieutenant Sidney Smith over to the *Leopard* to tell Humphreys the *Chesapeake* was his prize. But Humphreys did not want the American ship. He wanted several known deserters, especially Jenkin Ratford, a London native. He sent a team of officers and men to muster the crew of the *Chesapeake*. The searchers found some sixteen British deserters, but took only four. Their top find was Ratford. A notorious deserter, he enlisted on board the *Chesapeake* after running from the Royal Navy. He then went out of his way to taunt English officers on the streets of Norfolk. The other three, easily recognized, escaped together in February from their British ship lying in Hampton Roads. David Martin of Westport, Massachusetts and William Ware from Maryland clearly were American citizens. The third man, John Strachan, also claimed to be from Maryland. The four were taken back to Halifax, where Ratford was hanged and Ware died from wounds received while being flogged through the fleet. And five years later, on June 13, 1812,

1 Ibid., 18.
2 Ibid.
3 Ibid.
4 James, *Naval History of Great Britain*, 4:329-330.
5 *American State Papers: Foreign Relations* 3:20.

with considerable fanfare, Martin and Strachan were restored to the decks of the *Chesapeake* at Boston.

Barron declined Humphreys' offer of assistance. Despite three and a half feet of water in the hold, and the substantial damage to masts and standing rigging, the *Chesapeake* made an overnight return to Hampton Roads. A bipartisan uproar followed.

Outraged and shamed, the people of the Norfolk area promptly cut off all contact with the British navy. No longer would they provide pilots, provisions, water, and the like. Citizens of Portsmouth, Virginia met and unanimously agreed if anyone ignored the ban on aiding the British navy they would be "deemed infamous."[1] The British fleet commander in Hampton Roads sent a menacing message to shore about maintaining his access to the British consul. At Hampton, a gang of locals descended upon a schooner ready to sail to the British ships and destroyed upwards of 200 hogsheads of water. Thus challenged, the British threatened to invade Hampton to procure water and they blustered they were of a mind to retake the *Chesapeake*, now under the command of Captain Stephen Decatur. Norfolk officials asked Decatur, commander of United States naval forces at the place, to protect them with his small force of gunboats. Decatur accepted the challenge. He told the secretary of the navy if the British "attempt to come up with the force they speak of, I think I am not over sanguine when I say I believe they will not all go down again."[2] Over 1,600 militiamen, some from as far away as Richmond and Petersburg, took up defensive positions, and volunteers rushed to repair Fort Norfolk.

Seething anger quickly spread throughout the country. The *Ledger* office in Norfolk got the ball rolling. Within a day, it put out a broadside presenting "the details of a most unexampled outrage in the perpetration of which the blood of our countrymen has been shed by the hands of violence and the honour and independence of our nation insulted beyond the possibility of further forbearance."[3] The reaction was nonpartisan. The *Federalist* reported: "We have never, on any occasion, witnessed the spirit of the people excited to so great a degree of indignation, or such a thirst for revenge. . . ."[4] The *National Intelligencer* thought if the British "refuse that satisfaction which we demand, the result . . . will be war."[5] The *Evening Post* concluded, "the national sovereignty has been attacked, the national honor tarnished, and that ample reparations and satisfaction must be given or . . . war ought to be resorted to by force of arms."[6]

New England newspapers expressed similar fury. At Portsmouth, the *New Hampshire Gazette* came out with an early report under the bold head-

---

1 *Newport* (RI) *Mercury*, July 4, 1807.
2 *American State Papers: Foreign Relations* 3:21.
3 Library of Congress, *Ledger Office*.
4 *Washington Federalist*, July 1, 1807.
5 *National Intelligencer* (DC), July 10, 1807.
6 *New York Evening Post*, July 14, 1807.

line: "BY THE MAILS. HIGHLY IMPORTANT!!! BRITISH OUTRAGE".[1] In Worcester, the local paper reported the incident under the heading: "The Nation Insulted".[2] The *Newport Mercury* thought the outrage "very naturally lead us to fancy that a war with England is inevitable."[3] The *Connecticut Courant* described the attack as "wanton and unprovoked,"[4] while the *Salem Gazette* concluded "an act of war has been committed upon us."[5]

Members of both political parties came together as one at numerous public meetings. Large groups gathered at New Haven, Newport, Providence, and Portsmouth to denounce the British insult. In Boston, the Republicans called a meeting for July 10, after the majority Federalists declined to call an official town meeting. When the Federalist did set a meeting for the 16th, some 2,000 citizens attended and pledged support for the national government. John Quincy Adams chaired the resolutions committee. The eminent historian Samuel Eliot Morison believed: "Had Jefferson then called for a declaration of war, Massachusetts would have accepted war with good grace."[6]

Some towns responded to a Norfolk Committee of Correspondence plea for expressions of outrage and support. Newport accordingly held a town meeting on July 9 and resolved the "insult . . . ought to be avenged. . . . Our national honour, our national interests, our national happiness . . . all require it."[7] Newburyport met on July 7 to consider the "alarming outrage" on the *Chesapeake*. The meeting resolved, "that we consider the attack made upon the United States Frigate Chesapeake . . . a violation of our national rights and an insult on our national dignity, no less humiliating than unwarrantable." The resolution continued, "we unite with our Government in wishing ardently for the continuance of peace on just and honorable terms; yet we are willing and ready to cooperate in the support of any measures however serious, which may tend to secure the honor and safety of our Country, and we pledge our lives and fortunes to support the same."[8] And the town took the added measure of raising a 90-man force in anticipation of a war. Sudbury, Massachusetts took similar steps, voting $12 monthly pay for militiamen called upon for actual service during the crisis as well as "six dollars to each soldier as advance pay, that shall equip himself for said service."[9] Even inland Worcester reacted. The town's Light Infantry tendered its services, its members resolving "we are ready, at a moment's warning, to march wherever the executive authority may direct."[10] Not to be outdone, two other Worcester infantry companies, the town's company of artillery and its cavalry company

1 *New Hampshire Gazette*, July 7, 1807.
2 *Massachusetts Spy*, July 8, 1807.
3 *Newport (RI) Mercury*, July 18, 1807.
4 *Connecticut Courant*, July 8, 1807.
5 *Salem (MA) Gazette*, July 10, 1807.
6 Morison, *Maritime History of Massachusetts*, 186.
7 *Newport (RI) Mercury*, July 11, 1807.
8 *Newburyport (MA) Freeholders 1790-1816, Vol. 2*.
9 Hudson, *History of Sudbury*, 465.
10 Lincoln, *Worcester*, 134.

likewise volunteered. And legislatures took up the cry. The Vermont General Assembly adopted a resolution "with but one dissenting vote," declaring "it is the duty of every American to rally around the constituted authorities of this county and to support them with his life and fortune."[1]

With a unified public behind him, Jefferson acted quickly to address the enormity. On July 2, he issued a proclamation telling the Royal Navy to leave "the harbors or waters of the United States, immediately and without delay," and to stay out.[2] Anticipating British insolence, he also prohibited all American intercourse with any ship disregarding his order. At the same time, he called upon the states to ready 100,000 militiamen to march at a moment's notice to defend the country. In contrast to Governor Strong's 1812 resistance to a similar call, on July 14, Massachusetts Governor James Sullivan took steps to detach 11,075 requested men. The governor projected a term of service of six months once the president made the call to active duty.

The president alerted his minister in London, James Monroe, about the volatile mood in America. The British, he said, "have often enough . . . given us cause for war before, but it has been on points which would not have united the nation. But now they have touched a chord which vibrates in every heart. . . ."[3]

While the focus remained on the British, like Phillips before him, Barron could not escape culpability. The navy department conducted a court of inquiry touching on the causes of the surrender of the *Chesapeake*. Barron drew no comfort from the fact his own officers, embarrassed by the affair, had requested the review. The panel determined that Barron had neglected to prepare his ship for action; acted indecisively; issued dispiriting commands; struck his colors before firing a shot; and surrendered prematurely. This resulted in a February 1808 court-martial. The court found Barron guilty of negligence and suspended him for five years. Stephen Decatur, unfortunately, served on the court even though he had asked to be excused. And Barron would not forget Decatur's role.

As the weeks passed, the British continued to inflame sensibilities by ignoring Jefferson's proclamation. They remained in Chesapeake Bay and continued to capture American commercial vessels, and impress and generally harass and threaten Americans. The clamor for war declined to a degree, but the dispute over neutral rights continued to fester in the following years.

In November 1808, Jefferson addressed the Congress for the last time. He acknowledged the "candid and liberal experiment" of the embargo had failed, and said "it will rest with the wisdom of Congress to decide on the course best adapted to such a state of things." As for the *Chesapeake* incident, "a subject on which the nation had manifested so honorable a sensibility," he had

---

1 Wilber, *Early History of Vermont*, 3:176.
2 *American State Papers: Foreign Relations* 3:24.
3 Coles, *War of 1812*, 7.

hoped the British government would fully redress the wrong. Instead, he reported: "It is found no steps have been taken for the purpose."[1]

Congress addressed the shortcomings and problems associated with the general embargo by passing the so-called Nonintercourse Act of March 1, 1809. This measure repealed the December 1807 embargo law and its amendments to allow Americans to trade with any nation except Great Britain and France. But, if either nation rescinded its edicts, commercial intercourse with America could resume. To an extent, the act eased the economic downturn in New England. Thereafter, up until the war, nonintercourse, in one form or another, became President Madison's basic tool to deal with the neutral rights problem, especially as it involved Great Britain.

At the same time, Madison tried to put to rest the smoldering *Chesapeake* issue. The United States sought satisfaction and reparations. Nonintercourse and the orders in council made their way into protracted negotiations on the *Chesapeake* matter. David W. Erskine, British minister to Washington, and Secretary of State Robert Smith came to substantial agreement in April 1809. The United States would resume trade with the British, and the latter would withdraw the offensive orders in council, restore the men taken from the *Chesapeake*, and "make a suitable provision for the unfortunate sufferers on that occasion."[2] But when Smith, nonetheless, suggested the minimal censure of Humphreys was insufficient, the deal collapsed for the time.

A more adversarial Francis Jackson succeeded Erskine in October, and reopened negotiations. Jackson's approach was so antagonistic that the United States requested and gained his recall. For more than a year, Britain did not have a minister in Washington. The protracted and interrupted talks promoted persistent ill feeling toward the British, especially since the Royal Navy continued to interdict United States shipping near the American coast. Under the conditions, another encounter was inevitable.

In May 1811, Commodore John Rodgers left Annapolis in the *President*, sailing under special instructions. Navy Secretary Paul Hamilton ordered him to repair to New York waters where British and French cruisers were harassing American traders. Hamilton had in mind a stop made by the H.M.S. *Guerriere*, 38. Early in the month, off Sandy Hook, the Briton waylaid the American brig *Spitfire* out of Portland and impressed John Diggio, a Maine native. Rodgers cleared Cape Henry on the 14th.

Although he was a fighter and did not need to be told, like other captains, Rodgers received the departmental order issued as a result of the *Chesapeake* embarrassment. The order instructed: "What has been perpetrated may again be attempted. It is therefore our duty to be prepared and determined at every hazard to vindicate the injured honor of our navy, and revive the drooping spirit of the nation . . .; and . . . you are to submit to none, not even a menace or threat from a force not materially your superior."[3] For good measure, when

---

1 U.S. *Senate Journal.* 10th Cong., 2nd sess., November 8, 1808, 295.

2 *American State Papers: Foreign Relations* 3:295.

3 Mahan, *Sea Power in its Relations to the War of 1812,* 1:256.

Rodgers forwarded the directive to his captains, he advised: "I should consider the firing of a shot by a vessel of war, of . . . particularly England, at one of our public vessels, whilst the colors of her nation are flying on board of her, as a menace of the grossest order, and in amount an insult which it would be disgraceful not to resent by the return of two shot at least."[1]

Two days later, a man-of-war under a press of sail stood towards the *President*, got close enough to look her over, and then turned and fled. Rodgers beat to quarters and took up the chase; holding out hope the stranger was the *Guerriere*. After dark, the two ships were within speaking distance. Unable to make identification, Rodgers hailed: "[W]hat ship is that?"[2] The other ship did not answer. Marine Captain Henry Caldwell recalled: "The commodore hailed a second time, and received no answer; but before he had time to take the trumpet from his mouth," the stranger fired into the *President*. "Commodore Rodgers, turning round to me, asked what the devil was that; and I replied, she has fired into us."[3] In a flash, the *President* returned a shot, only to be met with several shots in return, accompanied by musketry. "I had determined at the moment to fire only a single shot in return," said Rodgers, "but the immediate repetition of the previous unprovoked outrage induced me to believe that the insult was premeditated. . . . I accordingly . . . determined neither to be the aggressor, or suffer the flag of my country to be insulted with impunity, gave a general order to fire."[4]

The adversary turned out to be the British ship-sloop *Little Belt*, 20, Captain Arthur B. Bingham. The ensuing fight lasted as much as 18 minutes. At one point, both ships stopped firing. After a three-minute lull, the *Little Belt* recommenced firing, and the *President* promptly responded with vigor. In a few moments, the Briton once again stopped firing and someone on her declared her colors were down and she was in great distress. In the end, the British suffered 13 killed and 19 wounded. The *Little Belt* was severely cut up, but able to limp back to Halifax. The damage proved so extensive, she was sold out of service within the year. The *President* had one boy wounded, and relatively minor damage to rigging and the main and fore masts.

Much of the American public applauded the outcome, including most New Englanders. A few hardcore Federalists thought it a shame. New York City feted Rodgers, while Secretary Hamilton expressed concern for the captain. Within days, the secretary cautioned, "I am certain, that the chastisement, which you have very properly inflicted, will cause you to be marked for British vengeance." As for his own feelings, Hamilton said: "I declare, that my sentiments towards, & estimation of you, go beyond what may be expressed by the words, esteem & respect."[5] Indicative of the good feeling in Wash-

1 Ibid., 257.

2 *American State Papers: Foreign Relations* 3:478.

3 Ibid., 480.

4 *Niles'*, September 21, 1811.

5 Dudley, *Naval War of 1812*, 1:49.

ington, he wanted Rodgers' thoughts on rewarding the wounded boy with a midshipman's warrant.

An international controversy followed the incident. Both participants accused the other of firing first. The Royal Navy at Halifax convened a board of captains to examine the affair. The board and the English press accepted Bingham's version that the American fired first. The excitement prompted Rodgers to ask for a court of inquiry. Fifty witnesses provided sworn testimony over 12 days, and the court concluded the *Little Belt* fired the first shot. When the United States subsequently disavowed any hostile intent behind the engagement, the British dropped the matter. But a contributor to the *Norfolk Gazette* pondered: "There are men who consider this fracas an offset to the *Chesapeake* — I pray God it may not be an onset to War."[1]

In November, the two countries finally settled the *Chesapeake* issue. The new British minister to Washington, Augustus J. Foster, and the new secretary of state, James Monroe, reached an accord, years too late. Foster disavowed Humphreys' act; agreed to restore the impressed sailors; and provide "a suitable pecuniary provision for the sufferers in consequence of the attack."[2] Monroe accepted the conditions even though the United States continued to feel Humphreys got off lightly. As noted, the two *Chesapeake* survivors were returned in 1812, but the war interrupted payment of damages.

Once the abrasive *Chesapeake* issue passed, relatively minor incidents continued to arise with a cumulative effect. One of the most notorious dustups focused on New England. The case involved an Irish adventurer named John Henry who lived in Boston and Vermont before moving to Montreal. In 1808, Henry began to correspond with Herman W. Ryland, a confidential adviser to Sir James Henry Craig, governor of Canada. Henry offered his assessment of political conditions in the New England states. Ryland saw an opening and in January 1809, he offered to pay Henry if he accepted "a secret and confidential mission to Boston." He told Henry, "the Governor would furnish you with a cipher for carrying on your correspondence." Henry accepted and Craig said he was especially interested in learning about the secession sentiments of the Federalists in New England and "*how far, in such an event, they would look up to England for assistance, or be disposed to enter into a connection with us.*"[3]

The whole affair was silly, but inflammatory. Henry filed individual reports from Burlington and Windsor, Vermont, Amherst, New Hampshire, and a number from Boston. Full of opinion and gossip and short on intelligence, much of what he passed along could be found in the public prints. Before long, Henry complained about his meager compensation. He chased about Canada and England for two years seeking more money for his efforts.

In his travels he encountered another rogue, a Frenchman named Soubiron who passed himself off as Count Edouard de Crillon. Henry showed Soubiron purported copies of his reports to Craig. The pair hatched a plot

---

1 *Norfolk Gazette and Publick Ledger* (VA), June 7, 1811.
2 *American State Papers: Foreign Relations* 3:499-500.
3 Ibid., 546.

to sell the letters to the Madison administration. Anxious to embarrass the Federalists, the president paid $50,000 for the documents, and sent them to Congress in March 1812. As might be expected, an outcry followed. The two political parties tried to exploit the incident for partisan gain. When it became evident Henry acted alone and harmlessly, the initial uproar faded. But the escapade afforded another opportunity to think and talk about war. In much of the country, nationalism and bellicosity marched unrestrained and side by side.

CHAPTER 5. THE FINAL STEP

As the British and French interference with American maritime trade continued unabated, Madison prepared for armed conflict. In January, at his behest, Congress voted to raise 25,000 additional troops. And Democratic Republicans began to beat the drums of war. U.S. Senator Jonathan Robinson of Bennington, Vermont informed state party stalwart Reverend Ezra Butler of Waterbury about the measure, adding the hope that "every effort will be made by our friends to aid inlistments that we may have a short war and popular one." He added the postscript, "As we have passed the Rubicon we wish to know how the public Pulse beats."[1]

Butler, a man who would "run the gamut of judicial, legislative and executive experiences and yet remain always a person of Christian meekness, dignity and propriety,"[2] jumped to action. The Vermont party called a general public meeting to support Madison's policies for early February at Montpelier to be chaired by Butler. Daniel Thompson, a boy at the time, recalled: "We have seen some rather piping political times since that period, but none, which for intense excitement and party animosity, could at all compare with" the Montpelier gathering and others "that were everywhere exhibited on the approach of the war of 1812."[3]

On the appointed day, citizens poured into Montpelier, clogging the roads in the process. Many Federalists showed up, hoping to control the debate. Feelings ran high. The settled minister of the place, Reverend Chester Wright, citing conscientious considerations, declined to open the meeting. After a show of indignation, the assemblage began to cry out: "Uncle Ziba! Uncle Ziba!!" A committeeman jumped on stage and shouted: "Is the Rev.

---

1 Theodore G. Lewis, *History of Waterbury*, 43.
2 Ibid.
3 Thompson, *History of the Town of Montpelier*, 114.

Ziba Woodworth present? If so, he is respectfully invited to come forward and open this meeting with prayer."[1]

Woodworth had suffered a crippling leg wound at the infamous 1781 Battle of Groton Heights, forcing him to hobble about. He stumped his way to the platform, offered a brief, emotional prayer, and "entered into the political spirit of the meeting, showering a torrent of blessings on our rulers for their wisdom, patriotism and fearless stand in resisting the aggressions of British tyranny." He then asked "God's pity on the blindness of the enemies of the war, and enemies of our blessed country, and His forgiveness of their treasonable dereliction of patriotic duty, and still more treasonable opposition to the wise measures of our God-appointed rulers." A leading Democrat nearby reached out and whacked Woodworth's weakened leg, and in an undertone, exclaimed: "That is right! Give it to 'em, give it to 'em, Uncle Ziba!" Accounts indicate the old hero "did give it to 'em in a manner which very likely never had a parallel in the shape of a prayer."[2]

Congressman James Fisk of Barre led the pro-administration presentation before a generally sympathetic crowd. Nicholas Baylies, a Federalist lawyer, followed Fisk and attempted to stem the tide. He launched a spirited attack on Madison and his policies. Old Matthew Wallace of Berlin tolerated the discourse for a time before jumping to his feet exclaiming: "'Can't stand that! Can't stand that, Mr. Chairman! Anything in reason, but, by heavens, sir,' his eye flashing and fist raised, 'I sha'nt sit here to listen to outright treason!'"[3] The gathering went on to pester the lawyer with hissing and coughing and Baylies struggled to a conclusion. When the meeting failed to pass pro-Madison resolutions and the semblance of order evaporated, a disappointed Butler gave up as chairman. The opposition promptly filled the vacant chair with Charles Buckley, "one of the most high toned Federalists and decided opposers of the war in the whole country." But as if on cue, "the Democrats from abroad came pouring into the village" and "the hall was filled with the excited, war breathing friends of the Administration."[4] With the tide turned, in rapid order a set of pro-war resolutions was passed with overwhelming majorities.

In a few weeks, on April 1, 1812, President Madison sent a one-sentence message to Congress recommending an immediate 60-day general embargo on shipping. Both houses cleared everyone out of their chambers except members and aides, closed the doors, and took up the matter in expected secrecy. But the secret did not hold. Alerted by sympathetic members of Congress, scores of merchants and captains moved with haste to get loaded vessels to sea. At New York, over a hundred vessels were sent out ahead of the law, although the government cutters managed to detain four.

---

1 *Vermont Historical Magazine*, 4:10.
2 Ibid.
3 Ibid.
4 Thompson, 117-118.

At Boston, "the utmost exertions" were employed fitting ships for sea. In the several days leading up to the effective hour of the new embargo, 85 sail "were loaded, cleared and sailed principally for foreign ports." Deteriorating weather held about 20 in the outer harbor. Haze obscured a signal flag indicating "arrival of the law, and that the Revenue Cutter had been despatched to detain them." So, a messenger carried a warning to the ships and "the principal part of them cut, and put to sea."[1]

Captain Elijah Cobb of Brewster, Massachusetts fresh from carrying a cargo of flour to Cadiz received an alert while preparing to take on another load at Alexandria, Virginia. A merchant associate told Cobb "that he had just received a *dispatch* from Mr. Randolph, in Congress, saying to him, *what you do, must be done quickly* for the embargo will be upon you" in two days. Cobb found himself in a race "*to cheat the Embargo.*"[2] He had 100 tons of ballast to discharge, 3,000 barrels of flour to load, get provisions on the ship, find a new crew, and clear customs. Cobb managed to gain a clearance one hour before the deadline. Quickly, he got under way, out-sailed a customs boat, and made it to sea. He sold his flour in Spain at an inflated profit. While Cobb and a small minority of captains made it out ahead of the law, a large number did not.

In expectation of lost opportunity, when proposed, the bill met with understandable opposition. Federalist Congressman Josiah Quincy of Massachusetts summarized the opposition when he declared: "I look on this measure as an abandonment of our national rights; as impolitic; as deceptive; as calculated to impress on the American people an idea that it is . . . [the] intention to maintain commercial rights, which its true effect is to abandon."[3] A majority of the representatives disregarded such argument and voted to pass the measure by a 71-39 count. The Senate extended the effective period to 90 days by a 20–13 vote, and the House concurred with the change. The president signed the act on April 4, prompting Ellsworth, Maine to print and distribute throughout New England a broadside protesting that until the enactment "we remained ignorant that the ocean was not our own."[4]

The secretary of the navy promptly ordered the service to actively enforce the new embargo. Commodore Rodgers took up the task in the New York to Newport sector. To cover much of the rest of the northeast coast, he ordered Lieutenant William M. Crane in the brig *Nautilus* to patrol for violators "from Cape-Cod to Cape-Ann: you may nevertheless occasionally stretch as far north as Passamaquoddy. . . ."[5] The eastern states, as much as anything, objected to the timing of the embargo. An earlier growing season enabled the southern states to freely trade their flour and produce before the embargo took effect. Now that their season was at hand, unhappy eastern farmers,

1 *Columbian Centinel* (MA), April 11, 1812.

2 Elijah Cobb, *Memoirs of a Cape Cod Skipper*, 66.

3 Barry, *History of Massachusetts: The Commonwealth Period*, 372.

4 Silsby, *Maine Historical Society Newsletter*, 116.

5 Dudley, *Naval War of 1812*, 1:96.

blocked from their markets, felt put upon. Noncompliance with Jefferson's embargo, it will be remembered, thrived in the region. Rodgers considered these factors when he designed his enforcement plan.

Events moved at a rapid pace in a climate rife with talk of war. In the week of the embargo vote, a consequential and heated election took place in Massachusetts. Incumbent Republican Governor Elbridge Gerry faced off against Federalist Caleb Strong in a spirited if not bitter contest. Partisan newspapers called Gerry everything from a blasphemer and incendiary to a slanderer. The legislature reviewed the criticism of the newspapers and found 236 instances of libel against Gerry in pro-Federalist papers, and another 17 cases in pro-Republican papers. A grand jury looked into the libel charges, but declined to find bills of indictment.

The election introduced the phrase gerrymander to the political lexicon. Before the election, Governor Gerry signed a senate redistricting bill that contorted some district boundaries so as to favor his party. One new district looped up from Chelsea all the way to Salisbury, thus disregarding the usual practice of creating more or less compact districts made up of towns with common interests. A cartoonist touched up this district outline creating a caricature of a salamander and called the result a *gerry[sala]mander*. The ploy, forever after associated with Gerry, succeeded to the extent the Republicans wound up with a majority in the upper chamber. But the Federalists came out ahead in the House. Much more important, however, Strong prevailed over Gerry, 52,696 to 51,326, and positioned himself to oppose the coming war with authority and otherwise confound Madison. Gerry did not retire from the scene. He gained a promotion. His party quickly nominated him for the vice-presidency on the Madison re-election ticket and he won the office in the fall election.

Meanwhile, United States and Great Britain negotiators tried to resolve the thorny orders in council issue, the major stumbling block to peace. Lord Viscount Castlereagh, one of Britain's principal foreign ministers, on April 10, told the American State Department the orders would not be revoked in their entirety unless the French first repealed their comparable decrees. Madison considered the British response an unacceptable ultimatum, and he began to think about a war message.

Never reluctant to take sides, newspaper editors opined on the growing appeal to arms. A pro-administration Washington newspaper in plain terms called for war. Believing honorable negotiations were at an end, the paper declared: "The final step ought to be taken, and that step is WAR. By what course of measures we have reached the present crisis, is not now a question for patriots and freemen. It exists: and it is by open and manly war only that we can get through it with honor and advantage to the country. Our wrongs have been great; our cause is just; and if we are decided and firm, success is inevitable."[1]

---

1 *National Intelligencer* (DC), April 14, 1812.

In Baltimore, Hezekiah Niles allowed "a state of war is desired by no man," but likened armed conflict to a summer thunderstorm that "excites general apprehension and frequently does partial damage — but purges the atmosphere." He thought the "war will not last long," because Great Britain could not afford the added costs. Furthermore, he believed: "During the war there will be ample employment for all. Some part of the labor and capital of the United States, at present devoted to commerce, will be directed to objects calculated to seal the independence of the country, in the establishment of a thousand works, needful to the supply of our wants." Niles promised conscription would not be necessary. In a lengthy commentary, he lashed out at Governor Strong, who, he said, was "barely elected" in the recent campaign, and only then because "the exertions of his friends were greater than ever." He castigated former Senator Pickering who "calmly proposes a separation of the states", a notion supported "by a very contemptible portion of the people" who "will be eradicated by the war, and their eradication will indemnify the expense of it."[1]

Just as many editors saw another side. A New York paper, observing a war with England would require "numerous armies and ample treasure," asserted: "The war-hounds that are howling for war through the continent are not to be the men who are to force entrenchments, and scale ramparts against the bayonet and the cannon's mouth: to perish in sickly camps, or in long marches through sultry heats or wastes of snow." Instead, "the honest yeomanry of our country" will send off their sons to fight a war which will amount to "perfect madness."[2]

The *Columbian Centinel* in Boston took note of the "universal sentiment against a British War which prevails among considerate men of all parties in this section of the Union." The pro-Federalist paper claimed: "With the exception of a few brawlers in the street, and some office-holding editors, we can find none who seriously wish to promote this calamity. It is evident that under the circumstances . . . a declaration of war would be in effect a license and bounty offered by our government to the British Fleet to scour our coasts — to sweep our remaining navigation from the ocean, to annihilate our commerce, and to drive the country . . . into . . . poverty and distress. . . ."[3]

The country did not arrive overnight at the doorstep of war. Perceptive observers saw the inevitable conflict years beforehand. The long drawn out *Chesapeake* embarrassment and the failure of Jefferson's embargo led to one conclusion in the minds of many. Virginia Republican Congressman Wilson C. Nicholas, a Jefferson ally, resigned his seat in 1809 in protest over Madison's reluctance to abandon the general policy of his predecessor. "We have tried negotiation until it is disgraceful to think of renewing it," he explained to Jefferson. "Commercial restrictions have been so managed as to operate

---

1 *Niles' Weekly Register* (MD), May 30, 1812.
2 *New York Evening Post*, April 21, 1812.
3 *Columbian Centinel* (MA), May 20, 1812.

only to our own injury. War then or submission only remain. In deciding between them I cannot hesitate a moment."[1]

A few weeks after the upcoming declaration of war, former President John Adams made much the same point in a letter to a Pittsfield friend. He said his only surprise was the fact that "persons in authority, ecclesiastical and civil, and political and military" expressed surprise when the war came. He mused, "[How] it is possible that a rational, a social, or a moral creature can say that the war is unjust, is to me utterly incomprehensible.

"How it can be said to be unnecessary is very mysterious. I have thought it both just and necessary, for five or six years."[2]

John A. Harper, a first-term Republican congressman from New Hampshire, saw the same writing on the wall. Harper is usually included in that somewhat mythical band of representatives known as War Hawks, a militant group led by Henry Clay of Kentucky and John Calhoun of South Carolina. During his brief stay in Washington, Harper maintained a correspondence with William Plumer, his state's Republican governor. Much of what he had to say related to the war question. As early as December 2, 1811, he told Plumer, despite his inexperience, "I feel no hesitation in saying, that the present session will not be closed, without an *arrangement*, or actual *war* with Great Britain."[3]

Later, after passage of the embargo in early April, Harper advised the governor he understood "that all who voted for this measure will vote for war, together with several who voted against it . . . and that war we shall certainly have." He added: "I believe that the President, the heads of Departments, and the majority of both Houses of Congress, are doing every thing in their power, to put the country into an attitude, to resist the wishes of that *'renowned nation, who is fighting the battles of the world.'*"[4]

On May 13, Harper wrote to tell Plumer about a House resolution adopted that day which directed the speaker to write to all absent members, asking them to return to Washington without delay. Developments were moving apace. "The crisis is important," Harper said, "and it is desirable that the people should be fairly and fully represented. The great question will undoubtedly be taken early in June."[5]

All of this would suggest the cause or causes of the war were well understood by national legislators. Nevertheless, over the years, especially in the latter part of the 20th century, historians, commentators, writers, and others have debated the question. One writer came up with twelve different causes. In the end, much of this conjecture makes something complex out of something simple. The principle cause is clear. Hostile interference in one form or another by belligerent powers, particularly Great Britain, with the neutral

---

1 George R. Taylor, *War of 1812*, 109.
2 Coggeshall, *History of the American Privateers*, xl-xli.
3 Egan, *Historical New Hampshire*, 153.
4 Ibid., 164-165.
5 Ibid., 173.

maritime commerce of the United States caused the war. A review of the president's war message, the congressional debate and action it prompted, and the diplomatic exchanges between the two countries, leads to no other conclusion.

On June 1, President Madison sent a confidential message to Congress reiterating much of what he said in a November 5, 1811 message opening the 12th Congress. He alleged: "We behold, in fine, on the side of Great Britain, a state of war against the United States; and on the side of the United States, a state of peace towards Great Britain."[1] In making his case, he outlined four antagonistic policies that constituted the British system of dealing with American seagoing commerce. The first policy was the outrage of impressment. The second involved continuous harassment of the American coast. The third related to a sweeping system of pretended or paper blockades. And, the fourth, the contentious orders in council and associated edicts consolidated and expanded on the first three. To strengthen his argument and make the point the British did not deal in good faith in protracted talks on the maritime issues, he noted the Henry affair and British-Indian intrigues on the western frontier went forward as ministers of the two nations negotiated on the maritime issues.

Madison did not recommend war in so many words. He appreciated the solemn step of declaring war was a congressional prerogative. But he did urge early consideration of the question: "Whether the United States shall continue passive under these progressive usurpations, and these accumulating wrongs; or, opposing force to force in defence of the national rights, shall commit a just cause into the hands of the Almighty Disposer of events. . . . "[2] The president closed his message with a paragraph acknowledging the behavior of France was little better. Despite the revocation of French decrees, that country continued its depredations and violations of American neutral marine rights. Madison abstained from recommending congressional action relative to France at the time in expectation that the outcome of continuing Franco-American discussions in Paris would point to the course Congress should adopt.

Right after Madison delivered his earlier November message detailing the country's difficulties and differences with Great Britain, House Speaker Henry Clay appointed a nine-member select Committee on Foreign Relations to examine the issues raised by the chief executive. Harper and fellow Republican Ebenezer Seaver of Massachusetts were the only New Englanders named to the committee chaired by Calhoun. The assignments impacted the futures of both men. The committee assumed a bellicose stance and in a couple of weeks called for military and naval preparedness.

Prompted by Madison's war message, on June 3, Calhoun's committee issued another report, one that reflected the president's views, point by point, and took the next step. The committee recommended "an immediate appeal

---

1 *American State Papers: Foreign Relations* 3:407.
2 Ibid.

to arms."[1] In reaching its recommendation that the country declare war for the first time, the committee first censured Britain's attack on American neutral trade by its system of blockades, some legal and many pretended and unlawful. The committee moved to a discussion of the orders in council, by which "the British Government declared direct and positive war against the United States."[2] Impressment, according to the members, amounted to a third wrong, and harassment of the American coast was a fourth entrenched injustice.

Like the president, Calhoun's committee merely mentioned in passing the British connection to "the hostility of the savage tribes on our frontiers," adding it was "not disposed to occupy much time in investigating" the issue.[3] And Calhoun could not resist alluding to the bumbling Henry affair, partly, one suspects, because its mere mention made Massachusetts Federalists so uncomfortable.

Following Madison's approach, the Calhoun committee recognized the wrongs perpetuated by France, but argued they did not justify British transgressions. "The committee do not hesitate to declare, that France has greatly injured the United States, and that satisfactory reparation has not yet been made for many of those injuries. But that is a concern which the United States will look to and settle for themselves." And it "is a sufficient pledge to the world that they will not fail to settle it. . . ."[4]

Calhoun summarized: "The control of our commerce by Great Britain, in regulating at pleasure, and expelling it almost from the ocean; the oppressive manner in which these regulations have been carried into effect, by seizing and confiscating such of our vessels, with their cargoes, as were said to have violated her edicts . . .; the impressment of our citizens from on board our own vessels, on the high seas, and elsewhere . . . are encroachments of that high and dangerous tendency, which could not fail to" lead to war.[5]

The congressional war debate now started in earnest behind closed doors, although members began to beat the drums beforehand when the Foreign Relations Committee issued its November 29 report calling for a strengthened army and navy for no other purpose than to go to war. Calhoun's committee moved to implement its June report by filing a bill declaring war between the United States and Great Britain. Veteran Republican congressman John Randolph of Virginia, one of the most outspoken foes of the war, failed to have the measure rejected at its first reading. Quincy tried to perplex the majority by amending the bill to include repeal of the nonintercourse laws and the April embargo. The House defeated his amendments by a two to one margin, and the Calhoun bill was engrossed a third time. Randolph moved to postpone the bill until October, but suffered a two to one defeat of his

---

1 Ibid., 570.
2 Ibid., 569.
3 Ibid.
4 Ibid., 570.
5 Ibid.

own. Other members tried in vain to slow the march to war by moving to adjourn or postpone the up or down vote until the next day, June 5. Their minds made up, the representatives proceeded to vote 79 to 49 for war. This is the House vote most often cited as its war vote. In reality, the final House vote came two weeks later when Senate amendments were considered.

The House considered the question behind closed doors, so a record of the debate does not exist. But attentive people knew what was going on. A major New England newspaper told its readers: "Every letter from Washington pronounces the affairs of our country to have reached a crisis, and that the madmen who govern there will be left to declare War against *England* immediately."[1]

The secrecy so agitated a Massachusetts Federalist congressman opposed to the war that he had his speech printed in the *Alexandria Gazette* exactly as he had intended to deliver it before Congress. Samuel Taggart, an ordained Presbyterian minister from Colrain, also entered his prepared speech in a supplemental journal of the House, where it ran to 30 pages. "Having been long conversant in the quiet walks of civil life," Taggart said, "and in the exercise of a profession, one important part of the duties of which is to inculcate peace and good will both towards and among men, I cannot contemplate my country as on the verge of a war, especially of a war which to me appears both unnecessary and impolitic. . . ."[2] Taggart seldom debated in the House, but in this heartfelt speech he went on to touch upon just about all of the oft-repeated criticisms of the war. He deprecated it as an offensive war to conquer Canada, a place that has done no wrong, but is a nearby and vulnerable part of the British Empire. He believed the orders in council were not more antagonistic than the French decrees, and he thought our nonimportation and embargo policies were equally hostile.

Taggart leaned on the cost issue. Patriotism alone could not be relied on, he said. "[H]owever good a topic patriotism may be, to furnish materials for an harangue in a bar-room; for a newspaper or electioneering essay; or to embellish a war-speech on the floor of Congress, we must have money — money in large sums — to carry on the war."[3] He concluded: "Should the present war prove disastrous and unsuccessful; should we neither take Canada, nor obtain one single object for which we make war; yet if we only make war, and fight, and show our spirit, whatever may be the consequences, we may have a consolation similar to that of the gallant Francis, which he communicated in a note to the Queen Regent, after he was defeated and taken prisoner by his enemy and rival, Charles V, in the fatal battle of Pavia: 'Madam, we have lost all but our honor.' "[4]

The various positions taken on the war issue by other congressmen are documented in the *Annals* for December 1811 when the recommendations

---

1 *Columbian Centinel* (MA), June 10, 1812.
2 *Annals of Congress*, 12th Cong., 1st sess., 1637.
3 Ibid., 1659.
4 Ibid., 1676-1677.

made in the first Foreign Relations Committee report came before the House. Peter B. Porter, a committee member from Buffalo, New York, started the debate when he rose to explain the report. "Having become convinced that all hopes from further negotiation were idle, the committee, Mr. P. said, were led to the consideration of another question, which was — whether the maritime rights which Great Britain is violating were such as we ought to support at the hazard and expense of war? And he believed he was correct in stating that the committee was unanimously of the opinion that they were."[1]

Tennessee's Felix Grundy, another committeeman, picked up after Porter's beginning. He opened with a discussion of the "depredations on our lawful trade," actions traced not to "any maxim or rules of public law, but to the maritime supremacy, and pride of the British nation." At length, Grundy brought up what would be a controversial issue, the major strategic objective of a war. He favored driving "the British from our continent."[2]

Randolph then took the floor to respond. He wondered if the country could call upon Great Britain to leave American harbors and ports untouched until United States forces returned from a Canadian adventure. "The coast is to be left defenceless, whilst men of the interior are reveling in conquest and spoil." And "what will the merchants of Salem, and Boston, and New York, and Philadelphia, and Baltimore, the men of Marblehead and Cape Cod, say to this?"[3]

Robert Wright of Maryland argued "honest tars" deserved the protection of their country. He enumerated maritime incidents, such as the notorious *Chesapeake* affair, and declared: "[I]f these outrages, which cry aloud for vengeance, do not animate you, I fear the sacred fire that inspired your fathers in the Revolution is nearly extinguished, and the liberty of their degenerate sons in jeopardy."[4]

The earlier debate went back and forth. While he swayed few if any of his colleagues, Randolph seemed to get the best of things. In a second and lengthy December speech, he argued defense of maritime rights no longer motivated the advocates of war. Canada was the prize, fitting compensation; it was claimed, for the transgressions of the British. "Gentlemen from the North have been taken up to some high mountain and shown all the kingdoms of the earth," Randolph mocked; "and Canada seems tempting in their sight. That rich vein of Gennesee land, which is said to be even better on the other side of the lake than on this. Agrarian cupidity, not maritime right, urges the war." And then he delivered the most memorable line of the war debates. "Ever since the report of the Committee on Foreign Relations came into the House," he said, "we have heard but one word — like the whip-poor-will, but one eternal monotonous tone — Canada! Canada! Canada!" He stressed: "Not a syllable about Halifax, which unquestionably should be

1 Ibid., 414.
2 Ibid., 424-426.
3 Ibid., 448-449.
4 Ibid., 469.

our great object in a war for maritime security."[1] Few on either side, as well as American naval leaders, saw the same ripe strategic opportunity in Nova Scotia.

Upon receiving Madison's war message, the Senate printed it for confidential use. Thus, the upper chamber was prepared to proceed on June 5 when it received the House bill recommending war. All Senate proceedings remained private and confidential until the president signed the final declaration on June 18. But the Senate maintained a record of its limited debate on the subject, and the several procedural votes leading up to the final vote on the 17th. What was said mirrored the House debates of the previous December. Attempts to postpone the decision until November, October, and July failed. As in the House, New Englanders were not principal players in the Senate proceedings.

The Senate decision came on June 17. By a 19 to 13 count, the Senate voted for war. Except for Stephen Bradley of Vermont, all of the New England senators voted on the measure. Massachusetts and New Hampshire senators split, one from each state voting in the affirmative and one in the negative. Both men from Connecticut and both from Rhode Island recorded themselves against the war. Vermont's Jonathan Robinson sided with the majority. Other than Nicholas Gilman of New Hampshire and Jeremiah Howell of Rhode Island, both Democratic Republicans who came down against the war, the rest of the New England solons voted their party line.

None of the nine men clearly were penalized for their votes on the war, with the possible exception of Charles Cutts of New Hampshire. Chauncey Goodrich, a Federalist, resigned in 1813 to become the lieutenant governor of Connecticut. James Lloyd, a Massachusetts Federalist, also resigned in 1813, but he was reelected in 1822 only to resign again four years later. As for Cutts, a Democrat Republican, his term ended in March 1813, but he was appointed to fill the vacancy until a successor was elected. Jeremiah Mason, a Federalist, took the seat in June 1813. Cutts, however, longed for Washington. Apparently pushed by Vice President Gerry, in a crowded 1814 contest, he won election to the post of secretary of the United States Senate, serving until 1825.

The House took up the Senate's amendments on the 18th, and the fallout turned out to be dramatic. Opponents to war lost overwhelmingly in an attempt to postpone the bill indefinitely. Randolph then moved to postpone until October, but lost when only 49 men favored delay while 80 opposed. As events would decide, this was the final lost opportunity to avoid war. Randolph then tried to have the bill postponed until the first Monday in July. In the last recorded vote on the war, only 51 representatives sided with the Virginian, while 79 opposed his motion. The House promptly concurred in the Senate version without a roll call vote. The bill was enrolled, signed by the speaker, and sent on to the president for his signature.

---

1 Ibid., 533.

Unlike the present day, when incumbency for the most part assures representatives will be reelected if they run, after the 1812 war votes, eight New England congressmen were rejected at the first chance by their constituents or party. Six — Francis Carr (R-Mass.), Ebenezer Seaver (R-Mass.), Charles Turner, Jr. (R-Mass.), William Widgery (R-Mass.), Samuel Dinsmoor (R-N.H.), and John A. Harper (R-N.H.) — were unsuccessful candidates for reelection in the fall. Each man voted for the war, although Widgery did vote for the July delay. It was not enough. Harper, like some of the others, saw it coming. In a June 14 letter to Plumer he said: "I think I have pursued a tolerable *strait* course. At least I possess an approving conscience."[1]

The voters also turned out Richard Cutts (R-Mass.). Cutts did not vote on the June 4 motion, and, while he favored the July delay, he did not want to postpone indefinitely. Isaiah Green (R-Mass.) consistently voted for the war, and he also paid the price. He was so weakened in his Cape Cod district his party knew better than to renominate him for Congress. But for his support, Madison rewarded Green with appointment as collector of customs in Barnstable.

Two Massachusetts Federalists and war opponents — Leonard White and Josiah Quincy — seemed to have had enough and decided not to run for reelection. Similarly, two Massachusetts Republicans who did not vote for any of the June war motions called it quits. Peleg Tallman concluded one term in Washington would suffice. Ezekiel Bacon left Congress when his third term expired in March 1813, but he seemed to long for the capital. Within the year, he gained appointment as the first comptroller of the United States Treasury.

By any measure, this turnover was astounding. Ten out of seventeen Massachusetts congressmen did not return, six of them having been tossed out. This rate far exceeded the overall average biennial change in Congress for the period.

More dramatic, the entire New Hampshire delegation changed in the election after the declaration of war. In addition to the rejected Dinsmoor and Harper, representatives Obed Hall and Josiah Bartlett, both Republicans, and Federalist George Sullivan, all one-term members, did not return to the 13th Congress. Obviously, there was some change in other states, but nothing approaching this scale.

The emotionally charged and divisive war issue did not lead to similar outcomes in Connecticut and Rhode Island, two other antiwar hotbeds, because all the representatives in those states were members of the majority Federalist Party and they all voted against the conflict. Vermont's delegation also followed the party line, three Democratic Republicans voting for war, and the one Federalist, Martin Chittenden, came out against armed conflict. His stance obviously helped him gain the governor's chair in 1813 when his peace party made significant gains in the state.

---

1 Egan, 177.

Illustrative of Vermont's view of the issue, Norwich took a stand common in the state. Unaware of events of the day in Washington, on June 18, the town met to express support for the expected war. Displaying an unforgiving memory, the meeting set down "a lengthy and spirited arraignment of England, beginning with the persecution which drove the Pilgrim fathers across the sea in 1620." For some balance, it was noted: "France also in her turn has not been behind in violating our national rights." While the Norwich men agreed to support war with either country, their emphasis was on "demanding justice of Great Britain." When the town received word on the declaration of war, it rushed back into another meeting, and on July 6 voted "to raise a tax for defraying town expenses and to increase the wages of the detachment from Norwich."[1] The town granted enlisted militiamen an extra $3 per month.

Some places could not believe the action of Congress. Despite the fact the local newspaper the day before assumed "the painful duty"[2] of reporting the declaration of war, Salem went ahead with a planned town meeting on the 24th to plead with its members of Congress "to use all the means which the Constitution has placed in their hands to avert the impending calamity of war."[3]

The Salem meeting was part of a broad-based, last-ditch effort to avoid a frightful war. Boston held a town meeting at Faneuil Hall on June 15 described as an "Appeal to Peace." A "dignified proceeding" passed several resolutions "adopted with great unanimity. May the *God of Peace*," it was hoped, "grant they may be efficacious in averting from our country the dreadful calamity of war."[4] A few days earlier, New Bedford sent Congress a peace petition containing 1,150 signatures.

Three days after Madison signed the declaration of war, a much more significant peace proceeding took place in London. Unknown to anyone in America, on June 23, the prince regent, with the advice of the Privy Council, revoked the orders in council — the effective cause of the war. Great Britain simply concluded it had all it could do to combat Napoleon, who got across the Niemen River into Russia on the 24th. One war at a time seemed enough. Of course, weeks passed before the government in Washington learned about the significant repeal of the orders. In time, the country knew. And antiwar elements took note. Portland, Maine, for instance, "deeply impressed with the Melancholy & alarming situation of our beloved Country" petitioned Madison "to improve the present fortunate opportunity for the restoration of Peace. The revocation of the British Orders in Council . . . has essentially changed the aspect of the British measures, and we believe ought at once, to produce a correspondent change in American measures."[5] Administration

1 Goddard and Partridge, *History of Norwich*, 92-94.
2 *Salem* (MA) *Gazette*, June 23, 1812.
3 *Columbian Centinel* (MA), June 27, 1812.
4 Ibid., June 17, 1812.
5 *City of Portland* (ME) *Records*, Aug. 17, 1812 to Apr. 2, 1827, 2:2.

efforts to achieve an early peace, however, failed to make headway. Nonetheless, it remains, if John Randolph's motion to postpone a final House vote on war until October had carried, it is most probable the War of 1812 would not have occurred.

In reporting on the declaration of war, the *Centinel* correctly predicted "the first fruits of war will probably be on the ocean."[1] A somewhat vague but general war plan existed. The U.S. Army would conquer Canada in a brief campaign, a matter of weeks if not days. The small U.S. Navy with its 17 vessels and the state militias would defend the exposed Atlantic coast. And a fairly large unofficial fleet of private cruisers or privateers would prey on British merchantmen.

The centerpiece of the plan quickly turned into a disaster. U.S. General William Hull invaded Canada on July 12. Three days later the American garrison at Fort Michilimackinac on the straits between Lake Huron and Lake Michigan fell to an inferior enemy force. On August 15, Americans evacuated Fort Dearborn at the present site of Chicago. And the next day, Hull surrendered without a fight to General Isaac Brock at Detroit.

However, three days later, well to the east of Cape Cod, the U.S.S. *Constitution*, Captain Isaac Hull, defeated H.M.S. *Guerriere*, Captain James Dacres in one of the most celebrated victories in U.S. Navy history — the first American success of the war. When Hull returned to Boston on August 30, the town and New England showed its other side. "Boston was wild with fervor at the triumph of the favorite frigate. Partisan politics and hatred of the war were thrown aside in the general rejoicing."[2] In nearby Marblehead, the townspeople received the news "with the greatest enthusiasm; and so large a proportion of the crew of the victorious frigate were citizens of the town, it was considered almost a local victory."[3] Tradition places some 80 Marbleheaders on "Old Ironsides" during the epic fight.

The scene repeated itself a few months later. On December 29, 1812, Commodore William Bainbridge in the *Constitution* defeated the H.M.S. *Java*, 47, Captain Henry Lambert off the coast of Brazil. The *Boston Patriot* provided an early report of the sea fight, remarking: "It is with the most inexpressible joy, that we announce to the Friends and Supporters of the *Commercial Rights*, the *Honor* and the *Glory* of our *Common Country*, ANOTHER SPLENDID NAVAL VICTORY."[4] When "Old Ironsides" returned to Boston on February 18, 1813, the town celebrated with gusto. The ship berthed at Long Wharf as the North End Artillery fired salutes from Hancock's Wharf and the Washington Artillery saluted from Long Wharf. Commodore Rodgers, Captain Hull, General Wells "and other gentlemen of distinction" met Bainbridge, and the New England Guards escorted the entourage to the Exchange Coffee-House. Along the way, "the assembled citizens greeted him with repeated huzzas.

---

1 *Columbian Centinel* (MA), June 24, 1812.

2 Maloney, *Captain from Connecticut*, 195.

3 Roads, *History and Traditions of Marblehead*, 246.

4 *Boston Patriot*, February 17, 1813.

The concourse of people occupied nearly the whole space from the end of the wharf to the Coffee-House, and it was with difficulty the escort penetrated." Ships in the harbor and many stores "exhibited that flag which his services have contributed to honour. On one ensign which was extended across State street were enscribed the names of HULL, JONES [Master Commandant Jacob, of the USS *Wasp*, victor over HMS Frolic, October 18, 1812], DECA-TUR, and BAINBRIDGE."[1]

Although strongly opposed to the war, New Bedford, somewhat out of character, likewise celebrated the navy's victory over the *Java*. Lieutenant George Parker of the *Constitution* visited his in-laws at Fairhaven a few days after the ship's return to Boston. The town "tendered a public dinner" in his honor. Then, neighboring New Bedford sent its artillery company and "an excellent band of music from Taunton" to escort Parker to its Nelson's Hotel, "where an excellent repast was furnished by the landlord."[2]

This behavior of Bostonians and other New Englanders should not be surprising. After all, many in this region tied to the sea considered the U.S. Navy a child of New England, fathered by the Federalists, and starved by the Jeffersonians. Throughout the war, Boston and environs continued to closely follow and cheer on the navy. Out of the 234 officers in the navy at the outset of the war, 42 were born in the four coastal New England states. As well as Hull (a nephew of the disgraced general), Isaac Chauncey, Charles Morris, and Oliver H. Perry distinguished themselves during the conflict. John Downes, John Percival, Matthew Perry, and Joseph Smith were among others who stood out. Countless New Englanders, of course, served as enlisted seamen in what the *Centinel* called "our gallant little *Navy*."[3]

But once the war opened, the navy was not the only game in town for unemployed seamen. Privateering, the third component of the nebulous war plan held out the promise of quicker and greater rewards. A New York newspaper reported interest in securing berths on privateersmen was so keen owners and skippers had little trouble filling out their crews. "Sailors repair to the recruiting rendezvous in such crowds that the commanders have, in many instances, been obliged to draw lots who should go on board."[4] From the very first days of the conflict, privateering on both sides became a major theme and a colorful and important chapter in the nation's first war.

1 *Boston Gazette*, February 22, 1813.
2 Bordens, *Bristol County*, 331.
3 *Columbian Centinel* (MA), July 4, 1812.
4 *The War* (NY), August 8, 1812.

Chapter 6. The Peace Party at War

As General Henry Dearborn struggled to assemble his forces and New England governors, editors, legislators, and ministers postured in the limelight during the early weeks of the war, marine interests tried to cope with the hazardous changes in their environment. Some suffered losses. Some gave up for the duration. And some ran the risks and profited.

Captain Samuel Patterson of Wiscasset became an early victim of events. He arrived in his ship *Ganges* at Portsmouth, England with a load of lathe wood and timber from Amelia Island, Florida just days after Britain learned about the start of the war. The authorities detained him and his ship and impressed some of his crew. After being "demanded . . . to prison" and interrogated, at the end of two months, the British sent him off on parole.[1]

Elijah Cobb escaped the grasp of the Alexandria customs collector in April, but he failed to elude the Royal Navy on his return from Cadiz. The schooner H.M.S. *Alphea*, 10, Lieutenant Thomas W. Jones intercepted him on the Grand Banks. Shortly, the H.M.S. *Jason*, 32, Captain James W. King came down and put a prize master on Cobb's ship and sent it into St. John's, Newfoundland. Cobb and his crew were not alone. There were 27 other captured American vessels in port, all prizes. Within the week, the U.S.S. *Essex*, Captain David Porter, sent a cartel into St. John's. The cartel ship turned out to be the H.M.S. *Alert*, 16, Captain T.L.O. Laugharne, taken by the *Essex* on August 13. The American lieutenant in charge of the cartel explained to Admiral Sir John Thomas Duckworth, the commander-in-chief and governor of Newfoundland, Porter and Laugharne agreed on an equal exchange of prisoners. Well over 100 British prisoners were on the *Alert*. Duckworth, at first upset at Porter for making a cartel on the high seas, soon agreed with

---

1 *Ship Ganges of Wiscasset Log Book.*

the deal. "Now, commenced a Scene of confusion, and bussle; the Crew of the cartile was soon landed, and the Americans as speedily took possession, & the next morn, at about the suns rising, we weighed the anchors of the *Ellert*, left the harbour of St. Johns, and made sail for New York, with 246 Americans on board."[1]

Considering the state of affairs, once he made home Captain Cobb decided to stay on his farm until the end of the war.

Some seafarers weighed the risks faced by the likes of Patterson and Cobb and simply decided to stay out of danger altogether. Levi Gifford reached this conclusion. When hostilities broke out, he had his coaster at Norfolk, Virginia. The perils of the time prompted him to lose interest in the sea. In the idiom of seafaring, Gifford swallowed the anchor, and he walked all the way home to Sandwich, Massachusetts. After the war, he retrieved his ship and went back to sea. William Rotch, Jr. of the New Bedford whaling and merchant family recalled seeing over 50 sailors walking home because ships were not sailing. Rotch understood there were many more afoot out of New York.

Yet there were a fair number of owners and seamen who appreciated the Dutch proverb — "Men must sail while the wind serveth." To these mariners, the war meant one thing — opportunity. Opportunity took more than one form, including licenses to trade. The Rotch firm stayed afloat using this approach. Under the system, Great Britain issued licenses to unarmed vessels, including American ships, to carry various supplies to British recipients. The majority of the licenses went to vessels carrying provisions, especially grain and flour, to Wellington's forces on the Peninsular. Some licenses covered wood shipments to England and others permitted carrying provisions to New Brunswick and the West Indies. A license in theory protected the holder from interference from the Royal Navy and British privateers. Jefferson thought the system tolerable. He considered it advisable to feed the British army in Portugal and Spain rather than in America and turn a profit at the same time. Madison objected to licensing even though his opponents believed tobacco from his own plantation made it to England on a licensed ship.

In November 1812, the British refined the rules governing licenses by issuing a circular that required licenses be "confined to the ports in the EASTERN STATES EXCLUSIVELY."[2] With this, Madison acted to prohibit American participation in the program. His message to Congress recommending a ban on licensed exports said the policy rested on a "mass of forgery and perjury unknown in other times . . . having for its object to dissolve the ties of allegiance and the sentiments of loyalty" in the United States, "and to seduce and separate its component parts."[3] The House passed such a ban in March 1813, but the Senate delayed acting until the next session. President Madison

1 Elijah Cobb, *Memoirs of a Cape Cod Skipper*, 79-80.
2 *American State Papers: Foreign Relations* 3:608.
3 Ibid., 607.

got his way in August 1813 and signed an act prohibiting American use of licenses and similar passes.

The licensed trade, while lucrative to some owners, was a tame business compared to the legendary activity called privateering. The concept of privateering traces to the Middle Ages when during peace individuals held the power of reprisal when wronged. European countries eventually began issuing commissions, known as letters of marque and reprisal, authorizing retaliation by private individuals during war. Over time, the concept evolved to the point private ships were commissioned to prey upon enemy shipping.

The prize act of June 26, 1812 regulated American privateers and so-called letter-of-marque ships during the War of 1812. Privateers were distinguished from letter-of-marque vessels only in that a privateer received a letter or commission to seek out, seize, and make prize of any enemy vessel it could find. A letter-of-marque ship, on the other hand, held a letter authorizing it to carry cargo to a designated port while armed to defend itself as well as capture, if it so desired, any enemy vessel that crossed its path. Put another way, a privateer was commissioned to cruise, while a letter-of-marque was registered to voyage. The government issued most of the letters for straightforward privateering.

The declaration of war empowered the president to grant letters, and the prize act that followed spelled out the details and formalities. The letters served as licenses, and it was of no benefit to engage in the practice without such a commission. Before issuance of a letter, the ship-owner applicant had to give bond with surety. Everyone involved, from owners to crew members, were required to observe the treaties and laws of the United States. The president prescribed "suitable instructions for the better governing and directing the conduct of the vessels, so commissioned, their officers and crews. . . ."[1] In broad terms, naval rank, grades, duties, and rules applied on privateers.

Commodore John Rodgers relied on this provision when he arrested and tried First Lieutenant George W. Burbank of the privateer brig *Anaconda*. In the early months of the war, the feared Nova Scotia privateer *Liverpool Packet* created havoc along the coast of Massachusetts. Since his own ship was refitting in Boston, Rodgers could not respond to the problem. Therefore, local merchants purchased the *Commodore Hull*, a schooner built for privateering and armed with four 6-pounders. Rodgers manned the vessel with 50 navy men led by Acting Lieutenant Henry S. Newcomb and sent her out to convoy timid coasters.

Burbank, in temporary command of the 18-gun *Anaconda* while his captain conducted business on shore, confronted the *Commodore Hull* when she arrived in Provincetown harbor on January 16, 1813. Burbank sent another lieutenant out to the stranger, but the man returned without learning the identity of the ship. Newcomb thought the American flag on his ship as well as his United States officer's uniform were the only identification Burbank's

---

1 Act of June 26, 1812, ch. 107, 1 *Stat.* 759.

man needed and refused to name his ship. When the *Commodore Hull* began to move along, Burbank feared the stranger was the *Liverpool Packet*. To prevent an escape, he ordered his bow gun fired ahead of the schooner. In the confused haste, three guns accidentally fired at the *Commodore Hull*, wounding Newcomb and two sailors. Stray shot smashed into a store in town. Rodgers charged Burbank with insulting the flag of the United States and wounding his three men. After a lengthy trial, the court acquitted Burbank.

Captured vessels, or prizes, were brought into port for adjudication. The U.S. District Courts held original exclusive jurisdiction of the condemnation and forfeiture proceedings that followed. Captures were auctioned and the prize money realized was distributed according to written agreements between captor owners, officers, and crewmen. In the absence of an agreement, the prize act and the navy act dictated the distribution of profits. Noncommissioned or unlettered captors were out of luck. Their captures were made for the benefit of the government.

Under the depressing conditions along the shore, owners willing to venture their vessels found budding privateersmen in great numbers. Volunteers outnumbered available berths. Just a few days after the war began, Niles reported: "The people of the eastern states are laboring 'might and main,' to fit out privateers. Two have sailed from Salem, and others are getting ready. This looks well."[1]

Critics of the hypocrisy of some Federalist owners participating in a war for profit, a war most of them continued to revile, could not resist hurling a few barbs in their direction. Boston printer, publisher, and bookseller Nathaniel Coverly, Jr. came out with a broadside on "Privateering and pirateering alias, the 'peace party' at war: alias, the devil to pay in the Federal camps."[2] Nonetheless, the rush to get to sea went forward. "It will not much amaze us, bye and bye," observed Niles in referring to New Englanders, "if these people go out to fight the enemy in washing tubs."[3]

Federalist participants ignored people such as Coverly and, for once, sided with Jefferson. The former president thought "every possible encouragement should be given to privateering. . . . [B]y licensing private armed vessels, the whole naval force of the nation is truly brought to bear on the foe."[4] Jefferson, never an advocate of a sizeable public navy, correctly assessed the situation. Only 22 American public vessels made it to sea during the war. However, over 500 American privateers sailed.

During the War of 1812, the government granted privateering commissions to 150 Massachusetts vessels, more than from any other state in the country. New Hampshire sent out 16; Maine accounted for another 15; Rhode Island claimed 18; and 11 sailed from Connecticut. Forty percent of the American privateers were from New England. Little wonder, by the end

1 *Niles' Weekly Register* (MD), July 11, 1812.
2 Library of Congress, *Early American Imprints*.
3 *Niles'*, September 26, 1812.
4 Securest, *Privateering and National Defense*, n.p.

of the first month of the war, a Halifax, Nova Scotia newspaper warned the swarm of American privateers in the Bay of Fundy made it imprudent to sail except in convoy.

Within the Commonwealth, Salem led the way with 41 commissioned privateers. Boston followed with 31. The remainder sailed from lesser ports, but not New Bedford. Dominated by Quakers and fervent antiwar Federalists, the town acted in July 1814 to emphasize its long-standing opposition to privateering. A meeting voted to make it clear the town "have scrupulously abstained from all interest and concern in sending out private armed vessels to harass the commerce of the enemy." The voters asserted "private armed vessels, while cruising in various climates and visiting ships and vessels from every country, are extremely liable to contract and receive on board infectious diseases." This pretended concern rationalized the town's vote to establish a quarantine "of not less than forty days" for all privateers entering New Bedford harbor.[1] The famous Bristol, Rhode Island privateer *Yankee* arrived in the harbor a week earlier and the town fathers wanted no part of her lest she provoke a British attack on the place. The quarantine charade served to sidestep the fact federal legislation sanctioned privateering and the townsmen did not want to place themselves in clear violation of the national prize law.

Men in Salem looked at things altogether differently. Captain William Webb, 47, and an experienced merchant skipper, assembled a crew of two dozen unemployed shipmasters and sailed in the *Fame* on July 1, 1812 as soon as her commission arrived. Newly built in Annisquam for fishing, the fast 30-ton schooner carried two small cannons. The *Fame* moved into the busy shipping lanes around Grand Manan and quickly made the first captures of the war by a private American armed vessel. The 300-ton ship *Concord* out of Plymouth, England and the 200-ton brig *Elbe* from Scotland surrendered without fighting. Webb returned to Salem eight days after leaving. The captured vessels carried lumber, masts, spars, staves, and tar. After condemnation proceedings, the prizes realized $4,691 at auction, an amount some ten times the cost of building the little *Fame*.

In October, the *Fame* cruised Down East for 15 days and took five more prizes, all schooners. During a two-year privateering career, the *Fame* made 11 cruises before being wrecked in 1814 in the Bay of Fundy. Her early success prompted other owners and seamen to try the business. Before the year passed, 18 Salem privateers made it out. They captured 87 prizes, sent in 58, and earned a half million dollars for this work.

Salem privateering cannot be treated without mentioning the *Grand Turk*, rushed off the stocks in Wiscasset in the first weeks of the war. She did not get out until early 1813 when Captain Holton J. Breed and a crew of 95 left on a 100-day cruise to Brazil and the West Indies. She captured three well-armed ships, sending them to France for condemnation. On her second

---

[1] *Centennial in New Bedford*, 86-87.

cruise, she sailed about the British Isles for over three months. The *Grand Turk* took seven vessels, one of them twice. The brig *Catherine* was taken and sent in, but recaptured by the H.M.S. *Bacchus*, 18. Before the *Catherine* could make port, the *Grand Turk* came upon her again and made her a prize for the second time. The *Catherine* did not get another chance. The Americans removed the best of her cargo and burned her. One of the other prizes proved less troublesome and more valuable. She carried thirty thousand pounds sterling on board.

For her first two years, the *Grand Turk* avoided serious confrontations during her extended cruises, but she almost fell to a mail packet. On May 2, 1814, she spotted a strange sail and gave chase. About two miles away, Captain Breed raised the English colors. When within musket shot, he hauled them down and hoisted the American flag. The stranger ran up the English ensign and commenced firing. The two antagonists pounded away for more than an hour when the *Grand Turk* became unmanageable. The Briton turned out to be the mail packet *Hinchinbroke*. Badly mauled, the packet made the most of the situation and got away.

In March 1815, uncertain of the peace negotiations, the *Grand Turk* under the command of Captain Nathan Green cruised off Brazil and barely escaped from a British frigate. The man-of-war attempted to decoy the inquisitive privateer in close, but Green saw the trick in time and turned tail. He escaped only after laborious work on the sweeps. A week later, after a ten-minute skirmish, the *Grand Turk* took her last prize, the British brig *Acorn*, armed with fourteen 12-pounders and carrying dry goods. On April 16, Green boarded the American schooner *Comet*, and learned peace prevailed. He shaped a course for Massachusetts and entered Salem harbor at the end of the month. In her career, the *Grand Turk* captured three ships, twelve brigs, seven schooners, and eight sloops — one of the most successful American privateers in the war. She proved to be just what Congress had in mind when it passed the prize act in June 1812.

Maine men built some of the larger and unluckiest New England privateers, including the 367-ton *Hyder Ally*. Portland shipwright Samuel Fickett completed the ship for the firm of Bryant and Sturgis, and the Boston merchants armed her with twelve 18-pound carronades, two long 18-pounders, and a pair of long nines. Some of the armament and, apparently, some of its luck came from the captured H.M.S. *Boxer*, 18. At the end of January 1814, Captain Israel Thorndike of Beverly, Massachusetts took the *Hyder Ally* out of Portland for the Indian Ocean. She captured a valuable British East Indiaman after rounding the Cape of Good Hope. But the British recaptured the prize at the last moment as it passed Cape Elizabeth en route for Portland. Another prize, taken off Sumatra and placed under Lieutenant Henry Oxnard of Portland, made it all the way to the area of Mount Desert Island before the British recovered her. Meanwhile, in the Indian Ocean, the *Hyder Ally* barely escaped from the H.M.S. *Salsette*, 38, Captain John Bowen. And only days later, she fell to the H.M.S. *Owen Glendower*, 36, flagship of Vice Admiral Sir Samuel Hood, ending her brief, unprosperous career as a privateer.

The brig *McDonough* of Wells proved even more unfortunate. Built quickly and expressly for privateering, she carried a crew of 70 men and one long 24-pounder and four sixes. "She put to sea amidst the cheers and good wishes of the people."[1] Out only a day, the *McDonough* was chased by a British man-of-war. After running for five hours, her topmasts gave way, and she was overhauled. The British sent the vessel into Halifax and transported the Maine crew to the notorious Dartmoor prison in England.

Undeterred, the locals hastened to get another brig constructed and fitted for privateering. Peace rumors spurred the builders who "feared that unless the greatest despatch was made, all their hopes of acquiring wealth might be suddenly blasted." Named the *Ludlow*, unpainted, lightly armed, and scantily manned, the 208-ton vessel sailed for fortune on January 22, 1815. "But in the course of a few days," the crew "began to realize the effects of their folly in building too hastily." The pumps could not keep up with dangerous leaking, so the crew bent to it and bailed by hand with buckets. In this manner, the *Ludlow* limped into Saint John's Island in the Caribbean. Without funds, the men could not put the brig in shape for sea until they found a well-heeled man who wanted to get his family to Havana. He paid for repairs as news of the peace accord arrived. The *Ludlow* went on to carry its passengers to Cuba where the captain sold his now unneeded guns to obtain money for provisions. The dispirited crew sailed for home, arriving at Kennebunk in April. "Such was the result of privateering with the people of Wells and Arundel. Not a prize vessel reached an American port. Thousands of dollars were spent, but not a cent was earned."[2]

The three-masted, 40-ton schooner *Dart* was another Maine privateer completed with dispatch just after the declaration of war. Built at Cape Elizabeth for Joseph Cross and other Portland owners, she was low and sleek with a pink or narrow stern. So that she could present a low profile and hide from the enemy, especially in a cove, her masts were jointed above the deck, enabling them to be dropped in the manner of a canal boat. Commanded by Captain John Curtis, the *Dart* carried four guns. The *Dart* left Portland toward the end of July with 27 men, bound down the coast in search of more crew members. When she cleared Thomaston for the sea on August 1, she carried a complement of 46 men. And before the month passed, the *Dart* made prizes of three English brigs, sending them into Portland. "The next capture made the *Dart* famous, and *raised the spirits* of all Portland."[3]

Cruising off Cape Ray, Newfoundland on August 31, 1812, the *Dart* spotted a merchant brig headed into the Gulf of Saint Lawrence. The American fired two shots at the stranger, and brought her to. She turned out to be the

---

1 Bourne, *History of Wells and Kennebunk*, 604.

2 Ibid., 604-605.

3 Goold, *Portland in the Past*, 446.

Dianna, Captain Alexander Thom, bound to Quebec from London carrying 212 puncheons of rum. Curtis placed his first officer, William Thomas, in charge of the prize and directed her to Portland. "Her cargo proved famous as the 'Old Dart Rum,' which became more celebrated for the peculiar flavor than any cargo of spirits ever landed in the country."[1] For years, purveyors sold rum from the original casks, certainly refilled more than once.

On her final trip, the *Dart* sailed from Portland under Captain Curtis, never to return. In all likelihood, she foundered in a gale, much like the *Dash,* another of the numerous privateers registered in Portland during the war. Built in early 1813 at Porters Landing in Freeport as a letter-of-marque, the *Dash* weighed 222 tons. Pierced for sixteen guns, she originally carried a long 32-pound pivot gun, and six broad-side guns. The pivot gun had a tale to tell.

William McLellan ran a store in Portland in which he kept piano-fortes to let. He acquired the instruments secondhand in Boston. Captain John L. Lewis sailed a packet run between the two places, and took McLellan's order for a "forte-piano," a common way to describe the piece. McClellan's writing may have been unclear, or Lewis was not musically inclined. At any rate, upon the packet's return from Boston, the captain went up to McLellan's store on Temple Street and informed the shopkeeper: "I could n't find a forty-pounder, but I got you a long thirty-two, which was the biggest I could find; and I want it taken away, as it lays right across my hatch."

"The gun lay on the wharf several years, and was referred to as 'Billy Mac's piano,' until guns came to be more salable than pianos, and the 'long thirty-two,' from an object of ridicule, became a terror to John Bull, as the pivot-gun of Portland's crack privateer."[2]

Captain Edward Kelleran first took the *Dash* to St. Domingo and returned loaded with coffee and logwood. He saw the ship could bear added head sail, so he changed the rig to that of a long-legged brig. Thus improved, she could out-sail just about anything in her class. At this point, the owners "decided that it was more profitable, expeditious and satisfactory to take cargoes out of the enemy's ships than to purchase them in ports."[3] The *Dash* became a full-time privateer. In the months to follow, under four different captains, she made seven trips and took and sent in 15 valuable prizes. In January 1815, Captain John Porter sailed her on the final, fatal trip. East of Cape Cod in darkness and driving snow she disappeared from the sight of the *Champlain,* a companion Portland privateer. Most likely, the *Dash* foundered on the breakers of Georges Bank, carrying a 60-man crew to their death. But, like the *Dart,* she left a lasting memory. Poet John Greenleaf Whittier made the *Dash* the subject of his melancholy poem "The Dead Ship of Harpswell."

Grand Manan's isolated but strategic location made the island's waters a haunt for some of Maine's smaller raiders, especially the open boats known

---

1 Ibid.
2 Ibid., 450.
3 *New England Magazine* 16:570.

as shaving mills. Some shaving mills were no more than whaleboats. Powered by as many as 16 oars, lightly armed, and manned by crews as large as 30, they were held in low regard by both sides. A New Brunswick newspaper reported with gratification that the shaving mill *General Pike* quickly left Boston in October 1813 due to an unfavorable reception, "their Shocking Appearance creating general Disgust."[1]

The crew of one such pillager had their stomachs instead of riches in mind when they stopped at Joseph Blanchard's farm in Seal Cove, Grand Manan. Blanchard had immigrated to the island from the United States and took the oath of allegiance in 1805. When the privateersmen demanded Blanchard give them some potatoes, he replied he was a British subject and "would not afford succor or feed the enemies of King George.

"'However,' said he, pointing to his potato field, 'there are the potatoes, and if you are rascals enough to steal them — you must dig them.'"[2] The Yankees turned away in shame and left empty-handed.

But the captain of the shaving mill *Weazel* had little compunction when it came to the personal property of others. Edward Snow of Hampden, "a preacher of the gospel," commanded this boat commissioned in Castine. The *Weazel* ran up the Grand Manan Channel on June 9, 1813 and raided homes and a store at Beaver Harbour and Pennfield on the New Brunswick mainland. The owners, Captain H. Young and a Mr. White, were absent, so Snow made off with 15 barrels of sugar, family clothes, and the children's toys! Later the same night, the *Weazel* "took the little schooner and all the fishing lines upon which a third resident of Beaver Harbour, Capt. Cross, depended for a living."[3] The looters left, regretting they did not have a third boat to fill with plunder.

An alarm reached Campobello, and by morning two boats were in pursuit of the unblushing marauders. The Canadians drove the *Weazel* on shore at Grand Manan and chased Snow and his men into the woods. "Prior to this affair, the British cruisers in the Bay of Fundy had never interrupted American fishing boats in their pursuits; but Captain Gordon of the 'Rattler' now ordered them off, and gave notice that such as were found beyond certain prescribed limits would be captured and destroyed."[4]

The people of New Brunswick were not alone in detesting the conduct of the shaggy shaving mills and a few larger American privateers. Residents in and around Eastport observed a tacit neutrality with their Canadian neighbors so as to facilitate the lucrative smuggling business. The *St. John Courier* reported: "American privateers in the Bay of Fundy stop all boats they come across, and, report says, rob passengers of their money, Americans as well as British. Several of the inhabitants of Moose Island (American) who were re-

1 Snider, *Under the Red Jack*, 87.
2 Buchanan, *Grand Manan Historian*, 60.
3 Snider, 88.
4 Buchanan, 61.

moving their families have been taken by these privateers. They have insulted the inhabitants on that island and threatened to destroy their homes."[1]

Nova Scotia suffered its share. American privateers brought the Nova
Scotian fishery and coasting trade almost to a standstill. But again, the shaving mills and their mischievous crews provoked the greatest outrage. Mrs.
Thomas Doane of Barrington township saved her pewter spoons by hiding
them in a bed occupied by an elderly lady just before some of these raiders reached her house. Mrs. Hezekiah Smith defiantly stood in her dooryard
with a gun and intimidated a sea-robber about to take one of her sheep. Crew
members of one shaving mill stepped onto David Smith's dock and proceeded into the village, looting as they went. Most of the male inhabitants were
away on the fishing grounds at the time. William Greenwood became so
upset with losses suffered at the hands of such "bogus privateers" that he
"went in his boat to Boston to recover his vessel and a lot of fish which had
been carried off, and was partially successful."[2]

As one might expect, complaints about the business were not one-sided.
The Annapolis Royal privateer *Brooke*, 5, under Captain Daniel Wade, for
one, earned unfavorable American press coverage. In July 1813, her owner
petitioned the government in Halifax for a letter of marque and reprisal.
And although the authorization was not granted until the end of September,
Wade was prowling off Portland in early August. Just beyond the reach of
the Fort Scammel guns, he captured the sloop *Sally*, Captain John Preble and
the sloop *Freeport*, Captain Asa Dyer, both of Sullivan. He paroled the American officers and crews after directing the schooner *Nancy* to serve as a cartel
to carry the parolees to Portland. Local newspapers reported the officers of
the *Brooke* "did not behave with the generosity which has characterized so
many of the British cruisers, having taken the prisoners' clothing." As bad,
Wade "had the impudence to take a pea-jacket from Capt. Abner Cushing"
of the *Nancy*.[3]

Portsmouth, New Hampshire sent out 16 privateers during the war. The
schooner *Fox*, carrying a crew of 85 and mounting twelve carriage guns and
two swivels, led the pack. Referred to as the "million dollar privateer," she
went on seven cruises under three different masters and captured 24 prizes.[4]
The record of the *Fox* is remarkable when it is realized a majority of American privateering vessels did not return a profit. In fact, some commissioned
privateers did not get to sea. A 1932 study of the Portsmouth customs records associated with thirteen of the town's privateers revealed only six of
these privateers made money, while seven failed to return original invest-
ments. Nonetheless, all told, Portsmouth's privateers captured 419 prizes.
Four prizes alone were worth a total of $2.5 million.

---

1 Snider, 89.
2 Edwin Crowell, *History of Barrington Township*, 239.
3 *Columbian Centinel* (MA), August 7, 1813.
4 Winslow, *Wealth and Honour*, 151.

The privateering business made a few Portsmouth men rich. Samuel Larkin stands out. He made a fortune in commissions at the end of the process, auctioning prizes and their cargoes. Larkin held the hammer in some 34 prize auctions that realized total sales of $2,234,509. Larkin needed the money. His family numbered 22. "Such was Maj. Larkin's reputation as an auctioneer," reported the *Portsmouth Journal*, "and his great skill and facility in the despatch of business, that he was sent for in all directions to conduct those sales, and they were attended by merchants from Boston, New York, Philadelphia, &c., &c."[1]

The greatest accomplishment of a Portsmouth privateer did not relate to earnings. Although the schooner *Thomas* was among the half-dozen New Hampshire moneymakers, she gained national fame for capturing the feared Nova Scotia privateer *Liverpool Packet*, considered by many to be the premier privateer of the period. The *Packet*'s legendary record is touched upon below. But, for the time, on June 11, 1813, the Nova Scotian's career was interrupted when it encountered the superior *Thomas* near Cape Sable. The *Packet* carried five guns and 35 men. Under Captain Tom Shaw, the *Thomas* carried fourteen guns and a crew of 100. She chased the smaller vessel for more than six hours before closing. After a brief skirmish, the *Packet*'s captain, the redoubtable Joseph Barss, Jr., struck her colors.

The town of Bristol led Rhode Island in the privateering sphere, serving as the home port for nine cruisers. Providence sent out five, and Newport claimed four. Bristol harbored the vaunted *Yankee*, universally considered in the top echelon of American privateers during the War of 1812. In six cruises, she took nine ships, twenty-five brigs, five schooners, and one sloop, valued at as much or more than $3 million. During the war, "The *Yankee* was at sea for approximately eighteen months, and averaged one capture of an enemy vessel about every twelve days. An amazing record!"[2]

The *Yankee* was a "morphydite" brig of 168 tons, 120 feet long. She carried as many as 19 guns and a crew of between 120 and 200 men. Oliver Wilson, her first captain, claimed: "The crew was made up of the picked young men of Bristol, and a braver or more noble-hearted set of boys never trod the deck of a vessel. If there was ever a commander who had a right to be proud of his ship and crew it was I."[3]

Owner James DeWolf had the *Yankee* ready to sail as soon as Congress declared war. On June 30 he wrote with urgency to the secretary of war: "I beg you will cause a commission to be forwarded as soon as practicable to the Collector of the District, that this vessel may not be detained."[4] The commission issued on July 13, and by August 1, the *Yankee* sailed off Nova Scotia, about to be tested.

---

1 Ibid., 149.
2 Jones, *Journals of Two Cruises Aboard the American Privateer Yankee*, xviii.
3 Howe, *Mount Hope*, 181.
4 Munro, *Story of Mount Hope Lands*, 301.

Near Halifax, Wilson discovered and ran down on a large ship. When the stranger showed English colors, Wilson fired his first division of guns, and then gave her a full broadside. "The ship soon returned the compliment, and the action was continued with spirit on boat sides."[1] After desperate fighting, the *Yankee* sailed across the enemy's bow and delivered a raking broadside, prompting the Briton to strike. She turned out to be the 658-ton *Royal Bounty*, Captain Henry Gambles, in ballast bound for Prince Edward Island. She mounted ten guns, but had a crew of only 25. The English suffered two killed and seven wounded, while the American casualties amounted to three wounded. The encounter proved to be *Yankee*'s most severe test, a fitting way to begin a great privateering career.

Connecticut did not play a large role in privateering, sending out only 11 privateers. Six sailed from New London, including the *Anaconda*, the privateer that gained notoriety when it took on the *Commodore Hull* at Provincetown. The *Mars* made a 100-day cruise in 1812–13, took 11 prizes, and "brought rum, sugar, brandy, wine, dry goods, iron, fish, fruit and such into New London with not a man lost."[2]

Captain George Coggeshall of Milford made the state's most significant impact on privateering. During the war he commanded the letter-of-marque schooners *David Porter* and *Leo*, commonly sailing out of Providence. He captured nine prizes, and retired from the sea in 1841, returning to Milford. Coggeshall used his firsthand knowledge of the subject and his contacts to write a definitive history of American privateering in the war.

Privateering was not a unilateral activity. The British played the game effectively. The Maritimes alone sent out 37 privateers and 12 letter-of-marque ships. This relatively small force captured over a third of the American vessels taken during the war. They were so effective more and more New England traders resorted to overland transportation; and a concept that traced back some two hundred years to Miles Standish received renewed attention. Canadian privateers lurked off the busy backside of Cape Cod and fell upon any passing vulnerable vessel. A canal across the Cape in the area meeting the mainland would eliminate the hazard of sailing around the peninsula in infested and unguarded waters. Talk of such a cut fizzled and another 100 years would pass before a canal became a reality.

The privateering business also had plusses and minuses. Yarmouth, Nova Scotia is a case in point. During the war, the town lost nine vessels to American privateers. But its own privateers, the *Fly* and the *Broke* brought nine American prizes back to Yarmouth. In the end, the impact on the region proved so memorable, to this day, the town of Liverpool, Nova Scotia puts on an annual summer festival called Privateer Days.

The methodology of Canadian privateers varied slightly from the general practice of American counterparts. "[S]ea actions of New Brunswick and Nova Scotia privateers were less than heroic. Few shots were fired — in

---

1 Coggeshall, *History of the American Privateers*, 49.
2 Decker, *Whaling City: A History of New London*, 71.

anger or otherwise — and less than a handful of people lost their lives in battle."[1] A policy of show force, but do not unnecessarily damage a prize prevailed. Many captured prizes, in fact, were unarmed or taken while anchored. The difference between the two sides involved fishermen. Americans tended to avoid them, because, in their view, small, smelly fishing boats provided little amusement and little return. Canadians, on the other hand, went after enemy fishing boats. They considered any blow against United States commerce worthwhile and the risks were negligible.

Many observers believe the little *Liverpool Packet* out of Liverpool, Nova Scotia to be the greatest of the 1812–15 privateers. Subjective judgments of this kind are always open to debate. However, one thing is certain. The *Packet* holds her own in any comparison with the *Grand Turk* or the *Fox* or the *Yankee* and a few others. Just over 53 feet in length, she carried only five guns; one 6-pounder, two 4-pounders, and a pair of 12-pounders. One of her letters or commissions set her weight at about 67 tons. A conservative count credits the *Packet* with 50 captures. An authoritative source sets the total at "an even hundred captures."[2]

She first put to sea at the end of August 1812, and promptly took the 325-ton *Middlesex* bound for New York. Captain Joseph Barss, Jr. went on to haunt the waters just to the east of Cape Ann and Cape Cod and ventured south to Point Judith. In one week, reports indicated the *Packet* captured 11 vessels just off Cape Cod Light. She took the schooner *Columbia* within the glow of Chatham Light. On another night, in Casco Bay, Barss captured the schooner *Lydia* within hailing distance of the navy's *Argus* and *Enterprise*, 14. In early 1813, the *Boston Messenger* questioned why "an insignificant fishing schooner . . . should be suffered to approach the harbour of the metropolis of Massachusetts, capture, and carry home in triumph, eight or nine sail of vessels, . . . in the short space of 20 days" all of which "would seem incredible were the facts not placed beyond any doubt."[3]

"In Salem, Mass., excitement seethed higher over the *Liverpool Packet* than it had since the days of the witches."[4] On November 12, 1812, Captain John Upton told the townsmen he would borrow the schooner *Helen* and seek out the *Packet* if 69 men would volunteer to crew for him. In short order, 69 seamen stepped forward, formed in column, and "preceded by the American flag, and by James McCarthy with his drum and by Henry Hubon with his fife, they marched through the streets of Salem. . . ." That night, the men carried several cannons on board the *Helen*. And early the next morning, they set sail. Before the day passed, they received intelligence indicating the *Liverpool Packet* sailed for home the day before. "This, however, did not prevent the valiant seventy from returning to port with all the honors of war."[5]

1 Kert, *Prize and Prejudice*, 96.
2 Snider, 51.
3 Bird, *This Is Nova Scotia*, 163.
4 Snider, 20.
5 Maclay, *History of American Privateers*, 448-449.

The *Liverpool Packet* departed Halifax on June 8, 1813, her tenth cruise of the war. Three days later her good fortune ended when she met the wrong ship. Portsmouth's *Thomas* held a three-to-one superiority in men and firepower, and the fabled Canadian raider could not out-sail her. At the close of the pursuit, a confused struggle resulted in several deaths on both ships. But the end came quickly. Captain Tom Shaw led the mischievous captive back to Portsmouth. A crowd assembled along the harbor and gave the victors three hearty cheers. The prize master on the *Packet* acknowledged the approbation by firing a 17-gun salute.

Major Larkin auctioned the *Packet* for $3,350, and the marshal marched Captain Barss and his Canadian crew to the Portsmouth jail. Barss "was too savage a wolf to let loose on the New England flock."[1] The authorities held him in close confinement until the following April, and then placed him on restrictive parole. Barss escaped from the jailer's house on July 9, and made his way back to Canada.

While the career of Barss ended, the *Packet* returned to privateering on the American side. Renamed the *Young Teazer's Ghost*, she made an unavailing cruise to the Maritimes, and, upon return, went up for sale. The new owner called her the *Portsmouth Packet* and sent her back out. She got into the Bay of Fundy before the H.M.S *Fantome*, 18 turned on her. The H.M.S. *Epervier*, 20 joined the chase off Mount Desert. The odds were too great, and after a flight of 13 hours, the *Portsmouth Packet* succumbed. A Nova Scotian partnership took possession and restored her heroic name. Under two different commands, the *Liverpool Packet* cruised until the end of the war and captured at least 18 more American prizes.

Not to be confused with two American privateers with the same name, the little 47-ton *Dart* out of Saint John, New Brunswick made a name for herself. In May 1813, under the command of John Harris, she sailed to the Cape Ann area and took the ship *Cuba* loaded with flour. After escorting her prize back home, she returned to Massachusetts waters and boarded eight more vessels, sending two into Saint John.

Two months later, Captain James Ross took over the *Dart* and enjoyed immediate success. Within a month, he made 15 captures. One of the prizes, however, pulled a "*Yankee trick*," and escaped. Off Mount Desert, the *Dart* took a Penobscot schooner returning from Salem. Ross put two of his men on board and took all her hands out except an 18-year-old Mainer. Ross directed him to pilot the schooner to Halifax. "The young man . . . put into Machias harbor in a fog, where she was taken possession of by the revenue boat."[2]

In addition to obvious nautical skills, like so many in his position, Ross could empathize with fellow mariners. After he captured the schooner *Camden* of Bangor, Ross took a big chance to help the Americans on the prize. Benjamin Downs, the master of the schooner, pointed out he and his mate

1 Snider, 42.
2 *Niles'*, September 25, 1813.

were sick and the only other crew member was his nephew, a mere boy. Ross appreciated the situation and stood in close to Wood Island and put the trio ashore near their homes. The proximity of the United States naval presence in Portsmouth and Portland highlighted the risk of this adventure.

The *Dart*'s luck ran out a few weeks later, and she became a footnote in American service lore. The little cruiser made a nuisance of herself around the eastern end of Long Island Sound in early October. A U.S. Revenue Cutter Service officer assigned in support of the navy took notice and acted. John Cahoone augmented his regular crew with 20 navy volunteers and left Narragansett Bay in the 70-ton schooner *Vigilant*, 4, intent on engaging the Canadian privateer.

Cahoone found his quarry to the east of Block Island on October 22, 1813; boldly sailed down on her, and loosed a broadside. Stunned, the depleted crew of the *Dart* put up little resistance. However, in the rush to board her, two *Vigilant* men fell between the vessels and drowned. The only advantage the *Dart* enjoyed was in armament. She carried some swivel guns in addition to four carronades. But most of her regular 25-man crew was off on prizes. The well-received victory became an integral part of the early tradition of today's U.S. Coast Guard.

Engagements between public vessels and privateers were few and far between. Privateers generally proved swifter and could evade stronger men-of-war. But the American privateer *Prince de Neufchatel*, Captain John Ordronaux, did not have a choice on October 11, 1814. While towing a recent prize, the English merchantman *Douglas*, Captain Duncan Cameron, the *Prince* found herself becalmed close in on the Nantucket south side abreast of Maddequecham. Closing fast from the southwest, a pursuing H.M.S, *Endymion*, 50, Captain Henry Hope, enjoyed a fresh breeze.

The Briton narrowed the distance by evening, but lost the wind. Meanwhile, the current drew the *Prince* toward shore, so Ordronaux anchored and cast off his prize. The *Douglas* came to anchor about a quarter-mile closer to the *Endymion*, as both sides plotted tactics. Captain Hope did not want to risk running his ship into shoal water. He thought he could cut out the privateer under the cover of darkness by employing his boats. He assigned the task to Lieutenant Abel Hawkins putting him in command of five boats manned by some 111 men.

Meanwhile, the fearless Ordronaux prepared to meet the onslaught. The 37 British prisoners on the *Prince* received his immediate attention. They were manacled and confined to the hold. As well as her 17 heavy guns, the ship held a large supply of small arms taken from British captures during the cruise. He loaded several hundred of these extra muskets and pistols and put them in handy baskets along the inside of the bulwarks. During the fight to come, his men would not lose precious time in reloading their weapons. They could simply fire a gun, drop it, and grab another already loaded.

Ordronaux also brought out on deck a supply of cannon balls to drop down into the expected boarding boats, and he hoisted and secured the boarding netting, creating something of an impediment to boarders. Finally, Ordronaux made it clear he intended to fight to the finish. He would blow up his ship before he struck her colors. Out of a normal complement of 150 men, he had less than 40 left on the *Prince*. The balance of his crew was off on prizes, including the nearby *Douglas*. At about 9:00 p.m., a privateersman on the *Douglas* signaled the approach of the five enemy barges. When they loomed in range out of the darkness, the *Prince* opened fire with her great guns. Undeterred, Hawkins ploughed ahead past the *Douglas*, intent on carrying the *Prince*. The British tried to place a boat on each bow, one on each side, and the fifth under the stern of the 310-ton brigantine.

The log of the *Prince* understates the viciousness of the melee that followed. "A warm action was then kept up with muskets, pistols, cutlasses, &c." reads the entry, "and in every attempt the enemy made to board he was promptly met and repulsed."[1] This does not mean the British failed to gain the deck in their five-pronged attack. When some Englishmen came over the bows, Ordronaux fired a main deck gun trained beforehand in that direction. Bagged musket balls and canister shot repelled this assault. Later, the British pushed the Americans back. Ordronaux grabbed a lighted match and moved to the companionway above the ship's magazine. He shouted to his men that if they continued on their heels, he would blow the ship to kingdom come. The threat had the desired effect, and the Americans rallied and drove the English off for a final time.

Such savagery could not last. After 20 minutes of violence, the British asked for mercy. The *Endymion* casualties amounted to some 28 killed, 37 wounded, and 28 taken prisoner. The *Prince* reported 7 killed and 24 wounded. Ordronaux and his surgeon suffered wounds. Hawkins died in the fight as did one of his master's mates. A British second lieutenant, two master's mates, and a pair of midshipmen suffered wounds. The gallant stand made by the Americans received the plaudits of contemporary observers and historians on both sides of the Atlantic.

Although he had repulsed the assault, Ordronaux continued to have his hands full. Only a few of the Americans came through the fight unscathed. So, he allowed the wounded British lieutenant, the two wounded midshipmen, one of the wounded mates, and a third midshipman to remain on board his ship for the night. But the remaining *Endymion* prisoners were held in a launch — away from firearms and oars — under the stern of the *Prince*. The next morning, Ordronaux moved up the eastern side of Nantucket and at Sesachacha put off most of the wounded and 67 accumulated British prisoners. The *Prince* limped into Boston, while the *Endymion* headed for Halifax to replace her losses. The *Douglas* was grounded at Squam and was promptly stripped clean by the locals. A diarist noted: "There is a great stir among the Inhabitants' getting ashore the property out of the ship . . . . [T]hey that get the most is the best fellow."[2]

---

1 McManemin, *Privateers of the War of 1812*, 187.
2 Starbuck, *History of Nantucket*, 314.

Wagons carried the majority of the wounded to town for treatment and care. The desperately wounded remained at Sesachacha. One of the British officers was entrusted to travel by hired boat to the British fleet at Tarpaulin Cove, Naushon Island to seek aid for his wounded countrymen. He returned with a surgeon and a supply of clothing.

As might be expected, some of the wounded struggled under the conditions. The *Nantucket Inquirer* in 1823 described the difficulties experienced by two wounded seamen. One man had a shattered jaw while another had a hand amputated. Invited to a home for dinner, they "were observed to stick to each other pertinaciously. The company fell to: but our wounded heroes were disabled for the manual and maxillary exploits being performed around them. After having complacently surveyed the scene without any offer of assistance from the busy guests whose diffidence perhaps outweighed their inclinations, he with one flipper, thus sternly, though with much point of humor, addressed his broken-jawed companion: 'I say Jack, since you can't grind, nor I carve, and the land-lubbers are all tucking the beef under their jackets, what do you say for splicing? If you'll cut for me, I'll chew for you.'"[1]

As for Ordronaux, when he got to Boston, a number of admiring merchants and citizens took steps to present him with a special sword and a vote of thanks for his valor. He discouraged his admirers. Years later, a higher honor recognized his courageous fight off Nantucket. When the U.S. Navy in 1942 launched the destroyer DD-617 at the Fore River, Massachusetts yard, it named the warship the U.S.S. *Ordronaux.* In the fall of 1814, however, the captain simply wanted to fade away from the action much as American privateering would vanish forever within a few months.

Though some of the encounters between warships and privateers turned savage, such as in the case of the *Prince*, perhaps more exhibited amiability and civility. The experience of Jeduthun Upton illustrates. Captain Upton left Salem on December 7, 1812 in the privateer brig *Polly.* The next afternoon, he spotted another privateer and gave chase. He fired his 9-pound bow chaser without effect at the fleeing ship. "Kept sight of her until 11 o'clock, it being somewhat thick we lost sight of her and gave up the chase to our great sorrow, as we had no doubt of its being the English schr. privateer Liverpool packet. . . ."[2]

Upton's luck turned altogether sour on the 23rd. The H.M.S. *Phoebe*, 36, Captain Hilliard chased the *Polly*, firing more than 20 shots into her. "I with the advice of my officers, thought to hold out longer would be madness." Upton surrendered his ship, and, to his surprise, the British "treated us more like friends than enemies. I was put in the gun room with the Lieut [Ingraham] and officers of marines who I found to be gentlemen." The next day, his captors returned his sword, quadrant, and spyglass, leading him to note in his diary: "Good opinion of my messmates."[3]

1 Ibid., 313.
2 *Jeduthun Upton Diary.*
3 Ibid.

The good fellowship continued. "Christmas day, we had a church meeting on board, the Capt acting as priest. The day spent agreeably. Dined with the Capt. in the cabin, who is a fine man, much of a gentleman and a Christian. Sat at the table drinking wine, etc., until 8 o'clock. . . ." The next day Upton recorded: "Spend my time much pleasanter than I expected, having such fine company."[1]

But things changed when Hilliard landed his prisoners at Plymouth, England early in January. Upton and the others were sent to the Mill prison. Despite Hilliard's support, the authorities denied Upton parole, because while being chased by the *Phoebe* he tossed his guns over the side. Hilliard even invited the American captain to dinner, but prison officials refused to let him out for the evening. After enduring harsh and unpleasant jail conditions, Upton gained an exchange in May. He made it to Portland early in July.

In drawing down the curtain on the privateering campaign it will be seen, by some basic measures, the 1812–15 privateers realized greater success than the public elements of the war machinery. Salem's Reverend William Bentley, a chronicler of privateers associated with his fabled town, succinctly observed: "These little boats have done great service."[2] Admittedly, the relevant statistics are not as complete, reliable, and valid as one would like. Nonetheless, various accounts indicate, during the war, the 515 or so American privateers took from 1,300 to 1,350 prizes valued at some $39 million. The 22 navy vessels took about 244 prizes worth some $6 million. This does not denigrate the little navy and its overall performance. Yet, it should be noted, the privateers went out at no expense to the public. And they not only put up bond, but customs duties were paid on their proceeds. A final point is more telling. The privateers captured some 30,000 prisoners, while the U.S. Army captured only about 6,000 of the enemy. The army truly struggled throughout the war.

---

1 Ibid.
2 Bentley, *Diary of William Bentley*, 4:107.

Chapter 7. Imminent Danger and Perils

During the first months of the war, the British more or less followed a hands-off policy when it came to the five northeastern states. Great Britain did not see a threat in New England and it did not want to offend and turn its significant antiwar elements. To upset the status quo made little sense, especially since Vermont's northern border and Maine's Passamaquoddy boundaries continued to be porous, permitting supplies and provisions to be smuggled from the United States to Canada, some of it destined for British forces fighting around the lakes. Indeed, Halifax authorities promptly promoted a state of neutrality around Passamaquoddy Bay, a condition conducive to free trade.

This is not to say the time passed quietly without spirited activity and occasional incidents. The governors of Connecticut, Massachusetts, and Rhode Island, while steadfastly refusing to detach their militias for United States service, made energetic efforts to organize and equip these units for their own coastal defense. The consequences of opposition and obstruction took up much time. For its part, the federal government found some sections of New England a rich source of army recruits in a time of force expansion. All the while, enemy privateering and nuisance naval raids created widespread alarm and eroded local economies already hurt by crop failures. When the U.S. Navy suffered a major setback at New London as the first year wound down, the morale of the region dropped further, promoting even greater concern and consternation all around.

Rhode Island comprehended its precariousness weeks before hostilities broke out. The state understood the April 1812 embargo to be a prelude to armed conflict. State leaders gathered within a week of the law's passage and issued the "Providence Resolutions," a document that deplored the national administration's interest in war and higher taxes, and urged the election of officers who favored peace. The resolutions highlighted the special vulnerability of what we now call the "Ocean State." "When war arrives, what will give protections to our harbours and maritime towns?" Showing disdain for the continuing influence of Jefferson's controversial emphasis on a flotilla of small harbor and river craft mounting one or two cannons and known as gunboats, the gathering scornfully asked: "Can we expect it from Gun-Boats?" The enemy, it predicted, will "make a war of frequent, and sudden descent on our long, and defenceless sea-coast. . . . We are now without protection; and while that part of the militia, not drafted and sent to war in Canada, would be assembling, the hand of ruin would pass over the land; and the enemy, laden with our spoil, leave us with our houseless wives and children, amidst the smoking fragments of our habitations."[1]

Two months later, the Rhode Island General Assembly sent a similar set of resolves to the U.S. Senate. The legislature decried "the very limited appropriations made for the protection of commerce, and the defence of our seaports;" noted the embargoes operated "with particular severity upon this State;" stressed the "patience, fortitude, and patriotism" of "the citizens of this State during the revolutionary war" can be depended upon again; instructed its members of Congress "to oppose all measures which may be brought forward tending to involve the country in war;" and if war becomes unavoidable, the members must "claim . . . adequate and timely means of defence and security against those imminent dangers and perils to which we are unwillingly exposed."[2]

Following the declaration of war, a sense of uneasiness prevailed throughout the state. Providence set up a river guard and worried about the "grim and bloody visage of civil commotion."[3] Newporters feared a British attack. Citizens and capital left the exposed town. In response to the anxiety and the perceived danger, Governor William Jones asked General Dearborn for the federal arms held at Newport. Two weeks later Dearborn replied by indicating he was transferring federal troops at Newport to positions on the northern front. He asked the governor to replace the federals with four state militia companies, half artillery and half infantry. Jones called a council of war on July 21 and decided not to call out the militia due to the "deficiency of funds in our state."[4] Instead, Jones wrote to the president and asked for 2,000 stands of arms, six field pieces, and sufficient ammunition. The administration did not respond. On August 22, the governor repeated his request, and advised the secretary of war the Rhode Island militia would be ready for federal service when the constitutional exigencies existed. In other words, the conditions were such that Dearborn's call remained unconstitutional.

Three British frigates appeared off Point Judith on September 19, heightening the alarm in the area. Jones set about obtaining powder and lead, but

---

1 *Newport* (RI) *Mercury*, April 11, 1812.
2 *American State Papers: Miscellaneous* 2:185-186.
3 Bayles, *History of Providence*, 1:193.
4 *Niles' Weekly Register* (MD), November 21, 1812.

refrained from calling out the militia. And on September 28, he wrote a third letter to the president. Within two weeks, the secretary of war replied for the administration. He said 1,000 stands of arms were being shipped to Newport and *"that 500 had been delivered to the state before."* Apparently, these weapons went to army volunteers from Newport, so Jones renewed his plea for more arms. If an attack comes before federal support arrives, Jones told the legislature, "it will not only be the duty of every citizen to be prepared . . . but of the general assembly to make an appropriation" to cover defense costs.[1]

Connecticut Governor Roger Griswold shared Jones's policy. In an August 6 proclamation he told the General Assembly he rejected Dearborn's request "for certain portions of the militia to be placed in the forts at New-London and New-Haven." Griswold intended to "maintain the lawful rights and privileges of this State, as a sovereign, free and independent state." In the end, he exhorted "all those capable of bearing arms to be at all times prepared and equipped in obedience to the lawful authority of the State and nation, to repel invasion, and resist aggressions on the liberties and privileges of the United States, of this State, or of any individuals or portions of the community."[2] By mid-September, the perilous lack of defensive forces prompted Adjutant General Ebenezer Huntington to take the unusual step of asking so-called exempts to supplement the militia by volunteering to serve just in Connecticut as a "body of state troops."[3] Most of the regular army troops once in New England forts were off to New York and Canada, leaving the five states to fend for themselves.

In Salem, Massachusetts, a body of merchants and citizens did not scorn gunboats. Concerned that the town's enthusiastic embrace of privateering might invite Royal Navy retribution, on July 27, the group asked the secretary of the navy to assign a few gunboats to protect their harbor. And although Governor Caleb Strong, with great conviction, advanced the same States' rights and antiwar positions put forth by Jones and Griswold, he did compromise and answer one national request for deployment of Massachusetts militia elements. General Dearborn asked Strong to assign five militia companies to Eastport in the Commonwealth's District of Maine. Strong replied on August 5, informing the general that the inhabitants of the town and nearby Robbinston were not fearful of British forces, but were apprehensive of border outlaws. He would provide three companies for this purpose. Accordingly, Adjutant General William Donnison ordered "three full companies of the eastern detached division . . . to march as soon as possible. . . ." The men were to be taken "from the nearest counties and districts, and from places the least exposed to the enemy."[4] General John Blake's brigade from the Penobscot sent two companies to Eastport, and a Robbinston company under Captain Thomas Vose, Jr. activated for service in its own town.

1 Ibid.
2 *A Proclamation, By His Excellency Roger Griswold.*
3 *Niles'*, October 17, 1812.
4 Ibid., August 15, 1812.

Strong's appraisal of British intentions around Passamaquoddy was well-founded. Lieutenant General Sir John C. Sherbrooke, the lieutenant governor of Nova Scotia, issued a decree pledging peace along the Down East border. He declared: "It is . . . my wish and desire that the subjects of the United States living on the frontier may pursue in peace their usual and accustomed trade without molestation, so long as they shall act in a similar way to the frontier inhabitants of this province of New Brunswick."[1] Sherbrooke advocated a neutral zone or peaceful coexistence so that illicit American trading so beneficial to the British could continue. The small militia detachment at Fort Sullivan could not begin to stop the smuggling that his decree encouraged.

Ironically, while traders in contraband profited, the militiamen found their Eastport conditions wanting. Food, clothing, and shelter were inferior and in short supply. Discipline, of course, broke down. Pork rations usually consisted of legs and heads. The men foraged in the vegetable gardens of the townspeople. Upon complaint, one officer called his unit into formation and upbraided his men for such misbehavior. "After he had finished his harangue, a green, tow-haired Jonathan of a fellow stepped out of the ranks, and, with a knowing cant of his head, said, 'Why, Cap'n, don't you expect that your men will root, when you give them so much hogs' heads to eat?'"[2]

Hezekiah Niles tried to cast a favorable light on developments. "The *actual war* that the enemy has waged against us for many years past," he said, "was more truly destructive than the present undisguised contest will be, if we are faithful to ourselves."[3] And he seemed to delight in the problem faced by a couple of New England governors because of their strict construction of the Constitution. "All of the other governors have complied with the President's requisition," he noted, "and the marching of regular troops to Albany, will teach governors *Strong* and *Griswold* the necessity of being duly prepared 'to repel invasion, &c.'"[4]

The governors were not alone in their anxiety and concern. Town officials around the region began to prepare in earnest. Sullivan, Maine called a September 26 special town meeting at this "critical juncture." The men voted to place military stores "in a more central place" under "the care of the Capt of the Militia Company." Each militiaman received "ten rounds of cartridges."[5] Nearby Eden, by contrast, set up a committee of safety under Colonel Cornelius Thompson "to inspect the disaffected to Government to watch their movements to take lawful Measures to suppress dissention and publicly note those . . . who defile their mouths with Reproches against our lawful Government."[6]

---

1 David Zimmerman, *Coastal Fort*, 28.
2 Kilby, *Eastport and Passamaquoddy*, 161.
3 *Niles'*, August 1, 1812.
4 Ibid., August 15, 1812.
5 *1789-1831 Book of Sullivan (ME) Town Records.*
6 *Book 1 Records of the Town of Eden (ME) 1796 to 1827*, 98.

At Bath, Major General William King delegated authority to his divisional officers to call out their units on their own account whenever a threat appeared. Militia units came to life. The newly created Fifth Regiment, for one, consisting of companies from Camden, Thomaston, St. George, Hope, and Appleton, assembled in mid-August "'armed and equipped as the law directs,' prepared to fill all vacancies of officers, and parade on the occasion."[1] Towns around Waldoboro, concerned with British privateers, met on October 5 "for the purpose of consulting for the safety of the Commonwealth."[2]

Inevitably, some communities took militia affairs more seriously than others, even to the point of conducting business on the Sabbath. Benjamin Percival, a Sandwich, Massachusetts civic leader and farmer, recorded in his diary: "Sunday Octo 10th . . . we have all been to town to day to attend a court before Justice Pope a number of persons were tried on an information of the militia officers they stood trial but were all fined."[3] At the time, men in the 18-25 age group were required to serve in the militia or risk being fined.

In Vermont, on October 9, Governor Jonas Galusha allowed there were those who doubted the course of the national government, "yet, war being declared by the constituted authorities of our country, it ought no longer remain a question of policy, but it has become the duty of the state governments, and of every individual, with promptitude, to espouse the sacred cause of our injured country."[4] He went on to tell the legislature he received 1,000 stands of arms from the United States armory in Springfield, Massachusetts. But, since he ordered 1,500, the legislators would have to come up with a way to distribute the lesser number. A few days later, following the governor's lead, the General Assembly resolved to support the federal government while relying "on the great Arbiter of events for a favorable result."[5] Meanwhile, the ladies of Poultney gathered to knit socks and mittens for the men of their hamlet called into service.

The Madison administration received more bad news from the front, and a recalcitrant state militia turned out to be a major factor. American forces suffered a defeat at Queenston Heights just north of Niagara Falls on October 13. A body of several thousand New York militiamen under General Stephen Van Rensselaer refused to cross over to Canada and turn the tide of battle which played out before their eyes. They reasoned they signed up to defend their homes and New York, not to attack Canada — a position not far removed from the stance of the New England Federalists.

Three days after Governor Griswold died on October 25, his successor, John Cotton Smith, appointed Thursday, November 26 a day of Public Thanksgiving and Prayer. "[N]otwithstanding the unusual and calamitous events of the current year," the pious Smith felt the "competent supply of the

---

1 Locke, *Sketches of the History of the Town of Camden*, 95.

2 Aiken, *Records of the Lower St. Georges and Cushing*, 33.

3 *Benjamin Percival Diary*.

4 *Niles'*, October 24, 1812.

5 Ibid., November 7, 1812.

fruits of the earth" realized during the past year could be attributed to His Providence's mercy.[1]

The Republicans of Nantucket, however, did not sense such bounty and sought relief elsewhere. Once the war opened, economic conditions rapidly deteriorated on the island some 20 miles south of Cape Cod. A Nantucketer named Meader, it is said, asked a neighbor for a hammer. Out of curiosity, the neighbor asked why he wanted the tool. "To knock out my teeth. I have no need of them, for I can get nothing to eat." Generations of islanders would resort to the localism, "I have no more use for it than Nick Meader had for his teeth," when describing something as superfluous or useless.[2]

Probably a fable, the tale nonetheless fairly depicts the island's struggle as 1812 came to a close. Prompted by depressing conditions, the Republicans wrote to President Madison in behalf of the island's almost 7,000 inhabitants. Their November 21 plea pointed to Nantucket's "peculiar situation" and the general unemployment that followed the suspension of the whaling industry on the island brought about by marauding British naval and privateering vessels. They did not want unconstitutional preferential treatment, but expected "when a resort to arms is considered unavoidable, our Government will afford that consistent Relief to such parts of the Community as are deprived of the means of subsistence by a continuation of the war." Nantucket asked Madison to devise a way to protect its absent and vulnerable whaling fleet in the Southern Ocean, and requested a stipulation "be effected with Great Britain whereby the Cod and Whale Fisheries of both Nations may be exempted from the Ravages of war."[3] The petition fell on deaf ears for the time.

In New Hampshire, Governor William Plumer clearly set forth his position in a November 18 message to the legislature. "Pacific measures having failed, congress were brought to the painful alternative of *submission or war.*" He stressed: "At a time when we are actually at war, I conceive arguments are unnecessary to convince you of the great importance and real necessity of improving the state and condition of our militia."[4] With legislative support, the governor soon detached militia units to Stewartstown up north and to Portsmouth on the coast.

Militia manpower needs competed with U.S. Army recruiting in the Granite State. By mid-September, the Eleventh Infantry, based in Concord, enlisted 397 men and marched them off to Burlington, Vermont. And the First Regiment of New Hampshire Volunteers formed in Concord on November 29, 1812. Within weeks, the outfit made its way to Burlington. Army enlistees became such a fixture in Concord that some of them thought they deserved to vote as local citizens at the annual town meeting. Concord had become a camp town.

1 *A Proclamation, By His Honour John Cotton Smith.*
2 William F. Macy and Hussey, *Nantucket Scrap Basket*, 77.
3 Starbuck, *History of Nantucket*, 279-280.
4 *Niles'*, December 5, 1812.

In a related sidelight, House Speaker Henry Clay in Washington had his hands full with Massachusetts Representative Josiah Quincy, one of the most conspicuous antiwar legislators. Clay, in fact, wanted to shoot the man. The matter came to a head in January 1813. For two weeks the House heatedly debated a contentious bill to add 20,000 men to the existing 35,000-man army, and bring the total force to 55,000. The extended debate mirrored the debate leading up to the war vote in June. Quincy, this time, led the opposition in unsparing language in a memorable January 5 speech. "Whoever believes this bill to be a means of peace, or anything else than an instrument of vigorous and protracted war, is grievously deceived," he began. "I warn, therefore, my political opponents; those honest men, of whom I know there are some, who, paying only a general attention to the course of public affairs, submit the guidance of their opinions to the men who stand at the helm, not to vote for this bill under any belief that its object is to aid negotiation for peace."[1] To Quincy, the object was Canada.

Representative Bolling Hall of Georgia called Quincy to order for intimating members of the administration were friends of Napoleon. Clay ruled the Massachusetts member was not out of order, and "it was impossible to prevent gentlemen from expressing themselves so as to convey an *inuendo*" [*sic*]. Quincy retorted, "No man was ever materially injured by any mere '*inuendo*.' The strength of satire is the justness of the remark and the only sting of invective is the truth of the observation."[2]

He continued: "Among the causes of that universal disgust which pervaded all New England, at the administration and its supporters, was the general dislike and contempt of this invasion of Canada." Quincy argued, "An army may be raised, and that during the first years it may be supported by loans, and that afterwards it will support itself by bayonets."[3] The leadership did not want to hear any of this. But Quincy went too far when he made "certain offensive observations . . . which do not appear in the printed report of his speech, as corrected by himself. One of these expressions designated Eastern democrats, among other opprobrious epithets, as toads, or reptiles, which *spread their slime in the drawing room.*"[4]

On the floor, Felix Grundy of Tennessee said, "[I]t affords no pleasure to inflict pain on others, and therefore, although the gentleman from Massachusetts (Mr. Quincy) merits all the severity which can be permitted, I shall forbear."[5] In the end, the bill passed 77 to 42. But Clay was so upset with Quincy; he left the chair and challenged his antagonist from Massachusetts to "a duel or disgrace."[6] Quincy simply ignored the speaker.

---

1 *Annals of Congress*, 12th Cong., 2nd sess., 541.
2 Ibid., 544.
3 Ibid., 549-551.
4 Ibid., 600.
5 Ibid.
6 Higginson, *Larger History of the United States of America*, 364.

After, Grundy took Quincy aside and explained, "Except Tim Pickering .
. . there is not a man in the United States so perfectly hated by the people of
my district as yourself. By --- I must abuse you, or I shall never get re-elected.
I will do it, however, genteelly. I will not do it as that ---- fool Clay did it,
strike so hard as to hurt myself. But abuse you I must."[1]

In the middle of the additional military force debate, a major Boston
newspaper published an editorial that went beyond Quincy's argument and
envisioned secession.

The *Columbian Centinel* saw the states north of the Delaware, especially
New England, "separated in fact" from the country south of that river. The
editor felt the Northern states "are in a condition no better in relation to the
South than that of a conquered people. . . . We, whose soil was the hotbed
and whose ships were the nursery of Sailors, are insulted with the hypocrisy
of a devotedness to Sailors' rights, by those whose country furnishes no navigation beyond the size of a ferryboat or an Indian canoe. . . . The consequence
of this state of things must then be, either that the Southern States must
drag the Northern States farther into the war, or we must drag them out of
it; or the chain will break."[2]

At the state house in Boston, Governor Strong became more involved in
matters of defense. He requested an appropriation from the legislature for
that purpose. The General Court in January made $100,000 available to arm
the militia. The House also passed an order directing the state's adjutant
general to seek congressional assistance for coastal defense. When the Senate declined to approve the resolve, Strong communicated on his own to the
national authorities. His request for the state's proportional share of firearms
authorized by Congress was rejected. As of the end of December 1812, New
Hampshire had received 1,000 stands of arms from the federal government.
Vermont received 2,500 and Rhode Island had 1,000. Connecticut, like Massachusetts, was shut out by the increasingly spiteful Madison government.

As the months passed, the federal firearms allotment issue intensified.
The War Department told Strong it did not have enough arms for every state,
and it would "supply, in the first place, *frontier states, and the militia who have
come forward in the service of the country*." The General Court wondered why the
United States withheld arms "from the populous, respectable, and exposed
state of Massachusetts, and which had been delivered from its own manu-
factories" in Springfield![3] The legislature also called for compliance with the
federal statute of April 23, 1808 which required proportional distribution of
arms and military equipment to the state militias. Eventually, late in 1813, the
administration, having made its point, relented and sent 1,500 stands of arms
to Massachusetts.

The navy continued to enjoy brilliant successes. For a few days in December, New London became a focal point of the war. Commodore Stephen

1 Ibid., 364-365.
2 *Columbian Centinel* (MA), January 13, 1813.
3 *Niles'*, June 12, 1813.

Decatur arrived on the 4th in the frigate *United States* with the news he van-quished the H.M.S. *Macedonian*, 49, on October 25. Newport shared the glory when the captured *Macedonian* limped into that place on the following day. Within the week, Lieutenant Archibald Hamilton of the *United States* made his way to Washington and, to the surprise and delight of almost everyone gathered at a naval ball to celebrate the earlier defeat of the *Guerriere*, pre-sented the battle flag of the *Macedonian* to Dolley Madison.

However, in January, American land forces suffered yet another defeat. General William Henry Harrison moved to recapture Michigan. One column of his divided army routed a small British detachment at Frenchtown and then dropped its guard. A reinforced British contingent supported by First Nations warriors counterattacked on January 22 and forced the Americans to surrender. The Indians proceeded to execute several score of the prison-ers, many of them Kentucky volunteers. The atrocity became known as "The River Raisin Massacre." Harrison cancelled his winter campaign.

Despite several celebrated defeats at the hands of the U.S. Navy, the Royal Navy methodically applied pressure along the American coast. The British blockaded the Georgia and South Carolina coasts in November 1812. The Chesapeake and Delaware Bays were blockaded on December 26. And on March 30, 1813, Great Britain extended its naval blockade to cover the entire coastline from the Mississippi to Long Island purposely sparing New England.

Nonetheless, by the early months of 1813, people along the region's shore were troubled about the state of affairs. The generally pro-war inhabitants of Falmouth, Massachusetts, like so many others, showed their apprehension. They sent a petition to Congressman Isaiah Green "praying that measures may be taken to secure them against the attacks of the enemy."[1] Congress simply forwarded the petition to the secretary of war. Yet, even in the face of the widespread nervousness, a few, like Zachariah Marston of Portland re-mained hopeful. "Notwithstanding the present appearances I feel confident we shall have Peace before July," he told an associate.[2] Most of the people did not share Marston's optimism.

For certain, the hills of Vermont did not appear ready for peace. At Highgate, 30 armed smugglers attacked a detachment of 13 mounted Unit-ed States infantry. Seven infantrymen managed to escape, but five became prisoners and a sergeant suffered mortal wounds. Otherwise, partisan fer-vor continued to dominate state affairs. Party spirit ran so warm "the dread of civil commotion hung heavily" on the minds of moderates. And "a man's politics constituted his passport or his mark of rejection at his neighbor's door."[3] Beginning in the period leading up to the war, the political division in Poultney, for example, became so intense the two parties held separate celebrations on the Fourth of July, "and if they could spike each other's can-

---

1 U.S. *House Journal*. 1813. 12th Cong., 2nd sess., February 11.
2 Marston, *Letter*.
3 H.P. Smith, *History of Addison County*, 72.

non, steal each other's rum, or do other mischief . . . it seemed to be regarded as legitimate and proper."[1]

As one might expect, despite all the difficulties, some people knew how to catch the opportunity. When the first British men-of-war appeared at Block Island, they anchored near the Middle Pond. Almost a dozen local fishing boats followed behind. Since Benjamin Sprague's boat got closest, the British told him to come alongside while the others were to hold back. A Brit queried: "How do you sell your fish?"

"Twenty cents apiece," answered Sprague.

The British placed an order, and Sprague asked: "Please pass down a bunch of yarn to tie them up."

Down came the yarn, and up went the fish as Sprague admonished: "Please pass your money down as soon as you get your fish."[2]

Sprague soon emptied his boat of fish, and moved away to allow the second boat to come up. As he withdrew, he let his fellow fishermen know the price he set. In short order, every man sold out and went home with unexpected cash in his pocket.

Pleased with his fish profits, Sprague told his wife, "I am going to try my chances." He gathered some ducks and chickens, beans, and a jug of rum and set out for the British ships. As he passed the minister's lot, several British officers appeared on horseback.

"My heart jumped right up into my throat, for I knew they would ask what I had in that jug."

The officers stopped and touched their hats. With his hands full, Sprague nodded in return.

"What have you to sell?"

Sprague answered, "Ducks, chickens, and beans."

"What's in that jug?"

Sprague appeared tongue-tied, and the officers laughed.

"I'll buy your ducks, chickens, and beans, and go on and let my steward have them, and let my men have a drink apiece, but don't let any of them get drunk."

"Now," thought Sprague, "there's good sailing and I'll make a good voyage."

He found the steward and some marines on the eastern side of Middle Pond. The steward paid for the fowl and beans, and gave his approval to approach the marines. Sprague beckoned for two of the men to follow him down a bank and behind some bushes. "The rum was half water," he recalled years later, "and I sold each a pint for a dollar a pint; after they went back, two more came, and so on until I sold all out to them at a dollar a pint."

Since it was noon, the British marines invited Sprague to join them for dinner. "I did, and they had their English rum with their rations. They asked me to drink some, and I did. Then they asked me if I did not think their rum

1 Joslin, et al. *History of the Town of Poultney*, 74.
2 *Livermore's History of Block Island*, 110.

was better than mine. I told them yes, but did not tell them how much of mine was water."[1]

On the mainland, Governor Jones had little time for socializing. He continued his defense initiative, assigning half of the 1,000 federal muskets to the Newport militia. The other 500 went to Providence. A search for state-owned cannons turned up only six brass field pieces. Bristol, Newport, and Warwick each received a pair.

Well down the coast, Warren, Maine considered a different approach. A March town meeting voted "to choose a committee to instruct the representatives to the General Court to use their influence to furnish some armed vessel to protect the coasting trade, and to confer with other towns on the subject."[2] A legislative committee held a hearing on the proposal. Nearby towns with greater exposure to naval assault were not as enthusiastic. Such a warlike vessel, they thought, would only encourage aggression by superior British forces. The committee did not issue a favorable report, and the idea faded away.

Much more vulnerable, Rye, New Hampshire added to its earlier cautious preparations. At its March town meeting, the voters directed the selectmen to "purchase one hundred weight of good Powder and Led in proportion for the use of the Town." The selectmen were told to store the ammunition in the attic of the meetinghouse. And the meeting decided "to give each Man detached in Rye fourteen dollars a Month including United States pay, providing they are called into actual service to defend the United States."[3] On the 8th, the men of the town formed a militia company under Captain Jonathan Wedgewood and went into service on April 1st. A year would pass before the outfit saw action.

In Concord, a dramatic political shift took place. The New Hampshire state government at the outset leaned in favor of the national government. Governor Plumer, a Republican, supported Madison's efforts, and the legislature sustained the governor. Popular dissatisfaction with the war, especially the failed land campaigns to the west, tipped the balance in the March elections. Former Governor John T. Gilman, out of office for eight years, took back the governor's office by a narrow margin. Out of more than 35,000 votes, Gilman prevailed by the slim margin of 250 votes. Plumer became another prominent victim of the volatile political climate in New England. At the same time, both branches of the New Hampshire legislature assumed an antiwar character. "The minority of 1812 had now become the majority."[4]

With the arrival of more moderate weather, naval activity increased in New England waters. The H.M.S. *Rattler*, 16, Captain Alexander Gordon and the H.M.S. *Bream*, 6, Lieutenant C.D. Browne harassed the Pemaquid-Boothbay area, taking five coasters in one day. Captain W.M. Read of Boothbay

---

1 Ibid., 110-111.
2 Eaton, *Annals of the Town of Warren*, 313.
3 Parsons, *History of the Town of Rye*, 275.
4 McClintock, *History of New Hampshire*, 496.

learned one prize "was in the offing becalmed." He mustered 20 volunteers and in three small boats recovered the prize without a fight. She turned out to be the schooner *Hannabritta* of Cushing. From the British prize crew, Read determined the *Rattler* and *Bream* planned to rendezvous that night at Townsend. Sure enough, before long, the *Rattler* "run up within Squirrel Island and came to anchor." Read fired alarm shots and Captain Daniel Rose rushed up with his militia company from Damariscotta. A British contingent landed near Spruce Point in back of Read's house. The militia fired upon them, but the Brits escaped unharmed. In the morning, the *Rattler* left, only to be replaced by the feared *Liverpool Packet*. The Nova Scotia privateer in one day took a schooner and three sloops in sight of the Boothbay harbor. "We continue under arms," reported Read. "Some of our coasters are taken daily."[1]

The Royal Navy encountered equally determined resistance on Matinicus. A British ship sent a boat on shore in search of provisions. All alone, "old Aunt Green" knew what to expect. She did not have time to hide anything, and most of the men of the sparsely inhabited island were away fishing. She watched as the navy men entered her barn and came out leading a valued ox. Aunt Green flew from her house and grabbed the axe from the chopping block. Waving the weapon in the face of the team's leader, she admonished: "If ye must take suthin', take one of them cows, but ye tech them oxen at yer peril." Impressed with the spirit of the elderly lady, the officer ordered: "Put him back, boys; old Tolman has some nice fat cattle, we will go up and get his."[2]

A chivalrous British officer who visited Swan's Island seemed to be less restrained. Several women and girls returning from berry-picking on a nearby island were overtaken by the crew of a boat from an enemy cutter. The British did not detain the pickers, but on departing, an officer kissed one of the girls. "'Go home,' said he, 'and tell your parents that you have the honor of being kissed by a British officer.'"[3]

The audacity of the British prompted the Belfast selectmen to petition Governor Strong. The town stressed it was "peculiarly exposed to the sudden Depredations of the Enemy, with no other Means of Defence than two Companies of Militia, and one Company of Artillery, with two light Field-Pieces. . . ." The selectmen asked for "a Number of Heavy pieces of Ordnance" and a supply of small arms for the locals ready to volunteer in a crisis.[4] The request went unmet, but soon thereafter a small detachment of regular troops arrived across the way in Castine. This force reduced the pressure on Belfast.

As word of the American success at the Battle of York in Upper Canada spread, Lincoln County, Maine men grew increasingly upset at the brazen

1 *Eastern Argus* (ME), April 17, 1813.
2 Long, *Matinicus Isle*, 89.
3 Small, *History of Swan's Island*, 31.
4 Joseph Williamson, *History of the City of Belfast*, 1:434-435.

British cruisers plundering the midcoast. On the first of April, the enemy took 12 coasters between Monhegan and Damariscove. The English even went into Tennant's Harbor and cut out four schooners. Rumors circulated that the enemy operated under orders to capture anything afloat — even canoes. A group of Muscongus area men came together one Sunday afternoon and plotted retaliation. The gathering concluded the *Bream*, just a schooner, made an inviting target. But, would such an undertaking stand a chance? Nearby, in what is now Bremen, lived a man who would know.

Born in Marblehead in 1747, Samuel Tucker, now 65, began following the sea at age 11. He served with distinction in the Continental Navy, attaining the title of commodore. He took a number of prizes during the Revolutionary War and was captured twice. Congress accorded Tucker a vote of thanks for his outstanding service in the infant navy. His most notable command may have been his 1778 winter voyage to Europe in the little frigate *Boston*, 24. After a harrowing, eventful trip he delivered John Adams to his minister's post in France. Contrasting personalities, the two men came to admire each other. In terms understandable in his circle of maritime friends, Tucker summed up the future president in one sentence. "I did not say much to him at first, but damn and bugger my eyes, I found him after a while as sociable as any Marblehead man."[1]

Tucker not only supported the scheme, but he agreed to assume command. The old warrior looked forward to one more fight. Within a day, a 45-man group of volunteers chartered the 100-ton sloop *Increase*. Each man supplied his own firearm, ammunition, and rations. Tucker obtained the necessary commission from Joseph Farley at the customhouse in Waldoboro. Captain John Binney of the Fourth Regiment, U.S. Infantry at Fort Edgecomb loaned two small cannons, a brass field piece, and 30 men.

After fitting out, Tucker addressed his band, warning them he sought a fight. "If any one chooses, he has a right to withdraw. . . . Now is the time to make up your mind." One timid fellow decided to drop out and he asked for his gun. "'No,' said his comrades, 'that is pledged; you must leave it:' and he went away amidst the hisses of the crowd."[2]

Thus prepared, the *Increase* sailed from Boothbay beyond Pemaquid to the eastward. When Tucker did not find his quarry or a target of convenience, he turned to the west. After two unproductive days, the hastily gathered rations petered out and the band decided to return to Boothbay. Tucker discharged the soldiers, returned their artillery pieces, and, on April 26, moved to return the sloop to her home at Muscongus. As he rounded Pemaquid Point, Tucker spotted a sail to the east. He changed his course slightly, appearing to be headed for the St. George River. The old commodore ordered almost all of his men out of sight below. As expected, the stranger turned on him and gave chase. Tucker reversed his course as if attempting to escape. After a short run, he tacked and sailed down on the pursuer. He ordered a

---

1 McCullough, *John Adams*, 183.
2 Sheppard, *Life of Samuel Tucker*, 218.

sailor to hoist the American ensign and called his volunteers topside. Armed only with a little swivel cannon and their muskets, the men waited for close quarters.

A little more than a mile east of New Harbor, the antagonists came together. The enemy fired the first shot, but a withering return fire poured from the Maine boat. This proved too warm for the Englishmen, and all but the captain scampered below. He flopped on his back on the quarterdeck and, reaching up with one arm, tried to steer out of danger. When he saw a brawny American sailor prepare to hurl a kedge anchor as a grappling iron onto his deck, he decided to surrender. Once on shore, the British captain admitted: "When I beheld a giant standing at the bow with a huge anchor on his back ready to throw on board of us through a space of twenty feet, and heard his awful cry: 'Commodore, shall I heave,' I thought the devil was coming after my vessel."[1]

The enemy ship turned out to be the 35-ton Halifax privateer *Crown*, Captain Richard Jennings. In addition to the 25-man crew, having earlier captured an American brig, the *Crown* of six guns had on board a number of American prisoners. Not a man on either side suffered injury during the skirmish, but the privateer's mainsail had 370 bullet holes and another ball found its way through Jenning's hat. Both ships went into Round Pond. The *Crown* and the ample amount of ammunition and stores found on the privateer were sold, the profits going to the captors. The English crew wound up in the jail in Wiscasset, but Jennings at first went to Tucker's nearby home. After, the English captain was sent to join his men in the Lincoln County jail. Before long, however, he escaped in the disguise of a woman. Weeks later, he crossed paths with several of the fishermen who crewed for Tucker. He "treated them very kindly, and told them he had no idea the American character combined so much hospitality and bravery, and remarked, 'You will never catch me again in a privateer against you.'"[2]

The British presence impacted just about everyone on or near the midcoast. Alibeus Partridge of Camden wrote to his two sons living in Ohio to tell them the "times are exceeding dark, scar[c]ety and war." Hundreds of families lacked bread or potatoes. A severe frost damaged local crops, and "co[a]sting is almost cut off. The British take and carey of[f] and burn numbers of them so that . . . the southern trade is so stopt that no provisions is brought from thence to help the difucalty."[3] And North Yarmouth men met to consider "the situation of many families who by the stagnation of business the scarcity of money, and the high price of Southern Corn . . . in addition to the failure of the Crops last year are reduced to distressing circumstances; and make such provision for their relief as may be thought best."[4] In the end,

1 Stahl, *History of Old Broad Bay and Waldoboro*, 112.
2 Sheppard, 221.
3 Alan Taylor, *Liberty Men and Great Proprietors*, 239.
4 *North Yarmouth* (ME) *Town Records Volume Second*, 408.

the meeting decided to fall back on Yankee self-reliance, and dismissed the idea of public assistance.

Tiring of the St. George-Sheepscot area, the *Rattler* and the *Bream* moved along the coast to Kennebunk where on May 19 they drove the Salem priva-teer *Alexander*, Captain Benjamin Crownshield, ashore near the mouth of the Mousam River. Portsmouth, New Hampshire rightly became alarmed and called a town meeting to address the growing threat. Daniel Webster spoke to the gathering and declared: "'Talk is not what the crisis demands.'" The local forts, he said, need repairs and men to defend them, and the national and state governments have been asked to furnish both. He did not know "'that either will attend to our application. But one thing we do know, the crisis demands labor, and we can *labor*; we can repair the forts. And then we know another thing, we *can defend them*. . . . ' The meeting adjourned with a hurrah for pick-axe, spade, and shovel."[1] The next day, hundreds showed up for the task, including the godlike Daniel, properly armed with his shovel.

The Portsmouth preparations seemed timely. News accounts described the awful April 29 — May 6 British raids in the Upper Chesapeake Bay. Led by Admiral George Cockburn, a man who would become notorious for his 1814 role in the attack on Washington and who would in 1828 rise to the position of First Naval Lord, the Royal Navy menaced Annapolis and Balti-more and sacked Havre de Grace, Fredericktown, and Georgetown. Cock-burn created great anxiety with his harsh policy of destroying any place that offered resistance. New England enjoyed good fortune in this respect. Cockburn remained in the south. The leading British commanders in the northeast during the war, and most of their subordinate officers, generally behaved as principled gentlemen. Pillaging and wanton destruction were alien to their makeup.

The people of Tisbury on the Vineyard felt the growing economic squeeze and they did not like it. On May 13, the town petitioned Congress to put an end to the "Exportation of Bread Stuffs . . . during the present Scarcity." With many townsmen unemployed, "the present high price of bread considerably adds to their embarrassment." Tisbury attributed the price rise and want of bread to the fact American vessels under British license were carrying flour and grains "to the ports & Countries under the controul of the British Nation & their Armies In return we see the Manufactures of Great Britain filling our ports & Towns thereby aiding our enemies as well as drawing out precious Metals."[2] The appeal may have helped. The Senate finally went along with the House, and, on August 2, 1813, the president approved Chap-ter 57, an act prohibiting the use of British licenses and comparable passes. American ships using such licenses and passes henceforth were considered and treated as British.

Newport, Rhode Island residents remained uneasy. The illustrious Cap-tain Sir Thomas Masterman Hardy now led a permanent British squadron off

---

1 McClintock, 496.
2 Charles E. Banks, *History of Martha's Vineyard*, 1:421.

Block Island effectively closing the eastern end of Long Island Sound and the approaches to Vineyard Sound. "Precautions are taking against the consequences of their attempting a landing on this Island [Newport] —the specie has been removed from the Banks — Individuals have sent away their plate — and nightly patrols are established in the town, and upon Brenton's neck. . . . Let the State and United States do their duty to us," a *Mercury* writer urged, "and we shall be ready and willing to assist in defence of ourselves, our families, and property and of this important port."[1]

As if to emphasize the threat, a boat from the H.M.S. *Orpheus*, 36, Captain Hugh Pigot chased the letter-of-marque *Whampoa*, ashore near Narragansett on the western entrance of Narragansett Bay. The American crew fled to the cover of woods and, joined by Captain Pierce's Newport militia, fired into a British launch, mortally wounding Lieutenant William Collins. Other boats from the *Orpheus* went after the *Whampoa*. They burned her and fled ahead of approaching American gunboats.

Meanwhile, the Rhode Island General Assembly, while asking for the assignment of regular United States troops to the Newport forts, complained to Madison about a perceived unfair tax burden. The state paid more taxes than half the other states. The legislature assumed when the federal government accepted Rhode Island tax revenues it also assumed the responsibility for defending the state. Rhode Island responded in part by declining to participate in the federal direct tax collection process. To assure collections and save itself the expense of collecting, the national government allowed 10 to 15 percent discounts to states willing to do the federal collecting. Considering the burden or cost of the unpopular task, ten other states also declined to seek the deduction. The Rhode Island legislature decided if the state gathered the assessments it "would release the General Government from the odium of collecting a tax which their own mad policy has brought upon the country."[2]

As the first year of the war began to wind down, an unexpected turn of events faced the nation. While the army enjoyed unusual success on the frontier, the navy suffered a major strategic setback as well as a dispiriting loss of one of its valorous officers and his ship. On May 27, an American amphibious force captured Fort George near Niagara. On the down side, in the fight, the United States lost an outstanding general, Zebulon Pike, and failed to destroy the smaller British army under Brigadier General John Vincent. Two days later, combined American forces repulsed a British attack on the Sackett's Harbor base at the eastern end of Lake Ontario.

The navy's troubles put New London again on center stage before the focus turned to Boston. Commodore Stephen Decatur in the *United States*, accompanied by the *Macedonian* and *Hornet*, left New York by way of Long Island Sound. He took this uncommon exit route in order to avoid the tight British blockade in front of the usual way past Sandy Hook. On June 1, De-

1 *Boston Gazette*, April 22, 1813.
2 Hickey, *The War of 1812*, 123.

catur and his squadron moved out of the mouth of the Sound and dashed for the open Atlantic. An English ship of the line and a frigate spotted far away off Montauk could not reach Decatur's force. But, all of a sudden, dead ahead off Block Island, another pair of British warships, a 74 and a frigate, loomed. Decatur had only one option — turn and run for New London. The enemy followed as far as Gull Island and blocked the port for the rest of the war. Decatur saved his ships, but the *United States* and the *Macedonian* remained bottled up for the duration. The *Hornet* did not escape until November 1814. Thus, without firing a shot, the British neutralized one-seventh of the little U.S. Navy.

Apprehensive of an attack by the British, on June 10, Decatur moved his ships up the river, past the Gale's Ferry bar, and anchored three miles below Norwich. "The commerce of the Thames ceased at once. Sails were taken down, hulls packed together like logs, keels left to decay. . . . It was a period of anxiety, depression, and gloom."[1] New London exhibited greater concern. "The neighboring militia were summoned to the coast, the specie of the banks was conveyed to Norwich, and the city emptied of women, children, and the more valuable portable goods."[2] An attack never came, but New London remained on edge until February 1815.

While anxiety reigned in the New London area, Boston and its neighboring towns experienced the most depressing few days of the war. Embargo ruin, privateering misfortune, and privation in general produced much grumbling and complaint, but, in the end, were accepted and tolerated in the land of the hard-nosed Puritans. However, the unexpected loss of a seemingly invincible warrior and his prized frigate cast a pall over the place. The story is stirring.

---

1 Caulkins, *Norwich*, 36.
2 Caulkins, *History of New London*, 631.

CHAPTER 8. DON'T GIVE UP THE SHIP

Young Perez Hatch, Tommy Mitchell, and Tommy Stetson of Marshfield, Massachusetts were up an about early on the spring morning of June 1, 1813, anxious to launch a new boat. Over recent days, guided by Perez's father, the three boys devoted much of their time to constructing an open fishing boat suitable for conditions in deep water. As the sun rose higher and a light southwest breeze developed, oxen dragged their boat to the nearby North River. The trio put in and promptly set out for a day of fishing east of Scituate. By the early afternoon, the boys had all the cod they wanted, and turned for home. At that moment, an obstacle came in sight — a feared British man-of-war.

The boys picked up their pace, hoping to avoid a confrontation. But an officer on the closing frigate shouted: "Heave to!"[1] The youngsters ignored the order until a shot hurled over their boat gained their quick compliance. Only 12 to 14 years old, the boys more than anything feared impressment. They drew alongside and timidly made their way up to the quarter-deck where they came face to face with Captain Philip Bowes Vere Broke, a 36-year-old combat veteran of the Royal Navy. The ship turned out to be the impressive H.M.S. *Shannon*; its tense company at action stations with the guns run out and loaded.

Broke's pleasant manner began to ease the boys' apprehension. He initiated a casual conversation, asking about their families, and then directed them to bring their catch on deck. When Broke asked the price of the fish, one boy, intent on ending their discomfort, blurted: "Take them, take them for nothing."[2] No, that would not do, assured the captain. He gave a shilling to each boy. Now much more relaxed, the youths told their new friend

---

1 Hagar, *Marshfield*, 193.
2 Ibid., 194.

he should not dally hereabouts. The famous American Captain James Lawrence was fitting out the frigate *Chesapeake* in Boston and she was almost
ready for sea. Captain Broke astonished his guests when he told them he
read the Boston papers, knew all about the *Chesapeake*, and, in fact, today he
had sent a formal challenge to Captain Lawrence. He hoped to engage him
before nightfall. The conversation ended at 4:00 p.m. when a lookout announced the *Chesapeake*, seven miles away and bearing down, had just fired
a gun. Broke hastened the Marshfield trio to their boat and ordered them to
get clear of the area.

The sea fight that followed, it cannot be doubted, turned out to be a major
event in the war, especially around Massachusetts. Historians continue to
describe the engagement in superlative terms and the outcome created lasting controversy and second-guessing. To this day, the Royal Navy considers
the action the finest duel of the war.

In the days beforehand, the *Chesapeake* and her heroic captain created
quite a stir in Boston. The 31-year-old James Lawrence earned a bold reputation during his 14 years in the navy, including his late command of the
Hornet. Recently promoted to captain, the secretary of the navy assigned him
to the command of the *Chesapeake* in mid-May and ordered him to get into
the North Atlantic primarily to interdict enemy communications with its
army in Canada and its forces on the lakes. The townspeople expected great
things. The day after Lawrence sailed, the *Columbian Centinel* recalled: "The
public mind experienced much agitation all yesterday, in expectation of witnessing from the high grounds or house-tops a naval recontre between the
U.S. frigate *Chesapeake* . . . commanded by the gallant Capt. Lawrence, and the
British frigate *Shannon* . . . commanded by Capt. P.V. Broke. . . ."[1]

Bostonians and their neighbors knew something big was about to take
place. The purpose and intermittent presence in Boston Bay of the *Shannon*
and the *Tenedos*, H.M.S. *LaHogue*, 74, and H.M.S. *Curlew*, 18, was common
knowledge. Repeated reports of the activity of these ships made their way
to town. One report stood out because it included an insight into the thinking of Broke. On May 22, the *Shannon* captured the little coaster *Mary Ann* off
Cape Cod from New Haven bound for Eastport. The British removed her
cargo of corn, flour, and pork (almost certainly intended to be smuggled
across the border to the British), burned her, and put her captain and crew
on a fisherman to be landed at Boston. Once ashore, the captain reported it
was Broke's determination to engage either the *Chesapeake* or the *Constitution*,
also at Boston.

Early in the morning of the 1st, the *Shannon* defiantly passed close to Boston Light to look things over. Broke saw the *Chesapeake* lying at anchor in
President Roads with royal yards across and seemingly ready for sea. And
"the British colors were then hoisted on board the Shannon, and she hove to,
near the land," before moving along.[2] In town, as the last navy boat left the

---

1 *Columbian Centinel* (MA), June 2, 2813.
2 *Weekly Messenger* (MA), June 25, 1813.

wharf for the *Chesapeake*, a man in the crowd who had spent years working the yards in Halifax spotted a friend in the boat. He shouted to his acquaintance: "'Good-bye Sam; you is going to Halifax before you comes back to Bosting; give my lub to requiring friends, and tell 'em I is berry well.' For this harmless but inappropriate sally he was instantly thrown into the dock, amid the execrations and derision of the enraged citizens, and narrowly escaped with his life."[1]

Lawrence began to move the *Chesapeake* at 8:00 a.m., had her last anchor up by noon, and "passed the Light-House, at half past 1 o'clock."[2] All alongshore, people rushed to vantage points expecting to see a memorable fight. Crowds flocked to available heights from Lynn to Malden, from Cohasset to Scituate. Reverend William Bentley of Salem said Legge's hill appeared "black . . . like the swarm of bees."[3] Captain Nathaniel Spooner, Jr. of Plymouth, like others, raced to the state house roof, one of the most elevated spots around. Upon looking over the scene with a trained eye, Spooner had second thoughts. He correctly sensed any confrontation would take place out of view from the land. Spooner scurried down to India Wharf and got one of the last slots on a packet sloop about to depart to follow the action. The *Centinel* reported the "bay was covered with craft and boats . . . full of passengers."[4] Many tagged along at a safe distance behind the *Chesapeake*. And the three young Marshfield fishermen rested on their oars and prepared to take in the historic drama.

The two frigates seemed evenly matched. The *Shannon* carried 52 guns and a crew of about 349. The *Chesapeake* mounted 50 guns and had a complement of some 387. But this simple comparison does not go far enough. The British crew, completing a lengthy patrol, was experienced with its ship and the officers understood both. The *Chesapeake* manning presented an altogether different situation. Lawrence assumed command of the ship less than two weeks earlier. It is believed he walked in the Boston Common all the night before sailing, pondering the challenging task he faced. To begin, he had difficulty filling his crew. Many of the men from the previous cruise left the ship in April when their two-year enlistments expired, grumbling about the distribution of prize money. Fresh hands did not rush to enter the unlucky *Chesapeake*. Lawrence found it necessary to draft a contingent from the *Constitution*. Some of the new men did not make it on board until the last moment, "their hammocks and bags lying in the boats stowed over the booms when the ship was captured."[5] Dispute lingers as to the proficiency or experience of the crew as a whole. Nonetheless, setting questions of qualifications aside, the crew could not be considered a fine-tuned team. More critical, the officers under Lawrence were ordinary members of the service.

1 Brighton, *Admiral of the Fleet Sir Provo W.P. Wallis*, 111.
2 *Weekly Messenger* (MA), June 4, 1813.
3 Bentley, *Diary of William Bentley*, 4:172.
4 *Columbian Centinel* (MA), June 2, 1813.
5 Roosevelt, *Naval War of 1812*, 1:223-224.

The first lieutenant from the last cruise was taken off the ship mortally ill. The second lieutenant and an acting lieutenant were away sick, while the other acting lieutenant was judged disruptive and released from his assignment. Augustus Ludlow, just 21 with nine years of service and the previous third lieutenant, advanced to the first lieutenant post under Lawrence. George Budd, a lieutenant for only a year, sailed as his second lieutenant. Two teenage midshipmen received acting lieutenancies just before departure. William S. Cox became the acting third lieutenant, and Edward J. Ballard was named acting fourth lieutenant. With immediate combat so likely, William Bainbridge, the commandant at Boston should have intervened and delayed the sailing until the *Chesapeake* was in the abest possible order. Bainbridge even declined to reassign *Constitution* men to Lawrence's ship. He simply looked the other way and left Lawrence to his own devices. In fact, one report indicates "he did not see Capt. L. for several days previous to his sailing."[1]

Broke, on the other hand, felt fully prepared. After seven years in command of the *Shannon*, there was not much he did not know about his ship. As to the business at hand, probably more than any other British commander, Broke excelled in the field of gunnery, and he put his gun crews through repetitive drills. In a display of supreme confidence, he sent Lawrence a chivalric and provocative challenge, dated June 1. The British captain began his letter by expressing disappointment with Commodore John Rodgers who earlier declined to accept "various *Verbal*" challenges.[2] The *Centinel* seemed to support the point when it revealed: "Numerous reports of challenges, &c, were as usual in free circulation."[3] The veteran commodore avoided a showdown when he took advantage of weather conditions and in the *President*, along with Captain John Smith in the *Congress*, departed Boston on April 30 and eluded the British ships. Broke outlined to Lawrence his "assurance of a fair meeting."[4] He detailed his armament and manpower, "because a report has prevailed in some Boston papers, that we had one Hundred and Fifty Men additional lent us from *La Hogue*, which really never was the case." The Briton promised an even fight. "I will warn you, (if sailing under this promise) should any of my Friends be too nigh, or any where in sight, — until I can detach them out of our way; or I would sail *with you*, under a truce Flag, to any place you think safest from our Cruisers, hauling it down when fair to begin Hostilities;. . . ." He closed: "[C]hoose your terms, *but let us meet*."[5]

Broke signed the letter and placed it in an envelope addressed to the *Chesapeake* captain. He called for Captain Eben Slocum, one of his 30 American prisoners. Captured hours earlier in his cutter, Slocum could not control his tongue. The British gagged him, placed him in irons, and burned his

---

1 Irving, *Spanish Papers*, 2:58.
2 Dudley, *Naval War of 1812*, 2:126.
3 *Columbian Centinel* (MA), June 2, 1813.
4 Dudley, 126.
5 Ibid., 128.

boat. William Stack, *Shannon's* coxswain, recalled Broke would have released Slocum and his vessel if he "had not been so saucy to our Captain and told him if he had a ship of force he would soon drive him off the coast or carry him into Boston: and as soon as he would go into Boston that there would be a ship sent to bring us into or drive us off the coast."[1] Broke surmised the unruly Slocum would be a reliable messenger. Handed the envelope and put in a boat for Marblehead, Slocum gained his freedom by simply agreeing to post the letter. Lawrence left without receiving the written challenge, but he was well aware of Broke's interest in a fight, an interest he shared. Just before sailing, he wrote to the secretary: "An English frigate is now in sight from our deck. . . . I am in hopes to give a good account of her before night."[2]

Lawrence kept his eyes on the *Shannon* from the outset, gave chase, and cleared his ship for action. "At 4 o'clock the C. hauled up, and hoisted jib and staysails and fired a gun — the ships at this time about 7 miles apart."[3] As a result of the clear challenge, Shannon hove to at 4:30 p.m. on a line between Provincetown and Cape Ann, approximately 30 miles east of Boston Light. The letter-report ascribed to Broke said the *Chesapeake* "came down in a very handsome manner, having three American Ensigns flying."[4] The *Chesapeake* also carried at the fore a large white banner declaring FREE TRADE AND SAILORS RIGHTS.

The *Shannon* displayed a single Union Jack, prompting one sailor to approach Broke and ask: "Sir, can't we have a new ensign?

"No, lads," he answered. "We've always been an unassuming ship. One ensign at a time is enough for us. But roll up another one and seize it in the main-rigging, to be ready if our first is shot away. Then roll up another, and seize it on the mainstay, in case the second is shot away."[5]

At 5:30 p.m., the *Chesapeake* "hauled up within hail" of the waiting *Shannon*, went into fighting trim, and "the Battle began."[6] Captain Spooner, five miles away, in a next-day letter, recalled: "I had a good opportunity to observe them as we had a good Spy Glass on bd and the weather was very fine."[7] Spooner and the others afloat nearby witnessed what a Halifax newspaper described as the "fairest, shortest, severest and most decisive actions ever fought between two ships of equal force."[8]

Coming down rapidly on the Briton's starboard, Lawrence did not take the open opportunity of passing under her stern and raking her. Instead, the *Chesapeake* put her helm up to assume a parallel course within pistol shot of the enemy ship. Under orders to wait until he sighted the second main-deck port from forward, the captain of *Shannon's* 14th gun held back until 5:50 p.m.

1 Pullen, *Shannon and the Chesapeake*, 94.
2 Roosevelt, 227.
3 *Weekly Messenger* (MA), June 4, 1813.
4 Dudley, 129.
5 Snider, *Glorious Shannon's Old Blue Duster*, 4-5.
6 Dudley, 129.
7 *Massachusetts Historical Society Proceedings*, 1:376.
8 *Columbian Centinel* (MA), July 7, 1813.

As soon as he let loose, down the line, the other guns fired in rapid order. Lawrence answered with a full broadside. "The first broadside," wrote Budd, "did great execution on both sides."[1] For some eight minutes, the two antagonists pounded away. "They were warm at it enveloped in smoke and fire."[2] Nelson's summary of the 1801 Battle of Copenhagen is an apt description of the encounter. "Here was no manoeuvring; it was downright fighting."[3] People on Cape Cod distinctly heard the commotion similar to distant thunder.

After devastating exchanges, the *Chesapeake* fell on board the enemy ship, her mizzen (aft) rigging fouling the *Shannon*'s fore rigging. A British attempt to lash the ships to one another failed, but it became unnecessary. The pair locked together, and Lawrence called for boarders. Since the American bugler had fled from his post in fright, it became necessary for Budd to shout the boarding order. In the din of battle, this vocal approach proved ineffective and contributed to hesitancy and confusion. At this critical moment, a British marine shot and mortally wounded the conspicuous American captain at the center of the action. As young Cox and several sailors rushed to his aid, Lawrence continued to call for boarders. Without thinking, Cox made the error of leaving the deck where he was needed, and helped carry his captain out of the field of fire. Once below, Lawrence gasped: "Go on deck, and order them to fire faster and to fight the ship till she sinks; never strike, let the colors wave while I live." When he sensed defeat was at hand, repeatedly, he cried: "Don't give up the ship, blow her up."[4]

At the same instant, Broke ran forward on his ship to evaluate the situation. He noted great disorder and gunners flinching on the *Chesapeake*. Sensing the two ships might drift apart, he seized the moment. At 6:02 p.m., drawing his sword, he vaulted over the bulwarks and headed for the enemy's quarterdeck shouting, "Follow me who can!"[5] Ludlow, already wounded, fell mortally struck in the wild and chaotic resistance. According to Broke, the "firing continued at all the Gangways and between the Tops, but in two minutes time the Enemy were driven Sword in hand from every Post."[6] As he led the advance, three Americans engaged Broke in hand-to-hand combat, clubbing him with a musket and cutting him down with a broadsword before being overwhelmed by supporting British attackers. While his men attended to the seriously wounded Broke, one looked aft, turned back, and exclaimed: "There, sir, there goes up the old ensign over the yankee colours."[7]

The ceremonial finishing stroke, however, proved tragic for the British. First Lieutenant George Watt of the *Shannon* carried a large white ensign when he boarded the enemy. A small British blue ensign first made its way

---

1 Dudley, 134.
2 *Columbian Centinel* (MA), June 2, 1813.
3 Mahan, *Life of Nelson*, 480.
4 Lovette, *Naval Customs, Traditions and Usage*, 200.
5 Poolman, *Guns off Cape Ann*, 111.
6 Dudley, 129.
7 James, *Naval History of Great Britain*, 4:203.

to the *Chesapeake*'s mizzen gaff (spar). Watt wanted a more dominant visual indication of surrender and he moved to replace the small flag with his larger version. In the turmoil, halyards got tangled, and the Stars and Stripes moved up before the blue Union Jack. The captain of *Shannon*'s No. 7 gun mistook the flag raisers for Americans retaking their ship. He fired a charge of grapeshot at the group, killing Watt and six of his men and wounding other Brits.

John Collier, *Shannon*'s captain of the maintop, years later recalled the turbulent American defense. In the weeks following the battle, he often talked to Broke at Halifax. On one occasion, the captain asked Collier if after the fight he ever saw Samuel Livermore, the acting chaplain of the *Chesapeake*. "I said I had not. He said that he had a struggle with him on the deck of his ship. I merely mention this as it occurs to me to show what desperate resources they must have been driven to for a minister to have a sword in his hand, instead of the olive branch of peace. . . ."[1]

The fight took all of 15 minutes, but the carnage was awful. In the initial confusion that follows violence on such a scale, different casualty figures are to be expected. And the number of fatalities changed as some of the wounded succumbed in the days that followed. A universally accepted casualty figure, therefore, remains elusive. United States casualties are most often said to total around 148 (with 48 dead). British casualties, on the other hand, are commonly said to add up to 84 (with 34 killed). The American losses amounted to about 37 percent while the overall British losses came to about 22 percent. Every *Chesapeake* officer was killed or wounded. Ballard, as well as Lawrence and Ludlow, suffered mortal wounds in the early going; Budd suffered serious wounds as he tried to board the enemy.

Once the shooting stopped, British sailors gently carried their seriously wounded captain back over to his cabin. Second Lieutenant Provo W.P. Wallis and Third Lieutenant Charles Falkiner survived unscathed. The pair assumed the towering responsibility of saving the two damaged frigates and escaping to Halifax. Wallis, in fact, became what might be described as the ultimate survivor in the history of the Royal Navy or any other navy, the most enduring figure of the War of 1812.

Born in Halifax, Nova Scotia in 1791, the 22-year-old Wallis unbelievably entered upon the navy rolls at age four! His father Provo F. Wallis worked as the chief clerk at the Halifax dockyard and knew his way around the navy and knew its rules. He convinced Captain Robert Murray to enter his 4-year-old as an able-bodied seaman on the books of the frigate *Oiseau*, 36. The boy, of course, did not serve on the ship, but the not uncommon ploy started his seniority count. When young Wallis did report for active duty in 1804 as a 13-year-old midshipman on the *Cleopatra*, 32, he possessed almost a decade of seniority. But the best was yet to come. In 1863, still on the active list, he received promotion to full admiral. In 1877, his seniority enabled him to suc-

---

1 Pullen, 93.

ceed to the honorary slot of Admiral of the Fleet, theoretically placing him at the head of the Royal Navy. When he reached his late nineties, the Admiralty suggested he retire. Still on the active list receiving full pay, he was reminded this made him subject to sea duty. He replied he was ready for such a call. Wallis continued in the top post until he died just short of age 101. His career spanned 96 years, a matchless record.

For the time being, however, Wallis had his hands full. To begin, there were around five dozen dead to commit to a spacious grave. The melancholy task was performed with tenderness, "yet quickly; sadly, and with few words."[1] More important, some 150 wounded men needed medical attention. In the confusion of the moment, Ludlow found himself overlooked and unattended in *Chesapeake*'s steerage. He asked a British sailor: "Will you tell the commanding officer of the *Shannon* that Mr. Ludlow, first of the *Chesapeake*, is lying here badly wounded?"[2] With haste, the victors initially moved him to poor Watt's berth.

Wallis also faced the problem of restraining some 250 largely hostile prisoners. On the *Chesapeake*, the British found "some hundreds of handcuffs in readiness for us, so we ornamented them with their own manacles."[3] And both ships required repairs. Lower masts suffered considerable damage, and the two warships were hurtfully holed. Wallis had only around 250 men to help with these critical tasks.

Falkiner took charge of the *Chesapeake* and moved to secure his command. Keeping on the safe side, his cautious and vigorous policing measures received negative coverage. Parts of the American press portrayed him as "shameful and barbarous."[4] An outspoken Niles tied the Federalists to the lieutenant's reputed malevolence. "The brutality of the British," he wrote, ". . . has been constantly stated — were the facts different from the reports given the world, they would have been denied, for we have thousands that 'leave no stone unturned' to exhibit the enemy as models of perfection — 'the shield of afflicted humanity, and bulwark of religion.' But the verity of these things have not been impeached; and we accept them as incontrovertible truths."[5]

Midshipman William Berry stirred the pot as much as anybody when later he complained about prisoner treatment to New Jersey Congressman Lewis Condict. Berry alleged Falkiner unnecessarily ordered his men to shoot at two American midshipmen in the fore and main tops imploring them to "kill those damned rascals." After the Brits fired "without effect," the lieutenant spotted Berry in the mizzen top and sent three men up to "throw that damned Yankee overboard. They immediately rushed up, seizing me by the collar," reported Berry, "now, said they, you damned Yankee, you shall swim for it, attempting to throw me overboard; but I got within the rigging, when

1 Brighton, *Admiral Sir P.B.V. Broke*, 176.
2 Ibid., 175.
3 Pullen, 64.
4 *Baltimore Whig*, October 28, 1813.
5 *Niles' Weekly Register*, September 1, 1813.

one of them kicked me in the breast, which was the cause of my falling; being stunned by the fall, I lay some time senseless, and, when I came too, I was cut over the head with a cutlass, which nearly terminated my existence."[1]

Midshipman William A. Weaver also wrote to Condict and claimed Falkiner "ordered sentinels to be placed at the mizzen mast; and, said he to them, if you see any of the Chesapeake's officers abaft the mizzen mast, cut them down; if you see them conversing together, cut them down without hesitation."[2]

Washington Irving in his 1813 biography of Lawrence said British treatment of Chesapeake prisoners was not "dishonorable," and published accounts to the contrary tended to be "incredible or untrue."[3] Roosevelt dismissed the charges and countercharges, noting anybody could go to James for one side or Niles for the other view. Falkiner gave his drastic orders so he would be heard by the prisoners, hoping this would intimidate or discourage schemes of uprising or troublemaking. The approach seemed to work, because the guards did not find it necessary to cut down any prisoners. The matter of securing the Americans remained an overriding priority, however. During the first night, Falkiner became so concerned he signaled Wallis to stop and take another group of prisoners over on the Shannon.

The two undermanned and injured ships remained quite vulnerable en route to safety in Nova Scotia. William Stack said the two ships bore up for Halifax passing within three miles of Cape Ann "where the shore was crowded with people where we could have cheered them; but the Captain's head was bad, and we did not wish to disturb him."[4] Wallis feared the appearance of the President or the Congress, or both. He seldom left the deck, and barely slept. The gravely wounded Ludlow, in fact, now occupied his bunk. The Shannon and her prize finally made Sambro Light off Halifax on June 4, but heavy fog held them in place. In a state of clouded consciousness, Lawrence continued to mumble his famous final order until the end came that night. Both American and British surgeons had attended Lawrence even after it became obvious to everyone, including the patient, his case was hopeless. With solemn respect, the British draped his body in an American flag and laid him on the quarter-deck of the Chesapeake. The fog lifted on Sunday the 6th and both ships made port. The crew of the H.M.S. Boxer, Captain Samuel Blyth, was among the crews that manned their rigging and watched as the two frigates passed. Generally, the crews did not cheer. An American witness explained: "Captain Lawrence was highly respected for his humanity to the crew of the [H.M.S.] Peacock [earlier defeated by Lawrence in the Hornet], and marks of real grief were seen in the countenances of all the inhabitants. .

---

1 American State Papers: Military Affairs 1:382.
2 Ibid.
3 American Mercury (CT), November 9, 1813.
4 Pullen, 98.

. . I heard several say they considered the blood which had been shed on the *Chesapeake*'s deck as dear as that of their own countrymen."[1]

Under "a discharge of minute guns," the British removed Lawrence's body to the King's Wharf early in the afternoon. His sword was placed on his flag-draped coffin. A funeral followed on the 8th. Six companies of the 64th Regiment of Foot led the funeral party, and "six captains of the navy officiated as pallbearers." The "officers of the Chesapeake followed it as mourners — the officers of the navy generally attended . . . and the procession was closed by a number of respectable inhabitants."[2] Captain Blyth served as one of the pallbearers. The garrison orders for the occasion required the British officers wear "a piece of black crape round their left arm."[3] Five days later, the ceremony was repeated for Lieutenant Augustus Ludlow who expired on shore.

As might be expected, the local press celebrated. The *Halifax Journal* on June 7 detailed a "NOBLE DEED OF HEROISM."[4] *The Weekly Chronicle* of Halifax thought "the lightning like rapidity of the action (not exceeding 10 or 11 minutes) seems almost unparalleled, even in the annals of the British Navy."[5] The *Acadian Recorder* crowed: "The result of this action is what might reasonably be expected, but there are circumstances attending it, which will ever make it memorable, and which causes our regret that instead of the *Chesapeake* it had not been the largest frigate of the United States, commanded by their ablest Captain."[6] London went all out in its celebration of the turn of events. After all, as Captain Brenton later wrote, by the end of May, the Royal Navy, "depressed by repeated mortifications, had in some measure lost its spirits; and the dissatisfaction expressed in the public journals of the empire produced, as no doubt many of the writers intended, a feeling of discontent and disgust in the bosoms of our seamen. This melancholy impression was, however, removed by the fortunate and gallant action fought on the 1st of June, 1813."[7] Admiral Napier, another partial observer, offered a consanguine compliment when he observed the "Americans behaved with great bravery (and why should they not? they are our children), but nothing could withstand the discipline of the 'Shannon.'"[8]

Back in Boston, in the first few days after the fight, the people did not want to believe the obvious. One newspaper described the crowds that "collected at the corners of the streets, seizing with avidity at every tale which varies in every narration."[9] Another observed: "Among the officers of the *Chesapeake* were many young gentlemen of this town — and till the particulars

1 Ibid., 114.
2 *Niles'*, June 26, 1813.
3 *Weekly Messenger* (MA), July 3, 1813.
4 Pullen, 81.
5 Ibid., 85.
6 Ibid., 88.
7 Brenton, *Naval History of Great Britain*, 2:490.
8 Napier, *Life and Correspondence of Admiral Sir Charles Napier*, 1:74.
9 *Daily Advertiser* (MA), June 3, 1813.

of the battle are known, great anxiety will prevail."[1] Three weeks passed before the disaster gained general acceptance. An American army officer on the eastern shore of Maryland heard the news from an English navy officer while the two conferred under a flag of truce. Initially believing the report a lie, the American finally accepted the disheartening news. "That G_d d_n particular ship, I guess, is always bringing the States into some scrape or another."[2]

"I remember," said one man, "how the post-offices were thronged for successive days by anxious thousands; how collections of citizens rode out for miles on the highway, accosting the mail to catch something by anticipation. At last when the certainty was known, I remember the public gloom; funeral orations and badges of mourning bespoke it."[3] Finally, a cartel arrived in Boston from Halifax confirming the unhappy news that the Shannon indeed did take the Chesapeake and in the process "gave her a d----- drubbing."[4]

The papers began to fill with details and analysis. The Boston Gazette noted: "The recontre between the Chesapeake and Shannon has been the subject of more speculation and deeper interest than any which has occupied the attention of the public since the commencement of this strange war." The paper published a commentary from "A FRIEND TO THE NAVY" who supported Lawrence's tactics. "If he had engaged" the Shannon "at long shot, and she had escaped, serious complaints would have been made, that he did not lay his ship alongside, as all our brilliant victories have been so successfully gained by close fighting. We hope none will be so uncharitable as to inquire why the Chesapeake did not engage at long shot — If they should, the answer is at hand. It is not the American mode of engaging."[5]

A week later, the Gazette continued to rationalize the defeat "to alleviate our grief," a defeat that "created a pang of universal sorrow." The paper concluded, "[A] series of disadvantages and accidents occurred, against which no skill or prudence could have guarded." Foremost, the editor thought the tide turned when Lawrence did not receive Broke's challenge before sailing. Had he received the letter, "undoubtedly some of our oldest and most experienced Lieuts. would have volunteered for a fight. . . ." And "as far as we can judge one or two able officers, unhurt, would have turned the fortune of the day."[6] Livermore, speaking as a key participant in the ferocious struggle on Chesapeake's deck, made the same point upon his return to Boston. The idea that veteran supporting officers would have changed the outcome is sound. However, this simple position tends to blame wounded Cox, especially, and the seriously wounded Budd, as well as the deceased Ludlow and Ballard for the defeat and, as such, it misses a key factor.

---

1 New England Palladium (MA), June 4, 1813.
2 Scott, Recollections of a Naval Life, 3:129.
3 Paine, Fight for a Free Sea, 132.
4 Niles', June 19, 1813.
5 Boston Gazette, June 24, 1813.
6 Ibid., July 1, 1813.

Lawrence left Boston when he did with one immediate objective in mind — to take on and thrash the *Shannon*. Everyone at the yard knew this. "So great was the confidence that the *Chesapeake* would win, and swiftly, that a wharf was specially cleared to take the battered *Shannon*, and preparations were begun for a victory supper that night, at which the surviving British officers would be guests."[1] Plainly put, Bainbridge failed to meet his responsibilities as Boston commandant when he did not direct the dashing young captain of the *Chesapeake* to prudently follow the instructions of the secretary and get on station in the North Atlantic in the manner of Rodgers and Smith. A victory over the *Shannon* would not have any strategic value, while the loss of one of the few American frigates would be a major defeat. But, if Boston officers somehow felt it imperative to accept Broke's continuing and open challenge, there was little excuse for the absence of a more mature and experienced set of officers under Lawrence.

Although the *Gazette* continued to believe the "little Navy is surely the pride of the federalists,"[2] increasingly, some members of the party made it clear their deep-seated opposition to the yearlong war overrode such sentiments. Back in the Massachusetts Senate, Josiah Quincy enraged a good many people with one of his moves. After the fight, but prior to learning the fate of Lawrence, the Senate considered a resolution commending the officer for his earlier capture of the *Peacock*. Quincy blocked the measure, asserting "in a war like the present," it was not "becoming a moral and religious people to express any approbation of military and naval exploits."[3] The Republicans bellowed Quincy's action amounted to "moral treason."[4]

An incensed Captain George Crownshield, Jr. of Salem responded in a bold way. He hired the brig *Henry*, manned her with fellow shipmaster members of the Salem Marine Society, obtained governmental permission, and set out for Halifax under a flag of truce to recover the bodies of Lawrence and Ludlow. He returned in 11 days with the two corpses as well as seven *Chesapeake* crewmen. Meanwhile, the town planned a stately funeral for August 23 even though political feelings ran high. The chairman of the Proprietors' Committee of the North Meetinghouse refused the use of their building for the service, because the committee did not have the authority "to open the House for any other purpose than public worship."[5] In fact, he made sure their bell would not peel as the procession passed. As telling, the East India Marine Society decided to attend only on the strength of a 32 to 19 vote.

Despite pockets of partisanship, a majestic but melancholy observance proceeded.

"Early in the morning, almost every vessel in the harbour and at the wharves, and all the flag staffs in town, wore the American Ensign at half

---

1 Poolman, 80.
2 *Boston Gazette*, June 24, 1813.
3 Morison, *Maritime History of Massachusetts*, 198.
4 Barry, *History of Massachusetts: The Commonwealth Period*, 400.
5 *An Account of the Funeral Honours Bestowed on the Remains of Capt. Lawrence and Lieut. Ludlow*, 40.

mast."[1] Once the *Henry* came to anchor in the Salem harbor, attendants placed the two coffins in boats manned by sailors wearing hats decorated with ribbons bearing the slogan Free Trade and Sailors' Rights. The men rowed minute strokes to India Wharf, and all the while the U.S. brig *Rattlesnake*, 14, and the *Henry* alternated firing minute guns. "The immense concourse of citizens which covered the wharves, stores, and housetops to view the boats, the profound silence which pervaded the atmosphere, broken only by the sad reverberations of the minute-guns, rendered this part of the solemnities peculiarly grand and impressive."[2]

Vice President Elbridge Gerry led the mourners, and six navy captains, including Hull and Bainbridge, served as pallbearers. "The procession was such, in point of respectability and numbers, as was never before witnessed in Salem."[3] However, "not an Officer of the State Government appeared with any badge of Office."[4] Associate Justice of the Supreme Court of the United States Joseph Story delivered the eulogy. Of the two fallen officers, Story believed: "Their fellow countrymen shall turn with a fond and holy reverence to the place of their sepulture — and when time shall abate the anguish of unutterable sorrow, they shall delight to point to the young and the old, to the warrior and to the statesman, the example of those who never caused a sigh from their country, but at their death."[5] The *Essex Register*, quoted in the *Gazette*, reported the eulogy "was such . . . as made veterans weep."[6] The bodies were temporarily interred prior to movement within days to New York City for final burial. Washington Irving summed up Lawrence's hold on a great many Americans when he wrote: "He passed before the public eye like a star, just beaming on it for a moment, and falling in the midst of his brightness."[7]

The mournful episode did not end at this stage. Contentiousness typified the navy of the period as the service strived to establish its organizational identity. In the process, an inordinate number of officers became the subjects of or principals in courts of inquiry or courts-martial. In such a climate, the loss of a valuable frigate invited assessment of blame. Formal organizations, because of the nature of their protective power structures, habitually calculate to push culpability down to the lowest possible levels of their pyramids. In the *Chesapeake* disaster, those in power saw fit to blame the loss on a young acting lieutenant and a black bugler. A general court-martial held on the *United States* locked up in the Thames River below Norwich found William Cox guilty of neglect of duty and unofficer-like conduct for carrying Lawrence below instead of leading the fight on deck. The court banished Cox from the navy. Then it sentenced the bugler to 300 lashes for cowardice.

---

1 *Boston Gazette*, August 26, 1813.
2 Trow, *Old Shipmasters of Salem*, 110.
3 *Boston Gazette*, August 26, 1813.
4 Bentley, 191.
5 *An Account*, 43.
6 *Boston Gazette*, August 26, 1813.
7 Pool, *A Catalogue*, 15.

In the weeks to follow, veteran officers muted their criticism of Lawrence's rashness. Just a few editors questioned his impulsiveness as Washington Irving rushed a heroic biography to print. Cox became the public scapegoat in the unforgettable *Chesapeake* tragedy; although President Harry Truman signed a bill in 1952 restoring his rank and standing.

Shortly after serving as a pallbearer for Lawrence in Halifax, Captain Blyth took the *Boxer* to the Passamaquoddy area. Off West Quoddy, he halted a barge carrying several ladies, including the wife of Colonel George Ulmer, commandant of the American forces at nearby Fort Sullivan. "The first impulse of our noble-hearted seaman," reported *The Naval Chronicle*, "led him to use the gentlest words that the most bland and polished manners could dictate to assuage their fears." Blyth immediately released the ladies and their barge, prompting Ulmer to reply with a card "acknowledging the politeness shewn to his Lady."[1]

Ironically, Eastporters and their neighbors held Ulmer in especially low regard while they viewed Blyth with good favor. "Ulmer was much disliked. The citizens, unable to bear the insults and oppressions which he authorized or permitted," created a committee to examine his conduct and report the findings. The report charged, "the inhabitants suffered the most wanton and unprovoked injuries" as a result of Ulmer's officious approach to his duties.[2] For some months, Ulmer had struggled to restrict intercourse with New Brunswick and Nova Scotia. In January, he sent a strong letter to the Eastport selectmen ordering every person in town not an American citizen or subject to take an oath of allegiance or be considered a prisoner of war. "And every citizen who shall hereafter pass into the British dominions, except by permission from the commanding officer of this frontier," he said, "will be considered as carrying information to the enemy, and will be dealt with accordingly." As well, Ulmer declared anyone supplying the enemy or a British subject "with provisions of any kind . . . will be apprehended for treason."[3] None of this went over well.

By contrast, the 30-year-old Blyth earned respect "for his manly and generous conduct. . . . His visits were often ill-timed, for it was his fortune to intercept supplies at moments of absolute want; but, though in the course of his duty he caused distress, he was liberal in adjusting terms of ransom, and treated his prisoners with kindness."[4] Late in August, he halted another small boat close to shore manned by three locals. The conversation turned to the U.S. brig *Enterprise* preparing for sea at Portsmouth. Blyth indicated he hoped to encounter her, because "seizing upon craft like theirs was detestable business, and that he wished to make a prize honorable to his profession." One of the men cautioned, he "had better keep clear of the 'Enterprise,'

---

1 *Naval Chronicle*, 33:460.
2 Kilby, *Eastport and Passamaquoddy*, 161.
3 *The War* (NY), February 9, 1813.
4 Kilby, 168.

for she would surely prove a 'Scotch prize [no prize at all].'" The remark amused Blyth, and with a chuckle, he replied, "Oh, no!"

Blyth eventually became quite close to some businessmen operating Down East, and the alliance led to his downfall. While not tending to his important militia duties, General William King of Bath continued to oversee his substantial commercial ventures. He held half interest in the brig *Latona* which showed up in Saint John, New Brunswick with Swedish papers and the name *Margaretta*. Charles Tappan, a Portsmouth merchant, and others, were on board. As Tappan recalled, they "filled her with British goods, intending to take them to Bath, Maine, and enter them regularly and pay the lawful duties thereon. All we had to fear was American privateers; and we hired Capt. Blyth, of H.B.M. Brig *Boxer*, to convoy us to the mouth of the Kennebec river. . . ." The King-Tappan group paid Blyth 100 pounds by a bill of exchange on London. All of this was routine according to Tappan, since "many American merchants imported, via Halifax and St. John, N.B., their usual stock of goods."[1]

The *Margaretta* carried a heavy load, including bales of English woolens and 193 suspicious casks. When a thick fog around Quoddy Head threatened to separate the two ships, the *Boxer* took the struggling Bath ship in tow. As agreed, when the pair reached the area of Seguin Island Light, the merchant-man scooted for the river and the man-of-war lobbed two or three shots over the *Margaretta*. Tappan explained the charade would "have the appearance of trying to stop us, should any idle folks be looking on."[2]

Whether idle folks paid any attention is unknown. Local fishermen, however, did observe the performance. One sailed to Portland, 25 miles away, and, on Saturday the 4th of September, sought out Lieutenant William Burrows to report the British presence. Burrows had arrived in Portland at the end of August in the U.S. brig *Enterprise* for a two-week patrol to the Kennebec "to protect the coas[t]ing trade."[3] Just 27 years of age, he was away on business in China when the war began and he did not gain his command until the first of August 1813. Once he heard all the fisherman had to say about the action off Sequin, Burrows wasted little time in getting under way.

Blyth planned to remain in the area for a few days. Early on September 4, he stopped at Monhegan and allowed his surgeon, a Mr. Anderson, to attend to "a Cripple son of Mr. Starling an inhabitant of the Island." Also, Lieutenant John A. Allen of the 64th Regiment, on the ship to improve his health, and Midshipmen Nixon and Pile went on shore to shoot pigeons. The *Boxer* "suddenly & unexpectedly" left without the four men,[4] and moved across Muscongus Bay, eventually anchoring that evening next to Johns Island near the entrance to Pemaquid Harbor.

---

1 Goold, *Portland in the Past*, 481-482.
2 Ibid., 482.
3 Dudley, 233.
4 Ibid., 238.

"The inhabitants at Pemaquid, fearing an attack quickly withdrew into the woods, and at evening heard the music playing on board the enemies' cruiser."[1] The local militia company marched to the scene and set up at the site of old Fort Frederick. On the next day, Sunday the 5th, all "received a scare . . ., when a launch came ashore to pick berries and stretch their legs."[2] After a short period, a ship's lookout spotted a strange sail proceeding toward them from the west. The *Boxer* recalled her shore party "and immediately made sail, giving a parting shot over St. John's island into the village of Pemaquid by way of farewell."[3]

The *Boxer* soon fired three defiance or challenge shots downwind toward the distant stranger. This gained widespread attention locally. "Many left their homes to seek better places of observation, and multitudes on the shores and hills waited with anxiety the result of the contest."[4] Reverend Jabez Pond Fisher heard the commotion while leading services in his Boothbay church. He "hesitated in his discourse, listened an instant and then, with a brief word or two as to what he suspected it might be, dismissed his congregation."[5] The meeting adjourned to the high ground of Kenniston's hill. On Monhegan, Josiah Starling, then a boy, recalled many years later that at midday "we went t' the top o' the hill, takin' a spy-glass with us, 'n' there we wuz jined by three officers of the Britisher . . . who wuz ashore, gunnin', the day afore, 'n' didn't hear the signal."[6] With the glass, Starling's father discovered the two warships rushing toward one another. The little group on the hill behind the village appreciated they occupied one of the best spots to watch the drama unfold.

Once Burrows assessed the object and strength of his charging foe, he "hauled upon a wind to stand out of the bay, and at 3 o'clock shortened sail, tacked, and ran down with an intention to bring her to close action."[7] According to William Barnes, a youthful member of the *Enterprise* crew and later a respected Woolwich, Maine sea captain, "[I]n the anxious hours of preliminary tactics the contestants ranged and circled in free sea-room between Monhegan and Seguin."[8] The maneuvering consumed six hours due to intermittent calm winds. When the fight began, the two ships were about eight miles southeast of Seguin. When it ended, according to Barnes, the ships were "some four or five miles east from Pemaquid point, four miles southwest of East Egg Rock . . . and about seven miles west north west of Monhegan."[9]

---

1 *Bath (ME) Daily Times*, October 19, 1878.
2 Fearson, "The Scalping of the Boxer," 3.
3 *Bath (ME) Independent*, November 10, 1883.
4 Johnston, *A History of the Towns of Bristol and Bremen*, 407.
5 Greene, *History of Boothbay*, 254.
6 Proper, *Monhegan*, 237.
7 *American State Papers: Naval Affairs* 1:297.
8 Henry O. Thayer, *Sprague's Journal*, 66.
9 Beston, *White Pine and Blue Water*, 81.

Before engaging, Burrows moved one of his two long 9-pounders from the bow to one of the stern ports. Suspicion circulated among the men that he was preparing to flee. The grumbling reached Burrows and he forcefully assured the crew: "WE are going to fight both ends and both sides of this ship as long as the ends and the sides hold together."[1] For his part, Blyth sent men aloft to nail a Union Jack to the foremast and two on the main-mast. This done, the English captain turned to his crew and "in a short and pithy speech, pointing to his flag," he told them: "IT SHOULD NEVER BE STRUCK WHILST HE HAD LIFE, and that he trusted they would resolve to take the enemy or go with him to the bottom!"[2]

"At twenty minutes after 3, P.M.," according to U.S. Lieutenant Edward R. McCall, "when within half pistol shot," the fight began.[3] The British gave three cheers and fired their starboard broadside. The Americans returned three cheers and a larboard broadside. In the opening moments, Captain Blyth moved to rally his gunners in the face of a fusillade of cannon shot. "Great God, what shots!" he exclaimed just as an 18-pound ball struck him dead.[4] Within moments, Burrows suffered a mortal wound. While helping his men run out a carronade, he propped a leg against the bulwark, and a musket ball hit his thigh and ripped into his body. Burrows dropped to the deck, but refused to be carried below. The surgeon, Dr. Bailey Washington, made the critically wounded captain as comfortable as possible, but could do little more. As the battle raged, Burrows repeatedly admonished, "Don't give up the ship! We'll take her yet."[5]

The management of the *Enterprise* devolved on McCall, and after about 15 minutes of pounding away, he began to maneuver. Lieutenant David McGrery now commanded the *Boxer*. The American "ranged ahead, rounded to on the starboard tack, and raked the *Boxer* with the starboard guns."[6] Then, setting her foresail, she moved to the Briton's starboard bow and raked her some more. By 3:45 p.m., the *Boxer*, according to McGrery, was a "complete wreck; all the Braces and Rigging shot away, the Main top Mast and top gallt. Mast hanging over the side, Fore and MainMasts nearly gone, and to-tally unmanageable; with only our Quarter Deck Guns manned; Three feet water in the hold; No Surgeon to attend the Wounded. . . ."[7]

The flags on the mainmast were shot away, and the Englishman's colors remained nailed to the foremast; "but his tongue was not fastened and he called for quarters. . . ."[8] The fight took 30 minutes. McGrery came over and offered Blyth's sword to McCall. The American officer declined the offer, and said Burrows, still living, deserved the honor. The two lieutenants went aft

---

1 Snider, 267.

2 *Naval Chronicle*, 33:469.

3 *American State Papers: Naval Affairs* 1:297.

4 Beston, 80

5 Picking, *Sea Fight off Monhegan*, 43.

6 Roosevelt, 263.

7 Dudley, 234.

8 *Niles'*, September 18, 1813.

where Burrows lay bleeding to death. On receiving the sword, he said, "*I am satisfied, I die contented.*"[1] In his last act, Burrows directed McCall to send Blyth's sword to the Blyth family. The *Enterprise* captain died eight hours later as the two ships struggled to make Portland.

As in the *Chesapeake-Shannon* encounter, in the present case, personnel and casualty totals are not firm. The *Enterprise* appeared to go into the engagement with 102 men. A seaman died in the fighting and Burrows and a carpenter's mate died within hours. In the end, four Americans died as a result of the battle. Midshipman Kerwin Waters suffered mortal wounds, but lingered for two years. Ten other *Enterprise* men received wounds. On the British side, out of a crew of 66 men, 17 ended up with wounds, 4 of them mortally. The number killed outright is difficult to pin down. When the prize crew reached the *Boxer*, they reportedly observed crewmembers throwing bodies over the side. And six bodies were found on the deck, draped in the British flag. McCall initially said, "[I]t appears there were between twenty and thirty-five killed, and fourteen wounded."[2] However, based on interviews with *Enterprise* officers, both the *Portland Gazette* and the *Argus* reported the number of British killed was unknown. Be this as it may, casualty totals aside, the outcome proved decisive.

When the smoke cleared and the two ships turned west toward Portland instead of east toward Halifax, several men gathered on Pemaquid Point gave three cheers and drank to the victory. Captain Jotham Johnson of Harpswell found himself much closer to the action. The local mariner recalled the contest and the move to Portland. "On their way as I lay at anchor the Boxer drifted down on my vessel. I paid out all the cable that I had and then took an oar and put it against the side of the Boxer and shoved her off. I immediately got under way and followed into Portland."[3]

While the British surgeon found himself stranded on Monhegan, his American counterpart, Dr. Washington, labored alone throughout the night and into the next afternoon. The *Enterprise* reached Fort Preble at 2:00 p.m. on Monday, and Navy Agent Samuel Storer took account of the situation. He penned a hasty report to Captain Hull, the commandant at Portsmouth. Hull passed the news to Bainbridge at Boston. Hull also issued detailed instructions to Surgeon Samuel Ayer at Portland, telling him to assist Washington "as he may require." Hull emphasized, "that no distinction is made between the Crew of the *Enterprize* and that of the *Boxer*." The captain also wanted a weekly report on injured British prisoners, noting when they are "so far recovered as to enable them to desert you will deliver them over to the Marshal. . . ."[4]

News of the victory spread rapidly. In Wiscasset, Joseph Wood wrote to a business associate: "As to news, I have with much pleasure (for a Tory) to

1 Goold, 484.
2 *American State Papers: Naval Affairs* 1:297.
3 Jotham Johnson, *Statement.*
4 Dudley, 239.

say that yesterday my store windows were for a third time broken in the rejoicing for a naval victory, at the mouth of our River. . . ." He summarized the event and added, "[F]urther particulars we have not heard, the Wind being ahead they bore away for Portland."[1] The keeper of the Portland Observatory, Captain Lemuel Moody, with his telescope tracked the two ships as they progressed toward Portland and reported to a crowd gathered below.

Once the vessels arrived in the harbor, anybody could go on board and look things over. Many took the opportunity. One of the visitors went on a special mission. An attorney by the name of Kinsman represented the merchants who employed the *Margaretta*. They considered the bill of exchange they had given Blyth a potential source of embarrassment at a minimum. Kinsman went to McCall before the officer completed an inventory and persuaded him to give over the bill and replace it with an untraceable $500 in specie. The note, pleaded Kinsman, could injure the Blyth reputation and lead to the arrest of Charles Tappan and others.

"I trust that this will go no further," cautioned McCall.

"It will go no further."[2]

Ezra Carter of Scarborough happened to be in Portland at the time and he took advantage of the opportunity to go on the *Boxer*. He found the ship "terribly battered and the decks were covered with splinters and blood from stem to stern." Sailors from both sides of the fight freely fraternized. Carter heard a Britisher tell a Yankee, "You had too many guns for us." The American retorted, "Count them up, we had no more than you, but we fired three broadsides to your two, and our aim was true while your shots went wild."[3] In fact, the *Enterprise* went into the fight armed with 16 guns compared to the 14 on the *Boxer*. Weeks later, a London newspaper attributed the outcome to the conclusion that "the Americans have some *superior mode of firing;* and we cannot be too anxiously employed in discovering to what circumstances that superiority is owing."[4]

Regional and national newspapers carried reports in the days to follow. The *Boston Gazette* led its account taken largely from the Portland papers with the headline: "Another Brilliant Naval Victory."[5] Niles, as was his custom, mixed editorial comment in his report. "We have the high gratification to record an account of another naval victory," he wrote, "as splendid as any that preceded it. Again has the *bloody cross* descended in homage to the *"striped bunting"* — again is the naval column decked with a trophy most brilliant, and the fact made manifest that our tars (if fairly met) in defence of 'free trade and sailors rights,' are invincible. . . ."[6]

---

1 William D. Patterson, *Sprague's Journal*, 174.

2 Duncan, *Coastal Maine*, 267.

3 Moulton, *Grandfather Tales of Scarborough*, 112.

4 *The War* (NY), April 26, 1814.

5 *Boston Gazette*, September 13, 1813.

6 *Niles'*, September 18, 1813.

Patriotic broadsides appeared. One carried the subtitle: "Free trade and Sailors' Rights! Or we will BOX it out."[1] And Secretary of the Navy William Jones forwarded copies of the official reports of the action to the chairman of the Senate Naval Affairs Committee with the observation, the victory "for brilliancy and decision, it is believed, has never been surpassed in single action."[2] Congress went on to pass a resolution authorizing gold medals for Burrows and McCall and silver medals for the other commissioned officers of the *Enterprise* "in testimony of the high sense entertained by Congress of the gallantry and good conduct of the officers and crew...."[3]

After the action reports were filed and the wounded provided for, two important matters required attention. The country needed to pay homage to the dead, especially the two young captains. Funeral services followed complete "with all the honors that the civil and military authorities at the place, and the great body of the people, could bestow."[4] Following two days of planning, the impressive funeral procession got under way at 10:00 a.m., Thursday the 9th. A pair of oared barges manned by merchant masters and mates and draped in black moved toward the two anchored warships. One came alongside the starboard gangway of the *Enterprise*, and the other went to the *Boxer*. Crewmen placed a flag-draped coffin in each barge, and four bells struck. The two brigs fired a gun, matched by guns at nearby Fort Preble and Fort Scammel. The barges moved by minute strokes to Union Wharf as the two brigs and the forts fired minute guns at each stroke.

Once on shore, pallbearers placed the identical coffins on open hearses before they moved through town. A lengthy and distinguished procession formed. A military escort, led by the Portland Rifle Company and two infantry companies headed the lengthy contingent. Captain Hull, Dr. Washington, and the officers and crew of the *Enterprise* marched behind the body of Burrows. Next in line, the officers and men of the *Boxer* accompanied the body of Blyth. Officers of the navy, army, and militia, federal and state officials, shipmasters and mates, judges, congressmen and state legislators, and citizens in general entered the line of march.

The solemn procession moved to the Second Parish Meetinghouse. After the service, the gathering reformed and headed for the Eastern Cemetery. Church bells tolled throughout town and two artillery companies positioned along Fore Street fired minute guns across the harbor. "As the funeral escort arrived at the graves, the ranks were opened to the right and left, halted, and faced to the centre, and rested on arms reversed, during the placing of the bodies in the graves, which were deposited side by side."[5] Riflemen fired six volleys over the graves, and the assemblage turned and moved back to the courthouse to disband.

---

1 *Sixth Naval Victory*.
2 *American State Papers: Naval Affairs* 1:294.
3 Resolution of January 6, 1814, 3, 2 *Stat.* 141-142.
4 *Niles'*, September 18, 1813.
5 *Boston Gazette*, September 16, 1813.

The proceedings amounted to the most memorable event in years in the town. In fact, writing at the end of the 19th century, an historian said: "Portland has seen few sights more impressive than this funeral pageant."[1] All business ceased. Throngs from the countryside gathered along the lengthy line of march and at the cemetery. Onlookers made their way to "tops of houses and windows were filled with men, women and children, anxious to gaze on this new spectacle. The highest degree of order prevailed, and solemn silence was kept."[2] The six-year-old nephew of the late Lieutenant Henry Wadsworth, one of the heroes of the ill-fated *Intrepid* of the Barbary Wars, came away deeply impressed. Many years later, Henry Wadsworth Longfellow recalled the occasion in his poem "My Lost Youth."

In the days following the somber ceremony, American newspapers continued to cover the battle. But the British did not believe much of this reporting, especially "that the *Boxer was literally cut to pieces, rigging, spars and hull; while the Enterprise... was in a situation to commence a similar action immediately afterwards.*"[3] Editors such as Niles continued to boast. "It is impossible that the *British*, at-once, should get down from the pinnacle of pride they had erected for themselves, by their deeds on the ocean," he wrote. "Their high renown has been obtained by combating *Frenchmen* and *Spaniards*; who, whatever may be their worth on land, want a certain *indescribable something*, with a great deal of experience in the management of ships...."[4]

The British forever downplayed the significance of the fight and rationalized the outcome. Writing almost 40 years later, a well-regarded historian of the Royal Navy summarized a common view when he declared: "The two vessels were much disproportioned in every way;... The one was a fine roomy vessel, well manned and equipped, the Boxer a mere gun-brig, unfit for any other purpose than to protect a convoy of coasters from the attack of a French lugger. The result, therefore, cannot cause any surprise."[5]

With the funerals behind them, the authorities faced one more task. Even in victory, they found it necessary to resort to court-martial to conclude the event. Lieutenant McCall charged Sailing Master William Harper and Isaac Bowman, captain's clerk, with cowardice. When the fight raged, Harper allegedly hid behind the foremast to avoid shot and advised McCall to haul down the colors. Bowman supposedly left his station during the combat and went below to record the action. Hull quickly disposed of the complaint against Bowman, observing the clerk was "a poor, innocent lad and as little acquainted with the world, as he is with a ship."[6] Bowman exhibited bravery in the weeks that followed when the *Enterprise* pursued some British ships, so the navy did not prosecute McCall's charge against him.

---

1 "Letter," *Collections and Proceedings of the Maine Historical Society*, 1:174.
2 *Boston Gazette*, September 16, 1813.
3 *The War* (NY), April 26, 1814.
4 *Niles'*, September 25, 1813.
5 Joseph Allen, *Battles of the British Navy*, 2:438.
6 McKee, *Captain Isaac Hull and the Portsmouth Navy Yard*, 271.

The Harper case was another matter. Hull convened a general court-martial in Portsmouth on December 28, 1813. Early in the month-long proceeding it became obvious Harper's main problem involved his poor relationship with the crew. The civilian pilot, Samuel Drinkwater out of North Yarmouth, pretty much summarized the matter when he responded to a Harper question: "I have heard the crew, generally, say, they disliked you — that you was cross and crabbed."[1] McCall, alone, testified strongly against the accused. Harper worked on his spirited defense for several days. And it is clear he had help preparing his written statement. The language, logic, satire, and sense of law employed are not that of a sailing master. The court deliberated at length, and, in a unanimous opinion, acquitted Harper.

While the American court-martial played out at Portsmouth, the British, under the presidency of Captain Henry Hotham, convened their own court at Bermuda. The conduct of all of *Boxer's* surviving officers and company came under scrutiny. After a careful investigation, the court decided the British defeat "is attributed to a superiority of the enemy's force, principally in the number of men, as well as to greater degree of skill in the direction of her fire, and the destructive effects of her first broadside."[2] However, the court found an acting master's mate and three seamen "deserted their quarters during the action, and through cowardice, negligence, or disaffection, to have withdrawn themselves from their duty in the engagement."[3]

Thus, one of the most memorable chapters in the War of 1812 came to a close. In the space of some two months during an unpopular and indecisive war, two decisive single ship combats in New England waters spiked popular interest in the hostilities. Both of the American warships included a good many native New Englanders in their crews. Many more coastal inhabitants actually witnessed the epic struggles. In the end, the visible presence of the Royal Navy during the period foretold things to come. Before it all ended, New England would see much more of Britons afloat.

---

1 Picking, 155.
2 *Naval Chronicle*, 33:472.
3 Ibid., 473.

Chapter 9. Trouble on the Waves

The day after Burrows' and Blyth's funerals in Maine, a New Englander earned lasting fame on distant Lake Erie. Twenty-eight-year-old Captain Oliver Hazard Perry, born in South Kingstown, Rhode Island, performed one of the most memorable feats of the war. Leading a squadron of nine vessels, on September 10, he defeated Captain Robert Barclay and his British squadron of six ships. Perry's flagship, the newly built brig *Lawrence*, 20, displayed a battle flag emblazoned with the words: "Don't Give Up The Ship." Perry's initial dispatch reporting on his victory matched James Lawrence's immortal words. "WE HAVE MET THE ENEMY, and they are ours . . . ," Perry declared.[1] In addition to its strategic significance, the outcome, following on the heels of the *Enterprise* success, boosted American morale at a time of growing doubt, hardship, and danger.

Many of the regional news editors continued to vilify President Madison's war policies and express misgivings about the course of events. In Portland, the *Gazette* criticized the "astonishing and mysterious" conduct of the war. "Seamen as well as soldiers are constantly marching for the protection of the 'Back Woods' folks, whilst the seaports and nine tenths of the property on the seaboard is within the grasp of the enemy or exposed to attack. Still we are told that by invading the wilds of Canada our Commercial Rights are to be secured."[2] A Boston newspaper observed: "We went to war, it was said, for the conquest of Canada and the liberty of the seas. Instead of taking Canada, we have lost three armies, forts Detroit, Michillimackinac, and the Michigan Territory. As to the *Liberty of the Seas* we have not now left even the liberty of our own rivers and bays!"[3]

---

1 Roberts and Brentano, *Book of the Navy*, 56.
2 *Portland* (ME) *Gazette*, April 30, 1813.
3 *Boston Gazette*, May 6, 1813.

In May 1813, Massachusetts voters made a statement of their own when they handily returned highly visible antiwar Governor Caleb Strong to office. At the end of the month, Strong sent a message to the General Court detailing his steadfast opposition to the war and calling for an appropriation for the state purchase of arms and munitions. The legislature made the funds available and, prompted by petitions from a number of towns and "excited by the apprehension of still greater evils in prospect," it sent a remonstrance to Congress. The legislature pointed out that of the $215 million in taxes collected by the federal government, "Massachusetts has paid upwards of forty millions, an amount beyond all proportion to her political weight in the Union." Moreover, claimed the legislature, no state "can have a greater interest, or . . . desire to protect commerce, and maintain the legitimate rights of seamen . . ." since one-third of all vessels and "nearly one-half of all native seamen" hailed from Massachusetts. The "cruel policy" of the national administration "has brought the good people of this Commonwealth to the verge of ruin," the remonstrance declared. By way of conclusion, the legislature urged Congress to adopt measures to "stay the sword of the destroyer" and attain "a just and honorable peace."[1]

The Massachusetts legislature did not exaggerate conditions. Signs of hard times abounded. After the British captured and burned two Warren, Maine coasters and imprisoned their crews, one skipper of the town decided not to expose his new brig to the same fate. Yet to simply tie up for the duration in an isolated cove would bare his boat to deterioration and require costly upkeep. He, therefore, removed the *Alexander* to the Oyster River, sunk her, and planned to keep her submerged until the end of the war based on the novel theory "though there is trouble *on* the waves, *beneath* them there is *none*."[2] Hundreds of masters on the New England coast made the decision to stay in port to lessen the risks of war. Many employed a less radical but derisive measure to protect their gear from the ravages of weather. They placed empty tar barrels or canvas bags on the mastheads of their idle ships, and called the covers "Madison nightcaps."

A New York newspaper told its readers, "the situation of the poor inhabitants" of Maine "in regard to the supply of provisions, is deplorable, having neither flour, nor corn, nor even potatoes to live upon."[3] On Long Island (now Isleboro) in Penobscot Bay, the "harsh and frigid realities of war were sensibly felt. Commerce was at an end, and hardly a coaster dared venture out of the harbor."[4]

In Cohasset, Massachusetts, Thomas Stoddard gave up fishing after the 1813 season. A diary entry reveals his annual catch dropped 90 percent due to the omnipresent British cruisers. He turned to cutting firewood for a living, all the while knowing because of the town's "exposed and defenseless situa-

---

1 *American State Papers: Miscellaneous* 2:210-214.
2 Eaton, *Annals of the Town of Warren*, 315.
3 Johnston, *History of the Town of Bristol and Bremen*, 404.
4 Farrow, *History of Islseborough*, 71.

tion . . . we could not expect to be exempt" from the ravages of the war.[1] And a Boston Federalist complained: "Our coasts are not navigable to ourselves though free to the enemies and money-making neutral[s]."[2]

More and more, commerce left the waterways and took to the roads. Reuben Safford of Hope, Maine twice led his sluggish team of oxen to Boston for provisions. But he gave up on the system since a round trip took two months to complete. In the more populous towns, wagon brigades were formed to handle the work of abandoned coasters, and editors amused their readers by supplementing their "Marine News" with special columns for "Horse Marine News." A Kennebunk weekly thus reported: "Arrived: November 6th, at noon, two horse-cutters, 'Timothy Pickering' and 'Quincy Cannon Ball.' Commander Delande from Portland to Boston spoke on her passing sixteen ox-schooners from Bath to Portland, cargo, tin plate, all well. Also saw on the Scarborough Turnpike a suspicious looking cutter which he escaped by superior sailing."[3] A New Bedford newspaper advised: "October 11th, arrived, a squadron under command of Admiral Heaton, consisting of seven square-rigged wagon vessels, Capts. J. Bates, D. Bates, Whitcomb, Lyons, Cooledge, and Sherman, eight days from Albany, with flour. Had good passage. . . . Spoke nearly 100 sail from this port, all in good health and well provisioned."[4]

Although the British by this time dominated the New England coastline, the Royal Navy was not without its own problems. Desertion remained a major concern. Early in the war, the commander of the Halifax station issued a proclamation calling upon deserters to give themselves up and declare "their Sense of Error," and he would in turn pledge "to obtain for them the PRINCE REGENT'S Free Pardon."[5] The effort met with little success. Throughout the war, British tars deserted at alarming rates. When the H.M.S. *Albion*, 74, late in 1813 anchored in Tarpaulin Cove at isolated Naushon Island, three marines and nine seamen fled the ship. The captain threatened to destroy the few houses at the place if the deserters were not given up. The men remained at large and the warship moved away without firing a shot.

Fourteen crewmen from the H.M.S. *Acasta*, 48, picked a better location to take their leave. Late in September, off New London, around midnight a "boat came along side the frigate for a relief guard, when, by a concerted plan," once the officer and all but two men left the boat, a dozen seamen jumped in the boat and pushed off. The gangway sentinel was among the culprits, so "their design was not immediately perceived." The escapees rowed under the stern to avoid the ship's guns. Sentries fired small arms without effect "and the bold fellows answered with three cheers, and pulled away for the land."[6]

1 Bigelow, *Narrative History of the Town of Cohasset*, 343.
2 Babcock, *The Rise of American Nationality*, 118.
3 Robinson, *Coastal New England*, 100.
4 Borden, *Bristol County*, 331.
5 Lohnes, "The War of 1812 at Sea," 98.
6 *Columbian Centinel* (MA), September 25, 1813.

British deserters naturally found it easy to assimilate in a countryside populated largely by people of English stock. Moreover, many locals provided aid and comfort to the deserters. Dennis Doughty of Cumberland Foreside just east of Portland heard a pounding on his door one night. He found a disordered and thoroughly wet sailor begging for help. The man claimed to be a deserter from a British man-of-war in Casco Bay. Pursued by a boat to Clapboard Island, he swam the extra mile to the mainland. Doughty concealed his apprehensive visitor in a blind attic entered from a hayloft. He piled hay over the entrance, and returned to his bed. In a short time, he woke to another knock at his door.

"Open, in the name of the King."

"I know no king," said Doughty, "but I fear no man and will open to you."[1]

The British squad searched the house without result, and returned to the shore and their boat. Doughty learned his guest was in fact an American impressed by the Royal Navy. The next night, he escorted the man through the woods to West Cumberland, and turned him over to the care of his inland brother.

As if the manpower problem was not enough, a November 12, 1813 hurricane churned through Nova Scotia. Buildings were unroofed and forests "over a large extent of country were leveled as completely as they would be in a chopping frolic."[2] The storm devastated the British fleet at anchor in Halifax. Overall, 100 vessels in the harbor were driven on shore, including the navy's *San Domingo*, 74, *LaHogue*, *Maidstone*, 36, *Fantome*, *Epervier*, *Manly*, 12, and *Canso*, 10. Other warships suffered damage when running afoul of one another. Due to a shortage of naval stores and limited repair facilities, "many months elapsed before the squadron could put to sea in its former strength."[3]

To tackle such problems, the Royal Navy always could rely on a deep reserve of talented officers. At the time, none had more luster than the legendary Captain Sir Thomas M. Hardy. Since the 1798 Battle of the Nile, the service called him "Nelson's Hardy," an unexampled accolade. He served as Captain of the Fleet at the glorious Battle of Trafalgar in 1805. In 1813, he commanded the squadron off Block Island. Forty-four years old, Hardy earned among many Americans the reputation of a gallant gentleman. Once while anchored at Block Island, he hosted on the *Ramillies*, 74, a well-attended dinner party for the islanders. Better yet, he responded considerately to the plea of an elderly Norwich father. The man learned his long-absent son — John Carpenter — served as an impressed seaman on the *Ramillies*. He gathered up documentation and went off to Hardy under a flag of truce. Captain Hardy examined his paperwork, and, convinced of young Carpenter's American citizenship, released him to his grateful father. And since the son had served in the Royal Navy for five years, he left the ship with $300 in back wages and $2,000 in prize money.

---

1 Rowe, *Ancient North Yarmouth and Yarmouth*, 196.
2 George Patterson, *History of the County of Pictou*, 273.
3 Lohnes, *Mariner's Mirror*, 326.

A few folks around New London, however, put Hardy to an early test. In April, a Mystic privateer captured a vessel commanded by one of Hardy's officers and held the prize and its crew for ransom. Hardy sent a pointed letter to Governor John Cotton Smith in Hartford, warning he would blow down New London if his men and boat were not returned. After extended negotiations, the local collector of customs accompanied the British captives out to the *Ramillies*. Hardy wined and dined the collector, and returned him to shore with assuring messages for the American people. Captain Hardy made it clear he disapproved of Cockburn's recent ruthless tactics in the Chesapeake. The collector told Hardy some inhabitants of the shore planned to move inland for safety. Hardy urged the customs man to tell the people he would not fire on any dwellings unless he received a specific but unlikely order to do so. He added he hoped to visit New London in the near future as a guest and not as a combatant.

About the same time, another *Ramillies* visitor, U.S. Army Captain William Van Deursen of Fort Trumbull, found Hardy "a man of great simplicity of manners, apparently a perfect stranger to everything like pride or ostentation." Even so, upon entering Hardy's cabin, Van Deursen "was struck with admiration at the style and grandeur in which it was fitted. Everything appeared to be conducted on the most splendid and magnificent plan, and I think I may safely say I never have seen anything of the kind that compared with it."[1] Newspapers throughout the country took notice of Hardy's considerate and gentlemanly ways. The *Columbian Centinel*, for one, observed: "Com. Hardy discharges his duty more agreeably to the principles of high and liberal warfare, than many of his brother commanders."[2]

Not everyone, however, thought Hardy's high-mindedness made him immune. Two New York shippers conceived a plan to destroy the *Ramillies* and open up Long Island Sound to navigation. They relied on a new federal statute — "An Act to encourage the destruction of the armed vessels of war of the enemy." Approved on March 3, 1813, the law allowed "any person or persons to burn, sink, or destroy, any British armed vessel of war, except vessels coming as cartels or flags of truce; and for that purpose to use torpedoes, submarine instruments, or any other destructive machine whatever." The measure offered a bounty of half the value of a destroyed ship's "guns, cargo, tackle, and apparel."[3] The New Yorkers sent the schooner *Eagle* down the Sound, her hold carrying combustibles including 400 pounds of gunpowder in a cask concealed under a large quantity of stones imitating ballast. In plain view, the vessel carried enticing common naval stores and barrels of flour. Cords connected a pair of trigger devices in the cask to two of the barrels.

As the *Eagle* approached the *Ramillies* off New London on June 25, Hardy dispatched Lieutenant John Geddes and 13 men in a boat to take her. The schooner's crew did not wait. On the approach of Geddes, they dropped the

---

1 Henry Whittemore, *History of Middlesex County*, 340.
2 *Columbian Centinel* (MA), August 26, 1813.
3 Act of March 3, 1813, ch. 47, 2 *Stat.* 816.

vessel's anchor, jumped in a boat, and rowed to the safety of Millstone Point. Geddes took possession of the *Eagle*, and, as instructed by Hardy, placed her alongside another captured coaster three-quarters of a mile from the flagship. Moments later sailors moved the barrels of flour unknowingly engaging the triggers and igniting the explosives. The blast disintegrated the *Eagle*. Geddes and ten of his men died instantly. "A shower of pitch and tar fell upon the 'Ramillies;' timber and stones were hurled aloft, and the waters around thrown into great commotion."[1] If the prize had exploded alongside the *Ramillies*, as planned, it could have destroyed the great ship. "After the explosion, not a piece of the wrecks could be seen with a spy-glass at the lighthouse."[2]

A Boston paper noted: "The Commodore seems to be very angry, and he has a good right to be."[3] The British long deplored the action. One English historian thought: "A quantity of arsenic among the food would have been so perfectly compatible with the rest of the contrivance, that we wonder it was not resorted to."[4] Captain Edward Brenton of the H.M.S. *Spartan*, 38, later a historian of note, thought: "Should actions like these receive the sanction of governments, the science of war, and the laws of nations, will degenerate into the barbarity of the Algerians; and murder and pillage will take place of kindness and humanity to our enemies."[5]

The next morning, Hardy sent a message to Brigadier General Jirah Isham, the New London militia commander, asking him to let it be known Hardy no longer would "permit vessels or boats of any description (flags of truce of course excepted) to approach or pass the British squadron."[6] But David Bushnell got under the ban. He built a primitive submarine, and made three trips beneath the *Ramillies.* On his last foray, he almost succeeded in planting an explosive device on the ship's hull. A local newspaper reported: "So great is the alarm and fear aboard the Ramillies that Commodore Hardy keeps his ships under way at all times."[7]

Captain Thomas B. Capel of the H.M.S. *LaHogue* responded to the situation in typical fashion. A few days after the *Eagle* incident, he stopped the schooner *Friendship* and placed a notation on her papers. He wrote: "I have warned the fishing Boat Sally of Barnstable to return immediately to her own coast — and in consequence of the Depredations committed by the Young Teazer & other American privateers upon the British fishing & coasting vessels belonging to Nova Scotia but more particularly from the inhuman & savage proceeding of causing the American Schooner Eagle to be blown up after having been taken possession of by His Britannic Majesty's Ship Rami-

1 Hurd, *History of New London County*, 224.
2 *Columbian Centinel* (MA), June 30, 1813.
3 *Boston Gazette*, July 5, 1813.
4 James, *Naval History of Great Britain*, 4:240.
5 Brenton, *Naval History of Great Britain*, 2:495.
6 Hurd, 225.
7 "The Turtle," *Empire Patriot*, 5:5.

lies an act not to be justified on the most Barbarous principles of Warfare, I have directed His Britannic Majesty's Cruizers on this Coast to destroy every description of American Vessel they may fall in with (flags of Truce only excepted."[1] In short order, the English privateer *Fly* intercepted and took the *Friendship*. After reading Capel's permissive endorsement on her papers, the master of the privateer spread word of the open season among his fellow privateersmen.

In view of all the British protesting it is worth observing the complaints of foul play in the *Eagle* affair were artful at best since Great Britain used similar destructive weapons. For the better part of a decade, the Royal Navy had employed a bomb or torpedo with a clock-like mechanism that floated with the current just at or below the surface of the water. Known as carcasses, the British notably set the devices against Napoleon's gathering invasion fleet prior to Trafalgar. And by 1809, the British were using so-called explosion vessels. Described as "diabolical engines of warfare"[2] by Lord Cochrane, a principal proponent, the novel vessels, abandoned and set adrift in the last moments of their run toward targets, carried some 1,500 barrels of powder, several hundred shells, and 3,000 hand grenades packed together to simulate a great mortar. If the fuse ignited the massive charge at the right instant, the resulting destruction to enemy warships could be horrendous. As if these terrifying instruments were insufficient, the British supplemented them with fireships. Topped off with as many as 50 Congreve rockets, fireships were set loose and set off in the same manner as explosion vessels. When the flames reached the rigging, the rockets ignited in spectacular and possibly deadly fashion, but the burning hulk remained the principal threat to the enemy. The *Eagle* seemed no more infernal.

Shortly after the war, a Connecticut historian addressed the British outcry. "Two answers were given to their remonstrances on this subject: one, that their cruel and wanton outrages on the peaceable inhabitants of the coast warranted any mode of defence calculated to afford protection: the other, that stratagems in war are always justifiable; and the modes of attack of which they complained stood on the same ground as sapping, mining, and ambuscades on land."[3]

The charges of impropriety and inhumanness were not one-sided at the time. The Madison administration asked Congress to look into the "spirit and manner in which the war had been waged by the enemy." A committee report in July 1813 focused most of its attention on the treatment of American prisoners. The committee recommended the House ask the president to collect "evidence of every departure by the enemy from the ordinary modes of conducting war among civilized nations." One of the examples of prisoner mistreatment cited in the committee report covered the unhappy experience

---

1 Snider, *Under the Red Jack*, 184-185.
2 Dundonald, *Autobiography of a Seaman*, vol. 1, 368.
3 Samuel Perkins, *Political and Military Events of the Late War Between the United States and Great Britain*, 169.

of Salem's Captain Jeduthun Upton. Another case involved Captain William Nichols of the Newburyport privateer *Decatur*. Testimony indicated the British detained him for 34 days in a cell "about four feet in width, and about seven feet in length, on board a prison ship." And a band of 15 imprisoned privateers largely from Boston, Portsmouth, Portland, and New London had their earlier written protest from the Melville prison at Halifax entered in the record. They described undignified and barbarous treatment at the hands of the British. "Most of us have been robbed of every thing, even of necessary clothing."[1] Niles reported the prison commander disparaged the complaints and told the men "to die and be damned — the King has 130 acres of land to bury them."[2]

After learning that ten *Chesapeake* petty officers were confined in a Halifax dungeon, the administration retaliated in October 1813. The government took a group of English prisoners out of a prison ship at Salem and sent them to the notorious Ipswich stone jail. Later, the Madison administration revoked the tolerable house arrest of ten British officers and incarcerated them in the unpleasant Worcester jail. Nine promptly escaped, although five were recaptured at Barre, Massachusetts after the United States marshal offered a $500 reward for their arrest and return.

The Federalist controlled Massachusetts legislature and Governor Strong moderated the vindictiveness while taking a stand for States' rights by closing Massachusetts jails to federal military prisoners. A February 1814 act prohibited using Commonwealth jails by "any other authority than the Judicial Authority of the United States."[3] The law further required all British prisoners of war to be discharged from the state jails within 30 days. Connecticut, Rhode Island, and Vermont authorities implemented similar policies.

Although the Royal Navy did not proclaim a New England blockade until 1814, the hostile British naval practices and tactics of 1813 had much the same effect. Other than the *Boxer*'s drubbing, the enemy's men-of-war enjoyed relative invulnerability in the Gulf of Maine. They continued to range all along the Maine coast, from Lubec way Down East to Wells in the south. The operation failed to intimidate everyone, however. John Paul of Ash Point was taken by a British warship while fishing in the Mussel Ridge Channel. Interrogated about the location of a swivel gun maintained for the protection of Owl's Head, Paul told his captors, "[I]t may be in Merriman's barn, — it may be behind his barn, — or it may be in the guard house, — or it may be in the bushes, — and I don't knew where the d—l it isn't; and if I *did*, I wouldn't tell ye."[4]

But British cruisers and privateers were not the only threats. On occasion, danger came from friends. Moses Thorndike of Camden went out as the pilot on a local privateer, flying the English colors in an attempt to entrap

1 *American State Papers: Military Affairs* 1:339-343.
2 *Niles' Weekly Register* (MD), August 8, 1812.
3 Waters, *Massachusetts Historical Society Proceedings*, 48:503.
4 Eaton, *History of Thomaston*, 288.

an enemy boat. In little time, they spotted an American coaster and bore for her to learn if her crew knew of any British vessels in the area. The coaster assumed the approaching craft was just what her flag suggested — an English privateer. The coaster turned tail. Thorndike's boat attempted to slow the flight by running up the American ensign. This had the opposite effect, and the coaster ran on shore to escape capture. Terrified, the crew vaulted over the bow and into the woods. The American privateer sent its pilot and several men ashore to tell their timid countrymen about their mistake. Once it became obvious the landing party was not interested in plunder or confrontation, one by one, the frightened sailors made their way to the edge of the bushes. Recognizing the local pilot, one man bellowed: "What, is that you, Thorndike?"

"Yes! Come here you scarecrows; what d'ye run your vessel aground for?"[1] Everyone had a good laugh, and both crews went about getting the coaster back in deep water and on her way.

The Halifax privateer *Fly* attracted a great deal of attention in Penobscot Bay in June 1813. She captured six coasters in one day, although half escaped by beaching themselves. The *Fly* escorted the unlucky trio to White Island Harbor, just west of Vinalhaven Island. In the security of the seemingly uninhabited little island, the privateersmen transferred goods from two of the prizes to the larger captive. Unseen in the dark, a sizeable band of local men armed with muskets, fowling pieces, and fuses silently gathered and took up concealed positions at the harbor's edge. When daylight arrived, a voice from the rocks sung out: "What schooner is that?"

"The Shear-Water of Baltimore! Won't you come on board?"

"No; but we invite you to come ashore."

"I'll see you d—d first," replied the captain.[2]

This rude reply prompted a crash of gunfire from the shore, driving the privateer's crew below. Two balls struck Enoch Stanwood and he became the first Canadian captain to be killed in the war. Seventy-five crewmen huddled below, afraid to poke their heads on deck. One man, however, goaded by his captain's last words, crawled on deck below the hammock nettings and succeeded in cutting the cable. "But . . . he dearly paid for his temerity; for the bullet of some correct-sighted fisherman shattered his under jaw — he fell, but succeeded in creeping below."[3] A fair breeze and favorable current moved the *Fly* away from the land as one privateersman steered to open water by thrusting a bayonet through the skylight to reach the wheel. Once out of harm's way, her prizes abandoned and lost, the *Fly* escaped toward Matinicus.

In southern New England waters, the Royal Navy remained active. During the late summer, Captain Farmery P. Epworth in the *Nymphe*, 38, disturbed Cape Ann. He made a number of captures of coasters and fishing

---

1 Locke, *Sketches of the History of the Town of Camden*, 99.
2 Eaton, *History of Thomaston*, 290.
3 Ibid.

boats and sent their captains to town to obtain ransom funds. At one time, nine unfortunate captains were back in Gloucester, each seeking $200 to ransom his vessel. Along the coast, in September, a British brig chased a Duxbury sloop on shore at Plymouth. The enemy succeeded in refloating the vessel, "but an alarm being sounded, our militia kept up so warm a fire, that they had to leave the deck; and three boats pulling off from shore retook her, and brought her into port."[1] A few days later, a similar scene played out at Killingworth just west of the mouth of the Connecticut River. The H.M.S. *Atalanta* tried to take a grounded Haddam schooner in what is now Clinton Harbor. The militia rolled out two brass 6-pounders on Hammock Point and set up an iron 4-pounder on Sandy Point. Fire from the two gun emplacements as well as from the enemy sloop "produced quite a warlike scene" before the British retired.[2]

Captain Robert McKown of Woolwich refused to be bullied by the enemy's diligence. "He belonged to the war party, was zealous for 'sailors' rights'; fearless himself, he had a most ravenous appetite for the 'blood of an Englishman.'"[3] Late in September, McKown left Boston for Bath in his schooner carrying merchandise as well as several merchants and their ladies. Approaching Portsmouth, a brig supporting the H.M.S. *LaHogue* tried to intercept McKown's vessel. Thoughts of beaching the Maine schooner to avoid capture were dropped when the *Enterprise* and the *Rattlesnake* along with a schooner and several gunboats poured out of Portsmouth headed for the enemy. Instead of racing into the safety of the harbor, McKown turned and joined the armed craft seeking to engage the *LaHogue* and her consort. The passengers pleaded with McKown to turn back. "Argument was lost upon him; his throat breathed vengeance; his very eyes flashed fire; he was an old 'war-hawk' and could not be restrained," a passenger recalled.

David C. Magoun, a respected Bath merchant on board, passionately protested McKown's actions. "You are entirely unarmed and cannot possibly be of any service in the engagement."

"No matter for that," replied the skipper, "the British do not know that; they don't know but we are half full of arms and men; at least we shall add one to the number; I have one old shooting iron down below, and I know I can make a hole with it in some d—d red coat before we quit."

As McKown pulled abreast the *Enterprise*, the American commander inquired: "Where are you going?"

"Don't you see," shouted McKown, "we are going wherever you go, if that's to Davy's locker!"

"My friend," replied the officer, "let me advise you to put back; you can be of no possible service to us, and you may see bloody work before you return."

---

1 *Columbian Centinel* (MA), September 25, 1813.
2 *Boston Gazette*, October 11, 1813.
3 Reed, *History of Bath and Environs*, 130.

"That's just what I want to see," answered the Woolwich master, as he continued onward.[1]

Just as the American fleet neared gunshot range of the two waiting British warships, led by the *Enterprise*, they all turned and headed back to Portsmouth. Captain Isaac Hull at the navy yard received intelligence the H.M.S. *Tenedos* was moving to support the *LaHogue*, so he ordered the forts to signal his ships to return. Years later, one of McKown's passengers remembered Hull's recall. "Never did our young heart beat with a readier joy than when our captain concluded not to go and fight the ship and brig alone, but to return and make a port with the brigantines."[2]

In mid-October 1813, a combined army of Austrians, Prussians, Russians, and Swedes defeated Napoleon in Leipzig at what is called the Battle of the Nations. When the news reached America, the Federalists felt emboldened. The folly of the war with Great Britain would become more apparent as that country could afford to redirect added military and naval resources against the United States. In this climate, Governor Martin Chittenden of Vermont moved to retract his state's armed support of the war. His predecessor, Jonas Galusha, a member of President Madison's party, sent a brigade of the Vermont militia to duty in northern New York. Worse, according to Chittenden, a portion of the brigade wound up under the command of an officer of the United States Army, and the deployment left a large part of Vermont's frontier "unprotected, and the peaceable, good citizens thereof . . . in great jeopardy, and exposed to the retaliatory incursions and ravages of an exasperated enemy. . . ." As the head of the Vermont militia, Chittenden ordered the brigade back to Vermont. He explained, "The military strength and resources of this state must be reserved for its own defence and protection. . . ." To the delight of the national administration, the brigade officers replied to the governor's "most novel and extraordinary proclamation," as they labeled it, by declaring they "absolutely and positively" refused to comply.[3]

This act of unconformity on the part of the brigade officers proved too much for the partisans to overlook. Representative Harrison Gray Otis proposed a resolution in the Massachusetts House supportive of Chittenden. As expected, people such as Virginia congressman John Randolph embraced the Otis position. He told Josiah Quincy, "No occurrence since the war has made so deep an impression upon me. . . . I rejoice . . . to see him enlisted on the side of the *liberty of the subject and the rights of the States.*" The New Jersey legislature countered by expressing disdain for the "ravings of an infuriated faction, either as issuing from a legislative body, a maniac governor, or discontented and ambitious demagogues."[4]

Republican congressman Solomon P. Sharp of Kentucky thought the militia officers acted in a manner characteristic of the descendants of the Green

---

1 Ibid., 131-132.
2 Ibid.
3 Brannan, *Official Letters of the Military and Naval Officers*, 261-264.
4 Morison, *Harrison Gray Otis*, 334-335.

Mountain Boys. Chittenden's conduct, on the other hand, "must meet the decided reprehension not only of every member of this House, but of every good citizen in the nation." Sharp went on to move resolutions requesting the U.S. attorney general "institute a prosecution" against the governor, charging him with enticing "soldiers in the service of the United States to desert." Vermont representative James Fisk, a Democratic Republican, said the state delegation opposed the appearance of Sharp's resolutions, though none of the delegation disapproved their substance. "The act was unjustifiable; but it was the act of the Governor of a State." Let the proper tribunal take up the matter, he urged. "It was not proper that the House of Representatives should turn informers."[1] Fisk moved the resolutions lie on the table. Having made his point, Sharp did not object, and the House set aside the measures. In the end, the governor's order and the subsequent uproar proved little more than a hollow political sideshow. The enlistments of many of the Vermonters soon expired and the brigade drifted back home to Vermont.

As the war lengthened, entire communities tried to live in harmony with the changed conditions brought about by the enemy at their doorsteps. Provincetown offers an example. Royal Navy ships patrolling about Boston Bay found the isolated tip of Cape Cod an ideal haven and source of basic needs. Captain John Hayes of the H.M.S. *Majestic*, 54, reported the inhabitants of Provincetown "are disposed to be on Friendly terms, and have promised to allow the Ships to take water from their Wells, and on reasonable terms will supply them with fish, Fruit, & Vegetables, and also good firewood."[2] Of course, the wood did not originate in barren, windswept Provincetown. Local coasters obtained cordwood beyond Cape Ann, so Hayes issued them passes to go about their business so beneficial to the British in the harbor.

While relations with the natives went smoothly, coasters fared poorly at Provincetown. An early December northwest gale drove several Maine vessels headed to Boston to seek refuge in the harbor only to be grabbed by British warships at anchor. The schooner *Fame* bound from Portland with lumber, schooner *Friendship* out of Kennebunk with lumber, sloop *Catharine* from Bath with a mixed cargo, and the sloop *Jane* of Kennebunk with wood and bark fell into the hands of the *Majestic* and the *Junon*, 38, Captain Upton Clotworthy. The coasters ran into trouble off Cape Ann, each splitting sails. The *Catharine* got the worst of things. Once at Provincetown, she dragged her anchor, forcing the skipper to cut away her mast. In this vulnerable state, the British seized her. She was "plundered, and considerably mutilated" before being set adrift and ending up on the beach. The other three did not sense their danger "until it was too late to retreat."[3] Hayes offered to ransom the *Fame* for $800; the *Friendship* for $500; and the *Jane* for $1,500. The higher ransom for the less valuable *Jane* serves as a pretty good indication her master (a

---

1 *Annals of Congress*, 13th Cong., 2nd sess., 859-860.
2 Dudley, *Naval War of 1812*, 2:272.
3 *Boston Gazette*, December 9, 1813.

Captain Brown) abused the British officers. At any rate, the American captains raced to Boston for the ransom money.

To the west, off New London, the British squadron under Captain Hardy created a great deal more concern. Citizens of the New London area lived in constant fear of a British attack provoked by the presence up the Thames River of Captain Decatur's three trapped warships — the *United States, Macedonian,* and *Hornet.* Antiwar elements in town pointed to Decatur's impotence as an inevitable consequence of a foolish war. Decatur determined to "silence the tongues of his countrymen grown spiteful out of the harm the war had brought their purses."[1] He prepared for a dash to the sea. After moving his ships downstream, he waited for favorable tides on the moonless night of December 12 to make his move. A pair of guard boats slipped silently past New London leading the three ships to the mouth of the river. As they came up on Avery Point at Groton, an officer in one of the boats looked back and spotted an ominous blue light just below Fort Trumbull on the New London shore. In a moment, a lookout detected a second blue light, this one on the opposite bank close by Groton's Fort Griswold.

An outraged Decatur quickly concluded traitors placed the blue lights to signal the waiting British squadron that the Americans were attempting to escape to the open sea. With his secret movement apparently revealed, he ordered his ships to turn back up the river. But he was not finished. Decatur briefed the editor of the *New London Gazette,* who, in turn, denounced "the traitorous wretches who dare thus to give the enemy every advantage over those great and gallant men, who . . . have surrounded the American stars with a lustre which cannot be eclipsed."[2]

Instead of setting themselves against the wickedness of the lights, townspeople abused the bearer of unwelcome news. Indignant citizens rebuked the editor for doubting the loyalty of the place. Connecticut, Rhode Island, and Massachusetts newspapers took up the censorious attack on the *Gazette.* A Boston editor asserted the report of a treasonous blue lights plot amounted to "a foul misrepresentation" and "a gross libel on the People of that patriotic State."[3] Still angry, Decatur reported the incident to the secretary, lamenting the fact "there are men in New London who have the hardihood to disbelieve it, the effrontery to avow their disbelief."[4]

Decatur's letter, widely circulated in the press, prompted Federalist congressman Lyman Law of New London to call for a congressional inquiry into the awkward allegation of disloyalty in his hometown. In introducing a resolution to this end, he argued, the charge, if not one of giving the enemy direct aid and comfort, "is at least a charge of giving the enemy light and information. . . ." Law stressed, while Connecticut did not approve the war, when Decatur sought the safety of New London, the state's "patriotic sons"

---

1 Anthony, *Decatur,* 204.
2 DeKay, *Battle of Stonington,* 86.
3 *Columbian Centinel* (MA), January 1, 1814.
4 Anthony, 205.

responded to the beat of the drum, and "repaired to the scene of the danger; they occupied the adjacent heights; they guarded the points of the harbor;" and provided protection the general government could not supply.[1]

Fellow Connecticut congressman Jonathan O. Mosely, also a Federalist, supported the measure. He argued: "Blue lights, I presume, have occasionally been brought into debate, as certain other terms frequently are, without any real or specific meaning, but simply by way of ornament or embellishment to a speech, such as Old tory, British gold, Henryism, &c. . . ." And if anyone thought the use of the phrase "blue lights" sprinkled in his speech made the speech "more lucid or brilliant," he did not object.[2] But this was not such a case. He wanted the facts uncovered so as to find the culprits or remove the unfounded stain on the honor of his state.

But the administration did not want any public examination of pro-British feelings even if they rose to the level of treason. Led by Calhoun of South Carolina, members from New York, Pennsylvania, Maryland, and Virginia argued against the principle of the Law motion. Congress held the unquestioned right to inquire into subjects associated with legislation, the opponents claimed. However, the measure asked the House "be erected into a court of inquiry or judicature for criminal offences," an object outside of its constitutional role.[3] In the end, the members decided to kill the motion. The *Centinel* put the best face on the outcome. "Thus the majority, by a side blow, have got rid of an inquiry, which they well knew would have proved the charges so flippantly made against the citizens of Connecticut, to have originated either in the most accommodating infatuation, or the most wanton fabrications."[4]

Beyond the politics of the blue lights issue, Congress at the time had greater concerns. The ground war in the west continued to go pitifully. In the last days of December, Lewiston, Black Rock, and Buffalo were plundered by the British and Fort Niagara fell. And, "On New Year's day of 1814 the settlers along the whole length of the Niagara — those of them who survived — were shivering beside the smouldering embers of their homes."[5]

Of more immediate consequence, at the behest of Madison, on December 17, 1813, Congress passed another embargo "on all ships and vessels in the ports and harbours of the United States."[6] The embargo, more severe and restrictive than any that came before, created a firestorm of protest. Strict enforcement meant "the people of Nantucket must move or starve."[7] In Down East Maine, a region almost totally dependent on water transportation, town after town remonstrated. Belfast voters claimed their grief and

---

1 *Annals of Congress*, 13th Cong., 2nd sess., 1123-1124.
2 Ibid., 1126.
3 Ibid., 1127.
4 *Columbian Centinel* (MA), February 2, 1814.
5 Rossiter Johnson, *History of the War of 1812-15*, 167.
6 Act of December 17, 1813, ch. 1, 2 Stat. 88.
7 Starbuck, *History of Nantucket*, 283.

burdens "under the present Dynasty are tenfold greater" than those leading up to 1776. Deer Isle called the law "the stench of despotism."[1] Ellsworth advanced a common theme by comparing the president to the evil Napoleon. Gouldsboro complained government agents even stopped their sleighs and poked around in their family provisions searching for contraband.

Even if one felt inclined to obey the embargo law, certain provisions were so onerous, compliance proved impossible for some. By way of illustration, Section 7 required the owner of a licensed fishing vessel to post a general bond four times the worth of his vessel and its cargo to assure he would not run into a foreign port. Modest, unsophisticated fishermen pursuing mackerel on Georges Bank could not begin to put up this kind of collateral. Tales of woe multiplied. According to lore, one Gosnold man sailed across Buzzards Bay headed for a New Bedford gristmill with a bag of corn. When he prepared to return home, a customs man refused to grant him clearance to carry his ground meal back to his nearby island residence.

The year 1813, the first full year of the war, closed amidst melancholy, gloom, and despair. New England, so reliant on the sea, suffered along with the rest of the country. But, if possible, the next year would prove worse. The British were about to accelerate their efforts in the region and carry the war onto its shores.

1 Morison, et al., *Dissent in Three American Wars*, 10.

CHAPTER 10. ALL AMERICA BLOCKADED

In the first weeks of 1814, the Royal Navy, the great threat to the New England coast, curbed its operations due to the harsh weather of the season and the aftereffects of the November hurricane at Halifax. Nonetheless, the crews of the warships on station had to eat, and their officers knew how to find provisions. When the H.M.S. *Albion* lay in Tarpaulin Cove in the Elizabeth Islands as New Years Day approached, a man "habited as a Quaker" delivered to the ship a boatload of fresh beef for sale. Of the more than 40 American prisoners on the ship, several knew the purveyor, confronted him, and called him a traitor. They let him know that when they gained their inevitable release, the authorities would be informed of his disloyal business. In response to the threat, the Quaker "applied to Capt. [J.F.] Devonshire for his assistance, who caused the prisoners to be detained and those of them who had called the man a traitor, to be put in irons."[1] Weeks passed before the British released the agitated prisoners on a distant shore.

Two other Quakers did not fare quite as well. Late in the previous year, John Hussey and Ebenezer Hussey, members of the Society of Friends, gathered up 50 head of cattle from their own farms and those of their neighbors in Berwick, Maine and headed south "with a view of finding a good market." The pair sold some of the animals at Plymouth, and when they passed through Orleans, only 13 remained unsold. Considered "working cattle and not in good order for Beef," the Husseys knew where to find "a good market" for the remaining cows. They continued to Provincetown and unloaded their scrawny critters on the willing-hearted British navy anchored at the Cape-tip. But once they arrived home, on January 8, the federal government arrested the two entrepreneurs. Charged with "high treason, in giving aid and

---

1 *Columbian Centinel* (MA), February 4, 1814.

comfort to the enemies of the United States," the Husseys were denied bail and sent to the Ipswich jail by U.S. District Court Judge John Davis.[1] Further irritating area Federalists, the two presumably peace-loving Quakers were of the war party. A Boston newspaper reported they were "*democrats*, and voted for the democratick candidates at the spring election."[2] The two men remained behind bars until May 18, when a grand jury of the U.S. Circuit Court found insufficient grounds to prosecute and directed their release.

Still other Quakers played a role on the political front. Since the arrival of the first European settlers on its shores, Nantucket has tried to hold itself apart and advance the supposition it is different and should be treated accordingly. At times, the inhabitants succeed in this endeavor. The Madison embargo offers an example.

"The conditions of the act were such as nearly to cut off communication between Nantucket and the continent."[3] Town leaders, including a number of influential Quakers, drafted a plea for relief. A townsman carried the petition to Washington, where the president and some members of his cabinet commiserated with him, and agreed to seek a remedy. At the end of December, Congress received the petition and a presidential request for relief. A Senate committee reported a bill for the purpose. As the bill made its way through the upper chamber and the House, interests on Block Island, Martha's Vineyard, and a number of Maine islands failed to have their communities included in the bill's coverage. On January 25, Nantucket became special. Madison signed an act authorizing Nantucketers alone to apply for permission "to employ any ship, vessel, or boat, for the purpose of conveying from the main land . . . fuel, provisions and other necessaries," and to carry "oil, spermaceti candles and fish" from their island.[4]

As winter took hold, Captain Decatur paid little attention to the embargo debate and politics. He experienced impatience bottled up with his three ships behind New London. Consequently, he reacted with initial enthusiasm when word reached him that Captain Henry Hope of the frigate *Endymion* and Captain Hassard Stackpoole of the H.M.S. *Statia*, 38, expressed a wish to arrange an engagement with the *United States* and the *Macedonian*. Courtly negotiations proceeded on the details before Decatur suffered misgivings over the potential for perceived rashness on his part. He called an end to the talks, thus losing a last reasonable chance for the *United States* and the *Macedonian* to escape their confinement in Connecticut.

One Englishman, however, did manage to find some action. Operating out of Tarpaulin Cove for the season, the H.M.S. *Nimrod* became the only British ship to go on the offensive in New England during January. Other Royal Navy ships in the region limited their weather-bound activity to interdicting American merchantmen, fishermen, and privateers. At daylight on

1 Ibid., January 12, 1814.
2 Ibid., February 2, 1814.
3 Obed Macy, *History of Nantucket*, 178.
4 Act of January 25, 1814, ch. 5, 2 *Stat.* 94.

the 28th of the month, Captain Nathaniel Mitchell left the protection of the cove in his cruiser and sailed to nearby Falmouth, Massachusetts. A week earlier, three barges from the Nimrod managed to set a coasting sloop on fire after she got on a reef off Woods Hole. Local militia repaired to the site and poured a fire of musketry into the barges, killing one Brit, wounding another, and sending a ball through the lieutenant's hat. Mitchell determined to teach the Falmouthites a lesson.

He anchored off the town just before noon and sent a boat on shore under a flag of truce. Mitchell demanded a Nantucket packet sloop lying at the dock and the town's two brass 3-pounders. The head of the militia contemptuously suggested the British "come on and get them."[1] Mitchell countered by granting the town an hour to meet his demands before he would fire on the place. Otherwise, the time could be used to evacuate. As the minutes passed, "the militia was fast collecting; the town in utmost confusion; the inhabitants removing the sick, the women, children and furniture."[2] Benjamin Sanford recalled: "We were constrained to remove our sick a mile or two from town where they remained two or three weeks till the alarm subsided. . . ."[3]

At one o'clock, as threatened, Mitchell opened fire on the town with his 32-pounders. Captain John Crocker, unfortunately, held the prime spot to view the cannonading. On the following day, he wrote a letter for the Boston papers, detailing the aggression. "The greatest sufferer was myself," he reported, "having eight thirty-two pound shot through my house, some through my outbuildings, and many through my saltworks. The greatest part of the furniture in the house was destroyed."[4] But neighbor Elijah Swift could see a bright side to things. A ball slammed into his house and demolished his sideboard well stocked with brandy and rum. The shot broke every glass and decanter, but spared every precious bottle and jug.

A cannonball smashed through the front door of the Ichabod Hatch house. Defiantly, Hatch refused to flee. He poked his head through the destroyed entryway and yelled: "There, damn ye, John Bull, see if ye can do that again!" Having made his point, Hatch retreated to his pantry just as a second shot struck the front of his house. "Ichabod went out the back door, shaking his head and muttering that the ways of Providence in rewarding the valiant of heart were beyond all understanding."[5]

An estimated 300 rounds hit the town, altogether missing the people, but striking some 30 dwellings. The firing dropped off at nightfall followed by intermittent shots after dark. Falmouth leaders feared a landing assault by the British since the Nimrod remained in position off the town through the night. The selectmen called for the aid of nearby town militias. The Sandwich company responded late the next day, and "when they got there the

1 Charles F. Swift, Cape Cod, 242.
2 Columbian Centinel (MA), February 2, 1814.
3 Sanford, Letter.
4 Columbian Centinel (MA), February 2, 1814.
5 Digges, Cape Cod Pilot, 363-364.

enemy were gone and the Militia discharged all but the drafted men who are to stay 2 or 3 days longer."[1] This first British sustained bombardment of the homes of the people of a New England town foretold things to come. Heretofore, British forays almost always targeted American vessels driven on shore or amounted to no more than minor demonstrations or amusements.

Even without regard to the Falmouth attack, early in the year, New Englanders felt a heightened sense of anxiety if not hopelessness. Increasingly, citizens released frustrations by entreating their government. This seemed like the only available avenue to relief. A Machias town meeting petitioned the Massachusetts General Court, claiming "we have been preserved from the Sword of the enemy, yet the unavoidable effects of the War have been extremely offensive in depriving us of our usual and principle means of obtaining, not only money but also the common necessaries of life." The town suggested "an exemption from the state tax of the present year" would be appropriate.[2] A lengthy legislative petition passed by a Portland town meeting, while "lament[ing] the necessity of calling in question the motives of our Rulers," exhibited bluntness. The assemblage felt unhesitant "to declare, we are betrayed, and that the guilty authors of the war, instead of supporting 'Sailors Rights' have for their only objects, the conquest of canada, self agrandizement, and the destruction of New England." The Portlanders vowed to support a state remedy "with our lives and fortunes."[3]

Not to be outdone, on January 29, Buckstown, as a last resort, sent a frank and well-crafted memorial to the Massachusetts legislature complaining the fate of earlier appeals to the national government "forbids us under circumstances of unlooked for peril and accumulated suffering" to again try that approach. The memorial excoriated apparent national government ties to Napoleon before highlighting its central point. "We perceive with unspeakable pain the prodigal and profligate mode of conducting the present ruinous war; prodigal inasmuch as immense sums of money, and many valuable lives have been uselessly squandered, without the attainment of one beneficial object; and profligate from the pertinacity with which the dangerous and bloody doctrine of retaliation is maintained to an extent unexampled in the history of war."[4]

Several places in addition to Buckstown cultivated the art of petitioning government, New Bedford included. "After having been twice distinctly read and considered," a New Bedford town meeting "unanimously adopted and ordered presented to the Legislature" a memorial against the "unnecessary, impolitic and unjust" war; a war "without preparation, without hope of success, and which exposed the whole extent of our sea coast to the mercy of the enemy." The town asserted: "The fallacy of the pretences upon which this War was declared, has been too often demonstrated to require further

---

1 *Benjamin Percival Diary.*
2 *Machias* (ME) *Town Records 1795-1823*, 1:243-244.
3 *City of Portland* (ME) *Records, Aug. 17, 1812 to Apr. 2, 1827*, 2:36-39.
4 *Records of the Town of Buckstown* (ME), *No. 1*, 203-204.

elucidation."[1] New Bedford expressed full confidence in the wisdom of the legislature to chart a corrective course. This continuous clamoring accomplished little beyond keeping the pot boiling.

When the moderating weather of April arrived, the British navy let coastal interests know the war was about to intensify. On the 7th, the British set out on the first of their predatory landing assaults on the New England coast. Led by Captain Richard Coote of the *Borer*, 14, six barges carrying 136 men attacked Potapoug, six miles up the Connecticut River at the present town of Essex. Laboring against wind and current, the raiders reached the extensive shipyards before dawn on the 8th. "They gave out word to the inhabitants that if they made the least resistance, they would fire the town; in consequence, they were not opposed."[2] Thus unimpeded, with four exceptions, the raiders "destroyed all the vessels afloat or on the stocks within three miles of the place . . . twenty-seven in number, their united burthen exceeding five thousand tons." Judea Pratt, a Freemason, extended a mystic sign of recognition to Coote. After a brief conversation, Coote, seemingly a member of the international secret fraternity, spared Pratt's vessel. Jeremiah Glover saved his sloop by agreeing to pilot the raiders back down the river. Coote took possession of two privateers. Otherwise, he claimed while his men enjoyed the run of the town, they "maintained the most unexceptionable conduct towards the inhabitants."[3] As they finished their business, they loaded the two American privateers with naval stores and seven hogsheads of rum and took both vessels along as they retired back down the river.

Before long, one captured privateer grounded, so the British set her ablaze. At noon, Coote decided to wait until dark before attempting to run the fort at Saybrook. To reduce his responsibilities, Coote burned the second privateer. Militia forces from Potapoug, Lyme, and Killingworth lined both sides of the river below the raiders. As many as 300 locals manned the fort, among them Samuel Dickinson of Ferry Point. Just before he left home for his assignment, Dickinson told his oldest boy of 14 to take the wagon and carry his mother and younger siblings to the safety of his grandfather's Oyster River house. Young Dickinson had other thoughts. Once his father went out of sight, the youth gathered his fowling piece and headed for the fort. Upon his appearance, the elder Dickinson responded to the disobedience by beating his son with a stick and driving him away. "Thus are the fires of patriotism rudely quenched."[4]

A thick fog reduced the illuminating value of numerous American riverside bonfires. After darkness fell, the British passed by and "a brisk fire kept up" from the banks.[5] The enemy, however, managed to escape back to their ships offshore with a loss of two men killed and two wounded. The value of

---

1 *Columbian Centinel* (MA), February 9, 1814.
2 *Massachusetts Spy*, April 13, 1814.
3 *Naval Chronicle*, 33:171.
4 Henry Whittemore, *History of Middlesex County*, 470.
5 Ibid.

the destroyed shipping approached $200,000. The attack, one of the most destructive in New England during the war, received considerable national attention and promoted great concern in all the coastal towns. For a moment, it detracted from the concerted campaign against Madison's embargo.

As the spring arrived, the assault on the embargo picked up momentum. A persistent critic called the measure a "deplorable descent from national greatness, a determination to harass and annihilate that spirit of commerce, which has ever been the [basis] of civil and religious liberty. . . ."[1] More than 40 towns petitioned the Massachusetts General Court during the period urging state action. Noting such local restlessness, Governor Strong asked the legislature to respond by studying whether Massachusetts could adopt measures to induce Congress to repeal the embargo or to amend the law to make it less questionable from a constitutional standpoint. The Massachusetts House took up the matter and ended up castigating the war in general while objecting in particular to "the pretence of aiming to secure the freedom of commerce and of seamen, by regulations which compel both merchants and sailors to renounce the ocean of their professions."[2]

Several towns made direct appeals of one form or another to Washington. Machias townsmen told the U.S. House since the embargo deprived them of "our usual means of obtaining money to meet the Demands of Government, the object of taxation must fail with us. . . ."[3] A Tisbury town meeting sent a petition to Congress asking that the embargo law be amended so "wee can have communication by water with the State of New York & Connecticut" to sell whale oil, salt, and wool, and return with "Bread Stuff and all the other Articles of Necessity."[4] A move to generate a similar plea in Edgartown fizzled, which was just as well. Congress committed the Tisbury petition to a legislative grave in the Committee on Foreign Relations. Representative Daniel Webster's attempt to gain support for a Portsmouth entreaty likewise failed. Inhabitants of the seacoast town wanted to transport lime by water from Maine. His bill made it through a second reading, but, on April 12, a Committee of the Whole House postponed the measure indefinitely well aware the request was about to become moot.

On March 31, President Madison succumbed to the pressure and sent a brief message to Congress asking for a repeal of the embargo except as it applied to carrying specie and "the importation of articles not the property of enemies, but produced or manufactured only within their dominions."[5] John Calhoun of Madison's party shepherded a repeal bill from his Committee of Foreign Relations through the House. "True wisdom consists in properly adapting your conduct to circumstances," he explained. "Two things may change our conduct in any particular point: A change of our own opinion,

---

1 *Columbian Centinel* (MA), February 23, 1814.
2 Barry, *History of Massachusetts: The Commonwealth Period*, 402.
3 *Machias* (ME) *Town Records 1795-1823*, 1:245-246.
4 Charles E. Banks, *History of Martha's Vineyard*, 1:422.
5 U.S. *Senate Journal*. 13th Cong., 2nd sess., March 31, 1814.

or exterior circumstances, which entirely change the reason of our former conduct."[1] Calhoun rationalized altered conditions in Europe prompted the administration's move, but it is clear the bitter and heartfelt protests of Americans served as the motivation.

Madison's capitulation proved too much for Webster to let pass without commenting. "I am happy to . . . act a part in the funeral ceremonies," he exulted. Webster concluded the embargo "was originally offered to the people of this country as a kind of political faith. It was to be believed, not examined. They were to act upon, not reason about it. To deliberate was to doubt, and to doubt was heretical. It stood upon the trust reposed in its authors, not upon any merit which could be discovered in itself."[2] In the end, the opposition centered in New England again prevailed, and the president signed a repeal enactment on April 14. But rejoicing did not last. The British tightened the vise.

In March, the Royal Navy's Admiral Alexander Cochrane replaced Admiral John Warren as commander of the American Station at Halifax. More forcible and energetic, Cochrane appreciated New England was anything but neutral despite its unhappiness with the war and the extensive beneficial smuggling carried out along the region's borders. A substantial percentage of American manpower and financial support for the war came from New England, and the region harbored key elements of the U.S. Navy and many privateers. On April 25, Cochrane extended the blockade from Long Island to New Brunswick. One of his officers summarized the result with a terse journal entry: "All America blockaded."[3]

Cochrane's extension proclamation had little added effect on American public vessels. As of May, his resources were comparable to those deployed beforehand by Warren. Between New London and Halifax, he had four ships-of-the-line, seven frigates, thirteen sloops, and one schooner. The primary mission of these ships remained unchanged. They continued to watch and respond to the *United States, Macedonian,* and *Hornet* at New London; the *Constitution* and a 74 (*Independence*) building at Boston; the *Congress* and a 74 (*Washington*) building at Portsmouth; and any other American men-of-war, such as the *President* and the *Adams,*28, that might venture in the area. Except for the three ships permanently incapacitated at New London, American warships experienced little trouble passing through the blockade.

American privateers made up a second important target of the Royal Navy. However, these elusive craft did not receive greater attention under the extended blockade. This was not the case with a third category. The blockade that followed the embargo added to the woes of the coasting trade. Unfettered coasters became key targets largely due to their suddenly expanded numbers. Describing the flurry of heightened commercial activity, a British

---

1 *Annals of Congress*, 13th Con., 2nd sess., 1965.
2 Ibid., 1966.
3 Whitehill, *New England Blockaded in 1814*, 17.

lieutenant compared the situation to a spout that "rushes with double force when the impediment which stopped it is removed."[1]

The misfortune of the sloop *Three Sisters*, Captain Higgins, typified the fate of the vulnerable little vessels. Captured on May 11 by the H.M.S. *Nymphe* off Cape Ann, she was sailing from Frenchman Bay to Boston and New London with a load of shingles and plaster. An expired British trading license proved worthless, so Captain Epworth removed the five crewmen and four passengers and burned the vessel. Three of the passengers turned out to be women school teachers employed for the past year on Mount Desert. "[T]he people of which place being almost unacquainted with money, had been in the habit of paying for their children's schooling in shingles," Lieutenant Henry Napier noted in his journal. The ladies "had embarked on board the *Three Sisters* intending to sell their shingles at New London, where they hoped to receive $75 for their year's labour."[2]

Seasickness added to the teachers' sorrow. But on the following morning, the weather moderated. "The fair prisoners (one very pretty) much better and more reconciled to their situation on being assured they would be sent on shore in the first fishing boat." Captain Higgins understandably gave his captors "a deplorable account of the wretched state of trade throughout the States since the war." In the afternoon, the *Nymphe* hailed a boat headed into Cape Ann. Before transferring the passengers, Epworth and his officers took up a collection for the teachers, the total "nearly the amount of their loss."[3] All of their trunks and personal belongings were put on board the inbound boat, according to the *Boston Patriot*, along "with particular instructions to the skipper, upon his peril, to land them as soon as possible." A newspaper reported the teachers tendered "their grateful acknowledgements to the captain and officers of the *Nymph*, for the gentlemanly and polite treatment they received while on board their ship."[4]

After repeated embargoes, almost two years of war, and scores of destructive incidents similar to the *Three Sisters* taking, New Englanders struggled to get by. Typifying the travail, on Cape Cod, another town moved to husband its natural resources. Leaders of Yarmouth gathered and responded to the need to resort "to every means of economical support for themselves and families especially under the present alarming political aspect of the times." Neighboring towns secured the right to regulate and manage their alewives, eel, herring, and perch fisheries, and Yarmouth petitioned the legislature "to be indulged with similar & homogenious privileges." The town wanted statutory authority to prevent "the same from being taken and carried away by the inhabitants of other Towns without permission."[5]

---

1 Ibid., 10.
2 Ibid., 14.
3 Ibid.
4 Ibid., 59.
5 James Crowell, et al., *Petition*.

Zenas Robinson, a Falmouth, Massachusetts native removed to Ohio, wrote to a family member in his hometown: "I am sorry to hear . . . [the British] trouble you so much . . . though it is nothing more than I have been expecting but I hope you will be able to keep your ground and that every Fed and tory in that part will have their eyes open," Robinson said. "Without they do I am afraid they will be the means of undoing that eastern country by what I can learn they appear to be opposing our government in every respect."[1]

In such a climate, on May 29, the *Nymphe* and the *Junon* demonstrated off Portsmouth, New Hampshire. Militiamen assembled and the inhabitants feared an invasion. A party from the *Nymphe* carried a flag of truce to Star Island and watered at the wells on Smutty Nose and Hog Island. The visits prompted Lieutenant Napier to observe: "All the people exceedingly discontented with the war and all join in abusing the government." Two days later, the two British warships displayed a flag of truce in Wellfleet Bay enabling them to gather provisions, "which the inhabitants were very willing to supply us with, being very well paid." Napier added: "It is our intention to oblige the Yankees to supply us with stock and vegetables at the market price. This is very reasonable; we leave all fishermen unmolested."[2]

The *Nymphe* sent a barge under Napier to Halibut Point at Ipswich on June 5, "with the intention of laying in wait, like a spider for flies." He promptly took an empty 100-ton sloop, "the master miserably poor and this his all." The lieutenant let him go, and returned to his hiding place. Before long, he cut off a schooner valued at $4,000. Continuing his work, he captured another schooner loaded with potatoes. Over the next few days, Napier's team captured and burned two more sloops and a schooner. He thought: "Making prize money resembles killing sheep; one likes to eat it but cannot bear the distress of the animal's death."[3]

Still teaming with the *Junon*, on June 9, the *Nymphe* received the first green peas of the season from Boston. "Newspapers, and in short anything we choose to send for, is brought by these rascals. . . . Federalists pretend to be friendly to the English," noted Napier. "They hate the war on their own account, hate the war because it prevents their making money, and like the English as a spendthrift loves an old rich wife; the sooner we are gone the better."[4]

Early in June, the *Bulwark*, 74, Captain David Milne joined the fleet off Boston. This prompted the pro-administration *Boston Patriot* to editorialize: "It is somewhat remarkable, that in return for Gov. Strong's compliment to Britain as the *Bulwark of our Religion* the British should have sent out to us a *Bulwark of Wrath*."[5] On the 9th, the *Bulwark* and the *Nymphe* sent barges into

---

1 Zenas Robinson *Letter.*
2 Whitehill, 18-20.
3 Ibid., 21-24.
4 Ibid., 23.
5 Ibid., 60.

Beverly, where they burned a large merchantman. A national newspaper reported: "A British squadron, consisting of a 74 gun-ship, several frigates, and smaller vessels, with numerous launches, are now spreading terror and destruction on all the seaboard of the Bay of Massachusetts." Milne pledged fishing vessels and dwellings would not be destroyed during the operation "unless individual resistance was made from behind rocks, trees, &c."[1]

Throughout the war, sniping from cover was the certain way to provoke British wrath. Despite the fact Great Britain possessed decades of experience confronting the American frontier tactic of stealth, her military commanders seemed wedded to the European rules of structured, linear combat. General Braddock's 1755 disaster at the Monongahela River did not seem to register. In a French and Indian War encounter, his well-formed force of 1,300 suffered almost 75 percent casualties at the hands of 900 dispersed enemy fighters. His opponents, mainly Indians firing from the woods, reported only 39 killed or wounded. The farmers of Concord, Lexington, and nearby towns handed out the same lesson to the Redcoats fighting their way back to Boston in April 1775. A lieutenant of the King's Own Regiment remembered: "[W]e were fired on from all sides, but mostly from the rear, when people had hid themselves in houses till we had passed and then fired." And a lieutenant of the Royal Welsh Fusiliers recalled many minutemen "lay concealed behind the stone walls and fences . . . firing now and then in perfect security."[2] In 1814, the thought of being shot at from cover still irritated English sensibilities.

The increasingly active enemy naval force promoted widespread apprehension on the coast. Plymouth called upon the Duxbury and Kingston militia units for help defending its harbor. Cohasset remained alert while Milne settled on an initial attack at Scituate. On the 11th, he sent marines in two barges from the *Nymphe* to burn the shipping in Scituate's harbor. "By this act, hardly to be denominated honorable warfare, ten vessels, fishing and coasting craft, were lost."[3] The British left with two schooners and a wood sloop. They spared only one vessel, "the skipper of which was a Democrat and a traitor but for his good services to the boats was restored," noted Napier. "[I]t is right to keep one's word but I question whether the destruction of such a rascal would not almost justify its being broken."[4] Reverend Mr. Thomas of the North Society hastened to the *Bulwark* and demanded to know what added violence could the townspeople expect. The captain assured the minister he was finished with the place.

Cohasset remained on edge. The selectmen asked the Commonwealth for two cannons to defend their harbor. Lieutenant Governor David Cobb turned down the request and suggested the town raise a white flag. This uncharacteristic and timid recommendation unsettled the town fathers. Once

---

1 *The War* (NY), June 21, 1814.
2 Scheer and Rankin, *American Heritage*, 76-77.
3 Deane, *History of Scituate*, 141.
4 Whitehill, 24.

an aide-de-camp to General George Washington, while a judge during Shay's Rebellion, Cobb displayed great personal courage when he faced down an armed mob. Having expected more from Cobb, the town took other steps to defend its waterfront. Within a day or two, Captain Peter Lothrop, head of the militia, sounded a general alarm. The call found Thomas Stoddard and several others working at the Simons Farm saltworks. Stoddard detailed the events that followed in his diary. "We secured our tools and were off. . . ." All the responding men gathered at the meetinghouse before moving out and entrenching on Hominy Point, "a miserable defense, truly."[1]

That evening a boat from the British men-of-war now off Plymouth arrived to take possession of a sloop they earlier drove into Cohasset. Based on an understanding, the militia did not resist, but they managed to learn from the British party that 400 other men with ten artillery pieces in eleven barges were preparing to attack Cohasset. Two Hingham companies, two Weymouth companies, an artillery company from Hanover and one from Randolph, as well as the Hingham Rifle Company rushed to the scene for the first night, bringing the total number of defenders to about 600. All the next day, militia units from neighboring towns poured in, doubling the force stationed near the cove. Anxious spectators covered the nearby heights, while as many residents spent the early morning cooking for the troops or packing up their family valuables to be ready for flight in the event of an invasion.

At 9:00 a.m., the anticipated eleven enemy barges along with a sloop tender hove in sight. Several English officers landed to reconnoiter. "All was now perfect stillness and anxiety. The officers of each company were encouraging the men to fight manfully, and in case any should desert in time of action, they were told they would be immediately shot down." Shortly before noon, after observing and evaluating the large and determined defensive force, Milne recalled his barges. For a time, the "town presented the appearance of a military camp."[2] The *Bulwark* sailed to the east to plague Maine. The militia commander released most of his units, but kept a select company stationed at the cove for the next six weeks.

The *Nymphe* and *Junon* tarried off Cape Ann, where Napier took boats into Annisquam and burned the sloop *Diligence*, sunk another sloop, and carried away two boats full of fish. He let another craft go, because it was owned by an elderly man who had eight children to support and suffered $20,000 in losses during the war. "Destroying this, his last, would have ruined him. Spared another, as I told them, because her name was the *Federalist* but the truth is she is aground alongside of the town and I could not get her off, or set fire to her there, without burning a number of poor people's houses."[3]

Moving along, the men of the *Nymphe* spotted cattle grazing. Napier and others went ashore and tried to chase down and seize a few. But the cows ran too fast, so the seamen shot one and dragged it to their boat. "This kind

---

1 Bigelow, *Narrative History of the Town of Cohasset*, 345-346.
2 Ibid., 347.
3 Whitehill, 25.

of thing pleases sailors amazingly." However, it did not please the girl tend-ing the herd. She gathered up her frightened cattle and drove them away in front of 18 armed enemy men. "Very few females, or even boys, would have done this, which shewed as much goodness of heart as intrepidity of mind."[1]

A much more serious encounter took place in mid-June on the south shore of Massachusetts fronting Buzzards Bay. Seven barges from the *Nim-rod*, for the time under Captain Vincent Newton, and the *Superb*, 74, Captain Charles Paget tried to slip into New Bedford on the night of the 12th. Pro-tected by Fort Phoenix and two navy gunboats, the town turned out to be an ill-advised target for the British when they lost the element of surprise by failing to reach their objectives — shipping and wharves — well before daylight. When the alarm sounded, the raiders withdrew and moved down the bay to a softer target.

Wareham clearly hoped the war would pass it by. Unlike so many places, such as Falmouth across the way or Cohasset, the town did not take any extra steps to protect itself. A substantial body of state law required towns to maintain militia companies, and Wareham met this minimum obligation. The town derived a certain sense of security from the fact it promoted an appearance of neutrality. Actually, Wareham town meetings of the period gave more attention to the protection of shellfish beds than they did to the public's safety. Wareham was about to pay for its lack of preparedness.

When the *Nimrod* moved towards Mattapoisett early on the 13th, the lit-tle village of 40 dwellings agonized. But the warship passed and continued northeasterly. In time, the few inhabitants on Great Neck spotted the threat. "Everybody rushed to bury their valuables."[2] Captain Newton anchored at 11:30 a.m. south of Bird Island. Ebenezer Bourne earlier noticed the path of the ship, recognized the danger, and raced to Wareham to spread the alarm. Word circulated rapidly, and the major in charge of the militia hastened to form and arm his small band of a dozen soldiers.

Lieutenant James Garland led the raiders, some 220 men picked from both the *Nimrod* and the *Superb* anchored nearby at Quick's Hole. A white flag of truce flying in the lead craft, the British made their way past Indian Neck in six barges and landed at the lower wharf in town. Several commu-nity leaders, carrying their own truce flag, a handkerchief tied to a cane, met Garland as he stepped on the pier. Garland demanded identification of all the public property and, indicative of a grudge, all Falmouth property and Falmouth vessels. He required assurance his men would not be bothered or attacked. A violation of this understanding would result in the destruction of every dwelling within range. The Wareham men agreed to the condition, and, without hesitation, pointed out vessels belonging to Falmouth.

The British flag of truce came down and four Falmouth schooners went up in flames. The enemy burned a Plymouth vessel at the outset, and, once they completed their incendiarism, five vessels were destroyed. Another twelve

---

1 Ibid., 26.
2 Ryder, *Lands of the Sippican*, 95.

suffered fire damage before the residents extinguished the flames. Torched, in addition to an unrecorded vessel, were the ship *Fair Trader*, 444 tons; brig *Independent*, 300 tons; schooner *Fancy*, 250 tons; schooner *Elizabeth*, 230 tons; schooner *Nancy*, 230 tons; sloop *Wilmington*, 150 tons; schooner *Industry*, 136 tons; schooner *Argus*, 136 tons; brig *William Richmond*, 135 tons; schooner *New States*, 96 tons; sloop *Paragon*, 70 tons; sloop unnamed, ready to be launched, 70 tons; sloop *William*, 60 tons; sloop *Thomas*, 60 tons; sloop *Experiment*, 60 tons; sloop *William Lucy*, 50 tons; and the sloop *Friendship*, 45 tons; a total of 2,522 tons.

Town leaders strongly protested the ravaging of private property. In the aftermath, a Wareham letter to Commodore Oliver H. Perry in command at Newport reported townsmen reminded Garland and his men of "their agreement, and that they had taken advantage of us by false promises, but they threatened to set fire to the village, and put the inhabitants to the sword if any resistance was made or any attempts made to put out the fires."[1] William Fearing made his own plea when marines stopped at his store and sampled his liquor. "Fearing remonstrated with them, saying, 'I am your friend,' but the commanding officer replied, 'Then you are an enemy to your country.'"[2] The marines went out the door directly to Fearing's uncompleted sloop and set it on fire.

The British did not molest fishing boats, and a fortunate vessel benefited from its name. A raider "seeing the name of Washington on the stern of one of the vessels . . . ordered it to be burnt. One officer exclaimed — 'Not a hair of the head of this vessel shall be scorched,' and she was spared."[3] But the local cotton factory did not escape injury. A British detachment shot a Congreve rocket into the first floor of the building, setting it ablaze. In his report, Captain Paget estimated the loss of the facility at a half-million dollars, but the damage turned out to be much less. As the raiders hastened back to their barges, townspeople extinguished the factory fire. The selectmen reckoned the total monetary loss incurred during the attack amounted to $20,000.

Garland used good sense if not uprightness in withdrawing his force from the town. He took a dozen Wareham men and boys hostage, placing a pair in each barge. Then, he hoisted his flag of truce. A small band of militiamen fired a few shots at the barges as they passed down the narrow river. Once the militia captain learned about the presence of the hostages and their plight, however, he stopped the sniping from shore. When Garland got clear of the scattered militia, he put the hostages on shore at Cromeset Neck. And after firing a single rocket and the swivel gun in each barge, the raiders gave three cheers, and made their way back to their ships, arriving late in the afternoon.

Paget wrapped up the foray and his report by observing: "I cannot in justice omit to report to you the steady and exemplary conduct of the seamen

---

1 *Niles' Weekly Register* (MD), July 9, 1814.
2 Sibyl, *Wareham*, 152.
3 *Columbian Centinel* (MA), June 18, 1814.

and marines, who, though exposed to incessant temptation of liquor, &c. did not in any single instance fail to spurn the offers made to them, and strictly to hold sacred private property."[1] Wareham's report to Perry presented an altogether different assessment. Townsmen indicated "the second in command swore it was a damned shame and disgrace to any nation to enter a village under a flag of truce and commit the greatest outrage and depredations possible, and then return under a flag of truce."[2]

Beyond the widely publicized assault on Wareham, much of the focus remained on the uneasy coast north of Boston. After the enemy burned a schooner at Beverly, the townsmen met and established a guard. Gloucester followed suit, completing the line of posts running along the shore from Marblehead. Salem doubled its guard from 14 to 30 men. "We have from every quarter the most violent threatenings of the British," noted a diarist. He added: "We have had burnings enough around us. . . . The number destroyed exceeds twenty, chiefly coasters, the only property of their owners."[3]

British activity in Maine picked up. On the 6th, the *Junon* dispatched a barge after the sloop *Mary* outside of Waldoboro. The English burned the sloop and sent the four-man crew to the prison at Melville Island, Nova Scotia. On June 16, the *Bulwark* dispatched 150 men in five barges to attack Biddeford Pool at the mouth of the Saco River. Captain Thomas Cutts, the principal property owner of the place, met the force under a white flag. He offered to ransom his three vessels and store. Captain Milne jumped in his gig and went on shore to explain his orders required destruction of property and did not allow for considerateness. Raiders thereupon torched one vessel, cut up a second, and confiscated the third. Before departing, the enemy party looted Cutts' store of $2,000 worth of goods. Later, the British relented, and permitted him to ransom his stolen vessel for $6,000.

In concert with the *Endymion* and *Junon*, before moving along toward the midcoast, the *Bulwark* created great anxiety from the Piscataqua River to Casco Bay. A Portland town meeting responded by mounting a 24-man nightly watch and extinguishing the beacon on the lighthouse. Bath, however, appeared to be the next target. On the morning of the 20th, lookouts at the mouth of the Kennebec spotted the *Bulwark* lying off Sequin and offloading troops into attack barges. When the news reached Lieutenant Colonel Andrew Reed of the 1st Regiment at Phippsburg Center, he initiated a general alarm. The alarm gun was fired as a horseman raced to General William King at his office in Bath. When King received the alert, he shouted out his window: "The enemy is coming! Every man arm, and to his alarm post instantly!"[4]

Consternation and fear and rumors spread rapidly throughout the town. The inhabitants mistook the banging away of Reed's alarm cannon to be

1 *Naval Chronicle*, 33:257.
2 *Niles'*, July 9, 1814.
3 Bentley, *Diary of William Bentley*, 4:259-260.
4 Owen, *Edward Clarence Plummer History of Bath*, 151.

the opening round of an all-out enemy assault. Artillerymen rushed to their placements along the waterfront. A federal regiment supported the Bath Light Infantry as it took up a position on Trufant's Point. Brunswick and Topsham militia companies arrived late in the morning. Over 1,200 militiamen assembled. Banks nonetheless removed their specie from town, much of it secreted in nail kegs and carried across the river to relative security in Woolwich. And citizens concealed valuables in wells and gardens or carried them away as they fled the town.

Reverend William Jenks of the South Society, chaplain to Reed's regiment, acceded to a submissive move by a group of faint-hearted residents. They proposed to give the British invaders the extensive Bath shipping if they would spare dwellings and buildings. Militants got wind of the plot and overhauled and held the minister before he got out of sight. Some townsmen did not appreciate the unilateral behavior of Jenks, also a militia officer. But a court of inquiry later absolved him of misconduct.

After all the commotion and excitement, the Bath invasion failed to develop. A small British contingent did demonstrate against Montsweag, but it retired when challenged by the local militia. The enemy, at this point, proved noncombative. The *Bulwark* boats ignored the nuisance gunfire from the little militia unit stationed on Pond Island when they passed back to their ship. As it turned out, the British held a greater interest in the Sheepscot River and Wiscasset, just to the east.

Along with the *Tenedos*, later on the 20th, the *Bulwark* sent six barges up the Sheepscot as far as the Cross River. One hundred and sixty men landed at Fowles' Point and began to reconnoiter. They approached a farm where everyone but an old man fled upon their approach. The lady of the house left in such haste, her fresh batch of slipcoat cheese remained in plain view on the kitchen table. The old gent allowed the British could take the cheese "if they must but spare him his pants."[1] They left with the cheese as well as the pants.

Afterwards, the raiding party crossed to the Edgecomb side of the river and drove Captain John Erskine's small militia detachment into the woods. "They approached within a few miles of the fort, opposite this town, with the avowed intention of coming to the wharves and burning the shipping," a Wiscasset correspondent told a Boston acquaintance, "but hearing our alarm guns and ringing of the bells, judged that we were prepared for them and retreated to their ships at the mouth of the river, after robbing a few houses."[2] Men from the enemy ships sent word to the troops at Fort Edgecomb that they planned to dine in Wiscasset on the Fourth of July. The Maine men retorted: "If you dine Wiscasset, you'll sup in hell."[3]

Two days later, the *Bulwark* anchored at the entrance to the St. George River, poised to pillage Thomaston. Two barges moved up the waterway,

1 Fannie S. Chase, *Wiscasset in Pownalborough*, 346.
2 William D. Patterson, *Sprague's Journal*, 173.
3 Fannie S. Chase, 346.

guided by two local men taken off of an unfortunate lime-coaster. Late in the day, the party landed in front of George's Fort in the town of St. George. Constructed in 1809, the fort did not present a formidable appearance. It mounted two to three 18-pounders behind a simple rampart. A small block-house, sparse barracks, and a brick powder magazine completed the fortification. The military effectively abandoned the facility in 1813, leaving it in the care of Hezekiah Prince. He, in turn, employed Ephraim Wylie, an elderly Valley Forge veteran, to tend the place.

The British unit advanced on the fort, vaulted the rampart, and demanded surrender. Busy inside preparing his supper, Wylie did not become aware of the assault until an attacker fired a musket ball through his door. An officer once again demanded: "Surrender!" Wylie came to the doorway and ordered the trespassers off of the property. The British commander responded by asking for the American commander.

"I am the commander!" answered Wylie. And "this is 'Squire Prince's Fort, and he has put me in charge of it." Meanwhile, marines spiked the cannons and searched for powder to blow up the garrison. But the magazine proved as empty as the rest of the place, and the British officer was reduced to demanding the surrender of the fort's flag. "I told you once," the agitated caretaker replied, "that this was 'Squire Prince's fort, and if you want any flag, you must go to 'Squire Prince."[1]

Thus stymied, with night descending, the British decided to press on up the river. On the Cushing side, at Collin's Cove, the raiders torched a sloop and another vessel on the stocks. At Broad Cove, they cut out a pair of sloops and towed them away. Young Christopher Curtis failed to escape in a punt from the second sloop and was detained. All of the noise brought Captain Joseph Gilchrist with his fowling piece to the scene. He discharged a volley into the darkness in an attempt to intimidate the invaders. Instead, he aroused the Kelleran and McIntyre clans on the other side of the river. They commenced a spirited fire toward Gilchrist and those who joined him, thinking they were the enemy.

Although unsettled by the puzzling exchange and thick fog, the English officer concluded to forge ahead to the greater prize — Thomaston. He forced Curtis by gunpoint to pilot the barges to the target. As they got unknowingly close to town, the officer wavered. Curtis exaggerated the distance remaining as the first inkling of dawn appeared in the east. The Brit felt it prudent to leave well enough alone and turn back. On the way down the river, the officer set Curtis ashore at the lower narrows and made the best of his way back to the *Bulwark*. Another Maine harbor town escaped the fate of Wareham, Scituate, and Potapoug.

All of this activity unnerved the men of nearby Waldoboro to the extent they rushed into town meeting "to determine what mode of protection" the town should adopt. They appointed a "Committee of Arrangements" to

---

1 Eaton, *History of Thomaston*, 296-297.

come up with "some suitable system of defence," and to consult with Bristol, Friendship, and other towns in the area. The meeting went on to direct the selectmen to "immediately cause 50 pounds of Powder to be made into cartridges . . . with a Ball in each cartridge, deposit them in portable boxes with two flints to every 24 cartridges & lodge them in three places on the eastern side of the [Medomak] river & two places on the western side. . . ." And the meeting charged the militia officers "to see that no ammunition be wasted or expended carelessly."[1] While the British continued to plague the general vicinity, Waldoboro's preparations proved unnecessary and the town remained free of the enemy.

In the same period, the New Hampshire coast experienced an extended case of jitters. Around midnight on June 21, the authorities at Rye sounded a general alarm. The New Hampshire Gazette reported: "[T]he citizens of this and the adjacent towns assembled with alacrity which does them great honor, and evinces their readiness to fly to the post of danger in defense of their country and their firesides."[2] As the alarm bells and signal guns sounded, inhabitants poured onto the streets, most heading for the interior. "Drums beating, the clatter of horses' hoofs on the pavement, the crying of children, the shrieking of women, made the confusion Babel-like."[3] Within a short time, the chief of the militia concluded the enemy was not in the offing and the alarm proved false. But the rumor disturbed the countryside for hours.

The excitability traced to two factors — the recent Battle of Rye and the attractiveness and vulnerability of the nearby navy yard at Portsmouth. On May 30, the Junon and Tenedos anchored off Rye, and a barge from the Junon chased a coaster into the harbor. The local militia under General Thomas Goss took up positions behind a stonewall on Little Neck and exchanged small arms fire with the British boat. The meetinghouse bell tolled, couriers carried the intelligence to Portsmouth and the other neighboring towns, and Doctor John W. Parsons raced to the scene with his medical bags. Some of the militiamen fired so zealously, they ran through their complete allotment of 18 rounds. Commenting on the display, Lieutenant Napier observed the Americans "are not very good shots yet, or very enterprising, but they no doubt will improve."[4] Nonetheless, the militia wounded two Brits while avoiding casualties of their own. Missing a customary swivel or comparable heavy armament, the barge found itself outgunned, and, within moments, turned back to sea. Thus, what would turn out to be the only fight of the war in New Hampshire came to a quick end.

However, for some months, Isaac Hull, commanding at the Portsmouth Navy Yard, expected a British attack. The 74 building at Portsmouth attracted a great deal of British interest and scrutiny. An April town meeting asked Governor Gilman for 800 men and sufficient arms and equipment to staff

1 Town Records Vol. 3, 1813-1823 Town of Waldoboro, ME, 42-44.
2 Winslow, Wealth and Honour, 188.
3 McClintock, History of New Hampshire, 502.
4 Whitehill, 19-20.

the local forts. A few weeks later, Hull complained to the secretary of the navy about the "defenceless state of the Harbor." He did not believe the local militia could respond fast enough to counter the large force the enemy could throw at him. Hull told Secretary William Jones his 200 navy men could not match the one to two thousand attackers he expected, "and you can easily suppose what the result will be. . . ."[1] He wanted manpower similar to what he understood New London possessed. Jones replied Hull was on his own. The secretary acknowledged the difficulty of recruiting seamen, but asked, "If you cannot get them in the very quarter of the union where they most abound, where are they to come from?" Moreover, "If the people of a populous place, with such powerful means of defence natural and artificial, will not defend themselves, I see nothing to prevent the force you have mentioned from burning the town and everything in its vicinity."[2] Hull's concern was well-founded. On May 27, Commodore Hardy arrived in the area and went on board the *Nymphe* "for the purpose of reconnoitring the coast, particularly Portsmouth, preparatory to an expedition being sent there." Other than the Rye skirmish, in the end, the Royal Navy left New Hampshire shore facilities alone and concentrated its efforts elsewhere. Before leaving for Cape Cod, on May 30, the *Nymphe* fired "a few signals with guns to alarm the coast by way of a frolic, which succeeded."[3]

Maine continued to be the prime objective. The *Bulwark* tried to land troops at Boothbay on June 28, but aborted the effort when confronted by a determined defense. The next evening, in heavy fog, a barge or barges attempted but failed to gain Pemaquid Harbor. Captain John Sproul's Harrington Company stationed at the old fort heard them coming and fired at the muffled sound of oars, and received a return fire. Arthur Child thereupon rushed to the Falls to touch off the alarm cannon kept in Captain John Fossett's barn. He reached the barn at midnight and got several neighborhood men and boys to help him roll the heavy iron gun out of its hiding place. In their haste, they did not appreciate the fact the piece was pointed at Fossett's dwelling. The first discharge broke every pane of glass on the near side of his house. Nonetheless, the second shot "gave the people of the whole region decided intimation of their danger."[4]

On June 30, the *Bulwark* dispatched three barges to probe New Harbor. The continuing fog obscured the boats until two made it inside the harbor. William Rodgers approached the enemy, loaded gun in hand. An officer threatened dire consequences if he fired. Rodgers suggested they ought to leave, because 100 militiamen were on their way. Despite the threat, Rodgers fired his piece, primarily to alert the village. Within moments, a sizeable contingent of locals set up on the shore and poured a heavy fire of musketry into the barges. The raiders returned the fire with enthusiasm, but their small

---

1 Gardner W. Allen, *Papers of Isaac Hull*, 33-34.
2 Ibid., 35-36.
3 Whitehill, 18-20.
4 Johnston, *History of the Town of Bristol and Bremen*, 411.

cannons were aimed too high to be effective. "Soon the men in the forward barge began to show signs of discomfort, and the next instant were actually backing out of the scrimmage; but the other barge for a few minutes showed a disposition to take the place of her consort."[1]

The fight lasted only a few moments before the barges turned tail. "Quite a number" of British were killed or wounded, while the defenders reported only one casualty. A Yank suffered a minor wound. When William Elliot of Round Pond headed home in the forenoon, his hands and face still blackened with gunpowder, he remained "perfectly furious. He said he had been having the best sport he ever had in his life, shooting Englishmen."[2]

Not everyone from Maine, however, saw the British as enemies to be challenged and thwarted. There were a disturbing number of New Englanders who viewed the crews of the blockading ships as ready customers. A certain amount of innocence, of course, attached to the individual family farmers and fishermen who sold their meager livestock, produce or catch at fair prices to the Royal Navy. But the master of the *Polly* out of Northport tarnished his name and the reputation of his countrymen. On June 17, Captain Tyler P. Shaw appeared to invite capture by the *Nymphe* off Boston. He carried government stores, "which for the value of a few dollars, he, in conjunction with a rich merchant of Boston, forfeit their honour as men, their fidelity to their country and morality as Christians." Shaw assured the captain of the *Nymphe*, a rich uncle would load his vessel with freight, and "as soon as he got it he would immediately run down to us and thus fill his pocket by the basest ingratitude." Lieutenant Napier concluded: "My hope and prophecy is that he will be hung before his next birthday."[3] The authorities in Boston did detain Shaw for questioning, but could not develop a case against him. "No doubt is entertained," thought a Salem minister, "he went purposely with supplies."[4]

Despite scattered cases of avarice, most New Englanders, in one way or another, remained focused on the conflict or its effects. Intensified British activity promoted increased vigilance all along the coast. On June 24, a group of citizens met at the Lincoln Bank in Bath and petitioned General King to assign an infantry company for guard duty in and about the town. He answered by detailing a 77-man provisional company under Captain John Wilson to the duty. Freeport took its first specific steps of the war to protect itself. A June 30 town meeting directed the selectmen "to procure the full and lawful quantity of Powder and ball for the use of the town."[5] In addition, the meeting authorized the selectmen to purchase 15 muskets.

On Cape Cod, the town of Sandwich concluded it needed more than a standby militia. The town voted "for a sufficient number of the militia . . . to be detached and put under pay of the state, in order to guard the seashore of

---

1 Ibid., 412.
2 Ibid., 413.
3 Whitehill, 27.
4 Bentley, 262.
5 *Freeport* (ME) *Record Book 1789-1856.*

said Town."[1] An alarm sounded at Salem, and the state rushed cannons and other arms to the place. Boston anticipated an attack at any moment. The behavior of one of the most notorious junior officers in the Royal Navy added to the town's apprehension.

Master's Mate Charles Goullet, a 22-year-old Yorkshire man, commanded the *Nymphe*'s tender. During the night of June 21, he went into Boston Harbor, reconnoitered at will, and, in order to get attention, burned a sloop before he left at sunrise. But he did not stop at that. He sent a "gasconading note" to the *Boston Patriot*, an ardently Democratic newspaper. Goullet said he grieved over the fact he was not "a sufficiently good pilot to navigate as far as the *Navy Yard*," but he had some advice for the commandant. "I would strongly recommend Com. Bainbridge to place the *Constitution* in the best possible state of defence, not only for her own protection, but that of his *unfledged Independence*."[2]

The *Patriot* used the opportunity to criticize what it considered Governor Strong's inattentiveness to defense. The competing *Boston Gazette* retorted: "This is a totally false and shameless assertion."[3] The blame, according to the *Gazette*, belonged to the Madison administration and its unwillingness to put sufficient federal troops in the harbor forts. The battle of words continued unabated. The *Gazette* suggested the Goullet affair was a hoax, and the *Patriot* answered with corroborating details and testimony. Then the *Gazette* shifted to calling the war itself a hoax. The war's advocates, the paper claimed, "also thought they should be backed by Napoleon, and that he would stick by them forever — here was a hoax."[4]

Thus, the second year of the war closed much as the year began. New England, for the most part, remained opposed to the war and lamented the impact of national government policies. The conflict by now touched communities far from the shore. Joseph Dale of Norway, Maine had enlisted in a company of United States volunteers and marched off to Burlington, Vermont. After a year of service on the frontier, he returned home sick, and died a short while later. Dale left a widow and nine children destitute. As common folk like the Dales suffered, political factions continued their war of words. But the British coastal raids of recent weeks pointed to dire times ahead. The region was approaching its breaking point.

---

1 *Sandwich* (MA) *Town Records 1798-1829*, 4:138.
2 Whitehill, 67.
3 Ibid., 68.
4 Ibid., 69.

CHAPTER 11. AN ORDER TO DESTROY

Notwithstanding periodic seasonable fog, the mild weather of July enabled the British to intensify naval operations in New England waters. The tenders to the warships became increasingly bothersome. And Mr. Goullett of the *Nymphe* solidified his reputation as one of the most obnoxious enemy officers. He employed captured fishing vessels as tenders. After capturing and ransoming several coasters and wood sloops at Nantucket and threatening to fire the town, Goullett called on the towns of Dennis and Yarmouth on Cape Cod. On the evening of the 3rd, he demanded a $1,000 ransom, since he believed the towns' Bass River sheltered several vessels he had chased a few days earlier. When Goullett appeared, five local fishing schooners were anchored and vulnerable in back of the bar at the mouth of the river. He threatened to burn the five vessels and every other Bass River boat he encountered if the locals did not promptly pay the ransom.

The owners in the port struggled throughout the night to raise $660. They carried the sum out to Goullett at sunrise along with an assurance the balance was on its way. By eight o'clock in the morning, the remainder was in hand and sent out. However, before the messenger reached the tender, Goullett spotted a vessel off Hyannis and raced away in pursuit. The next day, he stopped some fishermen from Bass River and ordered them back in to get the balance due or he would return and commence burning.

At this point, the Dennis and Yarmouth men decided to appeal for relief to Captain Milne on the *Bulwark*. They set out their case in a detailed letter, explaining they were "much alarmed us having several fishing vessels on the fishing ground and being in a great measure dependent upon their earnings for the necessaries of life as we are much impoverished by this unhappy war."[1]

---

1 Men of Yarmouth and Dennis, *Letter*.

Abner Crowell of Yarmouth, as agent for the petitioners, carried the letter to Milne.

"Uncle Abner" played his role to the hilt. He presented himself as an impoverished and unsophisticated fisherman. Milne and his staff appeared amused, yet Crowell's determined delivery gained an accommodation. He did not get the $660 reimbursed, but he did reach an accord on fishing privileges. Hereafter, in order to remain unmolested, all men fishing out of Bass River had to sign a promissory note agreeing to pay Crowell $100 within 90 days. But, if a subscriber during the present fishing season did not "render nor allow any assistance in re-capturing or piloting any prize or Neutral Vessel or Vessels . . . ," the $100 obligation would be voided.[1] Anyone imprudent enough to offer such assistance was required to pay the $100 to Crowell, and he would forward the levy to the British.

Meanwhile, Goullett sailed off east of Cape Cod to better fortune. He captured the schooner *Bee* on the 6th carrying $3,000 and a load of fish. This easy and profitable capture contrasted with a humiliation a week before. On June 30, the *Nymphe*'s tender captured a Harwich boat returning from Nantucket with 16 passengers, mainly women, and a load of cotton and wool. The British carried the Harwich captain to the tender, and transferred an officer and two men, all unarmed, to the Harwich vessel. A thick fog soon caused the tender to lose sight of her prize, allowing a pair of young Americans on board to turn the table on their captors. Both carried throaters, or fish knives. Thus armed, the young men subdued the three Englishmen and struck a deal. They put the officer and his two men in a skiff after the officer pledged to obtain the release of their captain. The Harwich master made it ashore the next day.

Goullett moved to Nantucket and with ease captured a number of helpless vessels between Tuckanuck Shoals and Great Point. When a Brit from the tender went in town to demand ransom money, it aroused considerable agitation and anger. A gang gathered in the streets intent on taking the offensive against Goullett's band. The leaders, for the most part, were off-islanders. The selectmen and others convinced the strangers that retaliation would lead to punishing attacks on the defenseless island.

All of this prompted a pacifistic gesture from the sizeable Quaker community on the island. Obediah Mitchell and others sent a letter to Goullett to "inform thee that we are of the people called Quakers and of the discription of Pease makers and have not at any period been enemies to Great Britain. . . . In consequence we feal imbolded to solicit thy lenity" because "the most correct part of the Inhabitance are solicitous and ever have been for Pease with G. Britain."[2]

Goullett penned a characteristic reply. "I forthwith acquaint thee that I am of the description of pease breakers called Sailors," he wrote, "and being at this present time in extreme want of materials to supply my calling, I must

1 Silas Baker, *Note*.
2 Whitehill, *New England Blockaded in 1814*, 39.

pray and beseech thee, Obediah, immediately to cause to be sent unto this, my sloop, at sea four bushels of the said pease, of the colour usually denominated green. . . ." The swaggering master added, "and it being a known rule of thy sect to succour the unfortunate, more particularly friends in distress, I trust thou will let the Milk of Human Kindness flow freely from thee, and should it to my unconscious eyes assume the appearance of cow's milk, and thee, Obediah, the plain and upright pail that holds it, even then, respected friend, I should not be offended!"[1] In the end, the islanders capitulated and Goullett "carried away several thousands of dollars in specie, besides sundry other articles."[2]

Despite the coastwise intensive interdiction of all American vessels as personified by Mr. Goullett's exploits off Massachusetts, early in the month, it became clear the English coveted eastern Maine. In the spring of the year the New Brunswick provincial legislature petitioned the prince regent requesting "when a negotiation for Peace shall take place between Great Britain and the United States of America, His Royal Highness will be graciously pleased to direct such measures to be adopted, as he may think proper, to alter the boundary between those States and this Province, so that the important line of communication between this and the neighbouring Province of Lower Canada, by the River St. John, may not be interrupted." Lord Bathurst obviously felt a need to strengthen his hand prior to opening the matter to any negotiation. In June he directed General Sherbrooke to occupy that Maine territory "which at present intercepts the communication between Halifax and Quebec."[3] Sherbrooke took the first step by mounting an expedition to take Moose Island in Passamaquoddy Bay. As head of the government at Halifax, he assigned Captain Hardy and Lieutenant Colonel Andrew Pilkington to the mission.

Beyond 250 local militiamen, Fort Sullivan at the southeastern end of Moose Island provided the only defense for the place. Major Perley Putnam, six officers, and 73 troopers (11 of them sick) of the 40th United States Infantry from Salem manned the fort. Pilkington would find six officers and "about eighty men."[4] Whatever the actual number of defenders, it was clearly insufficient to contest an assault of any size.

Up to this time, duty at the Eastport fort proved indifferent and monotonous. Lieutenant E. Manning, fresh from an assignment with the nearby Robbinston detachment, knew one reason. "Robbinston is a fine place," he said in a June 10 letter to Lieutenant Andrew Lewis at Castine, "and the young ladies very agreeable, much more so than at Eastport." He closed his brief note with a humorous yarn. "I ordered two (women) drummed out of

---

1 Ibid., 40.
2 Starbuck, *History of Nantucket*, 290.
3 Stanley, *Journal of the Society for Army Historical Research*, 168.
4 *Naval Chronicle*, 33:253.

Camp yesterday, which caused considerable laughter in Post."[1] In just an-other month, monotony and laughter would disappear from Fort Sullivan.

In the afternoon of July 11, the primary invading force moved up the East-ern Ship Passage or White Horse Way with the H.M.S. *Martin*, 18, Captain Humphrey F. Senhouse in the van. Hardy followed with the *Ramillies*; the *Bream*, Lieutenant C.D. Browne; and the bomb-ship *Terror*, rated an 8, John Sheridan. Bomb vessels, it should be explained, were rigged to carry as few as one large mortar designed to hurl explosive shells, or bombs, farther than the range of common naval cannons. Several transports trailed carrying some 2,000 men of the 102nd Regiment of Foot and a company of Royal Artillery. At the same time, Captain Richard Coote in the *Borer* entered the West Passage and proceeded to a point off the northwestern end of the island so as to block the natural escape route from Eastport.

At three o'clock, the ships hove to off Hayden's Wharf, and Lieutenant Oats came ashore under a white flag. He hastened to the fort and presented Putnam with an ultimatum from Hardy. The commodore took note of "the weakness of the fort;" expressed a hope to avoid "the effusion of blood;" indi-cated a desire "to prevent ... the distress and calamities" which would follow resistance; and gave the major five minutes to decide.[2] The feisty Putnam, though sick himself, declared: "As long as the American flag is flying, I do not surrender."[3] However, several leading townsmen were on hand, and they im-plored Putnam to give in and save the town from destruction. He called his officers to a council, and they were divided on the question. Putnam angrily threw his sword away.

Oats returned to his boat bareheaded. He had arranged beforehand to signal the ships at the first moment. If he covered his head, it signified a capitulation. Hat in hand meant the Americans had rejected the ultimatum. Just as Oats moved away from shore, he turned and saw a soldier lowering the fort's flag. With a sense of accomplishment, he placed his hat back on his head. Putnam had agonized for a few minutes before coming to his senses and offering the surrender of his little contingent. He explained in a written response to Hardy: "This I have done to stop the effusion of blood and in consideration of your superior forces."[4]

Pilkington came on shore and marched a force of over 500 Redcoats to take over Fort Sullivan. Although British intelligence correctly assessed the approximate strength of the defenders, the colonel felt ill at ease directing so many soldiers to take up a few score of impassive prisoners. The editor of the *Boston Patriot*, like some of his counterparts, suggested the Eastport out-come actually amounted to an American victory. He mockingly concluded: "[W]hen the people of England learn that this expedition has cost John Bull more than half a million dollars and has resulted in the capture of 48 ... full

---

1 *Bangor Historical Magazine*, 10: 200.
2 Auchinleck, *History of the War Between Great Britain and the United States*, 344.
3 Holt, *Island City, A History of Eastport*, 1.
4 Auchinleck, 344.

blooded Yankees and 6 . . . pieces of cannon, no doubt they will think it a glorious victory."[1]

Almost immediately, it became certain the action amounted to much more than a hit-and-run raid. Over a thousand members of the 102nd promptly took up defensive positions around the island, and Fort Sullivan became Fort Sherbrooke. Within hours, the British landed a fair number of dependent women and children. And before 18 hours passed, they found a suitable building for their youngsters and opened a school "for instruction in the common branches of education."[2]

To remove any doubt, on the 12th, Lieutenant Colonel J. Fitzherbert, the British commander in New Brunswick sent a letter to Brigadier General John Brewer at Robbinston. The colonel told Brewer, the head of the Washington County militia, the purpose of the expedition was to "obtain possession of *the Islands in Passamaquoddy bay*; — as being within the British boundary line; that there was no design to carry on offensive operations against the people resident on the main, unless their conduct should provoke severities; and that if they continued quiet, neither their persons nor their property would be in the least molested."[3]

Two days later, Hardy and Pilkington issued a proclamation in behalf of the prince regent declaring existing laws designed to assure the public order would remain in effect, and all inhabitants were commanded to appear on the 16th to take an oath of allegiance to King George III. Two thirds of the people took the oath. About 500 islanders rejected the overture, and found themselves on the earliest boats for Portland. As the weeks passed, others sold their real estate to eager British buyers and departed the place. Those who stayed made the best of the occupation. For the few weeks he remained on the scene, Hardy enjoyed respect and popularity. He liberally entertained on the *Ramillies*, and participated in community activities. Hardy delighted spectators when he tried to ride a pacing mare. "He made poor work of it, indeed; for saddle, stirrups, and bridle were gear to which he was not accustomed, while the beast would not obey quarter-deck mandates."[4]

Elsewhere, there was little time for amusements. The omnipresent British navy and news of the Eastport subjugation combined to excite anxiety far and wide. Belfast finally got around to forming "a committee of safety in this season [of] peril and to make whatever other arrangements this crisis may demand for the public good."[5] The town of Sullivan held a town meeting to "determine in what manner and what path they will take in case the Enemy should take post in this part of the County."[6] People seemed on edge. At Marblehead, one armed guard shot a young man who challenged him, and

---

1 David Zimmerman, *Coastal Fort*, 47.
2 Kilby, *Eastport and Passamaquoddy*, 183.
3 William D. Williamson, *History of the State of Maine*, 2:640-641.
4 Kilby, 186.
5 *The Second Book of Records in the Town of Belfast* (ME) *1807 to 1825 inclusive*, 159-160.
6 *1789-1831 Book of Sullivan* (ME) *Town Records*.

another sentinel shot an unresponsive old gent returning from a nighttime frolic. All along the coast, towns strengthened their limited defenses.

Lieutenant Napier of the *Nymphe* went into Salem late in July under a flag of truce and observed signs of general distress. While arranging for the exchange of several prisoners, he found the "soldiers, miserable looking, ill-dressed beings, but the officers, if possible, worse." He noted that while before the war, 20 East Indiamen sailed out of Salem, "now hardly a coaster of fifteen tons escapes being captured." Many women came down to his barge, he said, "to find out whether Englishmen were Christians or Devils. The ladies on this coast are infinitely more violent than the males, perfect Amazons!"[1]

As the weeks passed, the long war disposed some of the British officers to become callous. In July, the *Nymphe* stopped a little fishing boat in Cape Cod Bay and sent the skipper into Provincetown for $200 to ransom his craft. He possessed permission to fish and trusted the enemy would not molest him. "The poor creature has a wife and seven children, no money, and was in debt for his salt and fishing lines even," wrote Napier. "He with great difficulty scraped up by sixpences and shillings the amount of the money . . . and came on board with tears in his eyes. This is an ungenerous war against the poor and unworthy of Englishmen. I am ashamed of Captain Epworth's conduct."[2] A Salem diarist made much the same point. "One of our poor fishing men has his little boat taken from him & burnt & he put adrift in his boat many miles from land, without anything to eat or drink," Reverend Bentley wrote. "These are the mighty feats of Ships of 74 guns in our bay."[3]

Be that as it may, a fair amount of ransom money found its way back into the subsistence economy of the isolated communities. The selectmen of Provincetown, Truro, and Wellfleet visited the *Nymphe* early in July, prompting Napier to conclude, "[S]electmen . . . of all the Yankee towns are certainly *very select.*"[4] During the visit, the navy made a purchase of beef which seemed to be facilitated by the town officers. The diplomatic niceties continued a few days later when the selectmen of Chatham and Wellfleet carried sheep to the frigate, sheep the British considered lost after sending them to graze on Thatcher's Island. Towards the end of the month, Epworth sent armed boats ashore to procure oxen. "Arms" explained Napier, "are put in to save appearances for the people are willing enough to supply us with whatever we want, indeed a deputation of Quakers came off to beg we would go a little further to the southward and we should be supplied with much fatter and better cattle."[5]

On occasion, a British sympathizer took too much for granted. Mrs. Rhoda Howes of Chatham delighted in reciting the misadventure of Squire

---

1 Whitehill, 35-36.
2 Ibid., 38.
3 Bentley, *Diary of William Bentley*, 4:273.
4 Whitehill., 33-34.
5 Ibid., 41.

Crow, a Tory and Anglophile. "He killed a creetur and carried the beef over to" a British warship "to make friends with them." Fishing boats and packets experienced great difficulty running the blockade, she remembered, "so we couldn't get fish or coin either." Crow later ran his schooner into Chatham on the way to Boston, but the British spotted her, chased her ashore, and burned her. Most people "thought it was good enough for him and he did not get much sympathy in town."[1]

Despite some troublesome conduct on the water, there is general agreement the British acted as gentlemen when on shore at places such as the Lower Cape. Years after the war, a Truro lady recalled meeting a group of Britishers while walking home from school with some young classmates. The Truro girls started to move to the side when a dashing lieutenant touched his hat and urged: "Don't turn out of the road, young ladies, we won't harm you."[2]

Hannah Cobb of Truro, 21 at the time and older than the schoolgirls, remembered the period. The navy men came up the road past her father's house. "They looked very nice in their flashy uniforms but their being British and our enemies was enough for us Cape Cod girls, and though they tried hard to form acquaintances, they found no favors from us." Cobb added: "They wanted milk, eggs and any other produce that we could sell, and would pay for it quite liberally too."[3]

Sylvia Freeman of Provincetown retained a pleasant memory of the war years. On the beach she encountered a sailor from the H.M.S. *Spencer*, 74, known around the Cape as the "Terror of the Bay." "Little girl, there is a man on my ship who is very sick. If you might get me a bucket of milk, I will give you two dollars."[4] Sylvia succeeded in coming up with the milk and received the promised payment. With the proceeds, she bought a pair of French calico dresses.

August 1814 may well have been the worst month of the war from the American perspective. The government determined a $25 million war loan authorized in March raised only $11.4 million. Further hampering war operations, just about every bank outside of New England suspended specie payments. And the British armed forces intensified their efforts on all fronts. To the east on the 6th, the *Tenedos*, Captain Hyde Parker, appeared off Northeast Harbor at Mount Desert Island. His crew spent the next few days watering the ship and taking on provisions including four oxen and over 300 pounds of potatoes. The animals and potatoes came from a Cranberry Island fisherman in exchange for an assurance that his boat would not be torched. Thomas Bunker watched the activity and suspected the British "meant mischief."[5]

---

1 William C. Smith, *History of Chatham*, 387.
2 Rich, *Truro-Cape Cod*, 357.
3 Hannah Cobb, "War of 1812."
4 Nancy W. Paine Smith, *Provincetown Book*, 30.
5 Hansen, *Mt. Desert*, 20.

Earlier, to avoid seizure, Bunker and Benjamin Spurling secreted their schoo-ners inside the Mill Pond at Norwood's Cove behind Southwest Harbor.

The British did not take long to learn about the two hidden vessels. In an attempt to avert conflict and avoid the loss of their schooners, Bunker and Spurling responded by making their way out to the *Tenedos.* After a brief conference, Parker decided to hold Spurling as a hostage and send Bunker back to shore to raise money to ransom the schooners. Once Bunker made it to town, word of the threat spread rapidly and as many as 70 armed locals gathered in the woods about the cove near the targeted vessels. Militia units from as far away as Ellsworth started for the site.

Old Jacob Lurvey, a Revolutionary War veteran living on the Somesville road, gave over his only musket to his son who hustled to the scene. As the hours passed, the elder Lurvey became increasingly agitated. He jumped from his sick bed and began to dress.

"'What are you thinking of, Jacob?' cried his wife. 'You, sick man, and going down to the fight!' And then, to head him off utterly, 'What could you do without your musket? Isaac's got that.'"

"'Yes, I'm going. By this time some of our men have been wounded, and there'll be a musket for me.'"[1]

Out on the *Tenedos,* Parker grew impatient and dispatched an armed landing party in a cutter and a barge equipped with a swivel gun. The British placed Captain Spurling in an exposed position in the barge as something of a shield. Bunker remembered: "When the barge approached near enough, she was hailed, and told to keep off as the woods were full of armed men."[2] An initial exchange of gunfire prompted young Robert Spurling to come out from the woods and plead for his endangered father's life. In reply, the elder Spurling yelled from the barge, "Never mind me, Rob, I am an old man, but give it to these dashed Britishers as hard as you can." Another exchange of musket fire followed, and the attackers employed their swivel "breaking branches, hitting rocks, but wounding no one."[3]

Always reluctant to take on concealed sharpshooters, the British backed off after just several volleys and returned to their ship. Two Brits suffered severe wounds in what proud natives called the Battle of Norwood's Cove. Another Englishman and one American received minor wounds. The next day, Parker released Spurling unharmed and sailed away to the south. Over the years, young Lurvey proudly pointed out the tree that had absorbed 17 bullets aimed in his direction.

A more memorable battle took place at the other end of the New England coastline. Stonington, Connecticut became the target of Captain Hardy, the conqueror of Eastport. He reappeared off the eastern Connecticut town in the *Ramillies* on August 9th and sent a blunt, one-sentence note on shore. "Not wishing to destroy the unoffending inhabitants residing in the town of Ston-

---

1 Street, *Mount Desert,* 215.
2 Hansen, 21.
3 Somes-Sanderson, *The Living Past: Being the Story of Somesville,* 104.

ington," he wrote, "one hour is given them from the receipt of this to move out of town."[1] Hardy brought the *Terror* with him from Maine, and added the *Pactolus*, 38 and the *Dispatch*, 18 and, later, the *Nimrod*.

The message threw the town in confusion. "The sick and aged were removed with haste; the women and children with loud cries were seen running in every direction."[2] Valuables were buried in gardens or secreted in wells. The able-bodied men had two choices — defend or run. Without hesitating, as committee of defence chairman Amos Palmer reported, "[T]hey all exclaimed they would defend the place to the last extremity, and if it was destroyed they would be buried in the ruins."[3] Stonington possessed only two 18-pounders, one 6-pounder, and insufficient ammunition. The five British warships carried a combined rating of 156 guns.

An urgent call went out to the militia of the area, primarily the Third Brigade of the state force. Eight companies of the 30th Regiment hastily marched to positions in Stonington. Eventually, elements of the 8th, 20th, and 33rd regiments made it to the field. A little more than 60 militiamen were in the borough at the outset, and they rushed to the small breastwork overlooking the harbor, nailed their colors to the flagpole, and dug in.

Sixty minutes passed and the feared bombardment did not start. "Nelson's favorite hero and friend was seized with the compunctions of magnanimity; — he remembered what ancient Britons were; he remembered that something was due to the character of Sir Thomas M. Hardy."[4]

But two hours later, Hardy sent in five barges and a launch loaded with men. Each vessel also carried a carronade in its bow. Shortly thereafter, at eight in the evening, the warships opened a sustained covering fire of bombs, rockets, grape, and canister shot. When the invaders got within small grape distance, the militia opened fire with their cannons and muskets. The British small craft backed off and tried to land on the east side of the harbor. But the militia responded by dragging a small cannon over to beat them back again. The ships pounded away until 11:00 p.m. when firing ceased for the night.

By dawn on the 10th, another 227 militiamen were in place, and the *Nimrod* joined the attackers. At 7 o'clock, the British renewed their bombardment and sent five barges and two launches to shore. Like the day before, the Connecticut men beat back the first attempt to land. The British retreated and again moved toward the east side. At this point, according to Palmer, "We checked them with our six-pounder and muskets till we dragged over one of our eighteen-pounders. We put in it a round shot and about forty or fifty pounds of grape, and placed it in the center of the boats as they were rowing up in a line and firing on us. We tore one of their boats all in pieces, so that two, one on each side, had to lash her up to keep her from sinking."[5]

---

1 Richard A. Wheeler, *History of the Town of Stonington*, 68.
2 *Independent Chronicle* (MA), August 22, 1814.
3 Richard A. Wheeler, 74.
4 Trumbull, *Defence of Stonington*, 10.
5 Ibid.

Once the invasion craft returned to the warships beyond the harbor, the militia trained its cannons on the nearby *Dispatch*. When they got down to their last five cartridges, the defenders simply hunkered down for the next four hours as the navy ships threw round after round into the town. Finally, an express arrived from New London with ammunition, and the militia renewed its interest in the *Dispatch*. They drove her from her anchorage after coming close to gaining her surrender. A favorable change of wind helped the brig escape at the last moment. Out of reach of the American guns, but just within range for their own larger cannons, the British ships continued the bombardment.

Later on the 10th, Stonington sent two civil officers, Isaac Williams and William Lord, under a flag out to the *Ramillies* to feel out Hardy about his continued intentions. Town officials felt "there must exist some latent cause of a peculiar nature to induce a commander who had heretofore distinguished himself for a scrupulous regard to the claims of honorable warfare, — to induce him to commit an act so repugnant to sound policy, so abhorrent to this nature, so flagrant an outrage on humanity."[1] The Stonington men learned their town became a target because the British suspected it was a primary manufactory of dreaded torpedoes. They denied the charge, and the commodore moved to another issue. He would "wave the attempt of the total destruction" of the town if the local authorities sent Mrs. Elizabeth Stewart, the wife of the former British consul at New London, and her children out to the flagship.[2]

The truce lasted until the next afternoon when a series of miscommunications coupled with the fact Stonington was powerless to produce the Stewarts resulted in a resumption of the assault. The *Terror* lobbed shells into town from mid-afternoon until sunset. She returned to her work the next morning, and the *Ramillies* and *Pactolus* moved in and each fired three broadsides at the village. The bomb-ship continued to fire until noon. And then the British ships moved away altogether, ending the Battle of Stonington.

At the outset of the intense cannonading, "the people of New-Haven were fearful that the city of New-London had fallen into the hands of the enemy," all because of the presence of Decatur's trapped squadron.[3] New Haven expected an attack on the next fair wind. "The enemy are probably advancing up the Sound, and other towns may be summoned, like Stonington, to *surrender or be laid in ashes*."[4] The pro-Federalist *Boston Gazette* opined: "It seems the British naval commanders are determined to drag the physical force of New England into a vigorous defence of our territory; they experienced at Stonington-Point, the sharp shooting of federalists, as they say themselves. . . . They say the d—d Yankees fight like the d—l."[5]

1 Ibid, 13.
2 DeKay, *Battle of Stonington*, 173.
3 *Boston Gazette*, August 15, 1814.
4 Ibid., August 18, 1814.
5 Ibid., August 25, 1814.

By the time it was over, the British warships threw a reported 60 tons of metal into the little town, set 20 buildings on fire at a total loss of $4,000, and wounded just one defender while killing a horse and a goose. During the days to follow, the townsmen salvaged 15 tons of enemy ordnance and two anchors. Though battle casualty counts are often unreliable or imprecise, a report based on a British source indicates the attackers suffered 21 killed and 50 wounded. Hardy reported only two Englishmen died. But Stonington actually buried four of the enemy found floating in the harbor. At any rate, even though the people of Stonington claimed victory, the episode got the attention of everyone close to the New England shore.

Hardy's lackluster performance at Stonington pointed to the fact he did not have his heart in the effort. He told Williams and Lord the mission "was the most unpleasant expedition he had undertaken."[1] And it was not his style of combat. A week after he withdrew, it became clear Hardy acted on a general order from Admiral Cochrane. The continuing conduct of elements of the American army on the frontier incensed the British. On December 10, 1813, for instance, as it evacuated nearby Fort George, the New York militia under Brigadier General George McClure burned the Canadian town of Newark. Similar destruction occurred at the Long Point settlement, the village of St. David's, and elsewhere. As recently as May, a band of unorganized Americans crossed Lake Erie and struck mills and homes in Dover. Governor General Sir George Prevost as a consequence became vengeful. He wrote to Cochrane at Bermuda and asked him to retaliate. On July 18, Cochrane sent an order to the commanders of all his warships on the Atlantic coast of the United States, directing them to "destroy and lay waste" any American community "you find assailable," sparing only "unoffending" or "unarmed inhabitants."[2]

The Cochrane directive became known to the American government when Secretary of State James Monroe received an August 18 advisory from Cochrane. The admiral said his "order to destroy and lay waste" was a response to "the wanton destruction" of the United States forces in Upper Canada. "I had hoped that this contest would have terminated without my being obliged to resort to severities which are contrary to the usage of civilized warfare," he declared, "and as it has been with extreme reluctance and concern that I have found myself compelled to adopt this system of devastation, I shall be equally gratified if the conduct of the Executive of the United States will authorize my staying such proceedings, by making reparation to the suffering inhabitants of Upper Canada, thereby manifesting that if the destructive measures pursued by their army were ever sanctioned, they will no longer be permitted by the Government."[3]

Monroe got around to replying on September 6. He countered Cochrane's claims of irregular conduct and concluded: "Should your Government adhere

---

1 Trumbull, 16.
2 DeKay, 110.
3 *American State Papers: Foreign Relations* 3:693.

to a system of desolation, so contrary to the views and practice of the United States, so revolting to humanity, and repugnant to the sentiments and usages of the civilized world, whilst it will be seen with the deepest regret, it must and will be met with a determination and constancy becoming a free people contending in a just cause for their essential rights and their dearest interests."[1]

Monroe did not reply right away, because he found himself otherwise occupied. On August 24, a smaller force of Redcoats engaged a mixed force of American regulars and militiamen at Bladensburg, Maryland northeast of Washington. In the face of a disciplined attack, the militia broke and precipitately fled from the field. The defeat became known as the "Bladensburg races," and it opened the door to the capital. The British went on to sack Washington, especially public property including the Library of Congress. At the low point of his administration, Madison called Congress back into session. The Treasury was down to its last $5 million as of the first of July. In order to meet the "increased violence" of the British, he said, "large sums should be provided." The president lamented, the enemy "has avowed his purpose of trampling on the usages of civilized warfare.... His barbarous policy has not even spared those monuments of the arts and models of taste with which our country had enriched and embellished its infant metropolis."[2]

Just before Congress returned, Madison issued a proclamation exhorting the American people to rise to the challenge presented by the British disregard for humane principles and civilized rules of war. But the town of Nantucket turned a deaf ear to the call for renewed patriotism, having set a different course weeks earlier. In July, islanders intensified their efforts to obtain the basic necessities by appealing to Captain Milne for British permits to carry goods to the island. Milne agreed to the private petition and allowed one Nantucket vessel to transport provisions for personal use and others to carry firewood from Maine for family use. However, the squadron found the first permitted vessel it examined to be carrying goods for sale and profit. "In consequence of such a wicked and fraudulent proceeding," Milne revoked his permitting policy on August 5 and prohibited vessels "to leave or go into the Island of Nantucket, so far as the Squadron under my Orders can prevent it and private property of any description will be captured or destroyed."[3]

At about the same time, the town tried its luck with Cochrane. An island group of 225 "Federal Republicans and Friends of Peace," feeling "wholly dependent on the clemency of a Generous and magnanimous enemy," outlined the "absolute want" of the inhabitants in a written appeal for relief to the British admiral. On June 17, the justices of the peace of Nantucket County sent a similar request to Cochrane. Then, on July 23, the selectmen called a town meeting to appoint a committee to employ all legal means to obtain

---

1 Ibid., 694.
2 U.S. *Senate Journal.* 13th Cong., 3rd sess., September 22, 1814, 525-527.
3 Starbuck, 292

provisions and fuel. The *New Bedford Republican* reported, "[A]n assemblage of about 100 democrats, including the most insolent brawlers for the present War, convened and voted, unanimously, to clothe the Selectmen with the authority desired."[1] The board appointed Isaac Coffin and Sylvanus Macy and directed them to go to Admiral Cochrane and present the town's case. On the 28th, the pair sailed in search of Cochrane in Chesapeake Bay.

Coffin and Macy did not reach the admiral until the end of August. When they talked to him, they highlighted the unique situation of the island. "The people of Nantucket are a Defenceless People and mostly Quakers," the two stressed. "They never did Address the President of the United States with a tender of their Lives and Fortunes to support the War with Energy against Great Britain. The Island of Nantucket doth not Raise provisions enough for One Quarter part of the Inhabitants — They never owned a Privateer nor Letter of Marque in this War nor have they had a man in the Sea or Land Service of the United States . . . neither has there been an Organized Militia there these Fifty years last past."[2] After their fervent presentation, the two commissioners learned Cochrane earlier authorized Captain Henry Hotham, head of Royal Navy forces between Nantucket and Delaware, to deal with the Nantucket matter. So, they set sail for Long Island Sound. And when the two men found Hotham on the *Superb* off Gardner's Island, they discovered others from Nantucket recently entered into an agreement with him. Coffin and Macy headed home, their extended journey proving needless. Late in August, the British reached out to the island in a way that embarrassed the American government all the more since it followed on the heels of the humiliating plunder of Washington.

On August 22, Captain Vincent Newton in the *Nimrod* arrived in the island's harbor and came ashore under a flag. A diarist noted a Federalist delegation treated the navy contingent "with more familiarity than any strangers ever here before."[3] Newton told the authorities Hotham sent him to negotiate a neutrality agreement with Nantucket. The selectmen realized such a compact required a town vote, so they called a town meeting for the evening of the 23rd. The town house could not accommodate the large turnout, so the meeting "adjourned out of doors Round and about the Town cistern."[4]

After a relatively brief discussion, the town voted to "not take up arms against Great Britain"; to "surrender up all . . . publick Arms, Ammunition, and other publick property"; to "not take up Arms to Defend any publick property"; and to "make no opposition against any Brittish Vessel Coming into this harbor to Refresh."[5] In return, some Nantucket vessels would be licensed to carry supplies to the island. A letter writer to the *New Bedford Mercury* said, "All the inhabitants are rejoiced at the prospect which this arrange-

1 Ibid., 293-296.
2 Ibid., 301.
3 Byers, *Nation of Nantucket*, 286.
4 Starbuck, 303.
5 Ibid., 304.

ment affords them — particularly the Democrats — who are the *first* to beg favors from the very enemy whom they have insulted and abused." In addition to gaining access to provisions and fuel, the writer saw another benefit. "Those who have not paid the Direct Tax, will get clear of the same — for the U.S. jurisdiction over the Island, ceases, I presume during its *Neutrality*."[1]

Celebrations followed. The next day, the Nantucket packet *Maria* carried "large numbers of gentlemen and ladies" to the *Nimrod* for a dance on board. Some of the guests actually "tarried till 9 o'clock."[2] A Boston paper reported that during the *Nimrod*'s stay, "Officers and sailors were frequently on shore, and behaved very civil and polite; and were received in a very friendly manner, and entertained by the inhabitants."[3]

After the partying, a committee of four Nantucket men — two Democrats and two Federalists — followed Vincent to meet with Hotham off Long Island and consummate a written neutrality agreement. "[A]ll harmony — the Demos are obliged to comply & fall in with the feds," an island lady wrote in her diary.[4] On board the *Superb*, formalities concluded on the 28th, and Hotham issued a directive to his squadron. In addition, he granted three permits for Nantucket vessels to sail to Delaware for provisions and three to go to New York. Fifteen ships received licenses to transport wood.

Right away, both sides had second thoughts. Nantucket sent a delegation to visit Vice President Gerry at his home in Marblehead and apprise him of the development and the island's motives. Gerry appreciated the predicament and promised to seek the government's good opinion of the action. For his part, Cochrane anticipated a need to strengthen any neutrality pact. When he sent Coffin and Macy to see Hotham, he added a postscript to the letter he gave them to carry to the captain. If Nantucket inhabitants continued to pay any federal taxes or duties, he declared, he would withdraw any neutrality agreement, and he would "call on them to pay double the amount to His Majesty's Government."[5] Hotham did not receive this directive until more than a week after he signed the accord with Nantucket. Hotham promptly informed the island about the added requirement and directed the authorities to assure him they intended to comply with the Cochrane proviso.

The island felt cornered. A town meeting petitioned Congress to consider "the peculiar, Multiplied, and overwhelming evils which assail" Nantucket and "suspend the collection of the Direct Tax and Internal duties which, by Law, are, or may be, liable to be exacted of them." Congress did not get around to considering the petition until December when it was referred to the Committee on Ways and Means as the war began to wind down. Aware the petition alone would not meet with Hotham's approval, the town took an interesting preemptive step. The tax collector "was prevailed upon im-

---

1 Ibid., 305.
2 Gardner, *Coffin Saga*, 179.
3 *Boston Gazette*, August 29, 1814.
4 Starbuck, 307.
5 Ibid., 308.

mediately to resign his commission." Moreover, the town told Hotham, it felt "confident, that no inhabitant of the Island will accept the appointment as collector, and that no stranger will expose himself so much, as he necessarily must, to hold this undesirable office." These moves failed to satisfy Hotham. Consequently, on September 28, a sparsely attended town meeting dominated by Federalist affirmed the town's position in a manner agreeable to the captain when it voted "That this Town will not pay any Direct Tax or Internal Duties during the present war between the United States of American and the Government of Great Britain."[1]

In the final analysis, the notorious neutrality affair did not result in any military or strategic advantage for the British. It simply provided Cochrane — and the Federalists — with an opportunity to try Madison's patience. As for the islanders in general, the limited permits provided limited relief. Before long, the passes created so much partisan animosity as well as jealousy on the part of masters who did not receive the protections that the system fell into disfavor. The necessities of life remained scarce on the island until after the war ended. But the agreement did produce one unexpected benefit. Nantucket men held at the notorious Dartmoor prison in England gained early releases. British Admiral Sir Isaac Coffin, born in Boston of Nantucket parents, interceded on their behalf and they were discharged because "like the citizens of Denmark and Sweden, they were neutral."[2]

The nature of the next British operation in New England, however, proved altogether different from the Nantucket caper. Responding to the British government's interest in securing a dependable line of communication between Halifax and Quebec, Sherbrooke recommended "the most desirable plan would . . . be for us to occupy the Penobscot with a respectable force, and to take that river (which was the old frontier of the state of Massachusetts) as our boundary, running a line from its source in a more westerly direction than that which at present divides us from the Americans."[3] On August 26, Sherbrooke, with Major General Gerard Gosselin and Rear Admiral Edward Griffith, initiated his plan, leaving Halifax in force intent on striking Machias before moving to the Penobscot River. His flotilla consisted of the *Dragon*, 74, Captain Robert Barrie; the *Endymion*; the *Bachante*, 38; the *Sylph*, 18; a large tender; and ten transports carrying the 29th (Worcestershire), 98th (Prince of Wales's), and 1st Battalion, 62nd (Wiltshire) Regiments of Foot; two rifle companies of the 7th Battalion, 60th (Royal American) Regiment; and the 1st Company of Royal Artillery — some 3,000 soldiers. Early on the 31st, the task force fell in with Captain Joseph Pearce in the H.M.S. *Rifleman*, 18. Pearce advised Sherbrooke that the little American frigate *Adams* under Captain Charles Morris had got in the Penobscot and was upriver at Hampden. Sherbrooke changed his plan and decided to go after the *Adams*. He rendezvoused off Matinicus and added the *Bulwark*, *Tenedos*, *Peruvian*, 18,

---

1 Ibid., 309-311.
2 Andrews, *Prisoners' Memoirs, or Dartmoor Prison*, 79.
3 Stanley, 170.

and the schooner *Pictou* (ex-*Zebra* and second ship of this name in America) to his fleet, and moved on Castine.

The turn of events had its origin weeks before. Early in July, Morris left the Irish coast for America. Miserable, wet weather persisted during the return. By the time the ship reached the Gulf of Maine, several men had died from scurvy and 58 were down with the illness. Morris intended to gain Portsmouth, New Hampshire. Foggy conditions impeded precise observations, but soundings at midnight August 16 suggested he was nearing Cape Ann, thus confirming his estimated position. But at 4:00 a.m. on the 17th, in darkness and fog, the ship ran up on a ledge at Isle au Haut. To this day, the spot off the southern tip of the island just to the east of Western Head is called "Morris's Mistake." He initially thought he struck Cashes Ledge east of Cape Ann, "and the reflection that, in case the ship should founder, its distance from the land would render it impossible for a great portion of the crew to reach it by our boats caused some of the most painful moments of my life."[1]

When daylight arrived, Morris assessed his situation and put his prisoners and the sickest sailors on shore and took steps to float the ship off the rock at the next high tide. All went well, and near noon, the men succeeded in heaving her off. The crew worked the pumps and buckets continuously, moved the ship away, and restored a semblance of order by sunset. When the next morning dawned relatively clear, Morris, to his bewilderment, saw he was in the area of Mount Desert. He met two fishing boats, and sent them off to carry his sick crewmen and prisoners on Isle au Haut to the safety of Camden. And then a lookout on the crippled *Adams* spotted an enemy brig of war. Morris appeared to give chase to the smaller ship, but, in reality, he strived to make his way to the relative security of the Penobscot. The brig turned out to be the *Rifleman*.

Early on September 1, Sherbrooke's Penobscot expedition entered the cove at Castine and approached the lower fort. The formidable force stunned the citizenry, and the local militia melted away. Twenty-eight regulars staffing the fort refused an opportunity to surrender, but they were not far behind the militia. After firing a token salvo at a reconnoitering schooner, Lieutenant Lewis spiked his four 24-pounders, ignited a string of gunpowder that blew up the magazine, and headed to Buckstown trailing two field pieces. Sherbrooke landed an artillery detachment and two rifle companies to probe the defenses. When it became apparent Castine would not be contested, most of the other troops disembarked in good order. They took over the second fort, the courthouse and the customhouse, using the latter two buildings for barracks. Officers secured some of the better homes for their quarters.

Sherbrooke and Griffith immediately issued a proclamation "to the effect that, if the people would remain quietly at their homes and continue to pursue their usual avocations, would surrender all their arms, and would

---

1 Charles Morris, *Autobiography of Commodore Charles Morris*, 75.

refrain from communicating intelligence to the Americans, they should have protection and safety insured to them."[1] Also, the existing municipal officers and laws would remain in power, and the troops would pay for any provisions received from the inhabitants. The proclamation made it clear, "it is the intention of the British commanders to take possession of the country lying between the Penobscot River and Passamaquoddy Bay. . . ."[2] Castine became an English port of entry. Vessels belonging to the place were permitted to do business with the British provinces, but intercourse with any place to the west of the Penobscot was prevented. In reality, the occupation regularized "a state of military neutrality and economic co-operation that already existed."[3] Then Sherbrooke turned his attention to the *Adams*.

Before dispatching forces up the river, Sherbrooke attended to his left flank and a principal line to and from Hampden. He sent Gosselin with most of the 29th Regiment to occupy Belfast across the bay opposite Castine. Once they saw the lower fort explode, the inhabitants of Belfast anticipated such a tactic and many carried their more valuable household belongings inland, some going as far as Searsmont. The little Belfast militia understood armed resistance would be foolhardy and futile. The captain of the local artillery secreted his two field pieces over Park's hill. Other men hid their muskets about their property. Nonetheless, some 1,200 militiamen from the surrounding countryside assembled three miles out of town at the Simon Watson farm. "They anticipated having an engagement with the British, and in case the enemy committed any act of violence, or depredations, or did not render obedience to the honors of war, they were determined to resent it at all hazards."[4]

Gosselin crossed in the *Bachante* trailing two transports. He anchored off town late in the afternoon of September 1 and sent in a flag of truce. A crowd gathered along the shore to watch the proceedings. An officer in the barge asked to talk to the chief magistrate of the place, prompting William Moody to conduct the party to Huse's Tavern to meet Asa Edmunds, the chairman of the board of selectmen. The British indicated they intended to stay for just several days and then leave in peace. As long as they remained unmolested, they would respect the citizens and their property. And, at fair prices, they wanted certain quantities of beef and other provisions by the next morning. Edmunds indicated the town did not object to the landing, but he doubted Belfast could fill the shopping order so quickly. "If we had known you were coming, — if you had given us notice, — we should have been better prepared for you." The visitors entertained the thought that Edmunds meant that with a little warning, the militia would have contested the landing. "It was said that the somewhat equivocal remark occasioned no slight merri-

1 George A. Wheeler, *Castine*, 51.
2 Locke, *Sketches of the History of the Town of Camden*, 118.
3 Harvey, *Dalhousie Review*, 207.
4 Locke, *Sketches of the Early History of Belfast*, 220.

ment when reported on board the frigate."[1] Before long, Gosselin and his staff also made their way to the tavern where they "tarried till after supper. . . ."[2]

At dusk, more than 600 picked troops, many veterans of Wellington's operations on the Peninsular, disembarked from the transports. Nicknamed the "Boston Regiment," it being the unit that had committed the infamous Boston massacre, the outfit marched behind a band up Main Street to quarters in various homes and buildings. Gosselin supervised the procession from the back of a chestnut-colored Spanish pony. Some of the men occupied the meetinghouse, filled the pews with straw, and bedded down. "As this house was neglected to be cleaned after the English left, the rotted straw emitted such an odor that . . . it was not again used until purchased by the Baptists in 1821."[3]

Officers maintained rigid military discipline during the Belfast occupation, and minor transactions resulted in immediate punishment. Desertion remained a major problem. In Castine, the British dug a canal 12 feet wide and 80 rods long across the neck, partly to prevent desertion. Two men were convicted of the crime and executed. Guards shot one soldier trying to cross the canal. At Belfast, to discourage desertion, officers told their men the town was situated on an island some distance from the mainland. An inquisitive sentry on Wilson's hill thought he would explore the western side of the "island". He did not stop until he got to Montville, a dozen miles inland, where he settled and lived out a respectable life.

Gosselin and his men remained in Belfast until the "object of the expedition up the Penobscot had been attained."[4] Sherbrooke ordered him back to Castine on the 6th. When the British began to embark, Sheriff Samuel Burkmar walked behind an officer riding the sheriff's horse. The officer appropriated the animal as soon as he landed in town, and Burkmar did not expect to regain his mount. "Arriving at the beach, the officer dismounted, and tendered the horse to Mr. B. with a guinea as compensation."[5] The departure of the troops proved just as orderly and uneventful. Belfast, of course, was a sideshow, while the main act played out to the north as soon as the British reached the *Adams*.

When Morris entered the Penobscot late in August he concluded Castine and Buckstown would offer little security for a ship under repair. He sailed 30 miles up the river and anchored at the mouth of the Sowadabscook Stream in Hampden, just below Bangor and on the western side of the river. He felt confident his men and the local militia could repel at least a modest attacking force. His crew dismantled the ship, carried armament and provisions ashore, and started the process of heaving the ship down. Word about the capitulation of Castine reached Morris on the 1st of September, and he

---

1 Joseph Williamson, *History of the City of Belfast*, 1:437.
2 Locke, *Sketches of the Early History of Belfast*, 221.
3 Ibid.
4 Auchinleck, 346.
5 Locke, *Sketches of the Early History of Belfast*, 223.

took steps to defend the *Adams*. He placed nine of the ship's guns in battery on a nearby hill and fourteen on Crosby's wharf commanding the river below. A single gun positioned in between the two batteries controlled communications. At the same time, Morris called for help from General John Blake at Brewer, the commander of the Eastern Militia and another veteran of the Revolutionary War.

Griffith put Captain Barrie in charge of the task force detailed to capture or destroy the *Adams*. Barrie immediately proceeded up the river in the *Dragon*, *Sylph*, *Peruvian*, the transport *Harmony*, and a prize-tender. Only a small number of British officers earned an unpopular or loathsome reputation among American citizens during the war. Barrie — "a total stranger to literature, to every generous sentiment, and even to good breeding"[1] — added his name to the short list. A citizen of Hampden in a position to make a judgment asserted Barrie "is what God almighty designed for a brute."[2] As for the cooperating ground elements, Sherbrooke assigned "the detachment of royal artillery, the flank companies of the 29th, 62nd, and 98th regiments, and one rifle company of the 7th battalion, 60th regiment" under the command of Lieutenant Colonel Henry John.[3] Comparing the colonel to Barrie, an observer said John "is some younger . . . but not so well favored; is somewhat cross-eyed, but has more of the man; has less bluster, but more ability."[4]

This assemblage amounted to a truly awesome force. Like the hardened 29th Regiment, the 62nd earned a distinguished combat record under Lord Wellington on the Peninsular. Yet there was more than their veteran status about these men. Wellington himself felt somewhat uneasy at the mere sight of his own troops. "The scum of the earth," he called them, "the mere scum of the earth. . . . The English soldiers are fellows who have all enlisted for drink — that is the plain fact — they have all enlisted for drink."[5] While he remained proud of the military accomplishments of his army, after the battle of Sorauren, Wellington complained, "There is no crime recorded in the Newgate Calendar that is not committed by these soldiers, who quit their ranks in search of plunder."[6] The inhabitants of Hampden and Bangor would soon share Wellington's assessment of the common British soldier.

By the morning of September 2, Barrie's command made its way past Frankfort. At 5:00 p.m., he landed the troops at Bald Head Cove three miles below Hampden. Skirmishers rousted a few militia pickets, and the British bivouacked in the rain by 10 o'clock. Barrie sent 80 marines and about as many sailors to augment the land units, bringing the enemy total strength on the field to 750.

---

1 William D. Williamson, 2:656.
2 Joseph Williamson, *Bangor Historical Magazine*, 3:27.
3 *Bangor* (ME) *Journal*, February 10, 1857.
4 Joseph Williamson, *Bangor Historical Magazine*.
5 Guedalla, *Wellington*, 210.
6 Ibid., 238.

The Americans countered with a force of comparable size. The navy men numbered close to 150, and Lieutenant Lewis and his two dozen or so regulars from Castine were on hand. Blake gathered about 550 militiamen. Questionable estimates placing the size of the American defending force at 1,500 may be traceable to the fact many militia companies were in motion at the time, but all of these units did not make the field. As one example, the Lincolnville regiment only got to within ten miles of Hampden before the fight ended.

Morris, Blake, their staffs, and civic leaders held a council of war at the academy in Hampden late in the day on the 2nd. "Blake opposed any resistance as he felt it would only serve to exasperate the enemy." This disturbed a Federalist lawyer named Gilman. He said "he thought the council was called in order to determine on the most effectual mode of making resistance, not to be determined after they had got on the spot whether resistance was or was not to be made."[1] Morris, in fact, unsuccessfully urged the Americans take the initiative and attack the British at their encampment. The recommendation to throw up breastworks and otherwise entrench met with similar disfavor. Blake's hesitancy to adopt vigorous measures did not generate a fighting spirit in his men, many of them inexperienced. Some even reported for duty without weapons.

In the end, Blake set up a simple defensive line along the crest of a high ridge overlooking a pasture to the south. The right rested on the old meetinghouse west of the north-south road running through town. A pair of brass 4-pounders and an 18-pound carronade commanded this road and the bridge over Pitcher's Brook — the expected route of a British advance. The left of the line ran to the river in front of the hill battery. Fearful of a surprise attack, the defenders remained awake and alert throughout the wet night.

Shortly after 7 o'clock on the foggy and rainy morning of the 3rd, Colonel John sent skirmishers toward the Pitcher's Brook bridge. A sharp engagement ensued, so the colonel sent half of the company from the 29th Regiment in support. John soon "discovered the enemy drawn out in line, occupying a very strong and advantageous position."[2]

Lieutenant Lewis directed the militia's two field pieces and the carronade near the meetinghouse and he raked the road at the bridge with grape. But "the British ignored the fire, crossed the bridge, deployed, and charged with drawn bayonets."[3] The Lewis guns killed two attackers, including a captain, as well as a local man forced to guide the British to town. The disciplined, veteran Redcoats advanced up the hill as if on parade. When the enemy's glistening bayonets appeared out of the fog, the cold, wet, and inadequately trained militiamen in the center broke and fled in disorder. The sudden gap in the middle of the American line panicked the right and left wings, and a general rout ensued. Men took "to the woods, their homes, hiding or throw-

1 *Bangor* (ME) *Democrat*, March 10, 1857.
2 Auchinleck, 348.
3 Trickey, *Historical Sketches of the Town of Hampden*, 18.

ing away their arms and removing all evidence of involvement from their persons."[1] The general flight exposed the Lewis battery, prompting a militia captain to take his two cannons and flee to the Bangor woods. An army sergeant fired the 18-pounder a final time before spiking the carronade and departing.

Morris controlled the wharf battery while his first lieutenant, Alexander S. Wadsworth, commanded the hill battery. At the same time the Pitcher's Brook assault jumped off, a flotilla of barges, launches, and rocket boats moved on the *Adams*. Morris swept the river with grape, but the British were beyond reach. "A few minutes only had elapsed" said Morris, "when lieutenant Wadsworth informed me that our troops were retreating, and immediately after that they were dispersed and flying in great confusion. We had now no alternative. . . ."[2]

Before the British overran his hill position, Wadsworth spiked his guns and left for the bridge over the Sowadabscook. Morris discharged and spiked his guns and ignited a train leading to explosives on the *Adams*. With her colors flying, she blew up before the British could intervene. Morris found the enemy advance "so near the bridge that a part of our force, myself among the number, had to ford the creek, which the state of the tide fortunately permitted."[3] All of the *Adams* men made their way to Bangor where they organized a departure from the area. Morris directed his crew to head west to the Kennebec River thence to Portsmouth by way of Portland. He felt it "impossible to subsist . . . in a body,"[4] so he sent them off in small groups. "Capt. Morris was destitute of money, and his men were in rudest garb. They all suffered incredible hardships before they reached . . . the Kennebec."[5]

With one exception, the few settlers along the first leg of the route "willingly relieved our wants to the extent of their means." An apparently well-off farmer refused to let the men help themselves to some of his potatoes in his field. Upon hearing the refusal, a sailor stepped up to Morris, touched his hat, and softly asked: "Shall we pull the house down?" Morris, of course repudiated the thought, but the question "seemed to excite no small apprehension in our uncivil countryman." The next farm along the way appeared distressed. But the young owners said the navy men were welcome to their five sheep. "Three were accepted and soon prepared in the potash kettle which our host provided for the purpose."[6] Morris compensated the man by allowing him to select a musket, accoutrements, and ammunition from his party's belongings. Morris felt grateful for the help provided by the citizenry all along the way, and he later complimented their "liberality and attention."[7]

1 Fernald, *In Defense of the Adams*, 17.
2 *Niles' Weekly Register* (MD), October 6, 1814.
3 Charles Morris, 81.
4 Hatch, *Maine: A History*, 1:76.
5 *Bangor* (ME) *Journal*, February 7, 1856.
6 Charles Morris, 81-82.
7 Hatch, 1:77.

On September 6, the Morris group approached the Kennebec at Waterville, some 50 miles through the woods from Bangor. An alarm spread through the countryside at the first report of an armed band marching on the town. "Preparations for defense were rapidly made and the bravest youths started out to meet the foe and to defend their homes." To the relief of most of the citizens, the marchers turned out to be the *Adams* crew. "The friendly foes soon entered the town and the event was celebrated in what was considered the appropriate manner."[1]

Captain Morris borrowed funds from the Bank of Waterville and continued on his way. Along with many of his men, he made Portsmouth on September 9. And "at the end of two weeks every man reported himself at the appointed place — not a single one missing."[2] Morris felt gratified. "Notwithstanding the facilities that offered themselves on such a march, and the general disposition of sailors to prefer a change, not a single desertion took place."[3] The captain gained as much satisfaction from the fact an October court of inquiry conducted by Captain Hull and Captain John Smith absolved the officers and crew of negligence and wrongdoing associated with the loss of the *Adams*. In fact, the court found reasons to compliment the conduct of the officers and crew.

Back in Hampden, the British assumed full control within an hour and detached 200 soldiers to secure the town. Eighty prominent men spent the night as prisoners on the *Decatur*, one of two merchantmen lying close to Crosby's wharf. Most of these men were paroled the next day in time to watch the victors return from Bangor and ransack the town on their way back to Castine.

While the battle raged in Hampden, some of the British tars remaining on the ships amused themselves by firing cannons into unprotected Orrington on the east bank of the river. A ball from the *Sylph* smashed through a cottage near the ferry killing an occupant. A farmer nearby headed for the woods with his children and cattle when a cannon ball passed close enough to blow off his hat. And the town's Methodists cancelled their quarterly meeting when a shot hit their meetinghouse.

As soon as the *Adams* exploded, the main enemy ground force pursued the dispirited militia to Bangor. The *Peruvian*, *Sylph*, *Harmony*, and a few smaller craft moved up the river and arrived at Bangor ahead of the troops. The town sent out flags of truce, and the attackers responded by firing Congreve rockets over the village and gave two cheers. Captain Barrie appeared on horseback at midday on the 3rd, accompanied by Colonel John and Major Riddle of the 62nd. The selectmen asked the terms necessary to spare the town. "The answer . . . was, unconditional submission, public offices and property to be given up, the People of the Town to give up their arms and parole themselves, and private property should be most sacredly respected, to all of which the

1 Edwin C. Whittemore, *Centennial History of Waterville*, 58.
2 Jonathan F. Morris, *Genealogical and Historical Register of the Descendants of Edward Morris*, 229.
3 Charles Morris, 82.

Town agreed."[1] Quarters and provisions were demanded and supplied, "since the commodore, who was a churlish, brutal monster," according to a correspondent, "threatened to let loose his men and burn the town if the inhabitants did not use greater exertion to feed his men."[2] Without hesitation, the town relinquished the courthouse, two schoolhouses, a dwelling, and another building for barracks.

Barrie ordered that "no liquor should be sold or given to the men." But a *Bulwark* lieutenant demanded a "pipe of brandy, which as an officer demanded it was delivered without ceremony, rolled into the street put on tap & under the direction of said officer served out in buckets to the men."[3] Barrie saw Thomas Hatch dealing the brandy, felt disrespected, and knocked Hatch to the ground and kicked and spilled his cask. Barrie ordered an officer to destroy all the liquor in town. Before the facts behind the apparent disobedience became known, six stores were plundered and $6,000 worth of property destroyed. Some of the benefactors of the errant lieutenant's largesse may have been the soldiers who took the feather beds from General Crosby's house. They proceeded to the grist mill "and after pouring the feathers into the hopper, hoisted the gates and tried the experiment of making flour of feathers."[4]

Highjinks aside, many citizens became "frightened and moved into the woods." A newspaper correspondent wrote: "I know not what we shall do. We can scarcely provide for ourselves, much less a numerous enemy." The next day, the 4th, the same writer indicated: "We are alive this morning — but such scenes I hope not to witness again. The enemy's Soldiery are tolerable civil, *when you give them every thing they wish*. . . . They have emptied all the stores and many dwelling houses — they break windows, and crockery, and destroy every-thing they cannot move. . . ."[5]

Townspeople, aware of their powerlessness, tended to be conciliatory. A Republican of some prominence met a British officer on Main Street, pointed to his garden, and said:

"Captain, there is some sauce in my garden to which you are welcome."

"I want none of your sass (was the insulting answer)."

"I mean there are vegetables you can take if you wish."

"To be sure I can, they are mine already."[6]

Personal abuse on the part of the British at Bangor did not recognize anticipated bounds. One man remembered that "in dealing out their vengeance upon property and individuals it fell with unsparing hands upon the 'Friends of Peace.' Those who expected protection received the greater indignities — the New England spirit was no shield against the 'tender mercies'

---

1 Flagg, *Sprague's Journal*, 126.
2 Trickey, 22.
3 *Bangor Town Records*, Collection 1141.
4 *Bangor* (ME) *Commercial*, July 24, 1914.
5 *Boston Gazette*, September 15, 1814.
6 *Bangor* (ME) *Commercial*, July 24, 1914.

of Strong's Bulwark." Barrie horsewhipped a Doctor Fiske, a noted merchant and Federalist, when Fiske failed to obey an order with alacrity. Another Federalist and the town's state representative had his store pillaged. The British seemed to delight in plaguing Federalist lawyers, breaking into their offices and destroying papers and records. And Lawyer Hill "had his House entered, his clothes taken, even his wife's stockings, and when he protested against it, was threatened to be run thro'."[1] An antiwar minister encountered similar ill-use, but former Republican congressman Francis Carr exhibited his political skills and fared better. Defeated for re-election in 1812 largely due to his initial vote for war and subsequent vacillation, Carr went out in the street and convinced the raiders to spare his dwelling.

During the night of September 3 and into the morning of the 4th, the British methodically burned 14 vessels including the brig *Caravan*, the schooners *Eunice and Polly, Gladiator, Neptune's Barge, Thinks-I-To-Myself*, and *Three Brothers*, the sloop *Ranger*, and three unlaunched vessels across the river in Brewer. When they started to burn four ships on the stocks at Bangor, selectmen Moses Patten and Thomas Bradbury, fearful "burning them would have involved our little village in one general conflagration," pleaded with Barrie to stop and make a deal.[2] The selectmen offered Barrie a $30,000 bond that the unfinished ships would be completed, launched, and delivered to the commodore at Castine by November. Barrie, along with Colonel John, accepted the proposition. The enemy carried away the *Bangor Packet*, the schooner *Oliver Spear*, the *Hancock*, the *Lucy*, the *Polly*, and the boat *Cato*.

Before returning down the river on the 4th, Barrie and John paroled 191 local men considered prisoners, General Blake among the group. The British also guaranteed all the men of Bangor and Orono who "shall within thirty days next coming sign a parole of honor not to serve against his British Majesty or his allies during the present war unless regularly exchanged as prisoners of war, their personal safety, with that also of their families not so old as eighteen years of the male sex, and all females."[3] The Bangor selectmen felt overwhelmed by the turn of events. The estimated losses and damages inflicted by the British amounted to $45,000.

The men of Orono assembled in town meeting at Perez Graves' house and decided not to act on a warrant article to see "whether the town thinks it expedient to give up their arms and equipments to the British and be paroled under the same form that the town of Bangor has." Instead, the meeting formed a committee "to make inquiry and to find out the intentions of the British towards the Inhabitants of this town, and if it appears to them that they intend to invade this town. . . ."[4] In time, it became apparent the enemy held little or no interest in the place west of the Penobscot, and Orono was off the hook.

---

1 Flagg, 127.
2 *Bangor Town Records.*
3 Ibid.
4 *Bangor Historical Magazine*, 3:168.

But the enemy expedition decided to spend more time in Hampden. On September 5, the retiring British burned the *Decatur* and the other vessel off the town — the *Kutusoff*. The temper of the visitors prompted a committee to appeal to Barrie to treat the place with a little humanity. His shocking reply more or less summarized the philosophy of his mission.

"Humanity! I have none for you. My business is to burn, sink, and destroy. Your town is taken by storm. By the rules of war we ought to lay your village in ashes, and put its inhabitants to the sword. But I will spare your lives, though I mean to burn your houses."[1]

Mrs. Martin Kinsley refused to cower. British officers spotted her stately house and figured to put up in the place during their brief stay. She ignored their rapping on her front door, and continued supervising her hired girls on the second floor. The Brits threatened to burn the Kinsley dwelling and its occupants if they were not admitted. Mrs. Kinsley leaned out of a bedchamber window and told the men to quietly leave her premises. The officers continued their pounding and threats. The lady decided to act. With the help of her girls, she opened a couple of the upstairs windows, and emptied several fragrant chamber pots on the stunned enemy below. Prior to departing the town, one British officer allowed "that if the militia had had Mrs. Kinsley in command, Hampden would have been celebrating a victory, instead of suffering a defeat."[2]

Revolutionary veteran Harding Snow handled a demanding officer in his own way. The Englishman commanded Snow to turn over a cow for slaughter, but the old man refused.

"I guess you don't know who you are talking to," exclaimed the Brit. "You never have seen a British officer before."

Unfazed, Snow retorted: "I have and I have seen 'em run."

"Where did you see them run?

"At Bunker Hill."[3]

The defiance so unsettled the officer he whacked a log with his sword so forcefully the weapon snapped in two.

Otherwise, soldiers terrorized the village, killing livestock at will, destroying gardens, furniture, books, papers, and whatever met their fancy, but they did not follow through on Barrie's threat to burn houses. Before he left, however, the captain managed to extract a $14,000 bond on several incomplete vessels on the stocks in town, requiring their deliverance to the Royal Navy in Castine by November 1. When the havoc ended, the town estimated its total losses at $44,000, a sizeable sum for the period and just about the same loss reported by Bangor.

The attack flotilla slipped down to Frankfort and rejoined the *Dragon* on the 6th. Barrie demanded 40 oxen, 100 sheep, and a quantity of geese to go along with a number of horses taken in Bangor and Hampden. In addition,

---

1 Abbott and Elwell, *History of Maine*, 422.
2 Trickey, 20.
3 Boileau, *Half-Hearted Enemies*, 158.

he required the townsmen to surrender all of "their arms and ammunition — a part of which only was delivered; and in general the sturdy republicans of this town were slow to obey any of his commands."[1] Barrie left on the 7th, vowing to come back and make the town pay for its delays.

The captain did not return, but a local farmer took action to make the town pay. The selectmen leaned on George Haliburton to turn over a yoke of oxen to help meet the enemy demand. Haliburton did so and after the war, like so many others throughout the country, sought recompense through litigation. He sued the town, and a lower court awarded him damages — the cost of the oxen. Selectmen appealed to the Massachusetts Supreme Judicial Court. Haliburton's lawyer argued that, "as the demand made by the enemy was on the town in its corporate or municipal character, and as the plaintiff's property was appropriated to the satisfaction of that demand, it was reasonable and just that the town should reimburse him for what he had thus advanced for their benefit, and had applied to their use." In contrast to today's verbose written decisions full of legalese, Chief Justice Isaac Parker got right to the point in two brief paragraphs. "However meritorious the plaintiff's claim may be, and whatever obligations may rest upon the inhabitants, in honor and equity, to pay him for property advanced to purchase the safety of the whole," the court found, "we are not able to perceive any legal principle upon which his action can be maintained. There was no contract by the inhabitants, nor by any person authorized to make one for them."[2] Therefore, the high court set aside the lower court's verdict.

The Yankees got one last crack at the Barrie task force before it reached Castine. Several inhabitants shot from cover at the retiring British ships as they passed through the narrows at Prospect. The marksmen reported killing three sailors and wounding four. While this claim is questionable and inconsistent with British accounts, the retaliatory firing scored. Two British cannon balls hit one house and managed to kill one sheep. The impudence of the Prospect farmers concluded the Penobscot River expedition for Captain Barrie.

However, the affair did not come to an instant end for General Blake. His weak-kneed defense prompted the Commonwealth to initiate a court of inquiry. Major General Henry Sewall of Augusta and Brigadier Generals James Irish of Gorham and David Payson of Wiscasset sat for most of a week in Bangor before absolving Blake of misconduct. Blake promptly pressed charges against Lieutenant Colonel Andrew Grant and Major Joshua Chamberlain. At Hampden, where the center first crumbled, Grant commanded the right wing and Chamberlain commanded the left. Courts-marital in 1816 resulted in a two-year suspension for Grant and an honorable discharge for Chamberlain. The major, a grandfather of the popular Civil War hero of the same name, suffered materially at the time of the raid. The British burned two vessels on the stocks in the Chamberlain shipyard.

1 William D. Williamson, 2:648.
2 *Haliburton vs. Inhabitants of Frankfort*, 14 Mass. 214 (1817).

With Eastport subjugated, the *Adams* out of the way, and the major settlements along the Penobscot whipped, one chore remained before the British could claim dominion over eastern Maine. The little Down East town of Machias, Sherbrooke's original target, supported a federally maintained fort overlooking Machias Bay. Fifty regulars of the 40th U.S. Infantry and a dozen or so militiamen under Colonel Samuel A. Morse garrisoned the installation called Fort O'Brien. Sherbrooke sent Colonel Pilkington on September 9 with a brigade made up of elements of the Royal Artillery, and the 29th and 60th regiments — between 900 and 1,000 men. Captain Hyde Parker commanded the naval component which included the *Bachante* and *Tenedos*. The attackers landed at Buck's Harbor late on the 10th.

Pilkington stepped off at 10:00 p.m., intent on taking the crescent-shaped fort in the rear. Two mounted 18-pounder cannons and one mounted 18-pounder carronade faced to the front toward the water. When word of the pending attack reached the village of Machias, Colonel Jeremiah O'Brien mounted a horse and rode up and down the streets pleading for volunteers to "go out and meet the advancing foe on the Port road and turn them back or kill them!"[1] "If I can get twelve men to go with me, I will go to Col. Morse's relief."[2] Apparently the men of Machias could count better than the optimistic O'Brien, because he did not get a single volunteer. Most of the townsmen harbored antiwar views and considered themselves "Strong men." Disgusted, O'Brien galloped away across the bridge "uttering imprecations not of a gospel tone!"[3]

The men in the fort also could count. Five minutes before the enemy arrived, the defenders vacated the place, "leaving their colours." Pilkington said, "[T]he retreat was so rapid that I was not enabled to take any prisoners."[4] However, the British did find 50 to 70 cattle about the fort. In the weeks preceding the raid, Morse and his men confiscated the animals as contraband in western Washington and eastern Hancock counties and intended for the British garrison at St. Andrews. The sight of all the cattle at Fort O'Brien prompted one British officer to crack, "[T]his was the first fort he ever saw manned with bullocks."[5] The invaders did not encounter any resistance in a swift march to the village. In fact, a local horseman met the troops, gave a friendly wave, and conducted them to the center of town. But a militiaman from Narraguagus felt so shamed by the submission, he fired a token shot with his musket at the British, the only shot fired in their direction during the advance.

General John Cooper, the sheriff of Washington County, openly greeted the conquerors and asked Pilkington to avoid harsh measures prior to a formal capitulation. Cooper summoned General Brewer to Machias to confer

---

1 *Maine Historical Society Collections and Proceedings*, 1:203.
2 Drisko, *History of the Town of Machias*, 310.
3 *Machias* (ME) *Union*, August 16, 1881.
4 Auchinleck, 350.
5 William D. Williamson, 2:651.

and represent militia interests. Cordial discussions proceeded apace. In short order, the local military and civil officials signed the capitulation document, and accepted parole for themselves. Two days later, Sherbrooke and Griffith paid a brief visit to Machias and approved the agreement. The next day, the entire British force sailed back to Castine with the compliments of the local officials for their tolerably good behavior while in town. In fact, during the Penobscot adventure, both Sherbrooke and Griffith strengthened their solid reputations. A respected American observer of the campaign considered Sherbrooke "a man of splendid talents and courtly manners." He judged Griffith "to be affable and easy in his manners, and mild in temper; a man of handsome talents."[1]

From Halifax, on the 21st, Sherbrooke issued a lengthy proclamation governing conquered eastern Maine. He directed magistrates and civil officers to continue to function consistent with the laws and usages in place. He initiated an accounting of arms, but allowed men to retain their personal weapons exclusively for personal use. Sherbrooke mandated individual oaths of allegiance or neutrality from all males older than 15 years, but the British did not press the requirement largely because few of the region's inhabitants held any interest in resisting the British occupation. In many respects, the eastern side of the Penobscot became a British district. The United States mail did not cross the river from the west. And His Britannic Majesty's forces looked elsewhere around New England for things to do.

---

1 Joseph Williamson, *Bangor Historical Magazine.*

CHAPTER 12. SEVERE AND DEGRADING TERMS

As Machias submitted, a momentous engagement took place in Lake Champlain opposite northern Vermont. Told and retold elsewhere, the story does not justify in-depth treatment at this point. As one recent observer noted, the Battle of Plattsburg "can hardly be considered virgin soil . . ., for it has been analyzed and reanalyzed by everyone from academics to military and naval officers to world leaders."[1] Yet it is worth noting Theodore Roosevelt considered the action "the greatest naval battle of the war."[2] Churchill echoed the assessment, calling the event "the most decisive engagement of the war."[3]

Early in September, Sir George Prevost, governor of Canada and commander in chief of its armed forces, invaded northeastern New York at the head of an 11,000-man army. Captain George Downie supported Prevost and his movement against Plattsburgh and its substantial munitions depot with a lake squadron of 16 vessels. The Americans countered with a land force of less than 2,000 effectives under General Alexander Macomb and a fleet of 14 vessels under Captain Thomas Macdonough. Burlington, Vermont served as Macomb's staging point, and Macdonough put his fleet together at nearby Vergennes. During the campaign, more than 3,000 Vermonters volunteered for Plattsburgh service. When word of Prevost's invasion reached Montpelier, old Captain Timothy Hubbard took to the streets, cane in hand. He found a drummer and a fifer to march at his side as he criss-crossed the town throughout the day imploring men to volunteer to march to Plattsburg. By nightfall, Hubbard enlisted nearly two-thirds of the eligible males. The men stepped off the next morning, eventually taking a place in the line of battle.

1 Vermont History: The Proceedings of the Vermont Historical Society, 8:210.
2 Roosevelt, Naval War of 1812, 2:108.
3 Churchill, History of the English-Speaking Peoples, 3:296.

On September 11, Downie's superior force attacked Macdonough's well-positioned squadron in Cumberland Bay, now Plattsburgh Bay. Before surrendering after little more than two and a half hours of fighting, the British lost nine ships and suffered over 300 casualties. The Americans lost six vessels and counted about 200 casualties. When the smoke settled, Macdonough wrote to Secretary Jones: "The Almighty has been pleased to grant us a signal victory. . . ."[1] Prevost retreated back to Canada, and the northern frontier of New England remained quiet for the rest of the war.

Coupled with the glorified defense of Fort McHenry at Baltimore on September 13–14, the Plattsburgh victory gave a welcome boost to the national administration. However, New Englanders did not feel assured. Governor Chittenden of Vermont warned of hard times ahead while expressing new-found support for the war. In a September 19 proclamation, he remarked, "the conflict has become a common and not a party concern." He urged his constituents to set aside party politics and nerve themselves. "After witnessing the severe and degrading terms imposed on many of our fellow citizens on the seaboard," Chittenden said, "no man who is mindful of what he owes to his country and to his own character, can advocate submission while resistance is practicable."[2]

Sherbrooke's Penobscot campaign created anxiety, if not dread, from Camden to Connecticut. A Portsmouth newspaper reported the British evacuation of Belfast, adding: "Their avowed objects are PORTLAND and PORTSMOUTH — but they may stop at Wiscasset on the way."[3] The Boston papers carried the same alert, allowing: "They committed no depredations" in Belfast "but paid liberally for every thing they had."[4] A feared attack on Salem "made great shaking" among the inhabitants. So much so, the local authorities asked Reverend Bentley "to use all influence to stop the frenzy." On September 10 he noted the "alarm is so great that we are nearly depopulated. The quantity of Goods removed is immense. . . ." Two days later he recorded: "The people of the neighbourhood express their surprise to see people tumbling over [one] another to get out of Salem."[5]

The proximity of Belfast and Castine to Camden caused early concern at that place. On September 2, Brigadier General David Payson of the 11th Division ordered Lieutenant Colonel Erastus Foote's 5th Regiment "to fly to arms."[6] Responding to the order, Major Isaac G. Reed called together his Waldoboro battalion, and it headed for Camden late on Sunday the 3rd, "followed a long distance by weeping mothers, wives and sweethearts."[7]

1 Muller, *Proudest Day*, 328.
2 *Niles' Weekly Register* (MD), October 15, 1814.
3 *Portsmouth* (NH) *Oracle*, September 10, 1814.
4 *Boston Gazette*, September 12, 1814.
5 Bentley, *Diary of William Bentley*, 4:281-282.
6 Fannie S. Chase, *Wiscasset in Pownalborough*, 349.
7 Samuel L. Miller, *History of the Town of Waldoboro*, 115.

The militia of the town of Union received the call-up at the same time, occasioning "a general sadness." Women and children would need to complete the harvest. "Besides, — let the people say what they may, — the prospect of facing bullets backed with gunpowder is not agreeable." As the town's companies formed, several militiamen asked leave to attend church services about to begin nearby. The commanding officer granted permission as long as the soldiers agreed to return to formation at the beat of the drum. Before the minister completed his sermon, all was in order on the parade field, and "the summoning sound was heard. The men simultaneously rose, and went out of the meeting-house. The novel movement, at such a solemn time, awakened deep emotion; and many of the remaining members of the congregation could not refrain from tears."[1]

Foote placed cannons at both sides of Camden's harbor entrance as well as on Mount Battie overlooking the town. Over the next two days, militia units from Appleton, Belfast, Hope, Montville, Thomaston, St. George, and Warren advanced to support the Camden militia. But the scare proved groundless and lasted only several days. Payson released most of the troops and it turned out to be just in time for the Union men. Like many others, they were running low on food, having stepped off with only three day's worth of provisions. Upon reflection, it was felt the shortage would not have developed "if the military had had more experience as cooks, or the selectmen as providers."[2]

The midcoast nonetheless remained on edge for days. On the following Sunday, a rider from McCobb's Narrows pulled into the town of Warren with a report the enemy was moving up the St. George River. The authorities fired the alarm guns and sounded the courthouse bell. The local artillery company hastened to its post on the Thomaston wharf. After passing an uneventful and peaceful night, the militia disbanded, concluding the danger to be unfounded. The excitement apparently traced to an innocent William Parsons. Two young men assigned guard duty on the Cushing side of the river convinced Parsons to take their place while they courted some young ladies in the neighborhood. After a time, Parsons tired of his post and fired a gun to signal the wayward pair to return. Each station up the river answered the shot until the presumed alarm reached Hope, some 24 miles away. "The result was that not only the young beaux were brought in on the double quick, but that a company of minute men came all the way from Hope to Warren, before it was ascertained to be a false alarm; while Parsons got out of it the best he could."[3]

In early September, Portland prepared in earnest for an expected attack. An order to mobilize the militia and begin to organize the town's defenses went out to Brigadier General James Irish at Gorham. The messenger found Irish working his fields, whereupon the officer made haste to respond to the

1 Sibley, *History of the Town of Union*, 344-345.
2 Ibid., 345.
3 Eaton, *Annals of the Town of Warren*, 318.

call. As he raced to the east, he could not get the parting words of his elderly mother out of his mind. "Don't be a coward, James, don't be a coward; do your duty like a man."[1]

As the general took initial defensive steps, citizens exhibited increasing anxiety. British warships daily sailed about Portland Head Light reconnoitering. Bankers moved their specie inland and shopkeepers did the same with their goods and stocks. Reverend Samuel Deane of the First Church sent out a number of possessions, including books, furniture, and $1,060 in funds. Many families pulled up stakes. Lieutenant Otis Robbins, Jr., writing from Portland's Fort Sumner, told his brother in Camden their uncle should not think ill of the editor of the *Argus* when the newspaper shows up on just a half-sheet. The editor had his hands full with his duties as a militia officer. Robbins continued: "If the enemy should get possession of this town they would not get much, for all the property is moved out, the Town is nearly a wilderness . . . no stores open, and the finest houses are used for barracks for militia."[2]

Major General Alford Richardson of North Yarmouth took overall command of the forces gathered in Portland. Cumberland and Oxford counties dispatched just about all of their companies, and Portland appropriated $10,000 for its own defense. Redoubts and gun mounts appeared at key points and sentinels lined the shore. The disarmed *Boxer* received the armament of the prize ship *San Jose Indiano* and took up a position in the harbor. Estimates of the militia's strength ranged from 6,000 to 10,000. "But the enemy expresses the utmost contempt for them," thought Niles, "and expects to possess himself of *all the Massachusetts and Maine ports in six weeks* to destroy the shipping." In Bangor, "They took what they pleased, and done what they liked."[3]

Sad to say, some of the militiamen at the Portland entrenchments proved equally light-fingered. Many "were rather lawless and much addicted to stealing. . . . Iron bars, hoes, shovels, scrap-iron, — anything that could be of use on a farm, — were conveyed to their barracks, and sent home by friends who came to Portland to see them." One company captain reimbursed 70 dollars to complainants, while Waterford officers felt complimented when it was said their men "stole less than the rest."[4]

If possible, greater alarm developed in Portsmouth, New Hampshire. The fall of Castine and the aggression in eastern Maine frightened the town. A September 3 meeting asked the governor to provide military aid. The *Oracle* told the "good people" of the town: "You seem at last awakened to your danger. The danger is real, impending, perhaps at hand. You are called upon to use your efforts and your means for the protection of your soil, your houses,

---

1 Oak, *Life of General Irish*, 24.
2 Eaton, *History of Thomaston*, 299.
3 *Niles'*, October 6, 1814.
4 Henry P. Warren, William Warren, and Samuel Warren, *History of Waterford*, 126-127.

your property — in a word for your homes and your firesides, and *all* that renders them *dear*."[1]

On September 7, Governor Gilman called out detachments from 23 regiments throughout the state. Two days later, he ordered the entire militia to "hold themselves in readiness to march at a moment's warning, completely armed and equipped according to law."[2] Towns throughout the state responded. At New Ipswich, the selectmen mustered eligible townsmen at the meetinghouse and offered a dollar bounty and 12 dollars per month to those willing to go to the coast. "The drum and fife struck up, and a march commenced through the aisles of the old church, reviving within its walls the scenes of 'Seventy-six.' The required number soon joined." Each man drew down powder and bullets from the town magazine, "most of which were expended in shooting cats, pigeons and tavern signs on the march to Portsmouth."[3]

Massachusetts Governor Strong dispatched 500 of his militiamen to Portsmouth to help defend the navy yard and environs situated on the east side of the Piscataqua River in the District of Maine. Military exempts (often men too old for mandatory militia service) formed military associations around the Granite State. "Over a hundred men" in Concord, "comprising some of the most respectable and venerable citizens of the town, were straightway organized into a company numbered the Sixth of Volunteers."[4] They committed to act at the direction of the governor if called upon. The little town of Amherst formed a similar contingent made up of some 50 exempts. In the end, sixteen interior militia companies joined the two coastal regiments at Portsmouth, forming a brigade under the operational command of Brigadier General John Montgomery. Gilman traveled to the seacoast and assumed the role of commander-in-chief. The *Oracle* said: "We are happy to hear that His Excellency intends to command his troops in person."[5] By the middle of the month, the papers reported: "The means of defence have been prosecuted . . . with great assiduity. An attack is expected, and a determination to . . . repel it, universally prevails."[6]

Meanwhile, Captain Hull fretted at the navy yard. He thought "no dependence can be placed in the inhabitants of the town to defend anything more than themselves."[7] He devoted considerable effort to transferring the supplies of the *Congress* and all portable government property to inland Exeter. Hull worried about the vulnerability of the *Washington*, still on the stocks. She was at least two weeks from launching, and work on the great ship had slowed since some craftsmen left their work for militia duty. In-

1 *Portsmouth* (NH) *Oracle*, September 10, 1814.
2 Lyford, *History of Concord*, 1:335.
3 Gould and Kidder, *History of New Ipswich*, 125.
4 Lyford, 1:336.
5 *Portsmouth* (NH) *Oracle*, September 17, 1814.
6 *Boston Gazette*, September 15, 1814.
7 Maloney, *Captain from Connecticut*, 250.

telligence indicated the enemy squadron off Portsmouth consisted of three 74s, a pair of frigates, and several tenders — more vessels than required for routine blockade duty.

On top of this, Captain Bainbridge at Boston ordered Captain Morris at Portsmouth to transfer 30 of his men to the Massachusetts yard. Hull asked Bainbridge to reconsider. "I am ashamed of all around me, and blush for my degraded country; all is going, and God only knows what can save it from ruin, unless by the hand of him, we can raise the people." Hull pleaded, for "God's sake leave the men."[1] Bainbridge refused to change his mind, so Hull asked Secretary Jones to intercede. An irritated secretary of the navy ordered the men back to Portsmouth, thus fueling an incident that contributed to an eventual contentious, permanent split between the two famous officers.

Within the gathering clouds, Hull saw rays of hope. Young Captain Daniel Fernald of the coaster *Sally* used his wits to help the navy. Fernald sailed from Portland with two 24-pounders, 130 kegs of gunpowder, and 100 boarding pikes and cutlasses for the navy in Portsmouth. Fernald stowed the contraband in the keelson under heaped spruce wood. For good measure, he stacked cordwood about the deck. However, Lieutenant Robert Lashley in the tender for the H.M.S. *Spencer* intercepted Fernald off Saco.

Lashley sent men on the *Sally* to verify Fernald's claim he carried just firewood. The Britishers labored until they unknowingly reached within a single row of logs away from the weapons and powder. Inexplicably, they ended their search, came back on deck, and reported finding only wood. The lieutenant returned Fernald's papers and advised the searchers left too much wood in the bows. The Americans, he said, better right the load before proceeding.

Word reached Hull about the encounter. He assumed the coaster and her precious cargo were lost. But in time, the plodding *Sally* appeared outside the harbor. Hull quickly sent out boats to tow her up to the yard. Once the spruce was unloaded and out of the way, the "'big *logs*,' and '*kindling*' were rolled out."[2]

The "more destructive" prosecution of the war also promoted a sense of urgency around Boston. On September 6, Governor Strong directed Adjutant General John Brooks to order "the whole of the militia to hold themselves in readiness to march at a moments warning."[3] And individual towns took defensive precautions. Dorchester formed a company of exempts. Salisbury town meeting directed the selectmen to prepare 5,000 cartridges for use at short notice, and to set up a system of alarms employing cannons, bells, and burning tar barrels. A Roxbury meeting authorized its selectmen to procure munitions, engage horses and wagons for transport, and "procure hard bread, beef and pork for all the militia of the town."[4] Sixteen-year-old Eliza Susan

---

1 Ibid., 251.
2 Brewster, *Rambles About Portsmouth*, 261.
3 Commonwealth of Massachusetts, *General Orders*, Headquarters, Boston, September 6, 1814.
4 *Boston Gazette*, September 8, 1814.

Quincy, daughter of Josiah, chronicled preparations in her journal. She concluded: "It appears that if England consults her interest, we shall have peace, if her pride, war. Which passion will predominate no one can tell."[1]

The selectmen of Boston asked the Boston Marine Society to participate in a plan to sink blocking hulks in the channel between the forts on Castle and Governor's islands. The officials wanted the society to locate suitable vessels and position them for greatest advantage. Once the emergency passed, the authorities would raise the hulks and return them to the owners. A committee of the society looked askance at the idea even though the general membership supported the scheme. Events outpaced bureaucratic negotiations, and the dramatic measure did not get beyond the planning stage. The town, however, did work on improving fortifications at South Boston and on the harbor islands. While militiamen carried most of the workload, Bishop Lefebvre de Cheverus, behind a wheelbarrow, led 250 men from his flock to the work sites. And the local schoolmasters supervised a band of 250 scholars employed on the task.

Strong also renewed his continuing pursuit of federal funding for Massachusetts militia expenses. He told Secretary of State Monroe Massachusetts was compelled to defend itself since the United States troops left a dangerous void when they marched to the west. The national government, he argued, had a minimum obligation to pay costs. Monroe responded by repeating the administration's long-standing position. He allowed, if U.S. Army General Dearborn required and received the state militia forces, the "expenses attending it would be defrayed by the United States." But, if the state called the militia into service independent of Dearborn, the attendant expenses are chargeable to Massachusetts. Monroe said the "desolating warfare" made "it difficult to provide immediately for all the necessary expenditures."[2]

Strong was not alone in his feud with the Madison government. For weeks, Governor Smith of Connecticut tilted with the federal authorities on the questions of militia control and funding. Ever since the Stonington attack, New Haven and Bridgeport feared invasion and clamored for state help. Smith wanted a state major general to command the state militia serving with United States troops along the Connecticut coast. Failing to gain this concession, he withdrew the brigade of drafted state militia from federal service. U.S. Brigadier General T.H. Cushing countered by cutting off supplies to the brigade. Monroe supported Cushing by sending Smith a letter similar to his correspondence with Strong.

In the case of Connecticut, its post-Stonington apprehension would prove groundless. British forces essentially ignored the state's shore west of the Connecticut River. That does not mean the inhabitants of this sector lived free of the jitters. When coasting captain Elijah Reynolds sailed into Myanos River at Greenwich ignoring a hail, the sentry, Peter Horton, presumed the enemy was at hand. Horton threw down his musket and cried:

1 *Eliza Susan Quincy Journal*, 4.
2 *American State Papers: Military Affairs*, 4:886.

"'Now legs! If you ever did your duty, do it now!' It is gravely said by those who heard and saw him, that he tore down three rows of standing corn, in making his exit from the place of danger."[1]

In another scare, alarm bells sounded following a report of a nighttime British landing at Greenwich Point. Colonel Ebenezer Mead gathered his militiamen and marched to the meetinghouse in Old Greenwich where the band halted some two miles short of the enemy. "None were willing to proceed farther," except Whitman Mead who volunteered to reconnoiter under a flag. He found a squadron of gunboats out of the New York Navy Yard and Commodore Jacob Lewis and his men enjoying breakfast on the shore. Whitman decided to join them and tarry. All the while, the militia agonized. Their volunteer eventually returned with good news, and the company "feeling that they had earned glory enough for one day, disbanded and returned home."[2]

Timidity also flickered around Stratford. When a strange vessel appeared off the mouth of the Housatonic River, authorities detailed Sergeant James Coe and a guard detachment to watch over things during the night. As dawn approached, some of the guards thought they saw men moving in groups. Charles Burritt, familiar with the spot, knew that what appeared to be soldiers on the move were, in fact, bunches of thistle swaying in the wind. Burritt asked Sergeant Coe, "'Shall I shoot? I have two in range; I can kill them both.'" "'No, no!' said the sergeant, 'don't fire, but *Scatter boys! Scatter!* Or we shall all be killed.' And scatter they did, in double quick, still carrying on the joke."[3]

The controversy covered in the Strong–Monroe exchange would continue for years, but during the war, Jefferson and others promoted the view Massachusetts provided little aid to the national effort. In fact, the numbers tell a different story. Only New York supplied more regular troops than Massachusetts. All told, New England furnished 13 regiments. The middle states of New York, New Jersey, and Pennsylvania provided 15, and the remaining or southern states from Delaware to South Carolina supplied 10 regiments. As for financial support, in 1814, Massachusetts generated $1,600,000 in customs revenue, while Madison's home state of Virginia produced only $4,000. The two states provided almost the same amount of internal revenue during 1814. Massachusetts came up with $198,400 and Virginia forwarded $193,500. Direct tax collections were one-sided. Massachusetts turned in $2,114,400, while Virginia provided only $566,500.

For the most part, New Englanders devoted little attention to the tedious intergovernmental debates. The Royal Navy occupied their consciousness, especially in the case of those living on or close to the shore. The first September raid outside of eastern Maine fell on Gloucester. On the 8th, the *Nymphe* sent two barges against the minor fort at Bearskin Neck. Moving out

---

1 Mead, *History of the Town of Greenwich*, 191.
2 Ibid., 193-194.
3 Orcutt, *History of the Old Town of Stratford and the City of Bridgeport*, 433.

at midnight, one barge went into Long Cove and put men on shore. They surprised the fort's sentinel, captured 14 soldiers, spiked the guns, and departed. The second barge landed its attackers to the west, but encountered resistance from villagers leading to disaster. The discharge of their large bow gun caused a butt to start, creating a leak and forcing the raiders to abandon their craft. The officer and several of his men stole a skiff and escaped back to their ship. However, a dozen or so Brits became captives of the aroused militia.

Some Gloucesterites urged an exchange of prisoners, but the colonel commanding local forces said he did not have the authority to take such action. Instead, he told Lieutenant Charles Tarr to move the British captives to Salem. That night, a band of townsmen in disguise seized Tarr's prisoners and initiated their own exchange with the British. "It is difficult to conceive any other design in this landing than a wanton destruction of life and property; and yet the English captain, in the conclusion of the affair, promised the Cape people unmolested use of their fishing-grounds during the rest of the fall; and he kept his word."[1]

In the second week of September, invasion fears gripped the valley of the Sheepscot River in Maine. Notwithstanding the apprehension in Portland, Portsmouth, and Boston, the important port of Wiscasset expected to receive the initial visit from Sherbrooke's force. General William King of Bath called out his entire militia division and established field headquarters in Wiscasset. The three Bristol companies and the Walpole and Broad Cove companies got an early jump and moved to the shire town. Captain John Sproul's Harrington company remained home to guard the Pemaquid peninsula. Around the 10th, companies from Lincoln, Kennebec, and Franklin counties and even some from Hancock and Washington counties trooped into town. Several thousand men assembled. A local letter writer told a Boston paper about the mobilization. "The whole town is a military camp. . . . If the enemy attack us, we are determined to dispute every inch of ground with them."[2]

As in other threatened communities, Wiscasset residents removed or secured their prized possessions. While Moses Carlton sent his valuables to his place at Head Tide, Squire Hodge's son filled a silver chest with precious belongings and told the family servant to "bury it west of the house."[3] When the danger passed in a few weeks, Hodge told the man to uncover and return the chest. For some reason, the servant began to fidget and stammer. Hodge, believing the man's behavior indicated he had pilfered the chest and its contents, struck the servant about the head. The pathetic man experienced a fitful seizure, lost his mind altogether and never recovered to reveal the whereabouts of the Hodge treasure.

---

1 Babson, *Town of Gloucester*, 514.
2 *Boston Gazette*, September 15, 1814.
3 Fannie S. Chase, 351.

As King and his officers set defensive measures in place, the *LaHogue* accompanied by the H.M.S. *Chesapeake* appeared off Sequin on the 10th. Within hours, the enemy, in several barges, landed on Barter's Island, spiked four guns, and stole a number of sheep. Colonel Andrew Reed commanding at Cox Head dispatched the Parker's Island and Phippsburg companies across the Kennebec in pursuit. Pickets found the returning British marines at Indian Point, opened fire, and drove them down river toward the advancing main body of militiamen. When the barges came down on this force, the Yankees poured a sustained fire at the passing enemy. The British returned the fire. An English ball shattered John Hunt's musket barrel and ricocheted through his hat — making the hat the only casualty on the American side. The skirmish, one of several over a week or so, became known as the "Battle of the Barges,"[1] or the "Indian Point Battle."[2]

At the same time he organized defenses around Wiscasset, King ordered similar preparations for Bath. Gun batteries at Cox Head and Hunnewell's Point received particular attention. Having weathered a near panic during the June mobilization, the inhabitants this time removed and secured property, and, in some cases, withdrew to the interior, in an orderly manner. King concealed four of his own merchant ships in the Cathance River in Bowdoinham.

Augusta became concerned with "the alarming situation" and called a meeting to "adopt such measures . . . as the town in their wisdom should think fit."[3] The voters directed the selectmen "to procure forthwith, two hundred pounds of powder, such quantity of materials for tents, and such number of camp-kettles and small arms" as they thought proper.[4] The town's action anticipated an inevitable request. The next day, King asked Major General Henry Sewall of the Eighth Division headquartered in Augusta to send a reinforcement of 1,000 men to the coast. Some regiments marched immediately and arrived in Wiscasset on the 12th.

Like many of his neighbors, Benjamin Robbins of Winthrop made the most of the advance warning. Two days before marching to the coast with his militia regiment, he rode to Hallowell, sold some wool, and used part of the proceeds to buy gunpowder. His September 10 diary entry adds: "Borrowed a mould and run balls after I came back." He made cartridges Sunday night, and stepped off "in defense of our country" on Monday morning, the 12th.[5]

A dramatic change spread over the normally pastoral countryside. Prodded by a flood of rumors about an expected descent by the enemy, citizens raced about making preparations. A wild report circulated "that 30 sail of

1 Ibid., 352.
2 Todd, "The Battle of Indian Point."
3 North, *History of Augusta*, 415.
4 Nash, *History of Augusta*, 136.
5 Stackpole, *History of Winthrop*, 152.

the enemy's vessels are off the mouth of the Sheepscot River."[1] Militia companies from as far away as Somerset County filled the roads in response to the need to support Sewall. Harvesting activity slowed. Thomas Hodgkin of Lewiston left his crops and prepared one of his boys "to March with the militia" and "let wm Brooks [a hired hand] have a Scabbard & belt." On the 13th, he went with his "mare & waggon to haul Baggage for the Company," arriving in Hallowell late in the day. For the better part of two weeks, Hodgkin, working for the selectmen, carried "wheat & beef" and other provisions to militia forces bivouacked at Pittston.[2]

In and about Wiscasset, quartering the 2,000 or more militiamen who descended on the community became a major logistical problem. Public buildings, taverns, and the meetinghouse were turned into barracks, along with barns and workshops. A letter from Wiscasset appearing in the *Salem Gazette* described the general situation of the town. "We are experiencing . . . all the horrors of war except being captured and destroyed. Since the British squadron left the Penobscot we have hourly been expecting an attack."[3]

Beyond several minor skirmishes around the entrances to the Kennebec and Sheepscot, the region averted a serious confrontation in the days to follow. By early October, Army authorities were reduced to fretting over procurement matters. Assistant Deputy Quartermaster General Joseph Wingate in Bath felt it important to scold Captain John Wilson in command of the Phippsburg garrison. "I . . . understand that a quantity of wood" has "been purchased recently at your post at the rate of three dollars per cord," he wrote. "You will permit me to observe that . . . it cannot be expected that this price will be allowed for wood at Phipsburg when at the same time they are bringing it from that place and disposing of it here at one half of the sum." Citing his duty to "the public interest," Wingate disallowed the purchase.[4]

Cape Cod towns did not enjoy such relative tranquility at the time. British captains operating out of Provincetown, particularly Richard Raggett of the *Spencer* became increasingly avaricious. Raggett received his captaincy in April 1799, and did not advance to rear admiral of the blue until May 1825. Whether this apparent stagnation had anything to do with his pursuit of outside income is open to conjecture. At any rate, he arrived on the North American Station late in the spring escorting a convoy with reinforcements for Quebec. Raggett's nature became evident in August off Portsmouth when he captured the Newburyport fishing boat *Friendship*, Captain Andrew Wilson. Raggett demanded a ransom of $180, but Wilson could produce only $142. Raggett thereupon "took out sundry articles such as *rum, candles, bladders of snuff, &c.* and gave up the boat, with her sails, rigging, &c. much torn and injured."[5]

---

1 Fannie S. Chase, 357.
2 *Diary of Thomas Hodgkin.*
3 Fannie S. Chase, 356.
4 *Maine Historical Society Collections and Proceedings* 10:426.
5 *Boston Gazette*, August 22, 1814.

Not long after this confrontation, Raggett found himself tested by a Cape Codder. Captain Matthew H. Mayo and Captain Winslow L. Knowles left Eastham late in August bound for Boston in a whaleboat loaded with rye. Upon arrival, they sold their produce as well as the boat and bought a larger vessel, filled it with domestic products, and headed home. Off Plymouth, a tender for the *Spencer* apprehended them, and Raggett demanded a $300 ransom. He sent Knowles back to Boston for the money. Knowles accepted advice on the street to forget about the deal, leaving Mayo at sea to fend for himself.

At the end of a week, the Brits put Mayo back on the tender to act as her pilot as she patrolled Cape Cod Bay. A northwest blow came up and Mayo advised his captors to seek shelter under Billingsgate Point at Wellfleet. At an opportune time, he cunningly slinked forward, and cut the cable with his pocketknife. When it parted a short time later, he suggested seeking safety in Rock Harbor, Orleans. Mayo earlier picked the lock of a writing desk, removed two pistols, and concealed them under his jacket. Before long, as Mayo expected, the tender grounded on the Eastham flats. He assured an agitated commanding officer they were merely on the outer bar and not in danger. He convinced the Britisher that in no time the wind and currents would carry them across into deeper water. As they waited, he said it would be prudent for all the Englishmen to go below to avoid creating suspicion on shore. For good measure, he gave them a gimlet to tap a cask of rum while they waited.

The ploy succeeded. By the time the vessel heeled over in an outgoing tide, not a few of the enemy were feeling pretty good. Mayo had thrown all their guns overboard. When some of the men sensed trickery, they tried to rush on deck. Mayo drew the pair of pistols and threatened to shoot any man who advanced on him. Having reached an understanding on this point, Mayo jumped over the side and splashed his way to shore. He hightailed to town and alerted the militia. They responded with promptness, seized the boat and its contents, arrested the enemy crew and locked them in a barn. After contemplation, the inhabitants retained little interest in holding the British. The prisoners were encouraged to escape. The marshal from Barnstable took possession of the prisoners' belongings and Mayo claimed the tender. When the escapees got back to their ship, Raggett plotted retaliation. He set his sights on Eastham.

Raggett dispatched a demand to the town for his sailors' bedding and baggage. The town sent a committee out to the captain to explain the articles were in Barnstable beyond Eastham's control. "They were told nevertheless that if every article found on board the tender, and $10 cash for each seaman for having been obliged to lie without their bedding, and $1200 as a ransom for the saltworks were not delivered at Provincetown in the course of this month, the town and the saltworks should be destroyed."[1] The selectmen

---

[1] *Niles'*, October 6, 1814.

promptly came up with the sum, "taking a receipt with a written promise" to hold Eastham free of attack during the rest of the war.[1]

This seemed like easy money, so Raggett told the Eastham selectmen to inform their Brewster counterparts they were next. On September 17, he sent a flag into Brewster and told the selectmen and owners of saltworks that it was his "intention to retaliate as far as lays in my power, the conduct of the American Forces towards the defenceless Towns in Upper Canada." He noted the "great public utility" of the saltworks and suggested "the very moderate Sum of 4,000 Dollars as a contribution to guarantee their safety."[2]

Brewster promptly called a Sunday morning town meeting to deal with "the very sudden and urgent occasion." The September 18 meeting took several steps. First, it sent out community leaders to appeal to neighboring towns to meet in Brewster at 6:00 p.m. that day. The commander of the artillery received authorization to engage five horses "to be in readiness . . . at the response of the town." And the safety committee was instructed to see "how many 45 & 60 years old, including exempts, may be found" to join the artillery. The meeting adjourned until 5:00 p. m. when it came back in and concluded, "[I]t appears . . . that the town of Brewster can make no Dependance on any neighboring towns for assistance." After much deliberation, the meeting voted to have the safety committee return to Raggett "and make the best terms they can."[3]

The committee went out to the *Spencer* and tried to negotiate at least a compromise with the British captain. Raggett held his ground, and the Brewster men reported to a Monday town meeting "they used their utmost to obtain a relinquishment of a part of the sum demanded but could not."[4] The meeting moved to come up with the funds, agreeing "the contribution-money shall be taxed upon the salt-works, buildings of every description, and vessels owned in this town of every description frequenting, or lying on, the shores." The meeting decided to "hire the money, until it can be assessed and collected."[5] A little later, Brewster successfully petitioned the General Court for authority to lay a special tax to raise the money. The town carried the ransom to Raggett one day before the due date, and he acknowledged "to have received the same as a contribution" and guaranteed "the safety of said salt-works and town at Brewster during the present war. . . ."[6]

Raggett, commanding British forces in Massachusetts Bay, did not overlook the role of Barnstable. He sent the *Nymphe* there to recover the belongings of the Britishers captured at Eastham. Barnstable rejected the demand and seemed to insult the lieutenant who came on shore for the purpose. As a result of the unfriendly parley, the commanding officer of the *Nymphe*

1 Charles F. Swift, *Cape Cod*, 247.
2 Captain Richard Raggett, *Letter*.
3 *Records of Town Meetings, 1803-1828*, Brewster, MA, 330-332.
4 Ibid., 333.
5 Ibid., 334.
6 Ibid., 339.

"threatened to destroy Barnstable. . . ." He claimed 500 Royal Marines with "seven cannon mounted on traveling carriages" were prepared to carry out the mission.[1]

The intimidating developments prompted neighboring Yarmouth to call a special meeting on the 18th. The town appointed a committee to meet with similar special bodies from other Cape towns. Yarmouth came back into a formal session the next day and appointed still another committee, this "to inquire into the demand or errand, if any shall be made, by flag of truce." For good measure, the Yarmouth meeting outlined its general feelings and voted unanimously: "That as this town have ever expressed their decided disapprobation of the present ruinous and unhappy war, and have hitherto refrained from engaging in the same; we are still determined not to engage in, encourage or support it any further than we are compelled to do, by the laws of the country of which we are citizens."[2]

Bolder people inhabited nearby Barnstable, where men hastened to mobilize. Of the twelve towns on Cape Cod, only four, perhaps, five, demonstrated a combative disposition. Along with Barnstable, the towns of Falmouth, Orleans, and Sandwich harbored a steadfast desire and willingness to fight. Prior to September 1814, Chatham took an unbelligerent if not pacifistic stance. However, with danger at the door, on September 26, the town went so far as to establish a safety committee and place "the 25 guns and other Equipment brought from Boston as part of this Towns shear . . . by an act of Congress" under the direction of the selectmen.[3]

With the threat delivered by the *Nymphe* before them and the Brewster situation apparently unresolved, on September 19, the citizens of Barnstable conducted a town meeting to form a public safety committee to assist the militia "in case of an invation in seeing evry man at his post to repel such invation to inquire into and find out the Business of all suspicious strangers. . . ."[4] More to the point, as recorded by a more scholarly penman, the meeting resolved "in time of danger . . . it is the bounden duty of every citizen to rally round the standards of his country and resist such invasion and depredations with all the means in his power." Barnstable agreed it had to choose "either *honorable resistance* or *base submission*." and declared "a line must be drawn somewhere."[5]

Barnstable men did not need more encouragement, but, just in case, Matthew Cobb in Portland wrote to inspire his brother Daniel. "I observe that you are threatened at Barnstable. They cannot injure you with their ships. If they land their sailors to destroy your houses you can with a little spirit

1 *Niles'*, October 6, 1814.
2 Charles F. Swift, *History of Old Yarmouth*, 184.
3 *Town Records 1789-1823, Vol. 3*, Chatham, MA.
4 *Barnstable* (MA) *Town Records*, 2:288.
5 Ibid., 289.

that may be got up, drive them into the sea." He added: "I hope you will not purchase your safety, for that would be very degrading indeed."[1]

The town managed to acquire four cast-iron cannons, and positioned them overlooking the entrance to the inner harbor on the north of town. At one stage of the ensuing standoff, from out in the bay, the *Nymphe* lobbed a cannonball the considerable distance into the village. A false alarm on October 3 prompted "about 14 or 1500 of the militia to collect" in Barnstable.[2] In the end, preparedness along with the difficulties associated with navigating the largely shallow waters in and about Barnstable Harbor kept the British away.

The increased hostilities on Cape Cod heightened anxiety in Rhode Island and places to the west. A group organized to build fortifications in and around Providence as the *Nimrod* remained active about Narragansett Bay. She captured a schooner loaded with iron, plaster, and molasses, after driving her on shore at Watch Hill. The *Nimrod* also chased a Newport sloop on the Charlestown beach. A spirited fight ensued when the militia assembled "with a cannon." The scrap ended without casualties on either side. The "cargo was landed on the beach and saved," reported the papers, "but the sloop will be lost."[3]

Tension remained high elsewhere. Boston's *Columbian Centinel* claimed: "We have Halifax advices to the 26th ult. The disposable troops from the Penobscot had returned there, and it was reported that an expedition of 4000 was fitting out for Newport, New-London, or somewhere East of them. There were eight or nine frigates in port."[4] A week later, the same newspaper said, letters "from Newport mention, that fears were entertained there of a fall visit from the British in the Chesapeake."[5] An attack never materialized, and the people of Rhode Island probably did not know they narrowly escaped the undivided attention of Admiral Cochrane's substantial force. In a September 17 letter to the Admiralty, Cochrane indicated he planned to attack the Ocean State or New Hampshire after assaulting Washington. He regretted deviating from his Rhode Island plan. General Robert Ross and Admiral George Cockburn, however, convinced Cochrane to instead go after Baltimore.

Despite all the nervousness in southern New England, as the sailing season began to draw to a close, the Royal Navy focused its activity northward from Cape Cod. On September 20, Captain George Collier in the *Leander*, 58 appeared off Gallops Folly at Salem and sent three barges into the cove. A 50-man detachment of militia reinforced with a 6-pounder beat them off. One barge returned under a flag of truce carrying a brief letter. "Sir George Collier believes the boat on shore a fisherman," the note began. "He desires to exam-

1 Trayser, *Barnstable*, 143.
2 *Benjamin Percival Diary*.
3 *Boston Gazette*, August 11, 1814.
4 *Columbian Centinel* (MA), October 14, 1814.
5 Ibid., October 22, 1814.

ine her without recourse to arms, and if objected to he will land and destroy every house within two miles of the cove. — This the inhabitants may rely upon." Meanwhile, Lieutenant Colonel James Appleton assembled the 600-man Cape Ann regiment. After due consideration, Appleton suppressed his pride and replied to the Collier demand. "This is permitted without reference to the threat connected with your request, *which is such as was not to be expected from a British commander.*"[1] The inspection proceeded without incident, and the *Leander* moved along on her way.

The Maine coast remained under the gun, much as Niles, for one, expected. He observed: "When the war commenced the enemy promised to respect Eastport; but they took it, and they meant to trouble no place to the westward of it." But they have taken Castine and eastern Maine, he continued, though "they mean to molest no other part of Maine; *and these assurances will probably be found as sincere as former ones.*"[2] Editor Niles may have based his outlook on another midcoast incident.

While fishing on September 21 off Owl's Head to supply the mobilized militia, Asa Richards and Peter Oat of Camden fell into the hands of marauding British in a cutter and several barges. The enemy towed the Camden boat loaded with cod, haddock, and hake to Fisherman Island and feasted on the catch. Two more local boats, a coaster and a pinky, fell victims before the English officer, a Lieutenant Robbins, decided to move along and cruise around Shore Village (now Rockland). Sentinels on night duty at Jameson's Point heard the splash of oars as the enemy approached Clam Cove. They fired blindly at the sound and managed to strike an oar, prompting Robbins in the lead barge to back away. The officer in the next barge asked: "What now?"

"Why, the d—d Yankees are bush fighting us!" answered Robbins. "Pull to your oars, boys, and get out of the reach of them."[3]

Thus repulsed, the little flotilla moved to the east and Laisdell's Island. Richards and the officers put up for the night at the Whaling homestead while Oat and the rest of the entourage slept in the boats. The next morning, the British sent a boy to dig potatoes. Asked to supervise the task, Richards "was careful not to give a 'Quaker measure,' for they offered to pay a liberal price for all they obtained." And Mrs. Whaling churned $45 worth of butter for the Englishmen to carry back to Castine. Robbins failed in his attempt to hire Richards as a pilot, the Camden fisherman declaring he would not accept money and become a traitor. The lieutenant appreciated Richard's stance, but paid him a guinea for help to this point, paid for the fish, and sent him and Oats on their way. "Being possessed of their freedom, they were not slow in exercising their strength on their oars."[4]

1 *Niles'*, October 6, 1814.
2 Ibid.
3 Locke, *Sketches of the History of the Town of Camden*, 125.
4 Ibid., 126.

As soon as the pair reached Camden, they contacted Major Jonathan Wilson to tell the militia officer that Robbins intended to attack Northport the next morning. Some 100 Camden men volunteered to march northward to the scene at dawn. Word reached Colonel Jacob Ulmer in Lincolnville and he called out his regiment. Companies from Belmont, Ducktrap, Lincolnville, and Searsmont started to meet the enemy.

Early on the 23rd, Mrs. Elizabeth Drinkwater spotted barges approaching Saturday Cove. She told Zachariah Lawrence, and he raced to the shore with his gun. As the Britishers came close to the rocky shoreline, Lawrence barked out military orders as if he commanded an unseen but sizeable force. He fired from cover at one spot and jumped to another clump of bushes to shoot again. The lead pair of barges backed off to await the following boats. Lawrence ran up the bank and asked Alban Elwell and others to get their guns and join him in welcoming the enemy. Robbins countered by bringing up the cutter armed with a one-pound swivel, and this served to blunt further resistance at the outset on the part of the locals. With the way open, Lieutenant Robbins led 30 marines on shore.

The attackers marched to Jones Shaw's house. They accused Shaw of assisting Lawrence. When he denied the charge, "they gave him a shaking and cuffing, knocking his hat off." Shaw operated a store out of his basement, and the British ransacked the place, taking sundry items of clothing. While the men in the cutter entertained themselves by firing their swivel gun at the houses in the settlement, the marines marched Shaw as their hostage around the neighborhood. They pillaged the Captain Amos Pendleton house after enjoying the family's breakfast set out on the kitchen table just before they arrived. "They then went to Capt. Aaron Crowell's house, and used insulting language to Mrs. Crowell, who resented it in a womanly style."[1] She was on her own since her husband was at the time a resident of the Dartmoor prison in England. The raiders stole her wedding dress and tore open her beds, scattering feathers aloft in the breeze.

The Lincolnville militia made it to the disturbance just as the British turned back to their barges. Both sides traded volleys, and the Camden men came up and joined in the exchange with the enemy. "Maj. Wilson, full of frolic, turned his back, and bade them hit him if they could." The attackers made it to their boats and crossed to Long Island. Residents claimed the British washed blood out of their boats before sailing for Castine. Several years later, Levi Mathews, a Lincolnville mariner, chanced upon an officer who participated in the raid. The Briton lamented, "[I]t proved to be an expensive expedition to his countrymen, as a number of their lives dearly paid the forfeit on the occasion."[2] The Americans did not suffer any casualties, but the residents of Saturday Cove experienced losses amounting to $300 to $400.

When Colonel Ulmer reported his part in the skirmish, he told Adjutant General Brooks about a continuing and bothersome issue. Ulmer dis-

---

1 Ibid., 128.
2 Ibid., 129.

cussed "the almost daily passing of beef, cattle, grain, and supplies of almost every description the country affords . . . in large quantities, bound towards the enemy at Castine. . . ."[1] The *Providence Patriot* supported Ulmer's assessment when it reported "trade at Castine is very brisk; . . . there is a constant and great influx and eflux of traders, to such an extent that the town is overflowing."[2]

None of this should have been surprising. On one hand, New England farmers and traders needed the market. Secondly, a great need for provisions existed in Castine. Beyond the naval traffic at the place, the garrison included about 1,800 troops. Castine was bustling. The town had become "quite a gay resort for the officers of the British army and navy." A theater opened along with other refined amenities. "Many of the officers were gentlemen by birth, culture, and instinctive sentiment."[3]

Yet the needs of the Castine outpost explained just a small portion of the trade. Castine, in effect, replaced Eastport as the center of the smuggling business and the so-called neutral trade. British goods arrived at Castine and that portion intended to pass through the neutral charade was transported up the Penobscot River across from Hampden. A "Swedish" schooner received the goods on the eastern or British side. Warped across the waterway, the schooner entered the goods at the customhouse on the western or American side, paid the duties, and discharged its load. Although many people considered the neutral trade censorious if not treasonable, in one five-week period, the collector's office at Hampden received $150,000 in duties. Wagons carried the English goods from Hampden to Boston, New York, and other westerly destinations.

As a result of the Jefferson and Madison embargoes, smuggling enjoyed great favor in the region. Numerous Yankee traders elected to follow this wholly illegal approach to business. They employed various ruses. Some men avoided customs by secreting their British merchandise in double-bottomed wagons. The Hancock County sheriff, an appointee of Governor Strong, resorted to this method and got caught as he rolled through Wiscasset. His political enemies enjoyed his embarrassment. "The next trip Mr. Sheriff ADAMS takes to *Castine*, we would advise him to make use of an *Air Balloon* as there appears to be no safety in traveling on the land," said the *Boston Patriot*. "The *double bottomed wagons* are not safe from . . . James Madison's sentinels; but in an Air Balloon there will be perfect safety, as the officers of government are not permitted to travel in the air, nor to make seizures there."[4]

The fuss around Camden and the Northport raid aside, as September passed it began to become apparent the British would not undertake a major offensive in the Wiscasset to Portsmouth sector. The alarm subsided. The assemblage of reserve troops at Pittston, Maine began to disband in the last

1 Joseph Williamson, *History of the City of Belfast*, 1:439.
2 *Bangor Historical Magazine* 3:175.
3 John S.C. Abbott and Elwell, *History of Maine*, 423.
4 Johnston, *History of the Towns of Bristol and Bremen*, 416.

week of the month. Thomas Hodgkin, the diligent provider from Lewiston, bought a heifer from William Dingley. On the 24th, he "Sat out with hir for pitston got to the further part of Litchfield met the Soldiers Comeing home I turned back with them drive the heifer back."[1] Before the month ended, the troops defending Wiscasset and Bath started a phased withdrawal to their homes. The command discharged Benjamin Robbins' regiment at noon on September 25. The men marched north through the night and arrived footsore in Winthrop at 8:00 a.m. the next day. Benjamin's diary entry concluded: "Very lame kept the house near all day."[2] The last company to depart Wiscasset left on November 7.

At Portsmouth, authorities felt comfortable discharging the greater part of the defenders early in October. As a sign of the hard times, the troops from Keene were dismissed without pay, "and most of them had to beg their way home."[3] The original fear of attack, however, had a fair basis. After the war, a British officer told a New Hampshire militia officer he looked around Portsmouth during the September mobilization disguised as a local fisherman. He made his way up the Piscataqua River and assessed the vulnerability of the town and the navy yard. The Briton concluded the place would offer a stiff resistance, and the fleet commander dropped the invasion idea altogether.

Massachusetts, on the other hand, remained in a relatively high state of alert and continued to prepare for a major assault. A prominent London map seller also prepared. He told an American customer who asked for a good map of the United States to delay his purchase for a short time. The Englishman advised he was keeping all his North American maps incomplete, because the boundaries were about to be altered with the return of a large section of the Union to the British Empire.

The October need for more troops led the Massachusetts legislature to repeal the 1811 law that considered fishermen to be mariners and, therefore, exempt from militia service. And Governor Strong continued to back away from his original, hard line position on state control of the militia. He placed a detachment approximating a brigade under the command of U.S. General Dearborn, sending the unit to federal Fort Warren in Boston Harbor. In the middle of October, demonstrating the state's readiness, two brigades of the Massachusetts forces marched into Boston and passed in review for the governor and the Board of War. After the parade, the troops "performed a great variety of field evolutions and firings with the adroitness of the best disciplined regulars." An "immense crowd of spectators gave evidence of this conviction by reiterated plaudits."[4] Despite the anxiety around town, an attack never materialized. For the most part, the mobilized troops "did no heavier

---

1 *Diary of Thomas Hodgkin.*
2 Stackpole, 153.
3 Griffin, et al., *History of the Town of Keene*, 360.
4 *Columbian Centinel* (MA), October 22, 1814.

or dangerous duty than to pass from dinner to drill, during . . . monotonous service" at Boston.[1]

A chronicler recorded one casualty, however. When the Acton company marched to Boston's defense, it received an enthusiastic reception all along its route. At every corner, men and boys cheered. The outfit's drummer and fifer "were expected to respond with a triple roll and salute. The poor fifer was so exhausted with his untiring efforts to pipe shrill for the honor of his corps and town," it was reported, "that he was taken with spitting of blood and had to return home . . . the only blood shed during the campaign."[2]

As the summer waned and peace talks advanced in Ghent, Holland, British naval activity moderated on the coast of the United States. For days on end, the Royal Navy ships based at Provincetown limited themselves to using the windmill on Mill Hill, Truro as a practice target and issuing an occasional "Chalinge into the Constitution American Ship" holed up in Boston.[3] The peace negotiations drew considerable interest in Boston and Maine when it became known Great Britain late in October proposed peace on the basis of *uti possidetis* — the principle that leaves belligerents in possession of the territory gained by their forces during the hostilities. For the most part, the only ground covered by this proposition involved British-occupied Maine east of the Penobscot.

While the navies slowed down, privateersmen remained somewhat active. But a few of the Canadian privateers pressed their luck, including Liverpool's great *Retaliation*, Captain William Potter, operating at the time out of Tarpaulin Cove in the Elizabeth Islands. In August, accompanied by a prize, she chased the Nantucket packet into Falmouth. Fifty local men immediately manned the packet, "with a field piece and musketry," and chased the *Retaliation* of five guns.[4] The privateer escaped, but the packet managed to retake the unprotected prize.

Later, Potter sent his sailing master and four men in his boarding boat to take the pinky *Clementine*, Captain Edward Crowell, becalmed off Falmouth. Unarmed, Crowell submitted without a fight. The British officer told Crowell to "pick up your duds and get ashore. The threat didn't sit well. Crowell went below for his clothes and, as he gathered them up, proposed" a plot to his three crewmen. Crowell bounced on deck and, "seeing a favorable moment, clinched two of the privateersmen with their loaded guns in their hands; which he got from them; threw one of the guns overboard and retained the other." In a flash, the three other Americans overwhelmed the remaining Canadians. "Four men with no arms against five armed men and not a drop of blood shed."[5]

---

1 C.M. Hyde and Alexander Hyde, *Centennial History of the Town of Lee*, 63.

2 Drake, *History of Middlesex County*, 1:206.

3 John Allen, *Memorandum of a Log on board His Maj. Ship Newcastle*.

4 *Boston Gazette*, August 8, 1814.

5 *Falmouth* (MA) *Enterprise*, May 8, 1942, quoting the *New England Palladium* (MA), November 4, 1814.

"'I might have known,' moaned the sailing-master bitterly, 'no Crowell ever quits while he has breath in his body. You've folks in Liverpool, haven't you?'"

"'Same family,' admitted Edward Crowell. 'Some of them went to Nova Scotia from Cape Cod sixty years ago.'"[1]

Crowell, back in control of his vessel, carried his prisoners to New Bedford and marched them over the river to the fort in Fairhaven.

By late October, Falmouth felt it had had enough of the *Retaliation*. Weston Jenkins fitted out his sloop *Two Friends* with a brass 4-pounder and a well-armed crew of 32. Leaving Woods Hole in a southeast rain, the little sloop reached Job's Neck as the wind dropped off. The Falmouthites rowed the rest of the way to the approach to Tarpaulin Cove. When they got within three-quarters of a mile from their target, the privateer fired its long gun. Jenkins interpreted the shot to be a signal to stop, which he did. As soon as he anchored, a boat put off from the enemy ship. Jenkins beforehand sent below all but two or three of his crew.

Captain Potter and five privateersmen manned the launch, leaving only six men on the *Retaliation*. When he came close, Potter hailed: "What sloop is this?".

Jenkins responded: "The *William* of Falmouth."

"Whose in command of this sloop?"

"By that time he was right alongside. Captain Jenkins said, 'I am,' and stamped his foot, — and they saw men enough then! We all jumped up at the signal," recalled crewman John Parker, "and the men below came right on deck. The man in the barge lifted his gun to fire, but it only flashed in the pan."

"One of our men was kinder excited and he jumped right into their barge and took that man and threw him neck and heels right on to our deck." According to Parker. "He couldn't ha' done it if he hadn't been so excited."[2]

Once he secured Potter and his companions below decks, Jenkins put a dozen of his men in the enemy barge and directed them to follow his sloop over to the anchored *Retaliation*. The six privateersmen on board assessed their chances against a two-pronged attack, and quickly concluded they were too few to fight their ship. The Yankees "carried her without resistance."[3] The victors released two American prisoners found on the *Retaliation*, and brought the prize and her plunder into Falmouth.

Jenkins and his crew, however, faced another hurdle. They did not hold a commission for a private armed vessel and they were not entitled to the proceeds of the sale of the prize. Consequently, the men contacted Massachusetts Congressman Artemus Ward, Jr., and he presented a petition on their behalf. The private bill made its way through the legislative mill, passing Congress in late January 1815. President Madison signed the measure on

1 Snider, *Under the Red Jack*, 162.
2 Emerson, *Early History of Naushon Island*, 331.
3 Ibid., 330.

February 8, directing the district court "to distribute among Weston Jenkins, his officers and crew, of the sloop Two Friends, . . . the proceeds . . . held to the United States as droits of admiralty. . . ."[1] Not everyone who captured a prize without a commission received such prompt and favorable treatment as the warriors from Falmouth.

Around the same period, off Maine, another Canadian privateer became the victim of a stratagem. The *Fame*, a Chesapeake privateer, captured by the enemy, went on to sail as a Canadian privateer, and sometimes worked as a coaster. While freighting a load of molasses and sugar from the Maritimes to Castine, she ran into trouble. An American fellow named Lowe shipped as her second officer. Since he signed on in Nova Scotia, the captain assumed he was a Canadian. When the *Fame* approached her destination, Lowe told the four or five crewmen that seamen were in short supply around the mouth of the Penobscot, and if they wanted to avoid impressment, they should get below. They took Lowe's advice. And once they were out of sight, "he fastened them down, and then went to the captain, told him he was an American, and demanded the surrender of the vessel as a prize."[2] Taken completely unawares, the captain decided his life was not worth the risk of contesting the issue and he yielded. Lowe gradually changed the ship's course and soon fell in with two Camden fishermen who guided him into Wessaweskeag.

Captain Alexander Milliken of Northport and others bought the *Fame* at auction and fitted her out as a renewed American privateer. She set sail on December 1 and took several smuggling vessels before carrying a fairly rich prize into Shore Village on January 2, 1815. Soon after, the advent of peace ended her privateering career.

The next private adventure on Penobscot Bay prompted a terrifying response from the Royal Navy. Late in October, Major Noah Miller of Lincolnville recruited West Drinkwater, Jonathan Clark, and John, Kingsbury, and Samuel Duncan of Northport to crew his armed reach boat. The little open hull boat barely exceeded 14 feet in length. A tradition in the Moosabec Reach off Jonesport, these boats were keeled and powered by oars and square sails. Cruising in Belfast Bay looking for smugglers on November 1, Miller's craft did not present an imposing sight. At least Captain Benjamin Darling of the little Halifax sloop *Mary* bound for Castine did not perceive a threat when Miller and his band approached off Long Island.

Miller fired a shot as a signal and ordered Darling to heave to. "This he at first refused to do, threatening them very violently."[3] But Miller possessed a combative streak. He overhauled and rushed the sloop, taking possession without bloodshed. The *Mary* carried $40,000 worth of bale goods. The sloop's supercargo offered a ten thousand pound ransom, but Drinkwater and the rest of the crew rejected his proffer. Miller departed his boat at Northport and sent his men along with the prize to Lincolnville. Miller

---

1 *A Bill Concerning Weston Jenkins and others*. HR 51, 13th Cong., 3rd sess., January 13, 1815.

2 Eaton, *History of Thomaston*, 304.

3 Locke, *Sketches of the History of the Town of Camden*, 136.

knew full well something was missing. He did not possess the necessary privateering commission.

Ducktrap storekeeper John Wilson advised Miller to apply to Philip Ulmer, deputy customs inspector at Lincolnville. Miller made his way to that place, but when the sloop arrived, Ulmer went on board and declared her a federal prize. Miller then went over the road to Camden, while the inspector sailed the *Mary* to that port. Upon her arrival, Josiah Hook, district collector, confiscated the vessel and cargo in the name of the United States. Within four hours, hands unloaded the shipment of clothes, shawls, satins, and laces and sent the cargo to Portland. Hezekiah Prince noted the event in his diary: "The roads are full of teams . . . removing the goods from Camden."[1]

The affair moves in two directions at this point. On one hand, Camden faced a serious problem — an unwanted, captured enemy sloop in its harbor. Sensing the potential for a punitive, retaliatory British raid, the selectmen paid Clark and two of the Duncan boys five dollars apiece to sail the *Mary* around to the distant St. George River and hide her from view. The trio jumped to the task.

On the other hand, a drawn out quest for compensation commenced. Miller convinced Hook to grant him a backdated revenue commission. In January 1815, the sloop and its cargo netted $66,426 at a Portland auction. One half went to the U.S. Treasury. Miller and Hook each garnered $14,107, and the four crewmen received only $1,000 each. However, the pursuit of more satisfactory recompense continued for years. Unlike the Falmouth captors of the *Retaliation* who obtained their due from Congress in little more than two months, it took Drinkwater and his mates 42 years! After repeated unsuccessful attempts, in August 1856, Congress authorized Drinkwater, Clark, and the Duncans (or their heirs) to receive and split $33,213, or half the original auction proceeds. Shut out from the 1856 distribution, the heirs of Miller, in 1858, failed in one last try to gain added compensation for the 1814 capture of the *Mary*.

Turning to Camden again, the town faced immediate peril. Hiding the *Mary* would not suffice. Just as the town's inhabitants feared, when word of the caper reached the enemy base at Castine, the British initiated a reprisal. Captain William Mounsey set sail for Camden in the H.M.S. *Furieuse*, 38. On November 2, lookouts on Mount Battie spotted the warship's approach and ran up a signal flag. Panic spread quickly. Families wasted little time getting out of town with their valuables. In the rush, Bathsheba Thorndike broke a leg, and another lady escaped fatal injuries when her chaise upset.

Early in the afternoon, the *Furieuse* anchored just outside the harbor. British Lieutenant William Sandom came into the inner harbor on a barge under a flag of truce. Collector Farley and key militia officers went out to meet him. Sandom informed the local officials that if the *Mary* or $80,000 was not delivered up in short order, Camden and Lincolnville would be laid in ruin. Con-

---

1 Eaton, *History of Thomaston*, 305.

sternation took hold. An *ad hoc* committee of ten men, including Selectman Robert Chase and Colonel Erastus Foote, went out to Mounsey intent on explaining the prize and her cargo were beyond their reach and control. As the Camden boat came alongside, from on board the man-of-war, Lieutenant Robbins, the antagonist of Saturday Cove, spotted an acquaintance — Asa Richards — among the visitors.

Robbins shouted, "Halloo, there's our pilot!"[1]

As Mounsey and the Camden leaders parleyed, Robbins took Richards aside and offered him a reward if he would reveal the whereabouts of the goods from the *Mary*.

"I don't know where they are," answered Richards, "as they are scattered all over the country, and as for collecting them together, it would be as impossible as it was to collect the bones of Capt. Cook, which were dispersed over the Sandwich Islands."

"Well," responded the Brit, "we'll not ask you about the goods, if you will only tell us where Miller is!"

"I couldn't answer that question either," replied Richards, "but what would you do with him in case you should catch him?"

"Why, we'd hang him for a pirate!" asserted Robbins.[2]

In the captain's quarters, the conference recessed after reaching the understanding the town would petition the district court to release the goods of the *Mary* and return with an answer by 9:00 p.m. The court's reply did not arrive by the deadline, so Chase and prominent merchant Benjamin Cushing, as part of the initial agreement, returned to the *Furieuse* as hostages. And Mounsey granted a three-day delay to await the ruling. Meanwhile, Colonel Foote mobilized his regiment and called for help from neighboring communities. On November 3, Hezekiah Prince of Thomaston made another entry in his diary. "All the militia are in motion and gathering," he noted.[3]

As the militia assembled, Squire Dorithy of Sedgwick, a justice of the peace, sailed to Camden on business. Mounsey halted the justice as he approached, and, learning about his peaceful mission, released him under one condition. The Briton directed Dorithy to assess the strength of the town's defenses and report his findings on his way out of the port. After completing his business in town, Dorithy stopped on the warship before setting sail for home. He reported a formidable array posted in the town and on the outskirts intent on repulsing any invader and punishing any bombardment.

The district judge took his time deciding the issue, eventually ruling against releasing the seized goods. Thus rejected, the British commander reviewed his options and cancelled the threatened destruction. On Sunday morning, the 6th, Mounsey weighed anchor, fired a single cannon shot at a conspicuous militia officer showing off astride a horse, and shaped a course for Castine. However, he did not give up altogether. He carried his two hos-

---

1 Locke, *Sketches of the History of the Town of Camden*, 139.
2 Ibid.
3 Eaton, *History of Thomaston*, 306.

tages, Chase and Cushing, back to the base hoping to use them as bargaining chips. With the passage of ten days, the British concluded the town of Camden was more or less innocent in the *Mary* affair. They shifted their focus to Noah Miller and his crew, offering liberal rewards for their capture. After spending the fortnight on parole in a private residence in Castine, Chase and Cushing gained their liberty and returned home.

And like so many others during and after the war, the two former hostages set about to gain from their experience. A January 1815 town meeting article presented in their behalf the question: "To see if the town will remunerate Messrs. Benj. Cushing and Robt. Chase for their going on board the British frigate Furieuse as hostages about the 1st of November last past, and other expenses incident thereto, and raise money for the same."[1] The meeting thought living large in Castine was not a compensable hardship and summarily rejected the motion.

When the British command at Castine terminated the *Mary* incident and released Chase and Cushing, the folks in Maine did not know this step effectively ended enemy operations in their district. Great Britain would not undertake any added hostile actions against the coast north of Cape Cod. The Royal Navy would continue to harass American smugglers, coasters, privateers, and fishermen and, of course, remain alert for a chance to engage the *Constitution* if she slipped out of Boston. But the approach of cold weather and the continuing shortage of ships, manpower, and supplies at Halifax constrained enemy naval activity for the remaining weeks of the war. While the abatement started the region on its way out of the throes of debilitating and unwanted hostilities, New England first had to pass through one of its most shameful periods. Only the region's covetousness, perfidy, and ruthlessness exhibited during King Philip's War (1675-76) merits as much lasting censure as its behavior late in 1814.

---

1 Locke, *Sketches of the History of the Town of Camden*, 144.

Chapter 13. A Great Pamphlet

The war began to wind down in November 1814 and peace talks continued in Europe. Inexplicably, unbelligerent Truro, Massachusetts took its only town meeting action to address its wartime security. The town voted to empower its committee of safety "to Petition to the Chief Admiral on this Station or in other words do what they think best to be done for the Safety of the town."[1] The town meeting, it should be noted, had in mind Captain Raggett or any successor at Provincetown, not some United States officer. In contrast, nearby militant Barnstable seemed to sense the end and began to wrap up its military affairs. The town called for its safety committee members "to lay their accounts before" the town, and thanked those members "who do not present any account for their services."[2] A patriotic majority of the members did not seek recompense, but the total bill came to $705.19. The state board of war kicked in $310.27 to cover this cost.

The U.S. Navy, however, was not ready to draw down the curtain. An obvious drop in British vigilance enabled James Biddle to escape New London in the *Hornet* on November 18. He went into New York, refitted, and left that port on January 22, 1815 bound for the South Atlantic. On March 18, Captain Biddle and the *Hornet* mauled the H.M.S. *Penguin*, 10, Captain James Dickenson in 22 minutes off Tristan da Cunha. The *Hornet*'s splendid victory after a short cruise accentuated the lost potential caused by her dormancy of 18 months. Her two companions, the *United States* and the *Macedonian*, never got out. They remained in limbo behind New London for the duration. But farther along the coast at Boston, "Old Ironsides" waited for her chance to elude the British watch and get to sea.

---

1 *Truro* (MA) *Town Records*, 3:197.
2 *Barnstable* (MA) *Town Records*, 2:296.

A day before the *Hornet*'s escape, way Down East, Captain Alexander Milliken took advantage of the lull in naval activity to make merry with the British. He prepared a written proclamation acknowledging Sherbrooke's capture of eastern Maine and announced: "I do by all the power in me vested declare it recaptured, excepting Castine and Eastport, for and in behalf of the United States of America, and the subjects thereof having again become citizens are hereby ordered to conduct themselves accordingly." He ridiculed the British practice of declaring extensive blockades "without a sufficient force to enforce" such edicts, and announced his own blockade of "all the Ports, Harbors, Rivers, Bays, and Inlets, from the River Penobscot to River St. Croix, that remain in the actual possession of the enemy."[1] To validate his pronouncement, Milliken went into Machias and nailed a copy to the flagpole at the fort. Observers on both sides appreciated the drollery

Elsewhere, especially north of Boston, with the invasion threats discounted and most of the militia units deactivated, people tried to get back to business. In Wiscasset, Abiel Wood, Jr. finally found time to explain his inattentiveness in handling the bookkeeping chores of merchant Charles Howard. The recent alarm led to the removal from town of "all books, Papers, &c.," he wrote, "so I have not had any opportunity of examining your Company accounts."[2]

Trade between the western side of the Penobscot River and Castine flourished. Goods were plentiful and fairly priced. Livestock enjoyed high demand to the east. When the river froze over, "smuggling was undertaken with obstinate determination."[3] A seizure at Buxton confiscated illegal goods worth $10,000. The collector at Hampden tried his best to halt the illicit flow of dry goods bought at Castine and carried across the river at night. Smugglers counteracted as they could. When a collector's agent seized a sleigh loaded with contraband, the owner resorted to a not uncommon ploy and had the agent arrested for highway robbery. The government man had to obtain a writ of habeas corpus to gain his freedom. And when the authorities took custody of a drove of 28 oxen moving eastward, a gang of more than a dozen men reclaimed the herd under cover of darkness.

Agents stopped one wagon driver and demanded: "What are you loaded with?"

"Quintals of Pollock, casks of oil, and dry goods from Eastport."

"Drygoods from Eastport!" blurted an excited revenuer. "They must be smuggled."[4] The wagoner assured the inspector the goods were of American origin. Nonetheless, expecting to uncover English cloth and linens, the inspector broke open the boxes — only to find dried herring.

Unrestrained smuggling at this time prompted Congress to strengthen the laws designed to control the problem. Early in February 1815, President

---

1 *Maine Historical Society Collections and Proceedings*, 2:332.

2 Fannie S. Chase, *Wiscasset in Pownalborough*, 357.

3 William D. Williamson, *History of the State of Maine*, 2:654.

4 Rowe, *Maritime History of Maine*, 96.

Madison signed a comprehensive measure prohibiting intercourse with the enemy and granting customs officials and naval officers strong powers to enforce the law. Underscoring the administration's seriousness, a key section stipulated: "*Provided always*, That the necessity of a search warrant arising under this act, shall in no case be considered as applicable to any carriage, wagon, cart, sleigh, vessel, boat, or other vehicle, of whatever form or construction, employed as a medium of transportation, or to packages, on any animal or animals, or carried by man on foot."[1] As passed, the law was to remain in force only during the war and no longer.

During these waning days of the conflict, the reduced British naval force on the coast enjoyed about the same level of success as the American customs men Down East. The *Newcastle*, 60, Captain George Stuart, operating out of Provincetown captured the brig *Elizabeth* loaded with salt and the brig *Baltic* loaded with spices and oil, but lost a sloop at Salem and a coaster near Boston. On November 26, along with the *Acasta*, the *Newcastle* pursued a stranger for 24 hours to a point 220 miles east of Boston before carrying away her fore topsail yard and giving up the chase. She resumed her watchful waiting for the *Constitution*, and, later, in returning to Provincetown on December 12, at 6:00 p.m., "ran aground on a sand Bank off Beach Point"[2] at Barnstable. The mishap did not surprise some on the ship. One *Newcastle* officer later observed, Lord Stuart "had been many years at sea but, strange to say, knew nothing, literally nothing, of his profession."[3]

At any rate, Stuart sent a yawl, gig, and launch in search of vessels fit to lend a hand, and he worked the crew until 3:00 a.m., off-loading boats, and spare tackle and equipment. Resuming work at 6:00 a.m., the crew made a raft of some of the spars to use in deploying a pair of spring anchors. "Waited with great anxiety for high water," wrote a *Newcastle* journalist. "[I]n the mean time numbers of Americans Came of[f] from the Neighboring coast Who was of an Opinion that the Ship could not Be got off at 11 oclock high water." With satisfaction, John Allen, the journalist, crowed: [W]e hove the Ship off with Great Ease."[4] In three hours, the ship returned to its base at the Cape-tip to refit. But the smiles of fortune disappeared and the grounding incident set the stage for two American successes — victory at the Battle of Orleans and a stunning triumph for Boston's revered man-of-war.

The three boats sent from Beach Point for relief met with immediate disaster. Gale winds sank the gig and drove the launch and yawl ashore along the Lower Cape. "[T]he Boats Crews were taken Prisoners or Deserted to the Enemy."[5] Although the British eventually recovered the abandoned launch, in a while, things got worse.

---

1 Act of February 4, 1815, ch. 31, 3 *Stat.* 197.
2 John Allen, *Memorandum of a Log on board His Maj. Ship Newcastle.*
3 Pocock, *Captain Marryat*, 69.
4 John Allen.
5 Ibid.

On the 16ᵗʰ, the *Acasta* returned from its watch about Boston to join the *Newcastle* at Provincetown, leaving only the H.M.S. *Arab*, 18, Captain Henry Jane to pay attention to the *Constitution*. Allen recalled: "[D]uring this time we carried on a friendly intercourse with the Natives of the Bay who Brought us of every thing the place afforded which their charge was very reasonable as far as is Bought."[1] Nonetheless, Captain Stuart did not view the inhabit-ants around nearby Orleans with equal favor. Some of his ship's spare masts and spars rafted during the performance off Beach Point drifted to Orleans and were injured or taken by locals. Moreover, the town earlier in the year displayed defiance when it arrogantly rejected a British ransom demand. Stuart sent Lieutenant Frederick Marryat to undertake a punitive recovery mission against Rock Harbor in the town.

Marryat at age 14 joined the Royal Navy in 1806 as a midshipman. At times appearing larger than life, he participated heroically in more than a hundred sea and land engagements, many under the tutelage of the legend-ary Captain Sir Thomas Cochrane. Lord Cochrane commended Marryat in 1808 for his role in defending the besieged fort at Rosas. Several months later, in April 1809, still in his teens, he volunteered for "the hazardous, if not desperate"[2] mission of helping guide a novel explosion vessel against the French fleet at Aix Roads. But Marryat may, in fact, be best remembered for his second career. He would leave the navy as a captain and become a Lon-don literary figure of note, drawing on his experiences and creating the genre of naval fiction followed by Forrester, O'Brian, Pope, and others. The Orleans assignment seemed like easy work for such a stouthearted fellow.

Marryat set out in four barges on the 19ᵗʰ. Ordering three barges to remain outside, he entered Rock Harbor in the lead craft and promptly cut out the schooner *Betsey* and the sloops *Camel, Nancy,* and *Washington*. The latter two vessels were set on fire after they grounded on the flats. Marryat loaded the three reserve barges with recovered masts and spars and sent them back to the *Newcastle*. And he put 10 men on the *Betsey* and sent her on her way. How-ever, the inexperienced midshipman in charge, Charles Underwood, allowed the Yank captured on the *Betsey* to take her helm. In nasty weather and dark-ness, he contrived to run her aground near the Bass Hole in Yarmouth. The area militia seized the British crew and sent them along to the Salem jail.

Meanwhile, as Marryat moved to punish the insolence of Orleans, he found warm going. Militiamen turned out in force and poured a withering fire into his ranks. Royal Marine Thomas Walker sustained a mortal wound and became the only fatality of the lively scrap. Lieutenant Marryat and his remaining men escaped in the *Camel* towing their barge, and the townsmen rushed to extinguish the fires set by the raiders, keeping damage to a mini-mum. "[T]he Barge which was in tow of the Sloop went adrift During the Night with 2 men in her and has not Since Been heard of During this time."[3]

1 Ibid.
2 Dundonald, *Autobiography of a Seaman*, vol. 1, 341.
3 John Allen.

Actually, it wound up back in Orleans where the authorities placed the two Brits under arrest. After a costly lesson, Marryat and his five remaining men reached Provincetown in the *Camel* late on the 19th. But his problems were not over. The *Newcastle* inexplicably had sailed. The lieutenant went out in the bay in search of her.

In ill humor, Marryat searched for the better part of two days before he found Stuart and the ship late on the 21st. "'I was mad with hunger and cold' he remembered, 'and with difficulty did we get up the side, so exhausted and feeble were the whole of us. I was ordered down into the cabin, for it was too cold for the captain to show his face on deck.'" Marryat quickly seized the captain's decanter of Madeira, poured a glass, and downed it "'without even drinking his Lordship's good health. He stared and I believe he thought me mad. I certainly do own that my dress and appearance perfectly corresponded with my actions. I had not been washed, shaved, or cleaned since I had left the ship three days before. . . . As soon as I could speak, I said, 'I beg pardon my Lord, but I have had nothing to eat or drink since I left the ship.' 'Oh, *then* you are very welcome,' said his Lordship, 'I never expected to see you again.'"[1]

On the 22nd, Allen made another disappointing entry in his journal. "Receved Accounts from the Arabb of the American frigate Constitution had gone to sea."[2] Catching the British with their guard down, Captain Charles Stewart escaped unimpeded to the open sea in the venerable warship during the afternoon of December 18; a day after the *Acasta* left her interposing position off Boston and joined the recovering *Newcastle* at Provincetown. The *Constitution* wound up off Madeira on February 20, 1815, where she defeated the H.M.S. *Cyane*, 22, Captain Gordon Falcon and the H.M.S. *Levant*, 20, Captain George Douglass in a single action extending over some three hours.

The encounter at Orleans turned out to be the last notable British military intrusion on New England soil. But the administration was not out of the woods. The Federalists of the region had one final move of their own. A long time in the making, it amounted to a sad last gasp.

By 1814, among diehard New England Federalists, bitterness replaced straightforward opposition to the war. Beyond the decided specific differences over issues such as embargoes, nonintercourse, impressment, war against the mother country, strategy, control of the militia, defense of the coast, and the like, the dominant political party in New England saw its national influence and the influence of the region slipping away. The war and its management drove home the fact the expanding South and West, largely Republican and led by a Virginia dynasty, were wresting control of national affairs away from the nation's oldest and wealthiest region. As early as 1804, Timothy Pickering lamented "the rapid progress of innovation, of corruption, of oppression. . . ." He thought: "The people of the East cannot reconcile their habits, views, and interests with those of the South and West." Pickering,

---

1 Pocock, 70.
2 John Allen.

in fact, did "not believe in the practicability of a long-continued union. A Northern confederacy," he said, "would unite congenial characters, and present a fairer prospect of public happiness...."[1] He envisioned a Federalist confederation made up of New England, New York, and provinces in Canada, particularly Nova Scotia. For the time, the confederacy concept remained just that — a notion.

As the war developed and followed its course, the real and perceived grievances of New England multiplied and the differences between the two sections of the country became more pronounced. Dividing the country at the Delaware River, Boston's *Columbian Centinel* opined: "There are not two hostile nations upon earth whose views of the principles and polity of a perfect commonwealth, and of men and measures, are more discordant than those of these two great divisions."[2] This kind of thinking attracted a fair amount of support and opposition in the partisan press of the period, but the thought of secession never gained serious advocacy among the powers in New England.

Nonetheless, after the national government abandoned the region and left it to defend itself in the summer and fall of 1814, influential state and local leaders, especially in Massachusetts, determined something had to be done to address the underlying issues. A traditional American response met with favor. After years of talking about the need to convene, authorities in Massachusetts finally called for an interstate convention. The procedure possessed a commendable history. Conventions such as the Albany Congress of 1754, the Stamp Act Congress of 1765, the First Continental Congress of 1774, and the Philadelphia Constitutional Convention of 1787 were important and memorable conventions called to deal with governmental inequity. And prior to and during the present war, local and county conventions intended to organize support for one course of action or another cropped up at all seasons. Conventions were not novel.

Harrison Gray Otis of Massachusetts first proposed a gathering of northeast states in 1808. Repeal of Jefferson's embargo ended interest in such a conclave at that time. During the first year or so of the war, the idea surfaced more than once, but never got off the ground. In the last days of 1813, the South Hadley town meeting revived the idea of a convention of regional states. Within weeks, "some of the most discreet and intelligent inhabitants" of Hampshire County met to consider the "awful crisis." At the meeting, Noah Webster, the lexicographer, brought up his year-old plan for a "Convention of Delegates from the Northern States to agree upon & urge certain amendments to the constitution."[3] The meeting assigned Webster the task of preparing a communication to area towns that would set forth the growing list of grievances against the Madison administration and urge the communities to petition the state legislature for redress. Numerous towns

---

1 Henry Adams, *Documents Relating to New-England Federalism*, 339-340.
2 *Columbian Centinel* (MA), January 13, 1813.
3 Banner, *To the Hartford Convention*, 314.

statewide took up the call and appealed to the General Court to support a convention and work for the "speedy termination" of the "unhappy war."[1] But a few, such as Eden, remonstrated against the idea of "Sending patitions praying for a division of the Country."[2]

The general alarm along the coast in the early autumn prompted Governor Strong to call a special session of the Massachusetts legislature. His October 5 message reported the "situation of the state is dangerous and perplexing."[3] The governor's message went to a joint committee chaired by Otis. The senator had discussed the sectional convention question with friends in the days leading up to the session, and a few editors were promoting the idea. The *New Bedford Mercury*, for one, called for a New England convention to create "a confederacy by which the safety of each [state] shall be guaranteed by the efforts of all."[4]

The Otis committee took only three days to file a measure proposing a convention. The report stressed the difficulty of mounting a unilateral defense while responding "to the heavy and increasing demands of the national government." After summarizing the state's grievances, the Otis report argued: "[D]ishonored and deprived of all influence in the national councils, this state has been dragged into an unnatural and distressing war, and its safety, perhaps its liberties, endangered." Continuing, the committee recommended "a conference should be invited between those states, the affinity of whose interests is closest ..."[5]

To implement the report, the committee included seven resolves. The first four dealt with immediate defensive measures, including authorization to borrow $1 million for the purpose. The fifth and most significant resolve recommended that "twelve persons be appointed as Delegates from this Commonwealth, to meet and confer with Delegates from the other states of New England ... upon the subjects of their public grievances and concerns, and upon the best means of ... defence against the enemy ... ; and also to take measures, if they shall think proper, for procuring a convention of Delegates from all the United States, in order to revise the constitution thereof, and more effectually to secure the support and attachment of *all* the people, by placing *all* upon the basis of fair representation."[6]

Two-thirds of the Senate accepted the key convention resolve and three-fourths of the Massachusetts House concurred. Governor Strong approved the entire report on October 15. Critics were aghast. Salem's Reverend William Bentley, an intimate of the late vice president, General Dearborn, and even the president, put it succinctly. "The Speculators will run all risks of

1 *North Yarmouth* (ME) *Town Records Volume Second May 1st A.D. 1784 to April 2nd A.D. 1821*, 438.

2 *Book 1 Records of the Town of Eden* (ME) *1796 to 1827*, 143.

3 Barry, *History of Massachusetts: The Commonwealth Period*, 407.

4 *New Bedford* (MA) *Mercury*, September 16, 1814.

5 Massachusetts General Court, *The committee to whom was referred the Message of his Excellency*, 1-3.

6 Ibid., 4.

their heads to fill their purses."[1] Nonetheless, an early historian believed "the vote of the legislature reflected quite faithfully the wishes of the people."[2] Immediately, Senate President John Phillips and House Speaker Timothy Bigelow sent letters to the four other New England states.

Connecticut wholeheartedly accepted the invitation. The state's legislature favored the plan by a 153 to 36 vote. Rhode Island went along, but with less single-mindedness. The Ocean State's House of Representatives endorsed the idea by a 39 to 23 margin. The losing side offered a minority report, but it was not recorded "on account of its indecorous language and foul aspersions on the motives of the majority."[3]

In both Connecticut and Rhode Island, recent administration proposals to fill military ranks played a role in the outcome. A federal bill to initiate conscription and another to permit the enlistment of minors as young as 18 years of age raised considerable ill will at the time. By a 168–6 vote, the Connecticut assembly asserted the conscription measure was unconstitutional. The negativism in Hartford found 23 Republicans, including the minority leader, voting against Madison's military draft proposal. Americans have always disliked a military draft, and the public outcry in 1814 initiated this tradition. The conscription bill did not pass. But, too late to make much of a difference in the war effort and contrary to the feelings of large segments of the population, Congress enacted a law to permit the enlistment of minors. In response to some of the opposition, the law included a novel probationary clause. In authorizing expanded recruitment, Congress stipulated: "That it shall not be lawful for any recruiting officer to pay or deliver to a recruit under the age of twenty-one years . . . any bounty or clothing, or in any manner restrain him of his liberty, until after the expiration of four days."[4]

When the Massachusetts invitation reached Federalist Governor Gilman of New Hampshire, he did not bite. He pointed out to Otis that his legislature was out of session, and he feared "the consequences of a call" for such a purpose.[5] An invite needed to pass through the Republican controlled council, and Gilman doubted it would call a special session for such a controversial reason. Nonetheless, Cheshire and Grafton counties and Lancaster town in Coos County, all dominated by Federalists, convened and elected a pair of delegates to attend the proposed convention.

Although a Federalist supported by a legislative majority of his party, Vermont Governor Chittenden also declined to participate. Prevost's invasion and the recent nearby battle at Plattsburg made a deep impression on Chittenden, and he reversed course to support the national war effort. He did not have time for conventioneering. But Windham County in the south of Vermont, bordering Cheshire County, New Hampshire and not that far

1 Bentley, *Diary of William Bentley*, 4:293.
2 Barry, 410.
3 James T. Adams, *New England in the Republic 1776-1850*, 291.
4 Act of December 10, 1814, ch. 10, 3 *Stat.* 146.
5 Morison, *Harrison Gray Otis*, 360.

from Hampshire County, Massachusetts, decided to send a delegate to the conclave.

Massachusetts selected 12 delegates. Seven men represented Connecticut, and Rhode Island had four attendees. And there were the two representatives from New Hampshire, and the single delegate from the Green Mountain State. In addition, the Vermont secretary of state showed up. Since he was not elected to attend, the convention denied him a seat. The meeting created enough concern in Washington to convince Madison to have somebody in town. He ordered Colonel Thomas Jesup, the local army commander, to keep his eyes peeled and watch for any insurrectionary conduct on the part of the delegates and their supporters. As the meeting progressed, Jesup reported little public interest in the proceedings.

An earlier proposal for a regional convention recommended "for the Wise and Good, of those states which deem themselves oppressed, to assemble with delegated authority."[1] For the most part, the men selected for the 1814 convention met this standard. With an average age of 52 years, the convention members were a mature, experienced, and respected group. In an era when lawyers were esteemed, it is worth noting 22 of the 26 delegates were attorneys. Nine were jurists. An observer described George Cabot of Brookline, Massachusetts, unanimously chosen president of the convention, as "a man of so enlightened a mind, of such wisdom, virtue, and piety, one must travel far, very far, to find his equal."[2] Another Massachusetts delegate, Nathan Dane, authored the Territorial Ordinance of 1787. Samuel S. Wilde served on the Massachusetts Supreme Judicial Court. Connecticut's delegation included John Treadwell, a former governor, and Chauncey Goodrich, the present lieutenant governor and a former U.S. senator. Rhode Island's contingent included Chief Justice Daniel Lyman and Samuel Ward, a member of the Annapolis Convention of 1786. Miles Olcott, treasurer of Dartmouth College, served as one of the New Hampshire delegates. And Vermont's member, William Hall, Jr., served in the state council. Gouverneur Morris, the founding father from Pennsylvania, was not far from the mark when he described the membership as the "Wise Men of the East."[3]

Goodrich made the council chamber in the state house at Hartford available for the gathering. Accordingly, the Convention of Delegates from the New England States became forever after known as the Hartford Convention. December 15 was set aside as the opening day of the meeting.

In the days leading up to the first session, the public debate intensified. John Quincy Adams declared the convention "Unconstitutional and treasonable . . . wholly abnormal and wicked."[4] In contrast, Samuel Rodman, a prominent citizen of peaceable New Bedford, told a friend he wished for drastic action at the convention, because "we are wholly tir'd of the present

1 Ibid., 355.
2 Barry, 412.
3 Beirne, War of 1812, 331.
4 Ibid., 322.

system."[1] Josiah Quincy had a better feel for things. "A GREAT PAMPHLET!" he thought would be the only outcome.[2]

Along predictable partisan lines, editors from beyond the region railed against the convention. The *Richmond Enquirer* urged Madison to set the army against New England. The future front for the Southern Confederacy, anticipating nefarious action in Hartford, asserted: "[N]o state or set of states *has a right* to withdraw itself from" . . . the "Union, of its own accord." To do so, it said, amounted to "Treason — Treason to all intents & purposes."[3] Always on top of national affairs, Hezekiah Niles in Baltimore also took exception to the meeting, but he allowed the organizers were acting true to form. "On several occasions of public rejoicing, they have fired *five* guns, as a national, or *New England* salute."[4] Such people, Niles thought, could not be trusted. Watching closely, the *London Times* simply declared: "New England allied with Old England would form a dignified and manly union well deserving the name of Peace."[5]

The radical segment of the Federalist press got into the act, and seemed to draw heavily on the reasoning presented in the Kentucky and Virginia Resolutions of 1798 and even Madison's Report of 1800. It will be recalled, at the turn of the century, Madison asserted, "that in case of a deliberate, palpable, and dangerous exercise" of constitutional power by the national government, "the States . . . have the right, and are in duty bound to interpose for arresting the program of evil, and for maintaining within their respective limits, the authorities, rights and liberties appertaining to them."[6] The Hartford delegates and their supporters thought as much. Significantly, an analysis of extensive press treatment of the convention found "practically all of the elements out of which Calhoun and Davis constructed their nullification and secession doctrines were asserted in these New England constitutional arguments of 1814."[7]

With so much attention concentrated on the upcoming convention, even insiders did not know about a secret overture to the British initiated by Governor Strong at the time. In fact, the clandestine mission did not come to light until 1938. At any rate, Strong quietly dispatched George Herbert to Halifax to explore with Sir John Sherbrooke the possibility of an extraordinary settlement with the British. Without putting anything in writing, Strong wanted to know how Great Britain would respond if the Commonwealth's differences with the national government escalated to use of force. Herbert did not carry any credentials, but Sherbrooke personally knew him to be a "Gentleman who is a most respectable Inhabitant" of eastern Maine.[8]

---

1 McDevitt, *House of Rotch*, 493.
2 Hickey, *War of 1812*, 274.
3 Morison, *Harrison Gray Otis*, 370.
4 *Niles' Weekly Register* (MD), November 26, 1814.
5 Caffrey, *Twilight's Last Gleaming*, 286.
6 Randolph, *Virginia Report of 1799-1800*, 191.
7 Anderson, *A Forgotten Phase of the New England Opposition to the War of 1812*, 15.
8 Martell, *American Historical Review*, 559.

Herbert, a prominent Ellsworth lawyer and avid if not radical Federalist, had long ties to Strong and other party leaders. While at Dartmouth College, for instance, he developed a lifelong friendship with Daniel Webster. As a member of the Massachusetts General Court during the war, he became a Strong loyalist. Sherbrooke formed his positive opinion of Herbert a few weeks earlier. When the enemy occupied Castine and environs in September, Herbert went to the British commander to gain understandings favorable to the inhabitants. The lawyer argued against the forfeiture of firearms by the citizens. In such an event, "Desporadoes made up of our own people would invade every night our defenceless houses with impunity. . . ."[1] Herbert also pleaded for a continuance of commerce and maintenance of the established system of justice. Sherbrooke appreciated the merit of Herbert's recommendations and more or less adopted them as policy.

On November 20, Sherbrooke reported the interesting overture to Lord Bathurst in London, the secretary for war and the colonies. Sherbrooke summarized the expressed grievances of Massachusetts and the reason for the upcoming convention at Hartford. He noted Madison loyalists existed in strength throughout New England and would join with the general government to resist any separation movement pushed by the Federalists. "It appears," he reported, "that the Federal Party wishes to ascertain at this early period whether Great Britain would under these Circumstances afford them Military assistance to effect their purpose should they stand in need of it."[2]

Having asked Herbert to set his points in writing, Sherbrooke attached the statement to his dispatch. Herbert covered now familiar ground. He also indicated the gathering of states at Hartford planned to explore the possibility of "taking into their own hands the Revenues of all kinds accruing to the general Government within their respective Territories, with a view to appropriate those Revenues to their own immediate and joint defence." Such action, he stressed, "will necessarily lead to collision between that Government and these States, and also that the credit of that Government already greatly impaired, and always founded principally on the basis of Northern revenue, must entirely fail."[3] Herbert wrapped up by expressing "extreme regret" over the "depredations on our Coasts." The policy "had the most painful effects" on the New England states "with very little benefit, perhaps none . . . to the British Interests. Indeed it is a measure pregnant with the most serious consequences to both Countries. The levying of Contributions has excited a great degree of feeling and alarm," he said, "and has undoubtedly produced a war spirit in some limited degree, where it did not exist before." George Herbert suggested: "If that mode of Warfare be thought advisable, it must operate altogether on the South. Punishment will then be brought

---

1 Silsby, *Maine Historical Society Newsletter*, 117.
2 Martell, 559-560.
3 Ibid., 561.

Home to the Doors of the guilty. In that Country the British Government and people have no affections to lose."[1]

Bathurst replied on December 13, advising Sherbrooke that the two countries were on the verge of agreeing to peace in the talks at Ghent. However, if the negotiations did not succeed within reasonable time, Sherbrooke could go ahead with a separate armistice as contemplated by Strong. Moreover, the general could provide materiel support to help the insurgents respond to the certain "Resentment of the American Executive." In a separate letter of the same date, Bathurst told Sherbrooke to get together with the naval commanders at Halifax "to mitigate in every possible manner the pressure of War, in favor of all such States as shall have satisfactorily shewn a disposition to conclude an Armistice" with Great Britain in the event the war continued.[2] But as Bathurst expected, events overtook the secret mission. Strong's idea never progressed beyond the exchange of communications between Halifax and London.

At the same time, a diametrically opposite plot also faltered. Just before Christmas, Samuel H. Whiting wrote from Bangor to General King in Bath telling him beyond "a few dastardly Tories," sentiment in eastern Maine favored a militia attack on the enemy at Castine. Whiting thought he could rely on 500 men volunteering, while local militia officers felt confident 1,000 men would offer their services for such an expedition. He assessed the Castine defenses and found them wanting. More important, he learned the British held a substantial amount of specie at Castine and Buckstown. "If a secret expedition could be got up it would tell well, if plunder was the order of the day." Whiting sensed Governor Strong and the Commonwealth could not be depended upon for assistance in such a venture, but, he told King, "let us make an effort to take care of ourselves."[3] Whiting expected to gather more intelligence before visiting Bath in three weeks to pursue his scheme. But winter weather and events ended the affair in the planning stage.

Be this as it may, the time set aside for the New England meeting arrived. On the morning of the 15th, Hartford Republicans greeted the gathering delegates with ringing church bells and flags displayed at half-staff. Concealing exuberance, a group solemnly and slowly circled the state house marching to a funeral dirge. Inside, as soon as the convention came to order, it attended to housekeeping duties. George Cabot received unanimous support for the presidency. Theodore Dwight, *Connecticut Mirror* editor and not a delegate, became secretary by another unanimous vote. A committee prepared and the gathering adopted a set of rules. A rule cloaking all proceedings in secrecy turned out to be a public relations disaster. Governmental closed-door meetings were not at all unusual at the time, but, in this case, the mystery created a widespread belief that rebellion and treason were on the agenda. Only ru-

---

1 Ibid., 563.
2 Ibid., 564-565.
3 Whiting, *Letter*.

mors, some of them wild, came out of Hartford. Members faithfully kept the pledge of secrecy throughout the convention.

They were just as unflagging when it came to daily effort. During the three-week session (December 15-January 5), the delegates skipped only three days other than Sundays. Christmas became an off day because it fell on the Sabbath. Elsewhere, some people did manage to observe what has become a special day, including the officers and crew of the *Newcastle* off Boston. "Celebrated Chistmasday in the good old English Style," noted the ship's journalist.[1] And unknown to anyone in North America, the peace commissioners in Ghent truly rejoiced on December 25, but for reasons unrelated to religious considerations.

The convention got down to business on the 16th, and set the agenda. Initial attention focused on the American president's power relative to the state militias and the chief executive's responsibility to supply and fund the militias. On Christmas Eve, the delegates agreed "to prepare a general statement of the unconstitutional attempts of the Executive Government of the United States to infringe upon the rights of the individual States, in regard to the militia . . ."[2]

Upon contemplation, the delegates appreciated the underlying problem rested beyond militia control. Accordingly, they proceeded to recommend seven proposed constitutional amendments; namely, (1) that congressional representation and direct taxes be based on a state's number of free persons; (2) that new states be admitted only by a two-thirds vote of each house of Congress; (3) that embargoes be restricted to 60 days; (4) that two-thirds of both houses must approve nonintercourse measures; (5) that two-thirds of both houses must approve a declaration of war; (6) that no person hereafter naturalized be eligible for Congress or federal civil appointment; and (7) that no president shall serve more than one term, and no state shall provide a president for successive terms.

The benefit and relevance to New England of all but one of the proposals must be obvious. The naturalized citizen restriction is less clear. It reflected Federalist antipathy toward the considerable influence and unappreciated policies of Albert Gallatin. Born in Geneva, Switzerland, and a longtime secretary of the treasury under both Jefferson and Madison, Gallatin at the moment served on the American peace mission at Ghent. In 1793, Pennsylvania sent him to the U.S. Senate, but the opposition contested his eligibility. In February 1794, the body voted 14 to 12 to void his election, "he not having been a citizen of the United States the term of years required as a qualification to be a Senator of the United States."[3] Just one year later, now eligible for Congress, Gallatin gained election to the U.S. House of Representatives and served there until 1801. George Cabot and Caleb Strong were among the senators voting to oust Gallatin in 1794. Federalist Party leaders did not

---

1 John Allen.
2 Lyman, *A short account of the Hartford Convention*, 29.
3 U.S. *Senate Journal*. 3rd Cong., 1st sess., February 28, 1794, 37.

want to see another Gallatin in national office, and this explains the thinking behind the idea of altogether barring naturalized citizens.

The product of the convention fell far short of the treason predicted by some critics and opponents. The *Connecticut Courant* printed the moderate report in its entirety in an extra issue on January 6. Reproduced in papers throughout the country, the account silenced what fears of rebellion might have existed. The temperate character of the document surprised many Republicans as well as some in the administration. Hard-line Federalists felt betrayed, however.

In order to maintain control of the agenda, put the Madison government on warning, and reassure the main body of Federalists, the convention delegates concluded their report with a final recommendation. They set a follow-up meeting for late in June 1815 at Boston. And they authorized Cabot, Goodrich, and Lyman to call the second session.

The possibility of a meeting in six months tempered the stridency and disaffection prevalent in many parts of the region. Newburyport, by way of example, held a town meeting late in January 1815 to treat the convention report. The meeting resolved that the time was fast approaching when it would "consider our State Legislatures as the sole, rightful & bounden judge of the course which our safety may require, without regard to the persons still assuming to be the National Government," and "that the laws of the United States shall be temporarily suspended in their operation in our territory. . . . "[1] But Newburyport was willing to hold off for a little longer. The town of Reading passed a similar resolution and waited.

The Connecticut and Massachusetts legislatures took up the convention's work, and both voted approval. Vermont, on the other hand, passed a resolution in opposition, as did seven states outside of the region. The Massachusetts House entertained "a high sense of the wisdom and ability" of the delegates and their "most satisfactory proofs of attachment to the constitution of the United States and to the national Union."[2] And it endorsed the convention report by a 159 to 48 vote. At the same time, the General Court granted the governor authority to name three commissioners to proceed to Washington to promote the report's recommendations. Strong appointed Bostonians Otis, Thomas H. Perkins, and William Sullivan. The trio struck out for the capital early in February.

A few days earlier, however, Congress passed and the president signed a remarkable law that just about fully addressed the militia concerns spelled out in the convention's report. The measure permitted the president to receive into the United States service "any corps of troops . . . raised, organized and officered under the authority of any of the states . . . which corps, when received into the service . . . shall be . . . employed in the state raising the same, or in an adjoining state, and not elsewhere, except with the assent of the executive of the state so raising the same. . . ." Just as important, the act

1 Banner, 345.
2 Barry, 418.

provided such state troops "shall be armed and equipped at the expense of the United States, and shall be entitled to the same pay, clothing, rations, forage, and emoluments . . . as the regular troops. . . ."[1] When he learned of this turn of events, Otis boasted, "The egg that was laid in the darkness of the Hartford Convention was hatched by daylight under the wing and incubation of the National Eagle."[2] Had this law been in place at the beginning of 1814, before the British assault on abandoned New England, it is doubtful the antiwar movement could have maintained its momentum all the way to Hartford. Instead of mounting their own unilateral defenses, the New England states would have found themselves active elements of the national war machinery.

Otis and his associates became the subject of much derision and jesting as they made their way to Washington. Shortly after passing through Philadelphia, they learned about General Andrew Jackson's stunning strategic victory at New Orleans. And on February 14, momentous news from Ghent effectively ended their mission. Practically nobody showed any interest in constitutional amendments, so the trio hung around town for a while attempting to gain federal reimbursement for defense costs incurred by Massachusetts during the war. The changed atmosphere in Washington also worked against them on this score.

Writing from London several months later, John Quincy Adams did not accept the accuracy of Josiah Quincy's prophecy of little harm. He summarized his feelings toward the wartime performance of the Federalists culminating in their Hartford Convention. "As to our beloved New England," he told a friend, "I blush to think of the part she has performed, for her shame is still the disgrace of the nation. . . . As a true New England man and American I feel the infection of their shame, while I abhor the acts by which they have brought it upon us."[3] Adams, of course, possessed a unique though distant perspective stemming from his key role in the final chapter of the war.

Decades after the convention, the site of the meeting — now called the Old State House — witnessed a belated epilogue. A gentleman from the South visited the historic building and asked to see the actual meeting room of the Hartford Convention. A guide directed him to the former senate chamber where a Gilbert Stuart portrait of George Washington hung behind the presiding officer's chair. The painting is vividly colored and had not succumbed to the dullness of age. The visitor wondered if the Washington portrait watched over the convention delegates. "Certainly," answered the guide. "Well," responded the gentleman, still studying the painting, "I'll be damned if he's got the blush off yet."[4]

---

1 Act of January 27, 1815, ch. 25, 3 *Stat.* 193.
2 Beirne, 332.
3 James T. Adams, 300-301.
4 Van Dusen, *Connecticut*, 186.

CHAPTER 14. GLAD TIDINGS OF PEACE

Winter and universal awareness of the advancing and promising peace talks combined to shut down military operations in New England by the first of January 1815, although privateering continued on a greatly reduced scale. Among the final episodes on the water, a trio of American privateers chased ashore a transport out of Halifax with 250 troopers bound for the Castine garrison. The troopers clambered over the side and marched the remaining short distance to the town. The enemy consolidated its hold on eastern Maine taking formal possession of Buckstown on February 6, and reaching into places such as Ellsworth. But Castine remained the site of just about all of the British activity in the region.

Anglo-American commerce continued to flourish through the town, and army personnel became fully integrated into community life. Initially, enlisted men, with much time on their hands and want of money for rum, worked at odd jobs for the townspeople. The command under General Gosselin soon halted this practice, so the troopers began to trade their bread for liquor. The officers, likewise, put an end to this exchange in order to cut the "disgraceful amount of drunkenness among the soldiers."[1]

British officers made every effort to enhance social amenities. They planned "to import . . . female performers from Boston" to entertain in their new theater. Niles grumbled: "If *Boston* was now as it was in 1776, they would have some other amusement."[2] A cantankerous local veteran of the Revolutionary War seemed to make a similar point in a different way. The aged Hate-evil Colson, known as "Haty Co'sn," asked to see the commanding general. Granted an audience, he demanded: "Are you General Gosselin?"

"I am."

---

1 George A. Wheeler, *Castine*, 53.
2 *Niles' Weekly Register* (MD), December 31, 1814.

"Damn the *goose* that hatched you, then!"[1]

On occasion, social intercourse became even more strained. In mid-January, lodgers at the James Perkins House committed a wrong against Lieutenant Kearney and used abusive language toward Captain Stannus. A court of inquiry found a Mr. Lang and a Mr. Rhode to be the chief offenders. The cause of the commotion according to the court involved "the neglect and want of inclination on the part of the landlord to provide suitable furniture for a British officer's apartment, though he accommodated five merchants in his house several days after the arrival of Lieutenant Kearney."[2] The court banished Lang and Rhode from Castine, pulled Perkins' liquor license, and, for good measure, quartered added officers in his house. After two and a half years of fighting and privation, the war in New England had degenerated to a squabble over furnishings in a lodging on the coast of Maine. The time had come to put an end to the war that neither country wanted.

Peace overtures actually appeared in the first days of the war. On June 26, 1812, Secretary of State James Monroe sent Jonathan Russell, late chargé d'affaires at London, instructions by way of Augustus Foster, the returning British minister. Monroe told Russell that if "the orders in council, and other illegal blockades, and the impressment of our seamen . . . were removed, you might stipulate an armistice, leaving them and all other grounds of difference for final and more precise adjustment by treaty."[3]

The proposal ran into a stumbling block before it crossed the ocean. On the way back to London, Foster met with Admiral Herbert Sawyer and Sir John Sherbrooke at Halifax. Among other things, the pair agreed to a reciprocal cessation of proceedings against prize vessels. At the same time, Foster wrote to Sir George Prevost, the commander in Canada, to propose a halt to land campaigns. Madison, however, rejected the overall proposal as it developed, believing he was powerless "to suspend judicial proceedings on prizes." Moreover, the arrangement "might not be observed by the British officers themselves;" security was not provided against the marauding Indian allies of England; the proposition left Britain "time to augment her forces;" and a suspension prior to hearing Great Britain's answer to the central impressment issue, "might be considered a relinquishment of that claim."[4] Lord Castlereagh, the foreign secretary, expressed surprise "that as a condition preliminary even to a suspension of hostilities, the Government of the United States should have thought fit to demand that the British Government should desist from its ancient and accustomed practice of impressing British seamen from the merchant ships of a foreign state, simply on the assurance that a law shall hereafter be passed, to prohibit the employment of British seamen in the public or commercial service of that state."[5]

---

1 Munson, *Penobscot*, 114.
2 George A. Wheeler, 53.
3 *American State Papers: Foreign Relations* 3:586.
4 Ibid., 588.
5 Ibid., 590.

The diplomatic exchanges and niceties continued until late in the summer of 1812. On September 12, Russell again called on Lord Castlereagh and told him "that I had once more been authorized to present the olive branch, and hoped it would not be again rejected." But his lordship noted Russell's diplomatic functions had ceased and his authority rested on a letter from Secretary Monroe. This would compel Castlereagh, as he put it, "to act on unequal ground."[1] He would pledge the faith of the British government, but Russell could not give a similar pledge. Thus, an early and solid opportunity to end the war came to an end.

The next serious attempt to negotiate a peace agreement came during the following winter. Acting out of self-interests, Czar Alexander I, in February 1813, invited the two warring countries to Russia where he would attempt to broker a settlement. His Imperial Majesty foresaw "the great shackles" which the war was "about to place on the "commercial prosperity of nations. The love of humanity, and what he owes to his subjects, whose commerce has already sufficiently suffered," commanded him "to do every thing in his power to remove the evils which this war" was "preparing even for those nations who will not take part in it."[2]

Madison, undergoing tough times at home, accepted the offer at once. In May, he sent abroad a two-man party to connect with a third member already in Europe to form an American peace delegation. James A. Bayard, Sr. from Delaware traveled with Secretary of the Treasury Albert Gallatin to St. Petersburg to join John Quincy Adams, the United States minister in Russia. In addition to regional balance, the team represented bipartisan competence. Gallatin, of course, represented the president's party. A three-term veteran of Congress prior to his lengthy stint at the Treasury, the Pennsylvanian later served as minister to France, minister to Great Britain, and president of the National Bank of New York. Bayard, a Princeton graduate and lawyer, represented the Federalist Party in the House from 1797 to 1803 and in the Senate from 1804 to 1813. And Adams, as discussed, left Massachusetts and the Federalist Party in 1809 to serve at the court in St. Petersburg.

Gallatin and Bayard made it to St. Petersburg on July 21, unaware the British rejected the Russian mediation proposition. The two men tarried and hoped for instructions before departing for London in January 1814, leaving Adams in Russia. Their move to Britain tied in with developments. Late in 1813, Castlereagh told Monroe: "I can assure you that the British Government is willing to enter into a discussion . . . for the conciliatory adjustment of differences subsisting" between the countries.[3] He proffered direct negotiations with Washington to be conducted in London. After expressing unhappiness with Britain's rejection of Alexander's overture, Monroe asserted: "Wherever the United States may treat, they will treat with the sincere desire they

---

1 Ibid., 593.
2 Ibid., 624.
3 Ibid., 621.

have repeatedly manifested of terminating the present contest."[1] The United States, nonetheless, turned down London as a conference site. The parties settled on the Flemish city of Ghent.

Madison also strengthened his peace team. Speaker of the House Henry Clay resigned his seat in Congress on January 19, 1814 and accepted a nomination to be a member of the delegation. The president also added veteran diplomat Jonathan Russell. The Senate approved the revised five-man delegation — Adams at its head — on February 9. Clay proved to be a strong addition. During the ensuing months, the Kentuckian impressed Adams with his diplomatic skills. When Adams became president in another decade, he placed Clay in the post of secretary of state.

A typical New Englander, John Quincy Adams hurried to Ghent, arriving well ahead of the others. The other commissioners arrived by July 12, and the men rented a house together. This turned out to be a mistake. James Gallatin, young son of the secretary, made a July 15 diary entry. "Mr. Adams in a very bad temper. Mr. Clay annoys him. Father pours oil on the troubled waters."[2] Adams did not approve of Clay's lifestyle. The son of Massachusetts adhered to the old maxim with Puritanical overtones that one who rises late never does a good day's work. An entry in Adam's diary reads: "There was another card party in Mr. Clay's chamber last night, and I heard Mr. Bentzon retiring from it after I had risen this morning."[3] The commissioners would live and work together for six months, and Adams and Clay lost their tempers all too frequently. Gallatin seemed to find "his most trying and perhaps most useful work in keeping the peace between the Americans rather than in making it with the British."[4] In time, the pair learned to respect and like one another.

In contrast to the American delegation, the British team was less in size, skill, and experience. Admiral of the Fleet John James Gambier headed the three-man delegation. Lord Gambier possessed a controversial record, both at sea and at the Admiralty. He had the reputation of "a brave but weak officer, chiefly known as what was called in the navy a 'blue light,' that is a pious man of a somewhat Methodistical turn."[5] His timid command at Basque Roads in 1809 prompted Napoleon to consider him an imbecile. Henry Goulburn, a 30-year-old undersecretary for war and the colonies, was the second member. William Adams, holder of a doctorate in civil law and an author of little distinction, rounded out the mission. Beyond the matter of competence, the British team suffered from the fact they held little delegated authority. They found it necessary to refer all points to London, a ten-day process. Complicating matters, Goulburn and Dr. Adams shared a "prejudice

---

1 Ibid., 622.
2 Beirne, 377.
3 James T. Adams, *Adams Family*, 147.
4 Ibid., 149.
5 Hannay, *Life of Frederick Marryat*, 38.

of disliking everything that is not English, and of taking no pains to conceal their taste."[1]

The first meeting of the parties took place in the Hotel des Pays-Bas on August 8. Both sides presented their agendas. The British considered the matter of an Indian territory or buffer state to be an essential element of any agreement. John Quincy, speaking for the United States commissioners, said they were not authorized to discuss such a concept. The Brits communicated with their government, and returned to the table on the 19th. Castlereagh instructed his delegates to insist on the Indian barrier between American and British possessions. The British also insisted on the right to navigate the Mississippi River and expressed an unwillingness to address the issue of American rights to the Newfoundland fisheries. The seemingly uncompromising terms led Adams to apprehend the conference would end in its first weeks.

Young Eliza Susan Quincy and her mother visited John Adams several weeks later, and in a journal entry Susan said he "read us a letter from Mr. J.Q. Adams in which he said there was no prospect of peace & was very bitter against the Bostonians for rejoicing over the victories of the Allies." She added: "He said that if there was a man who hated the Yankee, it was Lord Wellington, & that the people of Boston might soon have other forces than those with which they had illuminated their State House."[2] Her father returned from Boston that day and reported widespread despondency in town over the discouraging news from Europe.

Madison publicized the stance of Great Britain, and a public outcry resulted. "Don't Give Up The Soil" became an oft-repeated motto.[3] The barrier or buffer desired by London would take up land ceded to the United States by the Indians in 1795. Much of the national press took up the president's side. The normally anti-administration *Columbian Centinel* considered the "proposition *so outrageous*, that we ought not even to make it a subject *of negotiations*." The Boston paper went so far as to argue, "[A] treaty with this condition must be derogatory to the *honor* of the United States, or *more disadvantageous to her interests than a continuance of the War*."[4]

While the British negotiators at Ghent felt confident in their rigid position, Lord Liverpool's government in London stepped back. With Castlereagh now fully occupied at the Congress of Vienna, Bathurst took over the lead in the Anglo-American talks. And upon reflection, he told Gambier the Indian territory provision was no longer a *sine qua non* or an essential element of any agreement.

As the days passed, Clay and Adams began to drift apart. Clay the Westerner became the hardliner. He was adamant about the Mississippi navigation question. At the same time, he cared little about fishing matters. Fishing

1 James T. Adams, 151.

2 *Eliza Susan Quincy Journal*, 7.

3 Beirne, 381-382.

4 *Columbian Centinel* (MA), October 19, 1814.

rights were a New England concern, and Clay did not see any merit in sup-porting the region that flirted with treason during the war. "The navigation principle," argued the former speaker contemptuously, "is much too impor-tant to concede for the mere liberty of drying fish on a desert."[1] For his part, Adams prepared to decline signing any treaty that sacrificed the fisheries.

Adams remembered Clay "was for playing *brag* with the British Plenipo-tentiaries; they had been playing *brag* with us throughout the whole nego-tiation." Adams explained: "He asked me if I knew how to play *brag* [a card game similar to poker]. I had forgotten how. He said the art of it was to beat your adversary by holding your hand, with a solemn and confident phiz, and outbragging him." Bayard confirmed Clay's description, "but you may lose your game by bragging until the adversary sees the weakness of your hand." Senator Bayard added, "Mr. Clay is for bragging a million against a cent."[2]

Clay, certainly more than anyone at the table, had his career on the line. The leading War Hawk, in 1812 he predicted a swift march to Quebec and expeditious redress of maritime wrongs. Instead, Washington was in ruins, the American army floundered in disarray, and New England was looking for a way out of the mess. To make an unsatisfactory peace under such condi-tions would make his prophecies look foolish. He told Adams he favored "a war three years longer."[3]

John Quincy Adams held little interest in wagering "a million against a cent." He, instead, pushed for a more reasonable, attainable goal. He stub-bornly insisted on a *status quo ante bellum* settlement — a return to the state of affairs before the war. Such a position is always attractive when both com-batants are tired of a war neither really wanted. And it should not go unno-ticed that Adam's proposition could be described as the New England posi-tion. Under such an agreement, the eastern counties of Maine would revert to Massachusetts and New England fishermen would continue to enjoy the rights stipulated in the third article of the treaty of 1783 governing the con-duct of their work on the coasts of England's dominions in North America.

In November, as Adams anticipated, the prince regent moved to play his best card. He told Bathurst "nothing should be neglected to induce the Duke of Wellington to accept the Chief Command in America as soon as possible." Liverpool agreed and presented the proposal to Wellington. But the Duke demurred. He felt continuing unrest in Europe required his presence close at hand. More to the point, he declared "that which it appears to me to be wanting in America is not a General, or General officers and troops, but a naval superiority on the Lakes." Without such a force, he could not do more than "sign a peace which might as well be signed now."[4] In fact, he advised the government sign a peace accord without demanding territorial acquisi-

1 Beirne, 385.
2 James T. Adams, 154-155.
3 Ibid., 154.
4 Guedalla, *Wellington*, 259-260.

tions since British military accomplishments did not support or merit land claims.

Wellington's decision and opinion seemed to influence the British approach. The talks began to make progress, and by mid-December, only two issues remained unresolved. Both were important to New England. One question involved islands, especially the Passamaquoddy islands known as Moose, Frederick, and Dudley as well as Grand Manan in the Bay of Fundy. Each country claimed the British-occupied islands. The second question related to ancient fishing rights.

The delegations reached agreement on the islands by proposing "mutual restitution of territory" except for the four Down East islands. Britain would hold the islands for the time. Then, a two-member commission would meet in St. Andrews, New Brunswick after treaty ratification to resolve title to the four islands. Be this as it may, the American ministers insisted: "No disposition made by this treaty of the intermediate possession of the islands and territories claimed by both parties shall, in any manner whatever be construed to effect [sic] the right of either."[1]

The Passamaquoddy matter proved relatively easy to resolve because it was one of three major boundary issues taken up by the conference and treated in the same manner. The others involved the boundaries between the St. Croix and Connecticut rivers and lines in the Great Lakes region. But the fisheries question for the most part only impacted New England — especially Massachusetts. Largely as a consequence, Adams especially considered it a vital matter. Beyond its importance to his home state, an odd familial connection existed. At the peace convention between the two countries in 1783, the elder John Adams stubbornly fought the same fight. The British negotiators at the time attempted to define fishing as a *liberty*, not a *right*. "If Heaven in the Creation have a right, it is ours at least as much as yours," argued the elder Adams. "If occupation, use, and possession have a right, we have it as clearly as you. If war and blood and treasure give a right, ours is as good as yours. We have been constantly fighting in Canada, Cape Breton, and Nova Scotia for the defense of the fishery, and have expanded beyond all proportion more than you. If then the right cannot be denied, why then should it not be acknowledged? And put out of dispute?"[2] The father prevailed in 1783 and the son intended to prevail in 1814.

Great Britain came to the table considering the fishing rights conferred by the earlier treaty to be abrogated by the present war, but agreed to enter into negotiations on the subject. Led by Adams, the Americans came to feel leery of doing anything that would imply abandonment of rights in the fisheries. And to stipulate that the countries would hereafter negotiate concerning the topic appeared unnecessary to the United States team. The Americans offered to be silent on fisheries, and, on December 22, intent on eliminating

---

1 *American State Papers: Foreign Relations* 3:744.
2 McCullough, *John Adams*, 282-283.

the last obstacle to an overall settlement, the British delegation dropped the matter.

On Christmas Eve, the two sides came together and signed an 11-article peace treaty that sidestepped the principal issues that led to war. Impressment and neutral maritime rights were not addressed in the final agreement. The first article of the treaty restored all territory taken except the four islands at the east of Maine. The second article set a phased timetable for absolute cessation of naval hostilities. The third related to prisoners, while the next five articles set up procedures to handle the several boundary disputes. The ninth article was designed to end hostilities with the Indians, and the tenth supported mutual efforts to end slavery. The final article dealt with ratification. As before, both nations continued to disagree on just about everything but a shared desire for peace.

Four of the American commissioners sailed for home as soon as possible, leaving John Quincy to wrap up commission affairs in Ghent. Exhibiting traditional Yankee frugality, the last thing he did was to conduct an estate sale. He explained in a letter to his wife that "the good people of the place consider the Congress of Ghent as an epoch of so much importance in the history of their city, that they have given extravagant prices for some of our relics." Like a modern yard sale devotee, Adams delighted in his success. "I am told an old inkstand which was used at the conference, was sold for thirty francs, though it was not worth as many *sous*."[1] Adams enjoyed the task so much he did the British a favor and included some of their furniture in his sale.

On January 2, 1815, the H.M.S. *Favorite*, 18, Captain J.U. Mowatt departed from Plymouth, England headed for New York. Henry Carroll, one of the secretaries to the United States peace delegation sailed with Mowatt, as did Anthony Baker, the British delegation secretary. They conveyed final dispatches and signed treaty documents. Right after the Christmas Eve accord, Baker made it to London and on the 28th obtained the prince regent's approving signature. As the *Favorite* left for America, Christopher Hughes, Jr., another American secretary, sailed from Bordeaux for the Chesapeake in the schooner *Transit*. Hughes carried copies of the work of the peace commissioners and a copy of the treaty without the ultimate British signature.

The accelerated talks in early December led to an inevitable spate of rumors. One of British origin received wide attention in the Northeast. Early in January, a gun brig 18 days out of England hailed the H.M.S. *Spencer* off the New Jersey coast and handed up "exhilarating intelligence" of an accord at Ghent. Captain Raggett sent a boat under a white flag into Cape May with the report. The information quickly reached Philadelphia where the mail contractor at that place dispatched an express communication on the reported peace to Boston by way of New York. The *Spectator* summarized the news and allowed: "With much uncertainty and solicitude we shall await confirmation of this cheering intelligence."[2]

---

1 James T. Adams, 157.
2 *New York Spectator*, January 11, 1815.

Another month would pass before the *Favorite* reached New York late on Saturday, February 11. The receipt of official or conclusive word prompted an immediate reaction. The *Evening Post* said: "[T]he public expressions of tumultuous joy and gladness that spontaneously burst forth from all ranks and degrees of people . . . without stopping to enquire the conditions, evinced how really sick at heart they were, of a war that threatened to wring from them the remaining means of subsistence, and of which they could neither see the object nor the end."[1] Messengers fanned out to carry the news to the major towns in the Northeast as Baker and Carroll headed for Washington. Baker carried the ratified British copy. But Hughes arrived first, showing up on the 14th. Madison did not wait for Baker and Carroll. "The termination of hostilities depends upon the time of the ratification of the treaty by both parties," he told the Senate on the 15th. "I lose no time, therefore, in submitting the treaty to the Senate for their advice and approbation."[2]

And the Senate did not lose any time in acting. By a unanimous vote the next day, 35 senators consented to the ratification. When the Baker copy reached the White House on the 17th, the president promptly signed the official document just before noon that day. On the 18th, he sent the more complete Carroll package of treaty documents to the Senate and the House. "While performing this act," he said, "I congratulate you and our constituents upon an event which is highly honorable to the nation, and terminates, with peculiar felicity, a campaign signalized by the most brilliant successes."[3]

Niles euphorically and proudly reported the glorious news. *"Who would not be an American?"* he wondered. *"Long live the republic! All hail! Last asylum of oppressed humanity! Peace is signed in the arms of victory."*[4] The *National Advocate* exhibited similar enthusiasm and proclaimed the objectives of the war were narrowly defined as the assertion and defense of "our national rights; and to rescue . . . the drowning honor of the nation." And the *Advocate* concluded: "Those rights have been manfully asserted, and most gloriously defended."[5] The *Evening Post*, however, remained unconvinced. The editor listed four principal objectives of the war — Canada; orders in council repeal; definition of neutral rights; and eradication of impressment. "Well, we have not got Canada," he mocked. On the second point, "we have not obtained a repeal" of the orders; "for they ceased to exist before the declaration. . . ." Thirdly, he asked: "In what article of this Treaty, I pray you, is to be found, a syllable relative to "illegal blockades and neutral rights?" Likewise, the treaty ignored the issue of impressment, he said. "Sailors are not even mentioned or in any way alluded to."[6]

1 *New York Evening Post*, February 13, 1815.
2 *American State Papers: Foreign Relations* 3:730.
3 Ibid., 731.
4 *Niles'*, February 18, 1815.
5 *National Advocate* (NY), February 17, 1815.
6 *New York Evening Post*, February 20, 1815.

Americans did not wait for news of Madison's ratification or the reaction of the editors before celebrating. News of the *Favorite*'s arrival in New York spread rapidly, reaching Hartford before a day passed. The *Republican Farmer* of Bridgeport reported the good news in a February 13 extra edition. Abel Flint tended to business and delivered a discourse on the peace at the South Meetinghouse in Hartford on February 14. Word of the final action in Washington made it to Connecticut in handsome time. A messenger reached Philadelphia in fourteen hours, and it took a rider nine hours more to carry the report to New York. And in another nine hours, the *New Haven Journal* received a copy of the signed peace treaty and rushed it into print. A day later, the *Connecticut Herald* of New Haven reported: "*The glad tidings of peace . . . has diffused a joy throughout the community, never before witnessed. In every place it has been received with the shouts of rejoicing, the roar of cannon, illuminations, and indeed, in every other way in which the people could manifest their heartfelt satisfaction.*"[1]

When the initial report reached Norwich on the 13th, "all was enthusiasm and ecstacy, and the rejoicings exceeded any thing ever before witnessed in America." Cannonades and illuminations dominated. Ships in the Thames fired salutes, "and these were echoed from the fortresses at New London, and those again were responded to from the British blockading squadron at the mouth of the river, till the whole adjacent country was made glad with the tidings."[2]

Stonington began to celebrate in the same boisterous manner, but the jubilation turned solemn. In the August 1814 Battle of Stonington, it will be recalled, the Connecticut defenders came out of the ferocious bombardment without losing a man. In the February 1815 peace celebration, however, the town sadly suffered one fatality. Thomas Stanton, a young man from Pawcatuck, died instantly when a cannon prepared to salute peace discharged prematurely.

The memorable event passed in grand style at New London. On February 21, the inhabitants illuminated the town. British officers from along the coast — including Admiral Henry Hotham, and Captains W.F. Aylmer, Alexander Gordon, Henry Jane, Hyde Parker, and James Galloway — came on shore to attend balls and receptions. The password on Hotham's *Superb* became "America" and the countersign, "Amity." Captain Stephen Decatur and Captain John Shaw of the U.S. Navy received the distinguished guests. As much as anyone, Shaw welcomed the unnatural assignment after months of idleness on the *United States* bottled up behind the town. Decatur, for his part, made the festivities in a roundabout way. He left his frustrating New London assignment weeks before to take command of the *President* at New York and a squadron which included the *Hornet*. Unfortunately, the *President* sustained damage on the way out of port and quickly fell victim to a British squadron off New York on January 15. Sent to Bermuda as a prisoner, Deca-

---

1 *Connecticut Herald*, February 21, 1815.
2 Caulkins, *History of Norwich*, 565.

tur soon received a parole. Gordon carried him back to New London in the *Narcissus*, 32 in time for Decatur to receive his former antagonists in celebration of the end of the war.

Rhode Islanders also applauded the initial news when it reached the state. Providence citizens gathered in the streets amid the traditional ringing of bells and firing of cannons. In Newport, when the intelligence reached town well before dawn on the 14th, the *Mercury* rushed an "extra" to the streets. But within a week, disparagement appeared. The *Rhode Island American* thought it "natural for those who have not profited by the late calamities, to inquire, what beneficial object the treaty has secured to the country, in return for the sufferings it has endured — for the blood which flowed — for the dangers which were encountered — for the millions that were expended — for the debt and taxes that have been fastened upon the community?"[1]

The response in Massachusetts, as might be expected, turned out to be much more robust and organized. In Boston, shortly after the breakfast hour on Monday the 13th, the bells of the Old South and the Federal Street Church began to ring. The Josiah Quincy family thought of fire, when Elisa Cabot burst in exclaiming: "Mrs. Quincy! — do you know what these bells are ringing? — Peace! Peace! — uttering these words as if the last she would ever speak, she sank into a chair. — We thought she had lost her senses." Josiah rushed outside to confirm the news and found "the whole town was in an uproar, cannons firing, drums beating, bells ringing."[2]

Senator Quincy ordered his sleigh and drove from the South End to the North End. "In State St.," recalled Eliza, "you might have walked on the people's heads & all were crowded — gentlemen shaking hands & congratulating each other, ladies & women running wildly about." A military company paraded up Main Street followed by three horse-drawn sleds loaded with sailors cheering as they passed. "The joy of the poorer classes of society who had suffered most from the war was very touching."[3] Most businesses shut down, and school children enjoyed a holiday. "The forlorn ships at the wharves and docks, once more displayed their colors" as their crews prepared for sea.[4]

After the first hours, community leaders took a step back and decided to put off a full public celebration until after the national government ratified the treaty. Members of the Washington Benevolent Society met at the Exchange Coffee House on the 16th to draw up plans. The mechanics and manufacturers got together the same evening to organize a grand procession. A joint legislative committee made arrangements for fireworks "and in conjunction with the Selectmen of Boston, for a general illumination of all public buildings in Boston."[5] The *Centinel*, hoping for "dignified decorum" during the

---

1 *Rhode Island American*, February 24, 1815.

2 *Eliza Susan Quincy Journal*, 23-24.

3 Ibid., 24-25.

4 *Boston Gazette*, February 16, 1815.

5 Ibid.

festivities, thought it advisable to stress "all private illuminations are strictly voluntary. . . . No marks of censure ought therefore to be permitted to pass on those who may not find it convenient to illuminate their windows." After all, "in many families there is sickness; and that others, who are as desirous as any to express their gratification on the restoration of Peace, may be by poverty, or some other cause, prevented." In reality, the editor had in mind not the sick and poor but the many townspeople still deeply opposed to anything related to the war including recognition of its end. "Precautionary measures have been taken to prevent any disagreeable occurrences," he warned.[1] But the apprehensiveness proved unwarranted. In the end, "Federalist and Democrat clasped each other's hands," noted one observer, "like ancient friends."[2]

In Salem, upon receipt of the first news of peace on the 13th, the streets filled and "the acclimation of thousands rent the air."[3] The Sea Fencibles and Salem Artillery companies formed in the town square and fired a 54-gun salute. In the politically divided town, Reverend Bentley wrote in his diary: "The return of peace under the present administration is not a pleasing circumstance to the Opposition, yet they do not chuse to express publickly, what they murmur in secret."[4]

Gloucester organized a celebration at the First Parish Meetinghouse, "and, for the first time, its venerable walls resounded patriotic songs, mingled with shouts of merriment and joy."[5] Not to be outdone, Marblehead illuminated all of its houses, "and from nearly every housetop something was set flying to the breeze; those who could not procure flags, hoisting sheets, pillow cases, and in some instances, even petticoats, in honor of the great event."[6] Marbleheaders "rang their bells three days & began instantly to prepare for sea."[7]

Stephen Cushing raced on horseback south from Boston to Hingham carrying the exciting news. Royal Whiton then joined Samuel Simmons on the latter's sleigh, and the pair spread the word around town. "We went to South Hingham and all the way Mr. Simmons kept singing out at the top of his voice, 'Peace! Peace!'" Whiton said, Simmons "kept his voice going the whole distance." Men gathered in the public houses to celebrate. The rejoicings that went on at Captain Hobart's House "carried far into night" and "were quite worthy of the great occasion."[8]

The tidings took longer to reach the more remote communities. And when it arrived, some folks yielded to skepticism. A Provincetown man told his neighbor: "They say peace has got down as far as Truro, but it's hard

1 *Columbian Centinel* (MA), February 22, 1815.
2 Edmund Quincy, *Josiah Quincy of Massachusetts*, 360.
3 Babson, *Town of Gloucester*, 518.
4 Bentley, *Diary of William Bentley*, 4: 315.
5 Babson, 519.
6 Roads, *History and Traditions of Marblehead*, 252.
7 Bentley, 318.
8 Bouve, *History of the Town of Hingham*, 1:336.

telling, Bill D___'s boys lie so like fury."[1] A report of peace did not reach icebound Nantucket until the 16th. Solid ice surrounded much of the island and shut down the harbor. However, a boat managed to land at Smith's Point and its occupants got to town by sunset with the news. "Bells began to ring" according to a diarist — "rang till 9 shouting by the Boys & through the streets. . . ."[2]

Back in Boston, authorities set Wednesday the 22nd as the red-letter day. The General Court, "impressed with a deep and lively sense of the goodness of the Almighty Ruler of the Universe," designated the day for public prayer and thanksgiving.[3] When Salem adopted the state date, Reverend Bentley sensed artifice. The "Celebration of peace is thrown upon the birthday of Washington that the name of that Hero might be an apology for the festivity," he concluded. And "Wednesday as a day in Lent, is to be kept by a religious service in the English Church in Boston & Salem. So we submit."[4]

The Boston "oration in celebration of Peace was performed in the morning at the Stone Chapel." A crowd filled the place "and the presence of several British Officers in full uniform gave an occular demonstration that Peace had come." After the service, a procession stepped off under the lead of Josiah Quincy, president of the Washington Benevolent Society. Tradesmen of every kind followed on sleds performing symbolic by-plays. "The carpenters were erecting a temple of Peace. The printers worked a small press. Struck off hand bills, announcing peace, & threw them among the crowd."[5]

At nightfall, all the public buildings and many private dwellings were illuminated. "The fireworks chiefly consisted of rockets thrown from the roof of the State house."[6] Celebrants ignited bonfires on several of the higher hills about town. And a splendid feast took place at Faneuil Hall. The revelry carried over to the next day with a concluding Peace Ball at the Concert Hall. Eliza overcame a reluctance to attend because of her young age and had a beautiful time. "Several British Officers in full uniform were actively employed in flirting & dancing not in the most graceful manner."[7]

Portsmouth, New Hampshire did not learn about the New York arrival of the *Favorite* until early on the 14th. Bells sounded all through the night. One of the bell ringers sought compensation the next morning based on the fact nobody relieved him for five hours. Henniker put off its celebration until the 24th. As a large concourse gathered in front of the Congregational meetinghouse, a gang of boys paraded in the streets with a swivel "firing at will." Judge Darling scaled a hogshead and read a series of appropriate sentiments. "Each sentiment was responded to by the artillery. The Judge's sentiment

1 Rich, *Truro-Cape Cod*, 359.
2 Starbuck, *History of Nantucket*, 314.
3 *Boston Gazette*, February 16, 1815.
4 Bentley, 315.
5 *Eliza Susan Quincy Journal*, 26-27.
6 Ibid., 28.
7 Ibid., n.p.

was, 'Now we may again sit under our own vine and fig-tree, with none to molest us or make us afraid.'"[1]

A Boston messenger reached Captain William Webb's Portland inn with the initial welcome news late on the 13th. An observance committee rushed to print broadsides bearing the news, a common practice of the period. One proclaimed: "Peace concluded let all the people thank God and say amen."[2] Thomas Hodgkin of Lewiston happened to be in Portland at the time, selling butter, cheese, and oats. He put up at Stevens' Tavern after completing his stops, and "at 11 o'clock at night," he noted, "an express arrived in portland bringing the joyfull news of a Treaty of peace . . . the bells were ringing & guns fireing all the remainder of the night." The noisy celebration continued throughout the next day "so that there was but little chance to do business in Town."[3] Officials finding it necessary to urge "good order be observed," admonished "that houses not illuminated may be attributed to inconvenience or not being occupied," and asked "the people retire to their dwellings at an early hour" after the daylong jubilation.[4]

Bath celebrated peace in a rowdy manner on the 15th. The townspeople marched through the streets under a large white banner emblazoned with the word PEACE. Church bells rang out, seemingly calling in the people. In the foyer of the North Meetinghouse, revelers improvised a table made up of a plank placed across two barrels "over which liquors were passed in a lively manner to thirsty souls. When I arrived there," recalled John Hayden, a youth at the time, "sundry of those souls were in an oblivious state, lying rolled up against the partition dead drunk; the rest were fast coming to that state, but in the meantime constituted the most boisterous and noisy crowd I have ever been in. . . ." Hayden added: "The noise in the entry . . . was so tremendous that the bell could not be heard, notwithstanding one of the doors was constantly open."[5]

A private party was in progress at the Major Moses Carlton homestead when a post rider entered Wiscasset during the cold evening of February 14. The horseman was so excited about the peace news he carried, he spurred his steed through the front door into Carlton's main hallway. A startled maid dropped a tray full of flip glasses intended for the guests, but it did not matter once the rider shared his intelligence.

The citizens at Litchfield Corners celebrated peace by "rolling a barrel of rum into the street, knocking in its head, and partaking liberally of its exhilarating contents."[6] But Bristol responded with decorum, partly because the first news did not reach down the peninsula to the town as quickly as it did in places along the traveled way. Nonetheless, when informed, the inhabit-

1 Cogswell, *History of the Town of Henniker*, 356.
2 Daniel Tucker, *Broadside*.
3 *Diary of Thomas Hodgkin*, 1809-1819.
4 Daniel Tucker.
5 Owen, *Edward Clarence Plummer History of Bath*, 164.
6 Oramandal Smith, *History of Litchfield*, 490.

ants gathered at the townhouse to exchange tidings and joyous sentiments. Waldoboro, in contrast, received the early report on February 14 when the western mail entered town. Elation broke out as crowds gathered and the town band played patriotic tunes. Townsmen illuminated their houses and set bonfires here and there. The jubilant scene was repeated a short time later in Warren when the mail stage reached that town.

The stage did not arrive in Camden until midnight, but the driver's post horn stirred some of the villagers. Once they heard the peace report, they commenced firing guns and igniting bonfires. "Many of the crowd forthwith repaired to the places where they could get inspirited by the imbibing of liquor, and there they gave vent to the ebullition of their feelings in consonance with their ideas of the occasion." The 12-pounders at the two harbor forts "began to speak in loud accents, and thus they continued to speak until the dawn of day." Simeon Tyler led a group to the top of Mt. Battie and its pair of 12-pounders and single 18-pounder. "As the largest piece belched forth from its elevated position, in deep thunder-like tones, the habitations below were shaken to their foundations, while the echo's reverberations were heard resounding over adjacent waters, remote hills, and distant valleys."[1] The mountaintop cannonading continued throughout the next day, when the celebration closed with a public dance. All the while, nearby little Union tried to keep up, making its swivel "speak as loud and as often as practicable."[2]

The mail stage arrived in Belfast on the 15th. Townsfolk received the peace treaty news with subdued excitement. A strong British force remained in view at Castine a little more than ten miles across Penobscot Bay. Even so, militiamen recovered concealed field pieces and fired a salute at Nesmith's Corner, while the keeper of Whittier's Tavern illuminated his place. Belfast turned out to be the last seaboard town to celebrate outwardly. For the time, every place to the east remained under British domination.

This is not to say celebrating ended at the mouth of the river. When news of the September 1814 raid at Bangor reached some of the area's northern settlements, reaction was swift. Foxcroft and communities around Sebec quickly organized a 56-man volunteer company and moved toward the action. The men turned back when they learned about the British withdrawal. However, the unit remained intact and alert. At the end of the war, some of the gentlemen of Bangor sent several gallons of spirits to their supporters to the north "as a testimonial of their high consideration of the patriotic conduct of this company." Before disbanding in February, the outfit got together one last time, and "the present from Bangor was the most powerful stimulant of the occasion. Over this, and by this, they made merry, rejoicing loud and long that victory had declared in favor of their espoused cause."[3]

Within a few days, a joint committee in Washington requested the president "recommend a day of thanksgiving to Almighty God for restoring to

1 Locke, *Sketches of the History of the Town of Camden*, 144-145.
2 Sibley, *History of the Town of Union*, 347.
3 Loring, *History of Piscataquis County*, 227.

these United States the blessings of peace."[1] Madison responded and set aside April 13, 1815. But Reverend Humphrey Moore of Milford, New Hampshire could not wait. He delivered his oration of thanks on March 9, and his remarks seemed to sum up events as well as anyone. "When the sound of peace reached our ears, little or no inquiry was made what were its conditions," said Pastor Moore. "No one was heard to ask, 'are our impressed seamen restored; are sailors rights and free trade secured?' It seemed to give universal satisfaction that the horrors of war had ceased and peace was restored. This interesting event," said Moore, "swallowed up all other considerations. The war had languished in the hands of its owners; and as it languished its price increased. This bantling grew heavy on their hands; and they would gladly have concealed its pedigree by destroying it at the age of two years and an half."[2]

From another viewpoint, Reverend Bentley recalled the past while looking to the future. "A Strange perverseness obtains in New England," he noted. "In Boston every act was employed to divert the publick hopes from the administration. In Salem many expressions of the same spirit appeared at our festivities. We owe every energy to promote a better order of things in New England."[3]

Be this as it may, a large segment of the population simply agreed with a Boston newspaper when it concluded: "The unrighteous war is at an end."[4]

---

1 U.S. *House Journal.* 1815. 13th Cong., 3rd sess., March 2, 767.
2 Humphrey Moore, *Oration,* 8.
3 Bentley, 317.
4 *Boston Gazette,* February 16, 1815.

CHAPTER 15. EPILOGUE

Economic factors more than anything pushed Great Britain and the United States to peace at Ghent. And, from the outset, economic factors moved the New England opposition to the war. This is not to say, loss of life was ignored by the peacemakers. Combat casualties are always heartbreaking. Nonetheless, American casualties in the War of 1812 were not unendurable when compared to the European losses in the Napoleonic Wars of the period. Some 2,260 American military personnel were killed in action and another 17,000 or so died of accidents or diseases. Privateer, merchant seaman, and civilian casualties are difficult to compute. But, in the end, other numbers made the difference. Accumulated war debt well over $100 million and defense outlays around $13 million concerned the entrepreneurial young nation.

The shipping business, so important to coastal states and agricultural states alike, suffered great losses during the conflict. Beyond sizeable exports, in the year before the war, American vessels carried 921,750 tons of foreign imports. During the war, over 1,400 American merchant ships fell into enemy hands. By 1814, the total tonnage of imports alone tailed off to 58,756. Businessman John G. Ladd of Alexandria, Virginia in February 1815 told an associate, "[O]ur market is almost destitute of foreign articles."[1]

The economic indicators reversed direction close upon news of peace. Markets experienced a rapid change. Within one day, sugar dropped to $12.50 per hundredweight from $26. Specie plummeted from twenty-two percent premium all the way down to two percent. "Sailors' Rights beat time to the sound of the hammer at every wharf," reported one paper, "and free trade looked briskly up."[2] Anxious to return to prosperousness, a Charleston,

---

1 Rotch Papers, *Letter*, February 18, 1815.
2 *New York Evening Post*, February 14, 1815.

South Carolina merchant checked in with William Rotch, prominent New Bedford shipper. "As the joyful event of Peace has unfettered the shackles which have so long bound down all commercial enterprise in this country," he said, "I conclude a statement of prices of our produce, rates of freight etc. will not be unacceptable."[1] Unleashed, merchants like Rotch up and down the coast got back to business. Seafarers once again thrived. Tax revenues increased rapidly, and within two decades, the federal government retired its bonded debt. Albert Gallatin observed: "The war has renewed and reinstated the national feelings and character which the Revolution had given, and which were daily lessening. The people" he thought, "have now more general objects of attachment, with which their pride and political opinions are connected. They are more Americans; they feel and act more as a nation; and I hope that the permanency of the Union is thereby better secured."[2]

Now regarded abroad as a full-fledged nation, America also looked inward. Spurred by the embargoes and the war itself, an industrial revolution took hold. Francis Cabot Lowell visited England in 1813 to study that country's manufacturing system so far advanced over the household textile activity in the United States. Fearful of capture on his return voyage, Lowell did not take notes or prepare diagrams. He memorized what he observed. Once at home, with the able assistance of Paul Moody, he put together the first American power loom. He generated power for the machine by harnessing a little waterfall on the Charles River in Waltham, Massachusetts. With financial support from wealthy Bostonians, Lowell formed the Boston Manufacturing Company. The operation changed the face of textile manufacturing in the country. From this little beginning, the Waltham System spread to riverside communities throughout New England, giving rise to a score of thriving manufacturing cities — just what Jefferson urged all those years ago.

Otherwise, New Englanders focused on the fourth article of the Treaty of Ghent. This provision set up a two-man boundary commission to settle claims over several islands in Passamaquoddy Bay and the Bay of Fundy. Three other commissions stipulated in the agreement handled boundary matters beginning at the upper St. Croix River between Maine and New Brunswick and running all the way to the Lake of the Woods at present-day Minnesota. The Passamaquoddy commission held the greatest interest for New England, a region still tied to the sea, since it impacted fishing rights and involved key maritime locales such as Eastport.

The British claim to the Passamaquoddy islands traced to a royal grant in 1621, while the American claim rested on the 1783 Treaty of Paris and the Jay Treaty of 1794. Despite the potential for protracted negotiations, the two commissioners proceeded promptly to an agreeable settlement. Both countries began the talks bound to accept such an agreement as final. In a brief finding, in November 1817, commissioners Thomas Barclay and John Holmes

---

1 Rotch Papers, *Letter*, March 13, 1815.
2 Henry Adams, *Writings of Albert Gallatin*, 1:700.

decided "that Moose Island, Dudley (now Treat) Island, and Frederick (now Dudley) Island, in the Bay of Passamaquoddy which is part of the Bay of Fundy do and each of them does belong to The United States of America and we have also decided and do decide that all the other Islands and each and every of them in the Bay of Passamaquoddy which is part of the Bay of Fundy and the Island of Grand Manan in the said Bay of Fundy do belong to His said Britannic Majesty. . . . "[1]

As straightforward as the language appears, it nonetheless gave rise to subsequent disputes. Conventions and treaties in 1892, 1908, 1910, and 1925 tweaked the seaward boundary. More recently, in October 1984, the International Court of Justice in The Hague handed down a ruling drawing the line out across Georges Bank. This left open the matter of ownership of Machias Seal Island, "and the friendly dispute has yet to be resolved."[2]

The St. Croix commission engendered much less interest right after the war since it treated uninhabited spruce land considered the other side of sundown. Be this as it may, differences handled by the St. Croix or second commission festered for years. In 1832, King William I of the Netherlands tried but failed to broker a settlement between the United States and Great Britain. Late in 1838, the dispute gave rise to the bloodless and legendary mobilization known as the Aroostook War or the Pork and Beans War. Finally, in 1842, U.S. Secretary of State Daniel Webster and Alexander Baring, 1st Baron Ashburton reached an accord on the northern Maine–New Brunswick boundary.

Except for Eastport and the contested Passamaquoddy islands, the occupied country east of the Penobscot gained its freedom within weeks of Madison's ratification of the peace treaty. British troops evacuated Castine on April 25, 1815, "leaving behind such memories of balls and routs, of levees and amateur theatricals, as suffered for the tea-table gossip of a whole generation."[3] Their departure also triggered a flurry of lawsuits and congressional bills seeking remission of duties on goods imported into Castine during Great Britain's occupation of the town.

When the enemy possessed the port, British authorities, conformably to the laws of Nova Scotia, imposed duties on the large amount of goods introduced into Castine. Right after the peace, the United States collector "established his office upon or near the British lines, and required that all goods of foreign growth or manufacture which had been imported during the hostile occupation, and were still there, should be entered as if then originally imported into the United States in a foreign vessel, and threatened to seize and detain the goods unless the owners or consignees would immediately pay or secure to the United States duties thereon."[4] To evade large losses, some owners and consignees paid a second set of duties, trusting, upon appeal,

---

1 *American State Papers: Foreign Relations* 4:171.

2 *Bangor* (ME) *Daily News*, November 26, 2004.

3 Drake, *Pine-Tree Coast*, 284.

4 *American State Papers: Finance* 4:393.

the American government would return the duplicate payments. Conten-tiousness never in short supply among Yankees, many confronted with the problem refused to pay the demands. Federal suits were lodged against them, but were ordered discontinued by the secretary of the treasury as a result of a specific unanimous opinion of the U.S. Supreme Court written by Mr. Justice Story of Massachusetts.

In short, the court found the goods imported into Castine were not sub-ject to United States revenue laws. "By the conquest and military occupation of Castine, the enemy acquired that firm possession which enabled him to exercise the fullest rights of sovereignty over that place", wrote Story. "The sovereignty of the United States over the territory was, of course, suspend-ed, and the laws of the United States could no longer be rightfully enforced there, or be obligatory upon the inhabitants who remained. . . ." Therefore, "where there is no protection or allegiance or sovereignty, there can be no claim to obedience."[1]

A few astute men who paid the duplicate duties preempted the courts and sought a legislative remedy. In 1819, prior to the decision, Caleb Hall and others of Bucksport and Jonathan Stevens and others of Castine appealed to Congress for restitution. Senate Bill 13 provided for relief and made its way to the president's desk. He signed the measure on April 11, 1820, and Congress approved an open-ended appropriation to cover the costs. This left those who paid up, but were not covered by Senate 13, in straitened circum-stances. Congress saw the unfairness, and, in May 1824, passed an act for the relief of Joshua Aubin and others caught in the pinch. However, Henry Rice and several other men and firms failed to get their names on the Aubin bill, and, despite a belated 1826 effort, did not receive congressional relief.

What became of the British collections presents another story. General The Right Honorable George Ramsay, the 9th Earl of Dalhousie and a former member of Wellington's staff, became lieutenant governor of Nova Scotia in 1816. In 1818, he set aside 7,000 pounds of the Castine customs receipts as an endowment for a college at Halifax. Lord Dalhousie assigned another 3,000 pounds to construct facilities for the college. He soon left to assume the post of governor general of Canada, and, in his absence, the school got off to a fit-ful start. However, Dalhousie's dream blossomed in the 20th century and the school bearing his name now has an enrollment of over 13,000 and a faculty of some 1,800.

Eastport remained under British dominion until June 1818. Once occu-pied in 1814, the British treated the place as restored territory, not occupied territory. Inhabitants who remained and took an oath of allegiance to the crown spent the next four years as British subjects. A succession of officers served as the military governor of Moose Island. The first four typified the group. The initial man, Colonel Harris, "was neither respectable nor respect-ed." His successor, Colonel Gubbins, "was impatient of contradiction, and

---

1 *United States v. Rice*, (1819) 4 Wheat. 254.

not remarkably placable." Colonel Renney "was a favorite, and is remembered with feeling allied to affection." Major Anstruther, the fourth military governor, "was a rough man, but, unlike Colonel Gubbins, of a generous nature." A gentleman preparing to leave Eastport complained to the major that some locals had presented him bills, "though once paid, and claimed a second settlement. 'Never mind,' said the major. 'Pay them again, — pay everybody that asks you. You have money enough, — satisfy everyone.'"[1]

Eastport experienced its own tangled revenue dispute that required a postwar congressional remedy. Just before the town fell to the enemy, Jabez Mowry and others gave the United States collector bonds to secure duties on recent imports. The invaders took custody of the bonds, and the courts in Nova Scotia forfeited the bonds. Worse, the British demanded second payments of the revenue fees from Mowry and his fellow merchants. The British harassed the men for the money even after the ratification of peace. And, at the same time, the American authorities initiated suits to recover the missing fees from the merchants. Congressman Cyrus King of Saco shepherded a relief bill through Congress. Signed into law in April 1816, the measure indemnified the principals and sureties in the bonds, and saved "them harmless against the loss thereof, and for the expenses already incurred by them in consequence of said loss."[2]

For three and a half years after peace, the people of Eastport remained in limbo enduring many hardships. They were claimed by Great Britain and the United States but felt disowned by both countries. The government of New Brunswick denied them full privileges, and the Massachusetts General Court denied a seat to their legislator since he came from a conquered district. Inhabitants faced a continuous struggle to maintain a semblance of normalcy. One patriotic island man was determined that his child must be born under the American flag. He therefore spread the Star-Spangled Banner over his wife's bed as she gave birth to a daughter.

Despite the privations, when the time finally arrived for the formal restoration of the island to the United States, principal residents thanked the departing military commander and his predecessors, "who, in the discharge of their official duties have had the magnanimity and uprightness to refrain from all oppression, and to overcome the temptation *'to feel power and forget right.'* "[3] On June 30, 1818, arriving American troops, under Brigadier General James Miller, exchanged salutes with the departing British soldiers under Captain R. Gibbon. A band played "Yankee Doodle," and the American colors replaced the British flag. On the following day, the citizens gave a public dinner in honor of the happy and momentous change.

An underlying war issue between Connecticut and Massachusetts and the national government persisted for decades after the peace. States generally sought and received reimbursement for the costs of their militiamen

1 Kilby, *Eastport and Passamaquoddy*, 187-189.
2 Act of April 29, 1816, ch. 158, 1 *Stat.* 175.
3 Kilby, 214.

and volunteers who entered the service of the United States during the war. Connecticut and Massachusetts also sought reimbursement for militia costs associated with all gubernatorial mobilizations. Federal authorities, from Madison onward, refused to recognize service and pay for such musters unless a state called out its militia to repel actual invasion or a well-founded expectation of invasion or the militia mobilized under a recognized federal authority or at a federal request. Massachusetts found itself up against this principle. Speaking in 1825 of the Massachusetts claim, President James Monroe summarized the long-running dispute when he told Congress: "[I]t will be seen that the conduct of the executive of that State, in refusing to place the militia thereof at that difficult conjuncture under the direction of the Executive of the United States, as it was bound to do by a fair construction of the constitution, and as the other States did, is the great cause to which the difficulty adverted to is to be ascribed."[1]

The federal government did eventually recognize the service of 3,488 Massachusetts militiamen. An 1824 audit found most of the militia expenses incurred in Maine in 1814, beginning with General William King's June call to arms and running to the militia activity associated with the scare around Camden in November, as well as the Boston area mobilizations of September 1814, to be supportable costs.

In 1826, Congress and auditors reviewed open Massachusetts claims while a few outspoken members attempted to add another standard. They wanted the state to renounce the "unconstitutional doctrines" of Governor Strong and the wartime Massachusetts Supreme Judicial Court. After some agitation along these lines, a House committee found "the recent disavowal of her present executive and legislature furnishes at least a belief that all danger of a future collision" on the militia control issue "has been permanently removed."[2]

Another audit followed in 1830, and Congress ruled some of the Massachusetts claim came under the well-founded apprehension of invasion principle. Massachusetts Governor Levi Lincoln took advantage of the 1830 congressional climate and forwarded a set of General Court resolves requesting final adjustment since the state's claim had been "before Congress for thirteen years; the particulars of that claim having been repeatedly examined by the executive officer of the government, the Secretaries of War, the committees of Congress, and a large portion thereof declared by them to be admissible."[3] Led by Senator Nathaniel Silsbee, Congress went on to reimburse the state $419,748 in 1831. Counting an $11,000 payment made back in 1817, this reduced the state's outstanding claim to $412,601. An 1837 federal audit ruled only $227,176 of this latter amount to be supportable and due to the Commonwealth.

---

1 *American State Papers: Military Affairs* 3:104.
2 Ibid., 160.
3 *American State Papers: Military Affairs* 4:295.

In 1843, Massachusetts Senator Isaac Bates renewed the state's effort to recover the balance due. In debate, Ohio Senator Benjamin Tappan "alluded to the refusal of Massachusetts, during the war, when our soil was invaded, to permit her militia to muster into the service of the United States. He maintained that (with the exception of the claims for compensating the heirs of the traitor [General William] Hull for the surrender of our soil and our army) there never was a more iniquitous claim before Congress. It was as absurd and wicked as the Hull claim."[1]

Senator John Crittenden of Kentucky appealed "to permit the little aberrations from the straight line of duty of the old Bay State to be buried in oblivion."[2] This helped, and the measure passed by a 27 to 19 vote in the Senate in the last hours of the 27th Congress. But a parliamentary move by Ohio's other senator, William Allen, stalled the bill, and Congress went home without final House action. Similar failed relief measures appeared in the next Congress as well as in 1845, 1852, 1854, and 1857. Finally, in March 1859, against her original claim of $843,349, Congress paid Massachusetts another $227,176, bringing the total reimbursement to the state to $657,924. "She obtained it after every item objectionable in point of fact had been exposed to the unsparing criticism of her political opponents. She obtained it after every item objectionable in point of proof had been subjected to the protracted and vigorous examination of officials from a section of the country where ill will to her was, until recently, fixed and hereditary. She obtained nothing except what was extorted from overbearing and adverse political majorities; and the final appropriation was voted in a Senate where she had few friends, without dissent, and with a general expression of surprise and shame that the rights of a State had been so long denied."[3]

At the same time, Massachusetts and Maine sought interest on the delayed reimbursements not to exceed $767,947. The two states agreed that since the war costs preceded the separation of the two states, any interest realized would be shared with two-thirds going to Massachusetts and one-third to Maine. To make the interest request palatable to Congress, the two states consented to give any interest proceeds to the European and North American Railway Company to support construction of 112 miles of track running from Bangor to New Brunswick, "a work of national importance."[4] In July 1870, Congress settled the Massachusetts-Maine interest claim providing certificates of indebtedness totaling $678,362, the funds going to the railway company.

Connecticut's quest did not take as long. Facing the same kind of opposition, it took the Nutmeg State until 1837 to get its money. Congressman Samuel Ingham argued for the "same justice" accorded other states, particu-

---

1 *Cong. Globe*, 27th Cong., 3rd sess. 366 (1843).
2 Ibid.
3 Senate Committee on Foreign Relations, *Compilation of Reports on Claims, 1789-1901*, 56th Cong., 2nd sess., 1901, S. Doc. 231, 387.
4 Ibid., 396.

larly Tennessee. He noted the only tangible difference "between them was, that the demand of Tennessee originated within the last twelve months, while those of Connecticut had been twenty-two years standing." Within the month, Congress appropriated $100,000 to meet Connecticut's claim of "nearly one hundred thousand dollars."[1]

Finally, the War of 1812 also proved instrumental in the establishment of New England's sixth and final state, the 23rd overall. From the 1640s until 1820, Maine formed a part of Massachusetts. As early as the Revolutionary period, some Mainers had expressed a desire to end this somewhat unnatural alignment. Over the next several decades, varying interests — from agricultural to political — pushed the issue. The distance from the seat of power in Boston as well as indifference and neglect by those in power formed the basis of much of Maine's dissatisfaction. The seemingly negligent performance of the Massachusetts government in the wartime defense of Maine helped bring matters to a head. Remaining a dependency of the Commonwealth lost its presumed benefit with the 1814 fall of eastern Maine.

The steadily increasing strength of Maine's Democrat Republican party after the war, especially in the expanding farm towns, turned the tide in favor of statehood. Federalists in and around Boston feared the growth in the opposition party would soon produce statewide majorities that would wrest away control of Massachusetts state government. For the first time, the Federalist at the state house saw merit in permitting the separation of the District of Maine. Cutting away the Maine Democrat Republicans would tend to protect Federalist turf.

A districtwide referendum vote in 1816 achieved a slim majority for statehood, but not the five-to-four majority required by the General Court. In early 1819, as part of the continuing statehood campaign, Maine towns flooded the legislature with petitions seeking another referendum. Out of 130 petitions dispatched, 125 supported separation. Legislators approved another vote on the question. A July vote in the district easily exceeded a mandated 1,500-vote majority. But the General Court also mandated the need to gain congressional approval by March 4, 1820. This almost turned out to be a stumbling block.

Congress first took up a Maine admission bill on December 22, 1819, just as the slave-holding Missouri Territory began its push for statehood. Abolitionists throughout the nation strongly fought the Missouri claim thereby creating unforeseen resistance to the Maine request. Southern slave states thwarted the Maine application as long as Northern free states objected to the admission of Missouri as a slave state. The "Missouri Compromise" resulted, and both places gained admission — one free and one slave. For Maine, approval came just in time. On March 3, 1820, President Monroe approved a congressional enactment that effective on March 15, 1820 admitted

---

1 *Cong. Globe*, 24th Cong., 2nd sess. 225 (1837).

Maine "into the Union on an equal footing with the original states, in all respects whatever."[1]

March 21 found William King, one of Maine's prominent actors in the War of 1812, at the head of a great jubilation in Portland. The wealthy Bath merchant, militia general, separatist leader, Democrat Republican, and soon to be first governor of Maine, played the lead role in the final large public celebration with any connection to the war. In honor of Maine statehood, "salutes were fired in the morning, at noon, and at sunset — the independent companies were under arms, and appeared in their usual style of military ex-cellence — the ships in our harbour displayed their flags — the Observatory and adjacent buildings were brilliantly illuminated in the evening, and the celebration closed with a splendid ball." A news account added: "Union Hall, in which the ball was held, was filled to overflowing with all that Portland can produce of elegance and fashion and beauty. . . . In front of the orches-tra, our national armorial, an eagle, lately killed in this neighborhood, spread his capacious wings, bearing on his breast a brilliant star, the addition now made to our national constellation."[2]

With the Maine statehood celebration, the people of the region figura-tively closed the book on the War of 1812. It is unlikely that very many New Englanders appreciated the fact the Missouri Compromise formed an open-ing scene in a more momentous and terrible story. The compromise did little to resolve the wicked problem of slavery, and, despite Gallatin's expectation, a generation later New England men marched away to fight because certain states felt put upon by the national government.

---

1 Act of March 3, 1820, ch. 19, 1 *Stat.* 544.
2 *New England Chronicle* (MA), March 21, 1820.

Bibliography

Unpublished Sources

Allen, John. *Memorandum of a Log on board His Maj. Ship Newcastle 1814 & 1815*, G.W. Blunt White Library, CT.

Bangor Town Records, Collection 1141, Maine Historical Society.

Baker, Silas. Yarmouth, MA, *Note* to Abner Crowell, August 9, 1814, Historical Society of Old Yarmouth, MA.

Barnstable (MA) *Town Records*, vol. 2.

The Second Book of Records in the Town of Belfast (ME) *1807 to 1825 inclusive*.

Records of the Town of Bingham (ME), *Vol. 1, 1812–1846*

Boston Selectmen. *Petition* to the Selectmen of the Town of Halifax, MA, August 10, 1808, Boston Athenaeum.

Records of Town Meetings, 1803–1828, Brewster, MA.

Records of the Town of Buckstown (Bucksport, ME) *No. 1*.

Records, No. 1, 1796–1830, Castine, ME

Town Records 1789–1823 of Chatham (MA) *Vol. 3*.

Cobb, Hannah. "War of 1812," ms., March 22, 1891, Brewster Historical Society, MA.

Crowell, James et al., *Petition*, Committee in behalf of the Town of Yarmouth, MA, May 12, 1814, private collection.

Town Clerk's Record of Town Meetings, Vol. II, Deer Isle, ME.

Edward Drinkwaters Book, 1808–1816, Yarmouth Historical Society, ME.

Town Meeting Records 1805–1826, Eastham, MA.

Book 1 Records of the Town of Eden (Bar Harbor, ME) *1796 to 1827*.

Town Records 1796–1815 Pages 100-221, Exeter, NH.

Boundary and Meeting Records, 1811–1831, Falmouth, MA.

Town Records & Vitals, Vol. 2, 1750–1838, Town of Falmouth, MA..

Fearson, Ross E. "The Scalping of the Boxer," Collection S163, Maine Historical Society

Freeport (ME) Record Book 1789–1856.

French, John. *Letter*, to his wife in Newton, NH, August 21, 1812, New Hampshire Historical Society.

Ship Ganges of Wiscasset Log Book, 1812 Apr. 22–1819 Apr. 17, Maine Maritime Museum.

Records, Vol. 1, 1751–1835, Town of Hampden, ME.

The Diary of Thomas Hodgkin, 1809–1819, Lewiston, ME, Maine Maritime Museum.

Johnson, Capt. Jotham. Harspwell, ME, *Statement*, n.d., Pejepscot Historical Society, Brunswick, ME.

Ladd, John G. Alexandria, VA, *Letter* to William Rotch, New Bedford, MA, February 18, 1815, Sturgis Library of Barnstable, MA

Town Records Book 1, 1802–1823, Town of Lincolnville, ME.

Lohnes, Barry. "The War of 1812 at Sea: The British Navy, New England, and the Maritime Provinces" (master's thesis, University of Maine, 1971).

Machias (ME) Town Records 1795–1823, Vol. 1.

Marston, Zachariah. Portland, ME, *Letter* to Jacob Pennel, February 9, 1813, Pejepscot Historical Society, Brunswick, ME.

The Earliest Records of the Island of Mount Desert and Other Islands Thereto Belonging, From A.D. 1776 to About the Year, 1820, Mount Desert Island Historical Society, ME.

Newburyport (MA) Freeholders 1797–1811.

Newburyport (MA) Freeholders 1790–1816, Vol. 2.

North Yarmouth (ME) Town Records, Volume Second & Volume Third, May 1st A.D. 1784 to April 2nd A.D. 1821.

Town Records Vol. 1, 1762–1833, Orleans, MA.

Parker, Asa. Jaffrey, NH, *Letter* to Isaac Parker, Keene, NH, September 6, 1812, New Hampshire Historical Society.

Benjamin Percival Diary, 1777–1817, Sandwich Town Archives, MA.

City of Portland (ME) Records, Aug. 17, 1812 to Apr. 2, 1827, vol. 2.

Town Meetings 1784–1826, Town of Provincetown, MA.

Town Records 1785–1811, Vol. 5, Provincetown, MA.

Book No. 4 of Records, 1812 to 1837, Provincetown, MA.

Eliza Susan Quincy Journal, 1814–1821, Massachusetts Historical Society.

Raggett, Captain Richard. *Letter* to the Selectmen of Brewster, MA and Proprietors of the Salt Works of the Town, September 17, 1814, Town of Brewster, MA.

Robinson, Zenas. *Letter* to Charles Sanford, Falmouth, MA, May 18, 1814, Falmouth Historical Society, MA.

Letters, William Rotch Papers, February 18 and March 13, 1815, Sturgis Library Archives, MS Coll. 4.

Records 1797–1815, Salisbury, MA..

Sandwich (MA) *Town Records 1798–1829, vol. 4.*

Sanford, Benjamin. Falmouth, MA, *Letter* to Zenas Robinson, August 24, 1814, Falmouth Historical Society, MA.

1789–1831 Book of Sullivan (ME) *Town Records.*

Town Records Vol. 1, 1777–1825 Thomaston, ME.

Todd, Arthur L. "The Battle of Indian Point," ms., 1931, Boothbay Region Historical Society, ME.

Town of Topsham (ME) *Memorial to Thomas Jefferson*, August 20, 1808, Pejepscot Historical Society, Brunswick, ME.

Truro (MA) *Town Records, vol. 3.*

Jeduthun Upton Diary, 1812–1813, G.W. Blunt White Library, CT.

Town Records Vol. 2, 1801–1835 Town of Waldoboro, ME.

Town Records Vol. 3, 1813–1823 Town of Waldoboro, ME.

Town of Wareham (MA) *Town Records, 1805–1858.*

Town Records, Vol. B, 1775–1810 and Vol. C, 1811–1834, Wells, ME.

Town Meeting Highlights Wellfleet, MA.

Westport (MA) *Town Records, 1787 to the present.*

Whiting, Samuel H. Bangor, ME, *Letter* to William King, Bath, ME, December 21, 1814, Maine Historical Society, Coll. 165, Box 12/17.

Willson, Henry. Topsham, ME, *Letter* to John Kittell, Boston, MA, February 9, 1808, Pejepscot Historical Society, Brunswick, ME.

Town Records, Vol. 3, 1790–1813, Wiscasset, ME.

Yarmouth and Dennis (MA), men of. *Letter* to the Honorable Commander of his B.M.S.; on the coast of Boston Bay, Historical Society of Old Yarmouth, MA.

PUBLISHED SOURCES

Abbot, Willis J. *The Naval History of the United States.* New York: Dodd, Mead, 1886.

Abbott, Herman. *History of Belfast, Maine to 1825.* Belfast, ME: G.E. Burgess, 1900.

Abbott, John S.C., and Edward H. Elwell. *The History of Maine.* Portland, ME: Brown Thurston, 1892.

Adams, Hannah. *An Abridgment of the History of New-England.* Boston: Belcher and Armstrong, 1807.

Adams, Henry, ed. *Documents Relating to New-England Federalism, 1800–1815.* Boston: Little, Brown, 1905.

——. *History of the United States of America During the Administrations of Thomas Jefferson.* New York: Viking, 1986.

——, ed. *The Writings of Albert Gallatin.* Philadelphia: J.B. Lippincott, 1879.

Adams, James T. *The Adams Family.* Boston: Little, Brown, 1930.

——. *The Founding of New England.* New York: Atlantic Monthly, 1921.

——. *New England in the Republic 1776–1850.* Boston: Little, Brown, 1926.

Adams, Nathaniel. *Annals of Portsmouth*. Portsmouth, NH: C. Norris, 1825.

Adams, Silas. *The History of the Town of Bowdoinham, Maine 1762 — 1912*. Bowdoinham, ME: Bowdoinham Historical Society, 1985.

Adkins, Roy and Lesley Adkins. *The War for All the Oceans*. New York: Viking, 2007.

Aiken, Ruth J. *Records of the Lower St. Georges and Cushing, Maine, 1605–1897*. Cushing, ME: Driftwood Farm, n.d.

Albion, Robert G., William A. Baker, and Benjamin W. Larabee. *New England and the Sea*. Mystic, CT: Mystic Seaport Museum, 1994.

Allen, Charles E. *History of Dresden, Maine*. Augusta, ME: Bertram E. Packard, 1931.

Allen, Gardner W., ed. *Papers of Isaac Hull*. Boston: Boston Athenaeum, 1929.

Allen, Joseph. *Battles of the British Navy*, vol. 2. London: Henry G. Bohn, 1852.

American State Papers. Claims 1.

——. *Commerce and Navigation 1.*

——. *Foreign Relations 2, 3, & 4.*

——. *Military Affairs 1, 3, & 4.*

——. *Miscellaneous 1 & 2.*

——. *Naval Affairs 1 & 2.*

Annals of Congress, 5th Cong., 3rd sess.

——. 10th Cong., 1st & 2nd sess.

——. 12th Cong., 1st & 2nd sess.

——. 13th Cong., 2nd sess.

——. 16th Cong., 1st sess.

Anderson, Frank M. *A Forgotten Phase of the New England Opposition to the War of 1812*. Cedar Rapids, IA, 1913.

Anthony, Irvin. *Decatur*. New York: Charles Scribner's Sons, 1931.

Auchinleck, Gilbert. *A History of the War Between Great Britain and the United States of America During the Years 1812, 1813 & 1814*. Toronto: Maclean, 1855.

Austin, Samuel. *Sermon Preached in Worcester, Massachusetts, on the Occasion of Special Fast, July 23d, 1812*. Worcester, MA: Isaac Sturtevant, 1812.

Babcock, Kendric C. *The Rise of American Nationality, 1811–1819*. New York: Harper and Brothers, 1906.

Babson, John J. *Town of Gloucester, Cape Ann, Including the Town of Rockport*. Gloucester, MA: Procter Brothers, 1860.

Bailey, Thomas A. *A Diplomatic History of the American People*. New York: Appleton-Century-Crofts, 1958.

Baker, William A. *A History of the Boston Marine Society 1742 — 1981*. Boston: Boston Marine Society, 1982.

——. *A Maritime History of Bath, Maine and the Kennebec River Region*. Bath, ME: Marine Research Society of Bath, 1973.

Bangor Historical Magazine, vol. 1 (1885), vol. 3 (1887–1888), vol. 5 (1890), and vol. 7 (1891–1892).

Bangs, Ella M. "An Historic Mansion." *New England Magazine* 27 (February 1903).

Bangs, Mary R. *Old Cape Cod: The Land, The Men, The Sea.* Boston: Houghton Mifflin, 1931.

Banks, Charles E. *History of Martha's Vineyard*, vol. 1. Edgartown, MA: Dukes County Historical Society, 1966.

———. *History of York, Maine*, vol. 2. Portsmouth, NH: Peter E. Randall, 1990.

Banks, Ronald F. *Maine Becomes a State: The Movement to Separate Maine From Massachusetts, 1785–1820.* Somersworth, NH: New Hampshire Publishing, 1973.

Banner, James M. *To the Hartford Convention: The Federalists and the Origins of Party Politics in Massachusetts, 1789–1815.* New York: Knopf, 1970.

Barry, John S. *The History of Massachusetts: The Commonwealth Period.* Boston: Henry Barry, 1857.

Bauer, K. Jack. *A Maritime History of the United States: The Role of America's Seas and Waterways.* Columbia, SC: University of South Carolina Press, 1988.

Bayley, Kiah. *War: A Calamity Greatly to be Dreaded.* Hallowell, ME: N. Cheever, 1812.

Bayles, Richard M. *History of Providence, Rhode Island*, vol. 1. New York: W.W. Preston, 1891.

Beck, Emily M., ed. *Sailor Historian: The Best of Samuel Eliot Morison.* Boston: Houghton Mifflin, 1977.

Beirne, Francis F. *The War of 1812.* New York: E.P. Dutton, 1949.

Bell, Charles H. *History of Exeter, New Hampshire.* Boston: J.E. Farwell, 1888.

Bentley, William. *The Diary of William Bentley, D.D., Pastor of the East Church, Salem, Massachusetts*, vol. 4. Salem, MA: Newcomb and Gauss, 1914.

Benton, Everett C. *A History of Guildhall, Vt.* Waverly, MA: privately printed, 1886.

Beston, Henry, ed. *White Pine and Blue Water.* Camden, ME: Down East Books, 1978.

Bicknell, Thomas W. *A History of Barrington, Rhode Island.* Providence, RI: Snow and Farnham, 1898.

Bigelow, E. Victor. *A Narrative History of the Town of Cohasset.* Boston: Samuel Usher, 1898.

Bird, Will R. *This Is Nova Scotia.* Philadelphia: Macrae Smith, 1950.

"The Dispute With America," *Blackwood's Edinburgh Magazine* 80 (July 1856).

Bliss, William R. *Colonial Times on Buzzards Bay.* Boston: Houghton Mifflin, 1888.

Boileau, John. *Half-Hearted Enemies: Nova Scotia, New England and the War of 1812.* Halifax, NS: Formac, 2005.

Bordens, Alanson, ed. *Our County and Its People: A Descriptive and Biographical Record of Bristol County*, Massachusetts. Boston: Boston History Company, 1899.

Bourne, Edward E. *The History of Wells and Kennebunk.* Portland, ME: B. Thurston, 1875.

Bouve, Thomas T., Edward T. Bouve, John D. Long, Walter L. Bouve, Francis H. Lincoln, George Lincoln, Edmund Hersey, Fearing Burr, Charles Winfield, and Scott Seymour. *History of the Town of Hingham, Massachusetts*, vol. 1. Cambridge, MA: University Press, 1893.

Bradbury, Charles. *History of Kennebunk Port.* Kennebunk, ME: James K. Remich, 1837.

Bradford, Alden. *Biography of the Hon. Caleb Strong, Several Years Governor of the State of Massachusetts.* Boston: West, Richardson and Lord, 1820.

———. *New England Chronology: From the Discovery of the Country by Cabot in 1497 to 1820.* Boston: S.G. Simpkins, 1843.

Brannan, John, comp. *Official Letters of the Military and Naval Officers of the United States During the War With Great Britain in the Years 1812, 13, 14, & 15.* Washington, DC: Way and Gideon, 1823.

Brenton, Edward P. *The Naval History of Great Britain,* vol. 2. London: Henry Colburn, 1837.

Brewster, Charles W. *Rambles About Portsmouth.* Somersworth, NH: New Hampshire Publishing, 1972.

Brighton, John G. *Admiral of the Fleet Sir Provo W.P. Wallis, A Memoir.* London: Hutchinson, 1892.

———. *Admiral Sir P.B.V. Broke, Bart., K.C.B.,&c.: A Memoir.* London: Sampson, Low, Son, and Marston, 1866.

Bristol, William. *An Address, Intended to Have Been Delivered at the Late Town Meeting in New-Haven.* New Haven, CT: Oliver Steele, 1809.

"The Shannon and the Cheseapeake," *British Army and Navy Review* 19 (January 1866).

Brodie, Fawn M. *Thomas Jefferson: An Intimate History.* New York: W.W. Norton, 1974.

Brookhiser, Richard. *Alexander Hamilton: American.* New York: Free Press, 1999.

Brown, Francis. *The Evils of War: A Fast Sermon Delivered at North-Yarmouth, April 7, 1814.* Portland, ME: Arthur Shirley, 1814.

Brown, Roger H. *The Republic in Peril: 1812.* New York: Columbia University Press, 1964.

Buchanan, Charles. "American Privateers at Grand Manan During the War of 1812." *Grand Manan Historian* 5 (1938).

Buel, Richard Jr. *America on the Brink.* New York: Palgrave Macmillan, 2005.

Bukovansky, Mlada. "American Identity and Neutral Rights from Independence to the War of 1812." *International Organization* 51 (Spring 1997).

Burt, Alfred L. *The United States, Great Britain, and British North America from the Revolution to the Establishment of Peace After the War of 1812.* New York: Russell and Russell, 1961,

Butler, Francis G. *A History of Farmington, Maine 1776–1885.* Somersworth, NH: New England History Press, 1983.

Butler, James, comp. *American bravery displayed.* Carlisle, PA: G. Phillips, 1816.

Byers, Edward. *The Nation of Nantucket.* Boston: Northeastern University Press, 1987.

Caffrey, Kate. *The Twilight's Last Gleaming.* New York: Stein and Day, 1977.

Calnek, William A. and Alfred W. Savary. *History of the County of Annapolis.* Toronto: William Briggs, 1897.

Calvert, Mary R. *Dawn Over the Kennebec.* Monmouth, ME: Monmouth, 1983.

Campbell, Duncan. *Nova Scotia in its Historical, Mercantile and Industrial Relations.* Montreal: John Lovell, 1873.

Carr, Albert H. Z. *The Coming of War.* Garden City, NY: Doubleday, 1960.

Carroll, Charles. *Rhode Island: Three Centuries of Democracy*. New York: Lewis Historical Publishing, 1932.

Cartland, John H. *Ten Years at Pemaquid: Sketches*. Pemaquid Beach, ME: privately printed,1899.

Carter, Nathan F. and T.L. Fowler. *History of Pembroke, N.H. 1730–1895*, vol. 1. Concord, NH: Republican Press, 1895.

Caulkins, Frances M. *History of New London, Connecticut*. New London, CT: H.D. Utley, 1895.

———. *History of Norwich, Connecticut*. Hartford: privately printed, 1866.

Channing, William E. *A Sermon, Preached in Boston, August 20, 1812*. Boston: C. Stebbins, 1812.

Chapelle, Howard I. *The History of the American Sailing Navy*. New York: W.W. Norton, 1949.

Chapman, Harry J. "The Battle of Hampden." *Sprague's Journal of Maine History* 2 (October 1914).

Chase, Fannie S. *Wiscasset in Pownalborough: A History of the Shire Town*. Portland: Southworth-Anthoensen, 1941.

Chase, George W. *The History of Haverhill*. Haverhill, MA: privately printed, 1861.

Cheshire Farmer. *An Enquiry into the State of the Farm*. N.p.: privately printed, 1808.

Chidsey, Donald B. *The American Privateers*. New York: Dodd, Mead, 1962.

Churchill, Winston. *A History of the English-Speaking Peoples*. New York: Bantam Books, 1963.

Citizen of Vermont. *The Crisis: On the Origin and consequences of Our Political Dissentions*. Albany, NY: E. and E. Hosford, 1815.

Clark, Charles E. *Maine: A Bicentennial History*. New York: W.W. Norton, 1977.

Clark, Charles E., James S. Leamon, and Karen Bowden, eds. *Maine in the Early Republic. From Revolution to Statehood*. Hanover, NH: University Press of New England, 1988.

Cobb, Elijah. *The Memoirs of a Cape Cod Skipper*. New Haven, CT: Yale University Press, 1925.

Coburn, Silas R. *History of Dracut, Massachusetts*. Lowell, MA: Press of the Courier-Citizen, 1922.

Cochrane, Harry H. *History of Monmouth and Wales*, vol. 2. East Winthrop, ME: Banner, 1894.

Coffin, Joshua. *A Sketch of the History of Newbury, Newburyport, and West Newbury*. Boston: Samuel G. Drake, 1845.

Coggeshall, George. *History of the American Privateers and Letters-of-Marque, During Our War with England in the Years 1812, '13, and '14*. New York: privately printed, 1856.

Cogswell, Leander W. *History of the Town of Henniker, Merrimack County, New Hampshire*. Concord, NH: Republican Press, 1880.

Cole, Alfred and Charles F. Whitman. *A History of Buckfield, Oxford County, Maine*. Lewiston, ME: Journal Printshop, 1915.

Coleman, Peter J. *The Transformation of Rhode Island 1790 — 1860.* Providence: Brown University Press, 1963.

Coles, Harry L. *The War of 1812.* Chicago: University of Chicago Press, 1965.

Collins, Edward D. *A History of Vermont.* Boston: Ginn, 1903.

Coolidge, A.J. and J.B. Mansfield. *A History and Description of New England, General and Local,* vol. 1. Boston: Austin J. Coolidge, 1859.

Crowell, Edwin. *History of Barrington Township.* Belleville, ON: Mika, 1973.

Current, Richard N. *Daniel Webster and the Rise of National Conservatism.* Boston: Little, Brown, 1955.

Currier, John J. *History of Newbury, Massachusetts 1635–1902.* Boston: Damrell and Upham, 1902.

Curtis, George T. *Life of Daniel Webster,* vol. 1. New York: D. Appleton, 1893.

Curtis, Jane and Will and Frank Lieberman. *Monhegan: The Artists' Island.* Camden, ME: Down East Books, 1995.

Cutter, Daniel B. *History of the Town of Jaffrey, New Hampshire.* Concord, NH: Republican Press, 1881.

Davis, Albert H. *History of Ellsworth, Maine.* Lewiston, ME: Lewiston Journal, 1927.

Davis, Joshua. *A Narrative of Joshua Davis, an American Citizen, who was pressed and served on board six ships of the British navy.* Boston: B. True, 1811.

Davis, William T. *History of the Town of Plymouth.* Philadelphia: J.W. Lewis, 1885.

Deane, Samuel. *History of Scituate, Massachusetts.* Boston: James Loring, 1831.

Decker, Robert O. *The Whaling City: A History of New London.* Chester, CT: Pequot, 1976.

DeKay, James T. *The Battle of Stonington: Torpedoes, Submarines, and Rockets in the War of 1812.* Annapolis, MD: Naval Institute Press, 1990.

———. *A Rage for Glory: The Life of Commodore Stephen Decatur, USN.* New York: Free Press, 2004.

Deyo, Simeon L., ed. *History of Barnstable County, Massachusetts.* New York: H.W. Blake, 1890.

Dickey, John S. *The United States and Canada.* Englewood Cliffs, NJ: Prentice-Hall, 1964.

Digges, Jerimiah. *Cape Cod Pilot.* Provincetown: Modern Pilgrim, 1937.

Dodge, E.H. *Mount Desert Island, and Cranberry Isles.* Ellsworth, ME: N.K. Sawyer, 1871.

Dow, Joseph. *History of the Town of Hampton, New Hampshire.* Salem, MA: Salem Press, 1893.

Drake, Samuel A. *History of Middlesex County, Massachusetts,* vol. 1. Boston: Estes and Lauriat, 1880.

———. *The Pine-Tree Coast.* Boston: Estes and Lauriat, 1891.

Drisko, George W. *History of the Town of Machias,* 1904.

Dudley, Wade G. *Splintering the Wooden Wall: The British Blockade of the United States, 1812 — 1815.* Annapolis, MD: Naval Institute Press, 2003.

Dudley, William S., ed. *The Naval War of 1812: A Documentary History,* vols. 1 and 2. Washington, DC: Department of the Navy, 1985.

Dunbar, Robert E., and George F. Dow. *Nobleboro, Maine-A History*. Nobleboro, ME: Nobleboro Historical Society, 1988.

Duncan, Roger F. *Coastal Maine: A Maritime History*. New York: W.W. Norton, 1992.

Dundonald, Thomas (tenth Earl of). *Autobiography of a Seaman*, vol. 1. London: Richard Bentley, 1860.

Dunnack, Henry E. *Maine Forts*. Augusta, ME: Charles E. Nash and Son, 1924.

Dutcher, L.L. *The History of St. Albans, Vt*. St. Albans, VT: Stephen E. Royce, 1872.

Dwight, Timothy. *A Discourse, in Two Parts, Delivered July 23, 1812, on the Public Fast*. Utica, NY: Ira Merrell, 1812.

———. *Travels in New England and New York*, vol. 4. Cambridge, MA: Belknap, 1969.

Eastman, Ralph M. *Some Famous Privateers of New England*. Boston: State Street Trust, 1928.

Eaton, Cyrus. *History of Thomaston, Rockland, and South Thomaston, Maine*. Hallowell, ME: Masters, Smith, 1865.

———. *Annals of the Town of Warren in Knox County, Maine*. Hallowell, ME: Masters and Livermore, 1877.

Egan, Clifford L. "The Path to War in 1812 Through the Eyes of a New Hampshire 'War Hawk.'" *Historical New Hampshire* 30 (Fall 1975).

Elliott, Charles W. *The New England History*, vol. 2. New York: Charles Scribner, 1857.

Ellis, Alice V. *The History of Prospect, Maine, 1759 — 1979*. North Searsport, ME: Little Letterpress Print Shop, 1980.

Ellis, Joseph J. *His Excellency George Washington*. New York: Knopf, 2004.

Emerson, Amelia F. *Early History of Naushon Island*. Boston: Thomas Todd, 1935.

Emery, Sarah A. *Reminiscences of a Nonagenarian*. Newburyport, MA: William H. Huse, 1879.

Everest, Allan S. *The War of 1812 in the Champlain Valley*. Syracuse, NY: Syracuse University Press, 1981.

Farrow, John P. *History of Islseborough, Maine*. Camden, ME: Picton, 1991.

Fenstermaker, J. Van and John E. Filer. "The U.S. Embargo Act of 1807: Its Impact on New England Money, Banking, and Economic Activity." *Economic Inquiry* 28 (1990).

Fernald, William F. *In Defense of the Adams*. Farmingdale, ME: W. Fernald, 1992.

Field, Edward, ed. *State of Rhode Island and Providence Plantations at the End of the Century: A History*. Boston: Mason, 1902.

Feintuch, Burt and David H. Watters, eds. *The Encyclopedia of New England*. New Haven, CT: Yale University Press, 2005.

Flagg, Charles A. "Relating to the War of 1812." *Sprague's Journal of Maine History* 6 (November 1918, to January 1919).

Floyd, Candace. *The History of New England*. New York: Portland House, 1990.

Freeman, Frederick. *The History of Cape Cod*, vol. 2. Boston: W.H. Piper, 1869.

French, George, ed. *New England: What It Is and What It Is To Be*. Boston: Boston Chamber of Commerce, 1911.

Gardner, Will. *The Coffin Saga.* Cambridge, MA: Riverside, 1949.

Gifford, C.H. *History of the Wars Occasioned by the French Revolution*, vol. 2. London: W. Lewis, 1817.

Gleaves, Albert. *James Lawrence: Captain, United States Navy.* New York: G.P. Putnam's Sons, 1904.

Goddard, M.E. and Henry V. Partridge. *A History of Norwich, Vermont.* Hanover, NH: Dartmouth Press, 1905.

Goold, William. *Portland in the Past: With Historical Notes of Old Falmouth.* Portland, ME: B. Thurston, 1886.

Gould, Albert T. *The St. George's River.* Portland, ME: Anthoensen, 1950.

Gould, Augustus A. and Frederic Kidder. *The History of New Ipswich.* Boston: Gould and Lincoln, 1852.

Gould, John. *There Goes Maine.* New York: W.W. Norton, 1990.

Graham, Gerald S. *Sea Power and British North America 1783–1820.* Cambridge, MA: Harvard University Press, 1941.

Green, Joseph J., Charles Burnham and J.H. Merrifield. *Centennial Proceedings and Other Historical Facts and Incidents Relating to Newfane, Vermont.* Brattleboro, VT: D. Leonard, 1877.

Greene, Francis B. *History of Boothbay, Southport, and Boothbay Harbor, Maine.* Portland, ME: Loring, Short and Harmon, 1906.

Gribbin, William. *The Churches Militant: The War of 1812 and American Religion.* New Haven, CT: Yale University Press, 1970.

——. "The Covenant Transformed: The Jeremiad Tradition and the War of 1812." *Church History* 3 (September 1971).

Griffith, Henry S. *History of the Town of Carver, Massachusetts.* New Bedford, MA: E. Anthony and Sons, 1913.

Griffin, Simon G., Frank H. Whitcomb, and Octavius Applegate. *A History of the Town of Keene.* Keene, NH: Sentinel, 1904

Griswold, Roger. *A Proclamation, By His Excellency, Governor and Commander in Chief In and Over the State of Connecticut, In America, August 6, 1812.*

Guedalla, Philip. *Wellington.* New York: Harper and Brothers, 1931.

Gwyn, Julian. *Frigates and Foremasts: the North American Squadron in Nova Scotia Waters 1745 — 1815.* Vancouver, BC: UBC Press, 2003.

Hagar, Joseph C. ed. *Marshfield: The Autobiography of a Pilgrim Town.* Marshfield, MA: Marshfield Tercentenary Committee, 1940.

Hale, Judson. *Inside New England.* New York: Harper and Row, 1982.

Hale, Richard W., Jr. *The Story of Bar Harbor.* New York: Ives Washburn, 1949.

Haliburton vs. Inhabitants of Frankfort, 14 Mass 214 (1817).

Hannay, David. *Life of Frederick Marryat.* London: W.J. Gage, 1889.

Hansen, Gunnar, ed. *Mt. Desert: An Informal History.* Mount Desert, ME: Town of Mount Desert, 1989.

Harden, Brian R., chm. *Shore Village Story: An Informal History of Rockland, Maine.* Rockland, ME: Courier-Gazette, 1976.

Hardy, Anna S. *History of Hope, Maine.* Camden, ME: Penobscot, 1990.

Hart, Albert B., ed. *American History Told by Contemporaries,* vol. 3. New York: Macmillan, 1901.

Harvey, D.C. "The Halifax-Castine Expedition." *The Dalhousie Review* 2 (July 1938).

Hatch, Louis C., ed. *Maine: A History.* New York: American Historical Society, 1919.

Hatch, William C. *A History of the Town of Industry, Franklin County, Maine.* Farmington, ME: Knowlton, McLeary, 1893.

Hawes, Charles B. *Gloucester by Land and Sea.* Boston: Little, Brown, 1923.

Hayes, Lyman S. *History of the Town of Rockingham, Vermont.* Lynn, MA: Frank S. Whitten, 1907

Hemenway, Abby M. *Vermont Historical Gazetteer,* vol. 2. Burlington, VT: privately printed, 1871.

Herrick, William D. *History of the Town of Gardner, Worcester County, Mass.* Gardner, MA: A.G. Bushnell, 1878.

Hickey, Donald R. *The War of 1812: A Forgotten Conflict.* Urbana, IL: University of Illinois Press, 1989.

Higginson, Thomas W. *A Larger History of the United States of America.* New York: Harper and Brothers, 1886.

———. "The Second War For Independence." *Harper's New Monthly Magazine* 68 (December 1883, to May 1884).

Hildreth, Richard. *The History of the United States of America,* vol. 3. New York: Harper and Brothers, 1852.

Hill, Frederic S. *The "Lucky Little Enterprise" and Her Successors in the United States Navy, 1776–1900.* Boston: privately printed, 1900.

Hodgman, Edwin R. *History of the Town of Westford in the County of Middlesex, Massachusetts, 1659–1883.* Lowell, MA: Morning Mail, 1883.

Hobart, Benjamin. *History of the Town of Abington, Plymouth County, Massachusetts.* Boston: T.H. Carter and Son, 1866.

Holland, Josiah G. *History of Western Massachusetts,* vol. 1. Springfield, MA: Samuel Bowles, 1855.

Hollister, G.H. *The History of Connecticut,* vol. 2. New Haven, CT: Durrie and Peck, 1855.

Holt, John "Terry." *The Island City, A History of Eastport, Moose Island, Maine.* Eastport, ME: Eastport 200 Committee, 1999.

Horsman, Reginald. *The War of 1812.* New York: Knopf, 1969.

Hoskins, Nathan. *A History of the State of Vermont.* Vergennes, VT: J. Shedd, 1831.

Hosmer, George L. *An Historical Sketch of the Town of Deer Isle, Maine.* Sunset, ME: Deer Isle-Stonington Historical Society, 1983.

Hough, George. *Defence of the Clergy of New-England.* Concord, NH: George Hough, 1814.

Howard, R.H. *A History of New England.* Boston: Crocker, 1880.

Howe, George. *Mount Hope: A New England Chronicle.* New York: Viking, 1959.

Hudson, Alfred S. *The History of Sudbury, Massachusetts, 1638–1889*. Boston: R.H. Blodgett, 1889.

Humphrey, Zephine. *A Book of New England*. New York: Howell, Soskin, 1947.

Hurd, D. Hamilton. *History of New London County, Connecticut*. Philadelphia: J.W. Lewis, 1882.

Hyde, C. M. and Alexander Hyde, comp. *The Centennial Celebration and Centennial History of the Town of Lee, Mass*. Springfield, MA: Clark W. Bryan, 1878.

Ingersoll, Charles J. *Historical Sketch of the Second War Between the United States of America and Great Britain*, vol. 1. Philadelphia: Lea and Blanchard, 1845.

Irving, Pierre M., ed. *Spanish Papers and Other Miscellanies, Hitherto Unpublished or Uncollected by Washington Irving*, vol. 2. New York: G.P. Putnam and Son, 1867.

Jacobs, James R. and Glenn Tucker. *The War of 1812: A Compact History*. New York: Hawthorn Books, 1969.

Jalbert, Russell R. *The Battle of Rock Harbor*. Orleans, MA: Orleans Bicentennial Commission, 1997.

James, William. *Naval History of Great Britain*, vol. 4. London: Richard Bentley and Son, 1886.

Johnson, Rossiter. *A History of the War of 1812–15 Between the United States and Great Britain*. New York: Dodd, Mead, 1882.

Johnston, John. *A History of the Towns of Bristol and Bremen in the State of Maine*. Albany, NY: Joel Munsell, 1873.

Jones, Noah. *Journals of Two Cruises Aboard the American Privateer Yankee*. New York: Macmillan, 1967.

Jordan, William B. *A History of Cape Elizabeth, Maine*. Bowie, MD: Heritage Books, 1987.

Joslin, Joseph, Barnes Frisbie, and Frederic Ruggles. *A History of the Town of Poultney, Vermont*. Poultney, VT: Journal Printing, 1875.

Keene, Luther. "The British Cake. A Reminiscence of the War of 1812. *New England Magazine* 5 (February 1887).

Kendall, C. Wye. *Private Men-Of-War*. New York: Robert M. McBride, 1932.

Kert, Faye M. *Prize and Prejudice: Privateering and Naval Prize in Atlantic Canada in the War of 1812*. St. John's, NF: International Maritime Economic History Association, 1977.

Kilby, William H., comp. *Eastport and Passamaquoddy: A Collection of Historical and Biographical Sketches*. Eastport, ME: E.E. Shead, 1888.

King, William and Mark L. Hill. *Remarks Upon a Pamphlet Published at Bath, Me. Relating to Alledged Infractions of the Laws During the Embargo, Non-Intercourse, and War*. Bath, ME: Thomas Eaton, 1825.

Kittredge, Henry C. *Cape Cod: Its People and Their History*. Boston: Houghton Mifflin, 1968.

Labaree, Benjamin W., William F. Fowler, Jr., Andrew W. German, John B. Hattendorf, Jeffrey J. Safford, and Edward W. Sloan.. *America and the Sea: A Maritime History*. Mystic, CT: Mystic Seaport, 1998.

Lapham, William B. *History of Rumford, Oxford County, Maine*. Augusta, ME: Press of the Maine Farmer, 1890.

An Account of the Funeral Honours Bestowed on the Remains of Capt. Lawrence and Lieut. Ludlow. Boston: Joshua Belcher, 1813.

Lawson, John D., ed. *American State Trials,* vol. 3. St. Louis, MO: F.H. Thomas, 1915.

Lawton, Loring, and Jordan, comp. *The City of Ellsworth Register with Surry and Blue Hill.* Auburn, ME: Peter I. Lawton, 1908.

Leckie, Robert. *The Wars of America.* New York: Harper and Row, 1968.

Levermore, Charles H., ed. *Forerunners and Competitors of the Pilgrims and Puritans,* vol. 1. New York: Marion Press, 1912.

Lewis, Alonzo and James R. Newhall. *History of Lynn, Essex County, Massachusetts.* Boston: John L. Shorey, 1865.

Lewis, Theodore G., ed. *History of Waterbury, Vermont, 1763–1915.* Waterbury, VT: Harry C. Whitehill, 1915.

Library of Congress. *Answer to the Governor's Speech.* Printed Ephemera Collection, Portfolio 48, Folder 17.

——. *The Constitution gone!!* Printed Ephemera Collection, Portfolio 48, Folder 5.

——. *Dignified Patriotism.* Printed Ephemera Collection, Portfolio 190, Folder 14a.

——. *Important and Alarming Information.* Printed Ephemera Collection, Portfolio 168, Folder 3.

——. *Ledger Office.* Printed Ephemera Collection, Portfolio 182, Folder 5.

——. *Prompt Patriotism.* Printed Ephemera Collection, Portfolio 49, Folder 28.

——. *Sedition! Treason!* Printed Ephemera Collection, Portfolio 48, Folder 21a.

——. *Sixth Naval Victory.* Printed Ephemera Collection, Portfolio 50, Folder 6a.

Lilly, Lambert. *The History of New England.* Boston: William D. Ticknor, 1847.

Lincoln, William. *Worcester, Massachusetts, From Its Earliest Settlement to September, 1836.* Worcester, MA: Charles Hersey, 1862.

Livermore's History of Block Island. Forge Village, MA: Block Island Tercentenary Anniversary, 1961.

Locke, John L. *Sketches of the Early History of Belfast.* Camden, ME: Picton, 1989.

——. *Sketches of the History of the Town of Camden, Maine.* Hallowell, ME: Masters, Smith, 1859.

Lodge, Henry C. *Studies in History.* Boston: Houghton Mifflin, 1884.

Lohnes, Barry J. "British Naval Problems at Halifax During the War of 1812." *Mariner's Mirror* 59 (August 1973).

——. "The War of 1812 at Sea: The British Navy, New England, and the Maritime Provinces," (master's thesis, University of Maine, 1971.

Long, Charles A.E. *Matinicus Isle: Its Story and Its People.* Lewiston, ME: Lewiston Journal, 1926.

Loring, Amasa. *History of Piscataquis County, Maine.* Portland, ME: Hoyt, Fogg and Donham, 1880.

Lovell, Daisy W. *Glimpses of Early Wareham.* Taunton, MA: William. S. Sullwold, 1970.

Lovell, R.A., Jr. *Sandwich: A Cape Cod Town.* Taunton, MA: William S. Sullwold, 1984.

Lovette, Leland P. *Naval Customs, Traditions and Usage.* Annapolis, MD: United States Naval Institute, 1939.

Lovejoy, Evelyn M. W. *History of Royalton, Vermont with Family Genealogies, 1769–1911.* Burlington, VT: Free Press, 1911.

Lyford, James O., ed. *History of Concord, New Hampshire.* Concord, NH: Rumford, 1903.

Lyman, Theodore. *A short account of the Harford Convention.* Boston: O. Everett, 1823.

Maclay, Edgar S. *A History of American Privateers.* New York: D. Appleton, 1899.

———. *A History of the United States Navy From 1775 to 1893,* vol. 1. New York: D. Appleton, 1894.

Macy, Obed. *The History of Nantucket.* Boston: Hilliard, Gray, 1835.

Macy, William F. and Roland B. Hussey. *The Nantucket Scrap Basket.* Nantucket, MA: Inquirer and Mirror, 1916.

Mahan, Alfred T. *The Life of Nelson: The Embodiment of the Sea Power of Great Britain.* Annapolis, MD: Naval Institute Press, 2001.

———. *Sea Power in its Relations to the War of 1812.* New York: Greenwood, 1968.

Mahon, John K. *The War of 1812.* Gainesville, FL: University of Florida Press, 1972.

Maine Historical Society. *Collections and Proceedings of,* 2d Ser., vol. 1 (1890), vol. 2 (1891), vol. 8 (1897), vol. 9 (1898) and vol. 10 (1899).

Maloney, Linda M. *The Captain from Connecticut: The Life and Naval Times of Isaac Hull.* Boston: Northeastern University Press, 1986.

Marin, Albert. *1812, The War Nobody Won.* New York: Atheneum, 1985.

Marryat, Florence. *Life and Letters of Captain Marryat,* vol. 1. New York: D. Appleton, 1872

Martell, J.S. "A Side Light on Federalist Strategy During the War of 1812." *American Historical Review* 43 (April 1938).

Martin, A. Patchett. *Life and Letters of the Right Honorable Robert Lowe Viscount Sherbrooke with a Memoir of Sir John Coape Sherbrooke,* vol. 2. London: Longmans, Green, 1893.

Martin, Tyrone G. *A Most Fortunate Ship: A Narrative History of "Old Ironsides."* Chester, CT: Globe Pequot, 1980.

Marvin, A.P. *History of the Town of Winchendon.* Fitchburg, MA: Garfield and Stratton, 1868.

Massachusetts, Adjutant General's Office. *Records of the Massachusetts Volunteer Militia: Called Out by the Governor of Massachusetts to Suppress a Threatened Invasion During the War of 1812–14.* Boston: Wright and Potter, 1913.

Massachusetts, Commonwealth of. *General Orders.* Head-quarters, Boston, September 6th, 1814.

The Public and General Laws of the Commonwealth of Massachusetts from February 28, 1807, to February 16, 1816, vol. 4. Boston: Wells and Lilly, 1816.

Massachusetts General Court, *The committee to whom was referred the Message of his Excellency, with the Documents accompanying the same, respectfully REPORT in part -.* Boston: 1814.

Massachusetts Historical Society Proceedings, vol. 1 (February 1885), vol. 48 (June 1915), vol. 64 (June 1931), and vol. 65 (January 1933).

Massachusetts House of Representatives. *Report of the Committee of the House of Representatives of Massachusetts on the Subject of Impressed Seamen.* Boston: Russell and Cutler, 1813.

Matloff, Maurice, ed. *American Military History.* Washington, DC: United States Army, 1969.

Mattapoisett, Town of. *Mattapoisett and Old Rochester, Massachusetts.* New York: Grafton, 1907.

McClintock, John N. *History of New Hampshire.* Boston: B.B. Russell, 1889.

McCullough, David. *John Adams.* New York: Simon and Schuster, 2001.

McDevitt, Joseph L. *The House of Rotch: Massachusetts Whaling Merchants 1734-1828.* New York: Garland, 1968.

McKee, Linda A.M. *Captain Isaac Hull and the Portsmouth Navy Yard, 1813-1815.* Ann Arbor, MI: University Microfilms, 1968.

McLellan, Hugh D. *The History of Gorham, Maine.* Camden, ME: Picton , 1992.

McManemin, John A. *Privateers of the War of 1812.* Spring Lake, NJ: Ho-Ko-Kus, 1992.

McMaster, John B. *A History of the People of the United States From the Revolution to the Civil War,* vol. 3 and 4. New York: D. Appleton, 1901.

Mead, Daniel M. *A History of the Town of Greenwich, Fairfield County, Conn.* New York: Baker and Godwin, 1857.

Meinig, D.W. *The Shaping of America: A Geographical Perspective on 500 Years of History,* vol. 1. New Haven, CT: Yale University Press, 1986.

Melville, Doris J. *Major Bradford's Town: A History of Kingston 1726—1976.* N.p.: Parnassus, 1976

Miller, Marion M., ed. *Great Debates in American History,* vol. 2. New York: Current Literature Publishing, 1913.

Miller, Nathan. *Broadsides: The Age of Fighting Sail 1775-1815.* New York: John Wiley and Sons, 2005.

Miller, Samuel L. *History of the Town of Waldoboro, Maine.* Wiscasset, ME: Emerson, 1910.

Moody, Edward C. *Handbook History of the Town of York.* Augusta, ME: Kennebec Journal, 1914.

Moore, Humphrey. *Oration, Delivered at Milford, N.H. March 9, 1815, Occasioned by the Treaty of Peace.* Amherst, NH: R. Boylston, 1815.

Morison, Samuel E. *Harrison Gray Otis 1765-1848: The Urbane Federalist.* Boston: Houghton Mifflin, 1969.

——. *The Maritime History of Massachusetts, 1783-1860.* Boston: Houghton Mifflin, 1921.

——. *The Oxford History of the American People.* New York: Oxford University Press, 1965

——, Frederick Merk and Frank Freidel. *Dissent in Three American Wars.* Cambridge, MA: Harvard University Press, 1970.

Morris, Charles. *The Autobiography of Commodore Charles Morris, U.S. Navy.* Annapolis, MD: Naval Institute Press, 2002.

Morris, Jonathan F., comp. *A Genealogical and Historical Register of the Descendants of Edward Morris.* Hartford: privately printed, 1887.

Moulton, Augustus F. *Grandfather Tales of Scarborough.* Augusta, ME: Katahdin, 1925.

Muller, Charles G. *The Proudest Day.* New York: John Day Company, 1960.

Munro, Wilfred H. *The Story of Mount Hope Lands.* Providence: J.A. and R.A. Reid, 1880.

Munson, Gorham. *Penobscot: Down East Paradise.* Philadelphia: J.B. Lippincott, 1959.

Murdoch, Beamish. *A History of Nova-Scotia or Acadie.* Halifax, NS: James Barnes, 1867.

Murdoch, Richard K. "The Battle of Orleans, Massachusetts (1814) and Associated Events." *American Neptune* 24 (July 1964).

Napier, Elers. *The Life and Correspondence of Admiral Sir Charles Napier,* vol. 1. London: Hurst and Blackett, 1862.

Nash, Charles E. *The History of Augusta.* Augusta, ME: Charles E. Nash and Son, 1904.

Naval Chronicle, vols. 32 & 33. London: J. Gold, 1814.

Centennial in New Bedford. New Bedford, MA: E. Anthony and Sons, 1876.

"The Privateer Dash." *New England Magazine* 16 (July 1894).

"North Yarmouth Light Infantry Company." *Old Times in North Yarmouth, Maine* 3 (July 1877).

North, James W. *History of Augusta.* Augusta, ME: Clapp and North, 1870.

Nye, Everett I. *History of Wellfleet: From Early Days to Present Time.* Hyannis, MA: F.B. and F.F. Goss, 1920.

Oak, Lyndon. *The History of Garland, Maine.* Dover, ME: Observer Publishing, 1912.

———. *A Sketch of the Life of General Irish.* Boston: Lee and Shepard, 1898.

Osgood, David. *Solemn Protest Against the Late Declaration of War.* Exeter, NH: C. Norris, 1812.

Otis, Harrison Gray, comp. *Considerations and Documents Relating to the Claim of Massachusetts for Expenditures During the Late War.* Washington: E. DeKraft, 1818.

Owen, Henry W. *The Edward Clarence Plummer History of Bath, Maine.* Bath, ME: Bath Area Bicentennial Committee, 1976.

Packard, Aubigne L. *A Town That Went to Sea.* Portland, ME: Falmouth Publishing House, 1950.

Paige, Reed. *Obedience to the Laws of Civil Rulers; A Duty Enjoined in the Scriptures: A Sermon Delivered at Hancock, August 20th, 1812.* Concord, NH: I. and W.R. Hill, 1812.

Paine, Ralph D. *The Fight for a Free Sea: A Chronicle of the War of 1812.* New Haven, CT: Yale University Press, 1920.

Parsons, Langdon B. *History of the Town of Rye, New Hampshire.* Concord, NH: Rumford, 1905.

Patrick, David. *Chambers's Cyclopedia of English Literature,* vol. 3. Philadelphia: J.B. Lippincott, 1904.

Patterson, George. *A History of the County of Pictou, Nova Scotia.* Montreal: Dawson Brothers, 1877.

Patterson, William D. "Old Fort Edgecomb." *Sprague's Journal of Maine History* 14 (October-December 1926).

Peabody, A.P., ed. *Life of William Plumer.* Boston: Phillips, Sampson, 1857.

Peck, Byron D., ed. *History of Bedford, N.H., 1737–1971.* Somersworth, NH: New Hampshire Publishing, 1972.

Perkins, Bradford. *Prologue to War: England and the United States, 1805–1812.* Berkeley, CA: University of California Press, 1961.

Perkins, Samuel. *The Political and Military Events of the Late War Between the United States and Great Britain.* New Haven, CT: S. Converse, 1825.

Perley, Sidney. *The History of Boxford, Essex County, Massachusetts.* Boxford, MA: privately printed, 1880.

Picking, Sherwood. *Sea Fight off Monhegan: Enterprise and Boxer.* Portland, ME: Michigonne, 1941.

Pierce, Neal R. *The New England States: People, Politics, and Power in the Six New England States.* New York: W.W. Norton, 1976.

Pinkerton, John. *A General Collection of the Best and Most Interesting Voyages and Travels in All Parts of the World,* vol. 12. London: Strahan and Preston, 1812.

Pocock, Tom. *Captain Marryat: Seamen, Writer, and Adventurer.* Mechanicsburg, PA: Stackpole, 2004.

Pool, Eugene H. *A Catalogue of the … collection of Captain James Lawrence.* Salem, MA: Peabody Museum, 1942.

Poolman, Kenneth. *Guns off Cape Ann: The Story of the Shannon and the Chesapeake.* London: Evans Brothers, 1961.

Potter, Chandler E. *Military History of the State of New Hampshire From Its Settlement in 1623 to the Rebellion in 1861.* Concord, NH: McFarland and Jenks, 1866.

Pratt, Enoch. *A Comprehensive History, Ecclesiastical and Civil, of Eastham, Wellfleet, and Orleans: County of Barnstable, Mass., From 1644 to 1844.* Orleans, MA: Lower Cape Publishing, 1996.

Pratt, Julius W. *Expansionists of 1812.* New York: P. Smith, 1949.

Preble, George H. *History of the United States Navy-Yard, Portsmouth, N.H.* Washington: Government Printing Office, 1892.

"The Press-Gang in the Northern Counties." *The Monthly Chronicle of North-Country Lore and Legend* 5 (January 1891).

Proper, Ida S. *Monhegan, The Cradle of New England.* Portland, ME: Southworth, 1930.

Pullen, H.F. *The Shannon and the Chesapeake.* Toronto: McClelland and Stewart, 1970.

Quincy, Edmund. *Josiah Quincy of Massachusetts.* Boston: Fields, Osgood, 1869.

Quinn, William P. *The Saltworks of Historic Cape Cod.* Orleans, MA: Parnassus, 1993.

Randall, Henry S. *The Life of Thomas Jefferson,* vol. 3. New York: Derby and Jackson, 1858.

Randolph, J.W., ed. *The Virginia Report of 1799–1800 Touching the Alien and Sedition Laws Together With the Virginia Resolutions.* Richmond, VA: C. Sherman, 1850.

Rappaport, Armin, ed. *Essays in American Diplomacy.* New York: Macmillan, 1967.

Reed, Parker M. *History of Bath and Environs.* Portland, ME: Lakeside, 1894.

Reid, Nancy T. *Dennis, Cape Cod: From Firstcomers to Newcomers, 1639–1993.* Dennis, MA: Dennis Historical Society, 1996.

Rice, George W. *The Shipping Days of Old Boothbay.* Somersworth, NH: New England History Press, 1984.

Rich, Marshall N. "N. Yarmouth Privateers." *Old Times in North Yarmouth, Maine* 3 (July 1877).

Rich, Shebnah. *Truro-Cape Cod.* Boston: D. Lothrop, 1883.

Richards, Lysander S. *History of Marshfield.* Plymouth, MA: Memorial, 1901.

Rider, Raymond A. *The Fearings and the Fearing Tavern with the Bumpus Family.* Taunton, MA: William S. Sullwold, 1977.

——. *Life and Times in Wareham Over 200 Years, 1739–1939.* Wareham, MA: Wareham Historical Society, 1989.

Roads, Samuel, Jr. *The History and Traditions of Marblehead.* Boston: Houghton, Osgood, 1880.

Roberts, Andrew. *Napoleon and Wellington.* New York: Simon and Schuster, 2001.

Roberts, Kenneth. *The Lively Lady: A Chronicle of Arundel.* New York: Doubleday, Doran, 1931.

Roberts, W. Adolphe and Lowell Brentano. *The Book of the Navy.* Garden City, NY: Doubleday, 1944.

Robinson, Reuel. *History of Camden and Rockport, Maine.* Camden, ME: Camden Publishing, 1907.

Robinson, William A. *Jeffersonian Democracy in New England.* New Haven, CT: Yale University Press, 1916.

Robinson, William F. *Coastal New England: Its Life and Past.* Boston: Little, Brown, 1983.

Roosevelt, Theodore. *The Naval War of 1812,* vols. 1 and 2. New York: G.P. Putnam's Sons, 1900.

Rowe, William H. *Ancient North Yarmouth and Yarmouth, Maine 1636–1936.* Somersworth, NH: New England History Press, 1980.

——. *The Maritime History of Maine: Three Centuries of Shipbuilding & Seafaring.* New York: W.W. Norton, 1948.

Rutland, Robert A. *Madison's Alternatives: The Jeffersonian Republicans and the Coming of War, 1805–1812.* Philadelphia: Lippincott, 1975.

Ryder, Alice A. *Lands of the Sippican.* New Bedford, MA: Reynolds, 1934.

Saltonstall, William G. *Ports of Piscataqua.* New York: Russell and Russell, 1968.

Sanborn, Edwin D. *History of New Hampshire: From Its First Discovery to the Year 1830.* Manchester, NH: John B. Clarke, 1975.

Scheer, George F. and Hugh F. Rankin. "Rebels and Redcoats." *American Heritage* 8 (February 1957).

Scott, James. *Recollections of a Naval Life,* vol. 3. London: Richard Bentley, 1834.

Sears, Louis M. *Jefferson and the Embargo.* New York: Octagon Books, 1966.

Secomb, Daniel F. *History of the Town of Amherst, Hillsborough County, New Hampshire.* Somersworth, NH: New Hampshire Publishing, 1972.

Securest, Larry J. *Privateering and National Defense: Naval Warfare for Private Profit.* Oakland, CA: Independent Institute, 2001.

Shay, Edith and Frank, eds. *Sand in Their Shoes: A Cape Cod Reader.* Boston: Houghton Mifflin, 1951.

Sheppard, J.H. *The Life of Samuel Tucker, Commodore in the American Revolution.* Boston: A. Mudge and Son, 1868.

Sibley, John L. *History of the Town of Union.* Boston: Benjamin B. Mussey, 1851.

Sibyl, Jerome. *Wareham, 1776–1976: Revolution and Bicentennial.* Wareham, MA: Wareham Bicentennial Commission, 1977.

Silsby, Herbert T., II. "A Secret Emissary From Down East." *Maine Historical Society Newsletter* 11 (Spring 1972).

Small, H.W. *A History of Swan's Island, Maine.* Ellsworth, ME: Hancock County Publishing, 1898.

Smith, E. Vale. *History of Newburyport.* Boston: Damrell and Moore, 1854.

Smith, H.P., ed. *History of Addison County, Vermont.* Syracuse, NY: D. Mason, 1886.

Smith, John Cotton. *A Proclamation, By His Honour, Lieutenant Governour and Commander in Chief In and Over the State of Connecticut, October 28, 1812.*

Smith, Joshua M. "Murder on Isle au Haut: Violence and Jefferson's Embargo in Coastal Maine, 1807–1809." *Maine History* 39 (Spring 2000).

— *The Rogues of Quoddy: Smuggling in the Maine-New Brunswick Borderlands, 1783–1820.* Ann Arbor, MI: University of Michigan, 2003.

Smith, Nancy W. Paine. *The Provincetown Book.* Brockton, MA: Tolman, 1922.

Smith, Oramandal. *History of Litchfield and an Account of Its Centennial Celebration.* Augusta, ME: Kennebec Journal, 1897.

Smith, Philip C. F. *Captain Samuel Tucker (1747–1833) Continental Navy.* Salem, MA: Essex Institute, 1976.

Smith, William C. *A History of Chatham, Massachusetts.* Chatham, MA: Chatham Historical Society, 1971.

Snider, Charles H.J. *The Glorious Shannon's Old Blue Duster and Other Faded Flags of Fadeless Fame.* Toronto: McClelland and Stewart, 1923.

———. *Under the Red Jack: Privateers of the Maritime Provinces of Canada in the War of 1812.* London: M. Hopkinson, 1928.

Somes-Sanderson, Virginia. *The Living Past: Being the Story of Somesville, Mount Desert, Maine.* Mount Desert, ME: Beech Hill Publishing, 1982.

Spater, George. *William Cobbett: The Poor Man's Friend,* vol. 1. Cambridge: Cambridge University Press, 1982.

Spears, John R. *Captain Nathaniel Brown Palmer: An Old-Time Sailor of the Sea.* New York: Macmillan, 1922.

Squires, James D. *A History of New Hampshire.* New York: American Historical Company, 1956.

Stackpole, Everett S. *History of New Hampshire.* New York: American Historical Society, 1916

———. *History of Winthrop, Maine.* Auburn, ME: Merrill and Webber, 1925.

Stahl, Jasper J. *History of Old Broad Bay and Waldoboro.* Portland, ME: Bond Wheelwright, 1956.

Stanley, George F.G. "British Operations on the Penobscot in 1814." *Journal of the Society for Army Historical Research* 19 (Autumn 1940).

Statutes at Large of the United States of America, 1796–1870.

Starbuck, Alexander. *History of the American Whale Fishery.* Waltham, MA: privately printed, 1876.

———. *The History of Nantucket County, Island and Town.* Boston: C.E. Goodspeed, 1924

Stearns, Ezra S. *History of the Town of Rindge, New Hampshire.* Boston: George H. Ellis, 1875.

Stevenson, Richard T. *The History of North America: The Growth of the Nation, 1809 to 1837,* vol. 12. Philadelphia: George Barrie and Sons, 1905.

Stowe, J.M. *History of the Town of Hubbardston, Worcester County.* Gardner, MA: A.G. Bushnell, 1881.

Street, George E. *Mount Desert: A History.* Boston: Houghton Mifflin, 1905.

Supplement, 8 Mass. 548 (1812).

Sweetser, Phyllis S., comp. *Cumberland, Maine in Four Centuries.* Portland, ME: Casco, 1976.

Swift, Charles F. *Cape Cod: The Right Arm of Massachusetts.* Yarmouth, MA: Register Publishing, 1897.

———. *History of Old Yarmouth.* Yarmouth Port, MA: privately printed, 1884.

Swift, Samuel. *History of the Town of Middlebury in the County of Addison, Vermont.* Middlebury, VT: A.H. Copeland, 1859.

Taylor, Alan. *Liberty Men and Great Proprietors.* Chapel Hill, NC: University of North Carolina Press, 1990.

Taylor, George R., ed. *The War of 1812: Past Justifications and Present Interpretations.* Boston: D.C. Heath, 1963.

Thacher, James. *History of the Town of Plymouth.* Salem, MA: Higginson Book, 1991.

Thayer, Henry O. "Naval Combat of Enterprise and Boxer September 5, 1813." *Sprague's Journal of Maine History* 2 (July 1914).

———. *Second War With England: Sundry Papers, by Rev. Henry Otis Thayer.* Bath, ME: Times, 1915.

Thayer, Mildred N. and Mrs. Edward W. Ames. *Brewer, Orrington, Holden, Eddington: History and Families.* Brewer, ME: L.H. Thompson, 1962.

Thompson, Daniel P. *History of the Town of Montpelier.* Montpelier, VT: E.P. Walton, 1860.

Thornton, Seth S. *Traditions and Records of Southwest Harbor and Somesville,* Mount Desert Island, Maine. Bar Harbor, ME: Acadia, 1938.

Thurston, David. *Brief History of Winthrop From 1764 to October 1855.* Portland, ME: Brown, Thurston, Steam, 1855.

Thurston, Florence G. and Harmon S. Cross. *Three Centuries of Freeport, Maine.* Portland, ME: Southworth-Anthoensen, 1940.

Todd, Charles B. *In Olde Massachusetts: Sketches of Old Times and Places During the Early Days of the Commonwealth.* New York: Grafton, 1907.

Trayser, Donald G. *Barnstable: Three Centuries of a Cape Cod Town.* Hyannis, MA: F.B. and F.P. Goss, 1939.

Trickey, Katherine W. *Historical Sketches of the Town of Hampden, Maine.* Ellsworth, ME: Ellsworth American, 1976.

Trow, Charles E. *The Old Shipmasters of Salem.* New York: G.P. Putnam's Sons, 1905.

Trowbridge, Thomas R. *Action Between the American Frigate "Chesapeake" and the British Frigate "Shannon", June 1st, 1813.* New Haven, CT: George D. Bove, 1897.

Trumbull, J. Hammond. *The Defence of Stonington* (Connecticut): Against a British Squadron, August 9th to 12th, 1814. Hartford, CT: 1864.

Tuchman, Barbara W. *The First Salute.* New York: Knopf, 1988.

Tucker, Daniel. *Broadside*, Massachusetts Historical Society, 35582 Shaw/Shoemaker fiche.

Tucker, Spencer. *Injured Honor: The Chesapeake-Leopard Affair, June 22, 1807.* Annapolis, MD: Naval Institute Press, 1996.

Turner, Wesley B. *The War of 1812: The War That Both Sides Won.* Toronto: Dundurn, 1990.

"The Turtle." *Empire Patriot* 5 (August 2003).

Updyke, Frank A. *The Diplomacy of the War of 1812.* Baltimore: Johns Hopkins, 1915.

Urban, Sylvanus, ed. "Interesting Intelligence from the London Gazettes." *Gentleman's Magazine* 84 (November 1814).

U.S. Congress. Cong. Globe, 24th Cong., 2nd Sess.

——. *Cong. Globe,* 27th Cong., 3rd Sess.

House. *A Bill Concerning Weston Jenkins, and others.* HR 51. 13th Cong., 3rd sess. (January 13, 1815).

——. *House Journal.* 10th Cong., 1st sess., December 18, 1807.

——. *House Journal.* 12th Cong., 1st sess., April 1, 1812, May 21, 1812, June 4, 1812, & June 18, 1812; 2nd sess., November 4, 1812, & February 11, 1813.

——. *House Journal.* 13th Cong., 1st sess., June 15, 1813; 2nd sess., January 6, 1814, January 22, 1814, January 31, 1814, February 14, 1814, February 28, 1814, & April 12, 1814; 3rd sess., October 20, 1814, December 1, 1814, December 29, 1814, February 10, 1815, & March 2, 1815.

Senate. Committee on Foreign Relations. *Compilation of Reports on Claims, 1789–1901.* 56th Cong., 2nd sess., January 15, 1901, S. Doc. 231.

——. *Senate Journal.* 3rd Cong., 1st sess., February 28, 1794.

——. *Senate Journal.* 9th Cong., 1st sess., February 12, 1806.

——. *Senate Journal.* 10th Cong., 1st sess., October 27, 1807; 2nd sess., November 8, 1808.

——. *Senate Journal.* 11th Cong., 3rd sess., December 31, 1810 & January 2, 1811.

——. *Senate Journal.* 12th Cong., 1st sess., March 10, 1812, June 1, 1812, & June 17, 1812.

——. *Senate Journal.* 13th Cong., 2nd sess., January 12, 1814, January 18, 1814, January 24, 1814, & March 31, 1814; 3rd sess., September 22, 1814.

United States v. Rice, (1819) 4 Wheat. 254.

Van Dusen, Albert E. *Connecticut.* New York: Random House, 1961.

Varg, Paul A. *New England and Foreign Relations, 1789–1850.* Hanover, NH: University Press of New England, 1983.

Vermont Historical Magazine, vol. 1 (1867), vol. 2 (1871), and vol. 4 (1882).

Vermont History: The Proceedings of the Vermont Historical Society 68 (Summer/Fall 2000).

Vorse, Mary H. *Time and the Town: A Provincetown Chronicle.* New York: Dial Press, 1942.

Wallace, Burnette B. and Frances S. Maher. *History of Woolwich, Maine: A Town Remembered.* Woolwich, ME: Woolwich Historical Society, 1994.

Walton, E.P., ed. *Records of the Governor and Council of the State of Vermont,* vol. 5. Montpelier, VT: J. and J.M. Poland, 1877.

Warren, Henry P., William Warren and Samuel Warren. *The History of Waterford, Oxford County, Maine.* Portland, ME: Hoyt, Fogg and Donham, 1879.

Watts, Edith S. *Deer Isle, Maine: From Pre-History to the Present.* N.p.: 1997.

The Writings and Speeches of Daniel Webster Hitherto Uncollected, Volume Three, Miscellaneous Papers Legal Arguments Early Addresses, Etc. Boston: Little, Brown, 1903.

Weeks, Alvin G. *Massasoit of the Wampanoags.* Fall River, MA: Plimpton, 1919.

Wells, Frederic P. *History of Newbury, Vermont.* St. Johnsbury, VT: Caledonian, 1902.

Weston, Thomas. *History of the Town of Middleboro, Massachusetts.* Boston: Houghton Mifflin, 1906.

Whalen, Richard F. *Truro: The Story of a Cape Cod Town.* Philadelphia: Xlibris, 2002.

Wheatland, Henry, ed. *Standard History of Essex County, Massachusetts.* Boston: C.F. Jewett, 1878.

Wheeler, George A. *Castine Past and Present.* Boston: Rockwell and Churchill, 1896.

—— and Henry W. Wheeler. *History of Brunswick, Topsham, and Harpswell, Maine.* Somersworth, NH: New Hampshire Publishing, 1974.

Wheeler, Richard A. *History of the Town of Stonington, County of New London, Connecticut.* Baltimore: Genealogical Publishing, 1977.

White, E.B. *One Man's Meat.* Gardiner, ME: Tilbury House, 1997.

White, James, ed. *Experience and Labors of Elder Joseph Bates.* Battle Creek, MI: Steam Press, 1877.

White, William H. "Heroes of the Sailing Navy: William Henry Allen." *Sea History* 110 (Spring 2005).

Whitehill, Walter M., ed. *New England Blockaded in 1814: The Journal of Henry Edward Napier.* Salem, MA: Peabody Museum, 1939.

Whiting, Edward E. *Changing New England.* New York: Century, 1929.

Whittemore, Edwin C., ed. *The Centennial History of Waterville.* Waterville, ME: Executive Committee of the Centennial Celebration, 1902.

Whittemore, Henry, ed. *History of Middlesex County, Connecticut.* New York: J.B. Beers, 1884.

Wilbur, La Fayette. *Early History of Vermont,* vol. 3. Jericho, VT: Roscoe Printing House, 1902.

Wilkie, Richard W. and Jack Tague. *Historical Atlas of Massachusetts.* Amherst, MA: University of Massachusetts Press, 1991.

Williams, T. Henry. *The History of American Wars From 1745 to 1918.* New York: Knopf, 1981.

Williamson, Joseph. "British Officers on the Penobscot, in 1814," *Bangor Historical Magazine* 3 (July 1887).

———. *The History of the City of Belfast, Maine,* vol. 1. Rockport, ME: Picton, 2002.

Williamson, William D. *The History of the State of Maine.* Hallowell, ME: Glazier, Masters, 1832.

Willis, William. *Journals of the Rev. Thomas Smith, and the Rev. Samuel Deane.* Portland, ME: Joseph S. Bailey, 1849.

Wilson, Daniel M. *Three Hundred Years of Quincy 1625–1925.* Quincy, MA: City of Quincy, 1926.

Winship, George P. *Sailors Narratives of Voyages Along the New England Coast, 1524–1624.* Boston: Houghton Mifflin, 1905.

Winslow, Richard E. *Wealth and Honour: Portsmouth During the Golden Age of Privateering, 1775–1815.* Portsmouth, NH: P.E. Randall, 1988.

Winsor, Justin, ed. *Narrative and Critical History of America,* vol. 3. Boston: Houghton Mifflin, 1884.

Wood, Edward F. R., Jr. *Old Mattapoisett: A Summer Portrait.* Mattapoisett, MA: Quadequina, 1995.

Works Progress Administration. *Watertown Records Comprising the Eighth Book of Town Proceedings 1810 Through 1829.* Newton, MA: Graphic Press, 1939.

Zimmerman, David. *Coastal Fort: A History of Fort Sullivan, Eastport, Maine.* Eastport, ME: Border Historical Society, 1984.

Zimmerman, James F. *Impressment of American Seamen.* New York: Columbia University Press, 1925.

ACKNOWLEDGEMENTS

When authors recognize the people who aided their work, there is a tendency to compress the record. Judgments are made, and only those who provided substantial or particular contributions are listed. I am uncomfortable with this approach, valuing even the small gestures and hints. But to name every one of the persons who offered a moment of their time would produce a voluminous roll. The matter seems open to another approach — a straightforward listing of the entities that lent a hand. In the present case, even this method produces a lengthy list.

Municipal clerks and their staffs in Barnstable, Brewster, Chatham, Eastham, Falmouth, Newburyport, Orleans, Provincetown, Salisbury, Sandwich, Truro, Wareham, and Wellfleet, all in Massachusetts; Bar Harbor, Belfast, Bingham, Bucksport, Castine, Deer Isle, Freeport, Hampden, Lincolnville, Machias, Portland, Sullivan, Thomaston, Waldoboro, Wells, and Wiscasset, all in Maine; and Exeter, New Hampshire were helpful sources of original information.

Historical societies proved to be rich resources. Thanks are due to the American Antiquarian Society; American Historical Association; Boothbay Region (ME) Historical Society; Brewster (MA) Historical Society; Connecticut Historical Society; Essex (CT) Historical Society; Falmouth (MA) Historical Society; Historical Society of Old Yarmouth (MA); Maine Historical Society; Massachusetts Historical Society; Mount Desert Island (ME) Historical Society; New Hampshire Historical Society; Newport (RI) Historical Society; Pejepscot Historical Society (ME); Rhode Island Historical Society; Thomaston (ME) Historical Society; and the Yarmouth (ME) Historical Society.

Libraries, of course, were equally invaluable during the research phase. Personnel at the Barnstable County Law Library; Boston Athenaeum; Boston Public Library; Brewster Ladies' Library; Brooks Free Library (Harwich); Centerville Public Library; East Falmouth Library; Eastham Public Library; Eldredge Public Library (Chatham); Falmouth Public Library; Jonathan Bourne Public Library (Bourne); Osterville Free Library; Plymouth Public Library; Sandwich Public Library; Jacob Sears Memorial Library (East Dennis); Sturgis Library of Barnstable; State Library of Massachusetts; Truro Public Library; Wellfleet Public Library; Wilkens Library, Cape Cod Community College; and Yarmouth Port Library; all in Massachusetts; Belfast Free Library; Camden Public Library; Chase Emerson Memorial Library (Deer Isle); Davistown Museum; Ellsworth Public Library; Folger Library, University of Maine at Orono; Jesup Memorial Library (Bar Harbor); Maine Maritime Museum; Maine State Library; Merrill Library, University of Maine at Machias; Merrill Memorial Library (Yarmouth); Penobscot Marine Museum Library; Rockland Public Library; and Skowhegan Free Public Library; all in Maine; G.W. Blunt White Library, Mystic Seaport (CT); Library of Congress; the Mariners' Museum Research Library and Archives (VA); Bailey/Howe Library, University of Vermont; and the U.S. National Archives & Records Administration provided a great deal of help.

The folks at Acadia National Park; Cape Cod Genealogical Society; the Dalhousie Review (NS); Greater Portland (ME) Landmarks, Inc.; Imagine-Maine; Office of the Clerk of the U.S. House of Representatives; Massachusetts Foundation for the Humanities; and the U.S. Senate Historical Office made important contributions.

The foregoing covers all but one notable exception to the rule of generalized appreciation. Professor Richard W. Judd of the University of Maine History Department deserves special mention. He took a fair amount of time to critique my manuscript and offer important and useful suggestions. I remain indebted to Professor Judd as well as the countless unnamed contributors from the listed entities.

INDEX